COMPARATIVE GOVERNMENT AND POLITICS

Published

Rudy Andeweg and Galen A. Irwin
Governance and Politics of the Netherlands (2nd edition)

Tim Bale
European Politics: A Comparative Introduction (2nd edition)

Nigel Bowles
Government and Politics of the United States (2nd edition)

Paul Brooker
Non-Democratic Regimes: Theory, Government and Politics (2nd edition)

Robert Elgie
Political Leadership in Liberal Democracies

Rod Hague and Martin Harrop
* Comparative Government and Politics: An Introduction (7th edition)

Paul Heywood
The Government and Politics of Spain

Xiaoming Huang
Politics in Pacific Asia

B. Guy Peters
Comparative Politics: Theories and Methods
[Rights: World excluding North America]

Tony Saich
Governance and Politics of China (2nd edition)

Anne Stevens
Government and Politics of France (3rd edition)

Ramesh Thakur
The Government and Politics of India

Forthcoming

Tim Haughton and Datina Malová
Government and Politics of Central and Eastern Europe

Robert Leonardi
Government and Politics in Italy

* Published in North America as Political Science: A Comparative Intoduction (5th edition)

Comparative Government and Politics
Series Standing Order
ISBN 0–333–71693–0 hardback
ISBN 0–333–69335–3 paperback
(outside North America only)
You can receive future titles in this series as they are published by placing a standing order.
Please contact your bookseller or, in the case of difficulty, write to us at the address below
with your name and address, the title of the series and one of the ISBNs quoted above.
Customer Services Department, Macmillan Distribution Ltd
Houndmills, Basingstoke, Hampshire RG21 6XS, England

Also by Maura Adshead

Developing European Regions?
Public Administration and Public Policy: Theory and Methods (co-editor with Michelle Millar)
Contesting the State: Lessons from the Irish Case (co-editor with Paedar Kirby and Michelle Millar)

Also by Jonathan Tonge

Northern Ireland
Irish Protestant Identities (co-editor with Mervyn Busteed and Frank Neal)
The New Northern Irish Politics?
Sinn Féin and the SDLP (with Gerard Murray)
Northern Ireland: Conflict and Change
The New Civil Service
The UK General Election 1997, 2001, 2005 (series co-edited with Andrew Geddes)

Politics in Ireland

Convergence and Divergence on a Two-Polity Island

Maura Adshead
and
Jonathan Tonge

© Maura Adshead and Jonathan Tonge 2009

First published 2009 by
PALGRAVE MACMILLAN

Palgrave Macmillan in the UK is an imprint of Macmillan Publishers Limited, registered in England, company number 785998, of Houndmills, Basingstoke, Hampshire RG21 6XS.

Palgrave Macmillan in the US is a division of St Martin's Press LLC, 175 Fifth Avenue, New York, NY 10010.

Palgrave Macmillan is the global academic imprint of the above companies and has companies and representatives throughout the world.

Palgrave® and Macmillan® are registered trademarks in the United States, the United Kingdom, Europe and other countries

ISBN-13: 978–1–4039–8969–7   hardback
ISBN-10: 1–4039–8969–9   hardback
ISBN-13: 978–1–4039–8970–3   paperback
ISBN-10: 1–4039–8970–2   paperback

This book is printed on paper suitable for recycling and made from fully managed and sustained forest sources. Logging, pulping and manufacturing processes are expected to conform to the environmental regulations of the country of origin.

A catalogue record for this book is available from the British Library.

A catalog record for this book is available from the Library of Congress.

10 9 8 7 6 5 4 3 2 1
18 17 16 15 14 13 12 11 10 09

Printed and bound in China

Contents

List of Boxes, Figures and Tables

List of Abbreviations

ABR	area-based response
ACA	Army Comrades Association
AMS	Additional Member System
BIC	British Irish Council
CAP	Common Agricultural Policy
CBI	Confederation of British Industry
CCI	Chambers of Commerce of Ireland
CDB	County/City Development Board
CFNI	Community Foundation of Northern Ireland
CIF	Construction Industry Federation
CII	Confederation of Irish Industry
CORI	Conference of Religions of Ireland
CSW	Commission on Social Welfare
CWC	Community Workers Co-operative
DARD	Department of Agriculture and Rural Development
DETE	Department of Enterprise Trade and Employment
DETI	Department of Enterprise, Trade and Industry
DfEL	Department for Employment and Learning
DPP	Director of Public Prosecutions
DSD	Department for Social Development
DUP	Democratic Unionist Party
DWS	developmental welfare state
EC	European Community
EEC	European Economic Community
ECJ	European Court of Justice
EMU	European Monetary Union
EOI	Ecology Party of Ireland
EP	European Parliament
EPCU	European Policy and Coordination Unit
FDI	foreign direct investment
FF	Fianna Fáil
FG	Fine Gael
FIE	Federation of Irish Employers
FOI	Freedom of Information Act
GFA	Good Friday Agreement
IBEC	Irish Business and Employers' Confederation
ICTU	Irish Congress of Trade Unions

IDA	Industrial Development Authority
IDB	Industrial Development Board
IFA	Irish Farmers Association
ILCU	Irish League of Credit Unions
ILO	Independent Labour Organisation
IRA	Irish Republican Army
ITUC	Irish Trades Union Congress
IWLM	Irish Women's Liberation Movement
JAAB	Judicial Advisory Appointments Board
JMC	Joint Ministerial Committee
LAW	Loyalist Association of Workers
LEDU	Local Enterprise and Development Unit
MAFF	Ministry of Agriculture, Food and Fisheries
MLA	Northern Ireland Assembly Member
MSG	Ministers and Secretaries Group
NAPS	National Anti-Poverty Strategy
NATO	North Atlantic Treaty Organisation
NDP	National Development Plan
NESC	National Economic and Social Council
NESF	National Economic Social Forum
NIC	Northern Ireland Committee
NICS	Northern Ireland Civil Service
NIO	Northern Ireland Office
NIHE	Northern Ireland Housing Executive
NPM	new public management
NSMC	North South Ministerial Council
NWCI	National Women's Council of Ireland
ODA	Official Development Assistance
OFDFM	Office of First and Deputy First Minister
PAFT	Policy Appraisal and Fair Treatment
PD	Progressive Democrats
PESP	Programme for Economic and Social Progress
PMB	Private member's bill
PPF	Programme for Prosperity and Fairness
PPS	purchasing power standard
PR	Proportional Representation
PSNI	Police Service of Northern Ireland
PUP	Progressive Unionist Party
ROI	Republic of Ireland
RTE	Radio Telefis Eireann
RUC	Royal Ulster Constabulary
SDLP	Social Democratic and Labour Party
SEA	Single European Act
SEUPB	Special European Union Programmes Body

SF	Sinn Féin
SIPTU	Services, Industrial, Professional and Technical Union
SMI	Strategic Management Initiative
SPC	Strategic Policy Committee
STV	Single Transferable Vote
TD	Member of the Dáil
UDA	Ulster Defence Association
UFU	Ulster Farmers' Union
UUP	Ulster Unionist Party
WTO	World Trade Organization

Acknowledgements

For lots of reasons, not least because you write them last, acknowledgements are the best bit of a book to write. In what is otherwise to be a fairly serious read, this may well be the most interesting page. It's often the first page that academics look at and the only page that friends and family read. So, whilst we have your attention, Maura would like to acknowledge: first and foremost, the two men who made this book possible – Jon Tonge and Neil Robinson. It is said that in life you should definitely try at least one of three things: build a house, have a child or write a book. I've tried all three and I'm not sure I'd advise anyone to do any of them, but if you are for writing a book, you should definitely do it with Jon. For everything else, I can't recommend a better man than Neil. Thank you for enabling me to find time to write this book, for looking after me and for ignoring the mess in the kitchen.

Special thanks to my wonderful PhD students (past and present) who provide 'pure thoughts', fresh insights and the most amazing scholarly support: Elaine Byrne, Liam Coen, Chris McInerney, Éidín Ní Shé, Gerardine Neylon and Gabriella Hanrahan.. Also thanks to all of my colleagues in the Department of Politics and Public Administration for being so very nice to work with, but especially those colleagues at the University of Limerick whose research focuses on Irish politics and who gave me ideas, inspiration and most helpfully copies of their publications – Bernadette Connaughton, Peadar Kirby, Helena Lenihan, Eddie Moxon-Browne, John Stapleton.

Prior to commencing this work, I was in receipt of a Combat Poverty Research Grant (RA/2004/01), which most usefully contributed to the foundations of much of this book. I would like to acknowledge this support for my research and give very special thanks to my colleague Tom Lodge and to the former Vice President of Research at the University of Limerick, Vincent Cunnane, both of whom helped me to expedite that research brief and thus most practically contributed to the completion of this book.

Finally, three generations of Irish women have contributed to this work: my grandmother, Madeleine Kelly, whose first-hand accounts of IRA action and Free State politics inspired my interest in the study of Irish politics; my mom, Theresa Adshead, 'because it wasn't off the grass I licked it'; and Éidín Ní Shé, whose excellent, energetic and enthusiastic research assistance made this book a pleasure to write. Together they represent the best of Irish politics, past, present and future.

Last, but certainly not least, we would both like to note our appreciation for all of the excellent team at Palgrave Macmillan - Rob Gibson, Cecily Wilson, Stephen Wenham, Keith Povey (with Nick Fox), and, of course, Steven Kennedy, who without doubt was the driving force in so much of the design and execution of this book.

Jon's acknowledgements are less extensive but no less heartfelt: I would like to thank Maura for being a calm and friendly co-author; my wife Maria for being so tolerant over her husband's relationship with his lap-top, even amid the recent arrival of Joseph Francis and my elder son Connell, for whom the PS3 may rightly remain of greater interest at this stage. Liverpool University has always had a welcome focus on Irish politics and has provided a supportive environment. Finally, Dermot, Pete, Jim, Catherine, Andy and Lyndsey have never been found wanting in discussions on Irish politics.

MAURA ADSHEAD

JONATHAN TONGE

The author and publishers would like to thank the following for permission to reproduce copyright material: Oxford University Press for an extract from *Political Parties and Party Systems* by A. Ware (1996); Palgrave Macmillan for two extracts from *Politics* by A. Heywood (2002); The Institute for Public Administration for an extract from the article 'Public Administration in a Mature Democracy' by D. Kelly (1993) in *Administration*; Cambridge University Press for an extract from the article 'Unequal Participation: Democracy's Unresolved Dilemma' by A. Lijphart (1996) in *American Political Science Review*; The Institute for Public Policy Research for an extract from *Leading the Way: A New Vision for Local Government* by T. Blair (1998); The National Economic and Social Council for an extract from *Prelude to Planning* (1976); Sheffield Academic Press for an extract from *The Politics of European Union Regional Policy: Multi-Level Governance or Flexible Gatekeeping?* by I. Bache (1998). Every effort has been made to trace all the copyright holders, but if any have been inadvertently overlooked the publishers will be pleased to make the necessary arrangements at the first opportunity.

Note on Irish Language Terms

It will come as no surprise that a book concerned with Irish politics contains a number of terms and phrases in the Irish language. To treat them all as foreign language terms would be distracting and, for most readers, unnecessary. We have therefore adopted the contemporary Irish practice of treating some Irish words as being assimilated into Irish English: these are not italicized or translated in the text. For readers unfamiliar with the Irish names and acronyms, we offer a short glossary of essential terms.

Aireacht From the Irish for ministry, but referring to a small working group similar to the French-style (and now EU- styled) *cabinet*.

An Post The Irish national postal service.

Áras an Uachtaráin Residence of the President.

Ard-fheis National convention of a political party or group.

Bunreacht na hÉireann The Irish Constitution.

Ceann Comhairle Chairperson of the Parliament (Dáil Éireann).

Clann na Poblachta Political party literally meaning 'Family of the Republic'.

Clann na Talmhan Political party literally meaning 'Family of the Land'.

Cumman na nGaedheal Political party literally meaning 'League of the Gaels'.

Dáil Éireann Parliament.

Fianna Fáil Political party most commonly translated by the party into English as 'Soldiers of Destiny', but deriving from the Irish meaning 'soldiers of the Fál', where Fáil is the genitive case for Fál, an old, poetic name for Ireland.

Fine Gael Political party literally meaning 'Family or Tribe of the Irish'.

Garda Síochána Police, translated from the Irish for 'the Guardians of the Peace'.

FÁS (Foras Áiseanna Saothair) Training and Employment Authority.

Tithe an Oireachtas Houses of Parliament – deriving originally from the Irish family name MacOireachtaigh (Geraghty), traditionally believed to have been advisers to Gaelic King O'Connor.

Pobal Formerly known as Area Development Management Ltd, the agency responsible for the disbursement of EU structural funding, from the Irish for 'community'.

Seanad Éireann Senate of Ireland.

Sinn Féin Political party political party literally meaning 'We Ourselves'.

Tánaiste Deputy Prime Minister; *Tánaiste* was originally the Irish word for the heir of the chief (*Taoiseach*) or king (*Rí*), under the Gaelic system of Tanistry which was a system for passing on titles and lands.

Taoiseach Prime Minister, from the Irish 'chief'.

Teachta Dála (TD) Member of Dáil Eireann, from the Irish literally meaning 'Deputy of the Dáil'.

Introduction

Although I intend to leave the description of this empire to a particular treatise, yet, in the meantime, I am content to gratify the curious reader with some general ideas.

Jonathan Swift, 'A Voyage to Lilliput', *Gulliver's Travels*

Why a Book on All-Island Irish Politics?

Irish politics has been the subject of significant international attention in recent years, in terms of the Republic's remarkable economic success and temporary status as the 'Celtic Tiger' and as a consequence of the Northern Ireland peace process. In both contexts, international attention has been drawn to the politics and policies of the Republic of Ireland and Northern Ireland, with a view to discovering the lessons that might be learned from political and economic developments. Ironically, however, those living in either state on the island of Ireland remain largely ignorant of the other. For some time, in both the Republic of Ireland and Northern Ireland, this was the politically 'correct' or 'appropriate' disposition to hold towards the other. Many ordinary citizens in the Republic, appalled by the violence in Northern Ireland and seeking to disassociate themselves as far as was possible from it, were proud to claim to know nothing about the politics in (if not of) Northern Ireland. Many ordinary citizens in Northern Ireland, in their desire to accentuate their separateness from the Republic, were equally proud to claim to know nothing about the politics there. To many interested and impartial outside observers, however, the logic of looking at both seems inescapable. That two states with a common origin and many similar influences, yet with divergent political and economic approaches yielding quite different policy styles and stances, have not been considered obvious cases for comparison is indeed remarkable.

The ambition of this book, however, is more modest. Whilst the work does not provide a comparative treatment of the two states in a strict methodological interpretation of the comparative approach, we do develop a study of Irish politics as an entity that rightfully incorporates some understanding of the politics in both the Republic and in Northern Ireland. Our motivation to do this was entirely practical. First, for many people outside Ireland and interested in Irish politics, it is a convenient and commonsense economy to have the two states considered together.

1

Second, for many people inside Ireland and interested in the politics and/or policies of only one of the states, we suggest that it is time to acknowledge the necessity of becoming more familiar with the other. Our approach reflects the new political dispensation on the island, an approach which is, in an ever increasing system of global interdependence, an obvious necessity. In short, we believe that it is no longer politically 'correct' or 'appropriate' for politicians, policy-makers, students and scholars of politics in either the Republic or Northern Ireland to claim ignorance of the other.

Plan of the Book

The 12 chapters in this book are most easily understood when divided into three parts. These deal with political institutions (Chapters 1 to 4), political behaviour (Chapters 5 to 8) and public policy (Chapters 9 to 12). In Part 1, Chapter 1 focuses on the role of the President, the Taoiseach and the cabinet in the Irish Republic, and the roles of direct-rule ministers and, more recently, devolved-executive leaders, in the forms of governance in Northern Ireland. It examines their respective functions as well as their interactions and interdependencies, and gives consideration to the alternative ways that each of these institutions has evolved over time and in the context of EU membership. Chapter 2 focuses on legislative assemblies in the Republic and Northern Ireland, and examines their relationships with cabinet, government, political parties and the people. Consideration is given to their respective abilities to carry out budgetary, legislative and scrutiny roles as well as recent debates over their need for institutional reform. In Chapters 3 and 4 we examine the bureaucracy and judiciary respectively, both topics that have to date received little attention in considerations of Irish politics. In Chapter 3, consideration is given to the role of the civil service and bureaucratic culture in Ireland and to the development of alternative administrative procedures and organizational cultures. Critical examination is made of a series of reform proposals in the Republic, culminating most recently in the Strategic Management Initiative (SMI). The Republic's application of the Whitehall model is contrasted with its interpretation within the Northern Ireland Office; and the relationship between the London, Dublin and Belfast bureaucracies is explored. In Chapter 4 we consider the organization of the judicial system in the Republic and in Northern Ireland. In relation to the Republic, we discuss the judicial development of the constitution, as well as the critical role played by Irish judges in relation to a range of recent high profile corruption tribunals. Consideration is also given to the judiciary's role in developing and expanding women's (and other minority) rights in the context of broader European equality legislation and rights definitions. The uniqueness of the Northern Ireland judicial system, a legacy of 30 years of conflict, is also examined, as well as the future development of that system in a post-conflict polity.

In Part 2, Chapter 5 focuses on political parties and the party system. We begin by tracing the major cleavages in the establishment of party systems, north and south; and we go on to explain how these have been reflected in the evolution and development of political parties. In Chapter 6, we examine the electoral system and voting behaviour, as well as the 'Single Transferable Vote' (STV) system of proportional representation (PR) that pertains to the Republic and Northern Ireland, and we evaluate the political consequences of its operation. We will review the arguments for and against reform of the PR-STV system and the way that these have been made in the Irish case. Consideration is given to the impact of PR-STV on voting behaviour, and the impact that this has on the behaviour of elected representatives.

Chapter 7 looks at the organization of civil society and the range of groups that provide an 'alternative' source of interest representation to conventional political parties. We consider, in the Republic, the increasing formalization of interest representation through the policy-making arrangements of social partnerships and other legislative and policy-based initiatives designed to support voluntarism and active citizenship. This contrasts with the situation in Northern Ireland, where the formalization of civic society participation in policy-making (in the Civic Forum, for example) is less well developed, but where informal, local 'civil societies' have long operated. We assess the capacity and potential of voluntary activities to bridge community divisions. The culmination and particularistic configuration of all forms of political behaviour is evaluated in Chapter 8, which deals with political culture.

Part 3 provides a broad overview of key spheres of public policy. Chapter 9 looks at the territorial administration of the state and the organization of subnational government. We examine the centralized nature of the Irish and Northern Irish states and the traditionally weak position of local government. We will evaluate the debates surrounding devolution and regionalization as well as most recent government moves towards decentralization in the Republic and the attempts to construct permanent devolution and meaningful local government in Northern Ireland.

Chapters 10 and 11 focus on the management of the economy and social policies, respectively, in each state. In relation to the economy, the Irish Republic – once referred to as the 'basket case' of Europe – became acknowledged as an international success. Much of the credit for this success is given to the development of Irish so-called 'government by partnership'. Meanwhile, in Northern Ireland, the visible symbols of reconstruction fail to mask a state-dependent economy, largely bereft of indigenous industry. Here, the economy remains inward (UK) looking. Consideration is given to the prospects for developing an 'all-island economy' implicit in recent cross-border initiatives and investment proposals. Notwithstanding the Republic's economic success, prior to the global problems of the late 2000s, however, questions are still raised about the inverse relationship that pertains between economic wealth and social inequality. As a consequence, Chapter 11 explores the evolution of the Irish and Northern Irish welfare states by evaluating responses to vulnerable citizens. Particular attention is paid to the attitude of society to the state's role in welfare provision, and consideration is given to the popular acquiescence that currently prevails in relation to welfare services, north and south.

Finally, in Chapter 12, we examine the impact that EU membership has had on the Republic and Northern Irish states. Here we give detailed consideration to Ireland's changing fortunes and the perceptions of its place within the EU before we turn to the EU's management of cross-border cooperation before and after the 1998 Good Friday

Agreement. The role that the EU has played and might play in the future of all-island Irish politics is further examined in the Conclusion. Consideration is given here to the future prospects for Irish politics: both to Northern Irish politics and to the Republic's politics; and to the North and South jointly in the context of the cooperative arrangements between the Northern Ireland Executive and the Irish Government, and in respect of the UK and Irish intergovernmental arrangements. This will thus draw together the major themes and issues from the book in order to summarize and synthesize the key areas associated with Irish politics, both North and South.

Historical Contexts: A Short Pre-History of Government and Politics in Ireland

As mentioned, in this book we will be examining the dual polities on the island of Ireland and the similarities, linkages and differences between the two. It is necessary to provide a very brief historical context. Ireland was joined to Great Britain by the Act of Union of 1801. By the 1880s there was a strong movement for home rule for Ireland. This was conceded by the British in 1914, though its implementation was delayed by World War I, resulting in rebellion in Dublin in 1916 – the Easter Rising. Rebel activity against British rule continued under the leadership of Michael Collins (1890–1922) and through the creation of the Irish Republican Army (IRA), formed in 1919. In 1921, the British offered 26 counties of Ireland dominion status within the Commonwealth, whilst the six northern counties remained part of the United Kingdom with limited self-government. The Treaty was accepted by a delegation led by Michael Collins, but not by all of his colleagues. The result was the creation of the Irish Free State, the outbreak of civil war and the assassination of Collins.

Those in favour of the Treaty banded together in Cumann na nGaedheal (later reformed as Fine Gael) under the leadership of William T. Cosgrave. Anti-Treaty supporters formed the rival political party, Fianna Fáil, led by Eamon de Valera (1882–1975). In 1937, he too acknowledged the *de facto* partition of Ireland, but claimed *de jure* responsibility for the whole island in articles 2 and 3 of a new constitution. Ireland remained part of the Commonwealth until its withdrawal in 1949, when it declared itself the Republic of Ireland. Despite a series of constitutional amendments in various state referenda, articles 2 and 3, which laid claim to the northern counties, were not removed until 1998 in a referendum enacted as part of the Good Friday Agreement.

In the Republic, the 1937 constitution provides for a president, elected by universal adult suffrage, for a seven-year term and a two-chamber national parliament, consisting of a senate (Seanad Éireann) and a house of representatives (Dáil Éireann), both serving a five-year term. The Seanad has 60 members, 11 nominated by the Taoiseach and 49 elected by panels representative of most aspects of Irish life. The Dáil consists of 166 members elected by universal adult suffrage through the STV system of PR. The President formally appoints the Taoiseach – in practice the leader of the largest party or coalition arrangement in the Dáil. The Taoiseach selects a cabinet and all are collectively responsible to the Dáil, which may be dissolved by the President in the event of a no-confidence vote in the Dáil.

In Northern Ireland, the consequences of the British Government of Ireland Act of 1920 were to establish a six-county state under British rule, but with devolved powers. The Act established two parliaments, North and South, plus a Council of Ireland to promote cooperation between the two areas pending their eventual unification; but the Council was virtually ignored. The parliament in the North had considerable autonomy and power over domestic policy, including law and order. In Westminster, the convention developed of not discussing affairs held to be the responsibility of the Northern Ireland parliament at Stormont. As a consequence, there was little oversight of Northern Ireland affairs by the British Government. In order to improve minority representation, PR had been introduced for Stormont and local elections, but the Ulster Unionist Party (UUP) consolidated its position by abolishing PR for local elections in 1922 and later for Stormont. This, together with the redrawing of local government boundaries, ensured that the UUP won every election from 1921 to 1972 and that opposition parties – labourite or nationalist – were permanently excluded from power.

Whilst there is no doubt that Catholics were discriminated against, debate over the extent of such (intentional and unintentional) discrimination continues. An attack by the Royal Ulster Constabulary on a civil rights march in Derry in October 1968 provoked the beginning of the Northern Ireland 'troubles'. British army support for the police was introduced in 1969. Security steadily worsened, especially after the failure of internment in 1971. An IRA armed campaign for a united Ireland was to lead to thousands of deaths. It was met with strong security measures and a backlash from Loyalist paramilitary groups determined to keep Northern Ireland within the UK. In 1972 direct rule from the UK was reintroduced. Northern Ireland was given its own secretary of state, assisted by a small team of junior ministers. Following a brief but unsuccessful attempt to re-establish a devolved assembly under PR in January 1974 (through the Sunningdale Agreement of 1973), direct rule was resumed in mid-1974. Devolution was attempted again in 1982 but, without cross-community support, did not succeed.

Negotiations between the British and Irish governments culminated in the 1985 Anglo-Irish Agreement, in which the Westminster Government allowed its Dublin counterpart consultative rights on Northern Ireland affairs. Outraged by 'Dublin's interference', Unionists protested, but to little avail. Amid a growing realization on all sides that on the one hand the IRA's campaign would not yield a united Ireland, and on the other hand that the IRA could not be entirely militarily defeated, a peace process developed during the 1990s. Following the 'Downing Street Declaration' of 1993, made jointly by the British and Irish governments, on 31 August 1994 the IRA called a 'complete cessation of military operations'. They were joined by most other Northern paramilitary groups and discussions about representative devolved government for Northern Ireland began once more. These stalled in 1996 with the IRA's temporary (1996–97) break in its ceasefire, but they resumed again, culminating in the Good Friday, or Belfast, Agreement of April 1998.

The Good Friday Agreement provides for three interlocking and interdependent strands of governance. The first strand creates an executive authority comprising up to 12 ministers from the 108-member Northern Ireland Assembly, allocated in proportion to party strengths. The Assembly takes charge of the internal affairs of Northern Ireland in areas such as health, education and agriculture. Other areas such as security, taxation and justice remain the responsibility of the Secretary of State and the UK Government. Decisions taken by the Executive must be ratified by parallel consent rules; a substantial support is needed in the Assembly from nationalists and Unionists. The second strand of the Agreement provides for a North/South ministerial council, with members from the Northern Executive and the Irish Government. Its members engage in consultation, cooperation and action in areas of mutual interest. The third strand is a British–Irish Council comprising representatives from elected parliaments and assemblies in Northern Ireland, the Republic of Ireland, Scotland, Wales, the Isle of Man, the Channel Islands and the House of Commons. This council meets twice yearly to discuss matters of mutual interest.

Political structures in Northern Ireland have thus changed markedly in recent decades, from a Unionist majoritarian parliament to direct rule to devolved consociational government. Structural changes in the Irish Republic have been much less dramatic, but there economic growth and modernization have been remarkable. Amid improved social, economic and political conditions, the traditional hostility between the two polities on the island is waning. In this book we explore the changes that have occurred and we examine the extent to which Northern Ireland and the Irish Republic are marked by similarity or difference.

Part 1

Political Institutions

1

The Executive

The label 'parliamentary government' is a half-truth. It correctly emphasises that a prime minister does not stand alone; he or she depends upon the confidence of a popularly elected assembly at the pinnacle of a system of representation. But parliament does not in any meaningful sense govern; that is the responsibility of the executive in which a prime minister is *primus*.

(Rose, 1991: 9)

Introduction

The Executive is the branch of government responsible for the implementation of laws and policies made by the legislature, the group of decision-makers who take overall responsibility for the direction and coordination of government policy. Executives are usually centred upon the leadership of one individual. This may be the Head of State (e.g. the President in the United States), or the Head of Government (Prime Minister in the UK), or, more occasionally, a combination of the two (such as the semi-presidentialism in France). As has long been noted, 'because a parliamentary system links the legislature and the executive, the prime minister has greater potential influence upon the direction of government than a president subject to the checks and balances of an American-style constitution' (Rose, 1991: 9). This potential, however, is generally circumscribed by a variety of formal institutional constraints, political circumstances and conventions, as well as the broader socio-economic context within which the Prime Minister and government must operate.

In terms of formal institutional constraints, federal states and those with written constitutions usually present the clearest restraints to executive autonomy – in terms of the division of powers and responsibility between the Head of State, Head of Government, cabinet, Legislature and Judiciary. Still, even without these, prime ministers may find themselves equally constrained by the political conditions of their office. Thus, whilst the gift of political office lies in the hands of the Prime Minister, the power of patronage may vary a great deal depending on whether or not that person is leading a large strong and unified party, or is presiding over a coalition. The conventions of cabinet government in different states may also limit the choice or even the pool of talent available in the first place. In Northern Ireland, these conventions amount to formal legal rules of power-sharing. Last but not least, the room for manoeuvre of all prime ministers is also circumscribed by the broader socio-economic environment in which they must operate: increasing international interdependence in global security and economy, global trends in markets and finance, as well as regional and transnational arrangements to accommodate them, may all place limits on executive autonomy.

Symbolic Politics and Executive Authority North and South

Essentially, the Irish case follows the UK model of government. However, added to Ireland's British inheritance of Westminster standards and procedures (reflected in Irish parliamentarianism and the organization of the civil service), Eamon de Valera's redrafting of the constitution in 1937 suffused the state with more United States-style checks and balances (through the creation of the Office of the President and the requirement for popular consent to every constitutional amendment). The Government was to be led by the Taoiseach – the Irish for 'Prime Minister' and literally translated as 'chief' (O'Leary, 1991: 136–7) – reflecting de Valera's wish to underline the Irish character of the state as well as the increased authority that his constitution conferred on the office.

It is argued that the complete redrafting of the Irish constitution by de Valera in 1937 represents not so much the beginning of a 'new world' but rather the culmination of a series of measures designed to bring 'an old and – from de Valera's perspective – desperately unhappy world to a close' (Fanning, 1988: 34). De Valera's quick recalling of a general election in 1933, in order to strengthen his party and provide a democratic mandate for constitutional change, facilitated his new Government in embarking upon a series of measures to legitimate (in their eyes and those of their supporters) the state system that they had inherited (Adshead, 2008). In consequence, the oath of allegiance, the right of appeal to the Privy Council in London, and the Governor General's right to veto legislation were all abolished in 1933. In 1936, the Senate was abolished, together with all references to the Governor General in the constitution (Coakley, 2005b: 22). On a political and symbolic level at least, the redrafting of the 1937 constitution completed the process of Irish independence (Farrell, 1988).

The offices of the executive have also been used in more contemporary Irish politics to make strong symbolic claims about the nature of the state (Bresnihan, 1999). In 1990, the election of Mary Robinson, at the age of 47, as President of Ireland was widely viewed – by Irish political practitioners and commentators alike – as of enormous symbolic value, as the first woman (a Catholic, married to a Protestant) to hold such high office (see Box 1.1) and one whose views were often at odds with the Catholic Church hierarchy. Her CV included independent membership of the Seanad (Upper House of Parliament), professor of law at Trinity College Dublin and extensive experience as a practising constitutional lawyer – when she sought to liberalize contraception laws, advance women's rights and decriminalize homosexuality, as well as opposing the insertion of an anti-abortion clause into the constitution in 1983.

She supported the unsuccessful attempt to remove the ban on divorce in 1986, an effort which finally achieved success in a further referendum in 1995. One government spokesperson declared: 'anyone who doesn't know that Mary Robinson is in favour of divorce hasn't been living in this country for the past twenty years' (*Sunday Tribune*, 5 November 1995, p. 5).

Robinson was elected with 77 per cent of the vote, a level of support which she maintained throughout her presidency. The widespread and enthusiastic support for her seemed indicative of a developing self-image in Ireland: that of a modernizing state which is beginning to acknowledge diversity of tradition, religion and values across the island. It remains debatable to what extent she reflected or promoted the growth of these particular values, but the perception of their increasing importance in Irish society indicates how debates over the religious versus the secular have assumed huge importance in national life.

The devolved government of Northern Ireland is headed by a three tiered arrangement: a First and Deputy First Minister (who, formally at least, are regarded as of equal status); a governing Executive of ten departmental ministers, plus two 'assistants' to the First and Deputy First Ministers; and a third tier legislative assembly of 108 members. This form of devolved government is very different from that experienced under one-party Unionist domination during 1921–72. During those decades, the form of government, headed by a prime minister of Northern Ireland, aped many of the features of Westminster, with one very important exception: there was no recognizable system of opposition. Nationalists generally declined to enter the parliament, based at Stormont from the 1930s onwards, and the Nationalist Party only accepted the role of official opposition in 1965 (Lynn, 1998). The creation of the northern parliament, and the one party executive which dominated it, 'represented the final triumph of exclusivist unionism' (Jackson, 1999: 243). Theoretically, the Northern Ireland Prime Minister and cabinet were responsible to Northern Ireland's parliament. In reality, there was a close bond between the Unionist parliamentary party and its leaders, with sufficient loyalty to the party leadership to render irrelevant such constitutional niceties.

The British government transferred considerable executive authority to the Unionist government, which enjoyed control of all 'low politics', namely those matters not concerning foreign or financial policy. Bew and Patterson (2002) have convincingly confounded the idea that the Unionist executive was merely a sectarian monolith. Moreover, nationalist self-exclusion from a state perceived as illegitimate exacerbated the problem (Buckland, 1981). Nonetheless, the lack of willingness to incorporate nationalists into governing institutions and the perpetuation of sectarian headcount majoritarianism ensured that Northern Ireland's government presided over an 'Orange state' in which a Unionist executive governed on behalf of a Unionist community. Nationalists declined to invest any recognition in the executive and thus governing institutions were seen as partisan tools of domination or oppression. The prime ministers of the state (see Table 1.1) were invariably Unionist 'grandees' from wealthy backgrounds, belonged to the Orange Order and were sectarian (although the depth of their sectarianism varied considerably). Unionist leaders were concerned with supposed 'threats' to the state and adopted conservative outlooks, notwithstanding the reforms attempted by Terence O'Neill. The tone was set by the first Prime Minister,

BOX 1.1

Presidents of Ireland, 1938 to present

25 June 1938–24 June 1945: Douglas Hyde (FF)
The election result of 1937, allowing Fianna Fáil into government, but without an absolute majority and relying on Labour's support, precluded turning the choice of the first president under the constitution into a political contest. Dr Douglas Hyde emerged as a suitable 'non-party' candidate. 'An Irish language enthusiast, a former president of the Gaelic League, a professor and a Protestant, he satisfied sundry national self-images and, at the age of seventy-seven, seemed unlikely to be unduly assertive' (Lee, 1989: 211).

25 June 1945 to 24 June 1959: Sean T. O'Kelly (FF)
Confident of a Fianna Fáil victory in the upcoming election, de Valera departed from the non-party principle and nominated his popular Tánaiste, Sean T. O'Kelly, as candidate – placing Sean Lemass as newly appointed Tánaiste in a good position to succeed him in leading the party. A contemporary of de Valera's, O'Kelly, who 'liked company, particularly the company of women, and could drink a glass or two or more of whisky', was a popular party figure, but not considered as Taoiseach material (Lee, 1989: 239).

25 June 1959 –to 25 June 1973: Eamon de Valera (FF)
It is argued that de Valera 'retired from active politics to the Presidency at the age of 76' (Gallagher, 1977: 376). Born to an emigrant mother in Brooklyn, when his father died at the age of two, his mother sent him home to Ireland to be brought up by an uncle in rural Limerick. A teacher by training, 'De Valera regularly professed to know, not only what the people wanted, but what God himself wanted' (Lee, 1989: 334). These views were epitomized in his historic 'vision of Ireland' speech, printed in the *Irish Press* on 18 March 1943, where he stated that the 'Ireland that we dreamed of would be a land whose countryside would be bright with cosy homesteads, whose fields and villages would be joyous with the sounds of industry, with the romping of sturdy children, the contests of athletic youths, the laughter of comely maidens, whose firesides would be the forums for the wisdom of serene old age'.

25 June 1973 to 17 November 1974: Erskine Childers (FF), died in office
Born in London on 11 December 1905, after living in England and France he moved to Dublin in 1931 to become the advertisement manager of the newly former *Irish Press* newspaper. During 1936–44 he was Secretary of the Federation of Irish Manufacturers. Elected to the Dáil in 1938, he served in 1944–48 as a junior minister, and, in 1951–54 and 1957–73, he held a series of government ministerial appointments, serving as Tánaiste in 1969–73. Although Childers 'enjoyed considerable political authority and public affection', his attempts to push the boundaries of his office (by establishing a 'think tank' to examine the long-term needs of the country) met with failure, when the Taoiseach Liam Cosgrave vetoed the move (Elgie and Fitzgerald, 2005: 310). 'Pushing the limits of office' was not successfully achieved until Robinson's presidency in 1990.

19 December 1974 to 22 October 1976: Cearbhall O'Dalaigh (FF), resigned
A Fianna Fáil Attorney General during 1946–48, and again in 1951–54, he was Chief Justice in 1961–73 and served with distinction as Judge of European Court from 1973 until his nomination for president in 1974. 'Widely respected as a scholar and gentleman',

→

→

O'Dalaigh was 'no party hack' (Lee, 1989: 483). Arguably, it was this independence of mind that proved to be his undoing when – having referred the Emergency Powers Bill (invoked by the government in September 1976 following the assassination of the British Ambassador on 23 July 1976) to the Supreme Court to check its constitutionality – he felt obliged to resign from office when the Minister for Defence, Paddy Donegan, suggested that his behaviour was a 'thundering disgrace'. O'Dalaigh viewed the Taoiseach's refusal to demand Donegan's resignation (though proferred twice) as undermining this office and making his tenure as president untenable (Gallagher, 1977).

3 December 1976 to 2 December 1990: Patrick J. Hillery (FF)
Following O'Dalaigh's resignation, Fianna Fáil nominated Hillery, who secured office unopposed (coincidently ensuring that he was not available for an inevitable party leadership contest with Liam Cosgrave later; see Lee, 1989: 482–3). According to Joe Lee (*The Sunday Tribune*, 16 March 1997), his style was said to be 'so low key that opinion polls recorded substantial support for the abolition of the presidency' towards the end of his tenure. By the time of his death, on 14 April 2008, however, the state mourned 'a private and even shy man whose sense of fairness, kindness and hard work were based on the values he grew up with at his home in Milltown Malbay ... He was one of our own. You'd see him anywhere and he'd stop and chat to any of us. He was the family doctor and everyone loved him' (*Irish Times*, 17 April 2008).

3 December 1990 to 12 September 1997: Mary Robinson (L), resigned
Mary Robinson is 'not a back-slapping, hail-fellow politician. She won't feign chummy chat in the manner expected of photo-opportunities just to look like a player' (*The Sunday Tribune*, 16 March 1997). Building her presidency on the principles of inclusiveness and empowerment, Robinson's sweeping election victory gave her both a mandate for change and for greater autonomy from government. In all but the most obviously political areas, Robinson left it up to the government to intervene or not, thereby placing 'on the government the onus of either being seen to instruct the presidency or of accepting whatever the President chose to do' (Morgan, 1999: 270). According to Joe Lee, 'She is a feminist, but not a fundamentalist. She has succeeded in attracting women without repelling men. ... And she is so obviously intellectually gifted that nobody can claim she has not achieved all her distinctions' (*The Sunday Tribune*, 16 March 1997).

11 November 1997 to present: Mary McAleese (FF)
A former RTE journalist and presenter, barrister, Reid Professor of Law at TCD and pro-vice-chancellor of Queens University Belfast, McAleese was the first president to be born in Northern Ireland. A northern nationalist, schooled just off the Falls Road, she moved with her family to county Down following sectarian attacks on the family home and pubs. McAleese is a strong (but unpredictable) Catholic: she is opposed to contraception, *in vitro* fertilization, divorce, interdenominational schools and actively against abortion; yet she supported David Norris in his High Court case to have the legislation on homosexual conduct declared unconstitutional and has campaigned vigorously for women priests. On taking up office, following the biggest electoral victory by any president, McAleese declared her hopes of being 'a President for a new century and a new millennium' (*Irish Times*, 1 November 1997).

James Craig, who adopted an 'increasingly parochial and sectarian disposition', even though the 1920 Government of Ireland Act, which founded the state, expressly forbade discrimination (Patterson, 1996: 7).

With the onset of the 'Troubles' in Northern Ireland, the devolved executive was replaced by direct rule from Westminster, seen as more benign, less sectarian and mildly reformist, although not in the security arena, where a 'war' to defeat the insurgent IRA was fought for three decades. Under direct rule, the Secretary of State for Northern Ireland assumed the executive functions previously held by the local Prime Minister and cabinet. The suspension of the Unionist government in 1972 was bitterly opposed by Unionists and introduced as a temporary measure, designed to last one year (Boyce, 1996; Hennessey, 2005). In reality, it marked the permanent disappearance of one-party government and the end of Unionist devolution after 50 years. An experiment, the 1973 Sunningdale Agreement, created a devolved power-sharing executive, in which moderate Unionists and nationalists, plus the 'middle-ground' Alliance Party, shared power in a 'grand coalition' created via the association of political elites evident in the consociational political deal. With militants on both sides excluded and unsupportive, and amid diminishing public backing, the Sunningdale deal lasted a mere five months. A further quarter-century of direct rule from Westminster followed, prior to the return of devolved government in 1999 after the 1998 Good Friday Agreement, a multiparty deal in which Unionists and nationalists agreed to share power. Devolved government was unstable from 1999 until 2002, collapsing three times before the return of direct rule. In 2007, following the previous year's St Andrews Agreement, a deal was reached allowing the restoration of a devolved, inclusive, governing executive and legislative assembly.

Formal Provisions for Executive Authority

In the Republic of Ireland, Article 15.1.2 of the constitution declares that executive authority resides with the Oireachtas, comprising the President, the Dáil (Lower House of Parliament) and the Seanad (upper House of Parliament). The President is elected by universal adult suffrage for a seven-year term. Every citizen over the age of 35 is eligible to compete for the office, provided that they are nominated *either* by at least 20 members of the Houses of the Oireachtas *or* by at least four county or county borough councils. Despite the popular vote for election, the nomination procedure ensures that would-be candidates can 'not even reach the starting-post without the backing of one of the main parties or some combination of the smaller ones' (Gallagher, 1988: 79). Where only one candidate is nominated to the office, there is no need to proceed to election. This was the case with the presidencies of Douglas Hyde, Cearbhall O'Dalaigh and Patrick Hillery, in 1938, 1974 and 1976 respectively, and for Mary McAleese's second term of office in 2004. The office and functions of the President of Ireland are dealt with in Articles 12 and 13 of the constitution.

Although the President does not have executive powers and acts mainly on the advice of government, the office holds a limited number of significant functions for government. The President appoints the Taoiseach on the nomination of Dáil

Table 1.1　*Governing Northern Ireland 1921–2007: Prime Ministers and Secretaries of State*

Years	Prime Minister of NI	Secretary of State	Type of government
1922–40	James Craig		Unionist majoritarian
1940–43	John Miller Andrews		Unionist majoritarian
1943–63	Basil Brooke		Unionist majoritarian
1963–69	Terence O'Neill		Unionist majoritarian
1969–71	James Chichester-Clark		Unionist majoritarian
1971–72	Brian Faulkner		Unionist majoritarian
1972–73		William Whitelaw	Direct rule
1973–74		Francis Pym (to March 1974)	Direct rule
1974 (Jan–May)	Brian Faulkner	Merlyn Rees (from March 1974)	Power sharing
1974–76		Merlyn Rees	Direct rule
1976–79		Roy Mason	Direct rule
1979–81		Humphrey Atkins	Direct rule
1981–84		James Prior	Direct rule
1984–85		Douglas Hurd	Direct rule
1985–89		Tom King	Direct rule
1989–92		Peter Brooke	Direct rule
1992–97		Patrick Mayhew	Direct rule
1997–99		Mo Mowlam	Direct rule
1999–2002	David Trimble*	Peter Mandelson (Oct 1999–Jan 2001) John Reid (Jan 2001–Oct 2002)	Power sharing
2002–05		Paul Murphy	Direct rule
2005–07		Peter Hain (to May 2007)	Direct rule
2007–08	Ian Paisley* (from May 2007)	Shaun Woodward	Power sharing
2008–	Peter Robinson* (from June 2008)		

* The title is First Minister – officially the First and Deputy First Minister are of equal status. Seamus Mallon was Deputy First Minister alongside Trimble; Martin McGuinness alongside Ian Paisley and Peter Robinson.

Eireann and members of government on the advice of the Taoiseach. The Taoiseach also advises the President over the acceptance or otherwise of the resignations of ministers and on the summoning and dismissing of the Dáil. The President reserves the right to dissolve the Dáil due to a no-confidence vote taken against the Government. Subject to the 1954 Defence Act, the President is vested with supreme command of the defence forces. He or she receives and accredits all ambassadors and may, acting on the authority and advice of government, exercise limited executive functions in connection with international affairs. All bills passed by the Oireachtas are promulgated by the President, who may refer any bill (excluding money bills) to the Supreme Court to test their constitutionality. This power may be exercised only in consultation with the Council of State, comprising the Taoiseach, Tanaiste (Deputy Prime Minister), Ceann Comhairle (Chair of Dáil Éireann), Cathaoirleach (Chair of the Seanad), the Attorney General, the President of the High Court and the Chief Justice (other members may include previous Taoisigh, presidents, or chief justices willing to serve and up to seven nominees of the President). The final decision, however, rests with the President alone. This presidential power was employed on 14 occasions up to June 2004 (Gallagher, 2005a: 85). On eight occasions, the Supreme Court found the bill constitutional and on the other six found either the bill as a whole, or some part of it, to be unconstitutional. In the event of the President becoming incapacitated, the Council of State may carry out the functions of the presidency. The President's office, in practice, however, is far more clearly constrained by the Taoiseach and government, whose permission he or she must first obtain to address either the citizenry or the parliament (Art. 13.7), or even to leave the state (Art. 12.9).

According to the 1937 constitution, executive power was to be clearly vested in the Government (the equivalent of the cabinet in other liberal democracies, distinguished by the use of a capital 'G'), headed by the Taoiseach. In this set-up, although the Office of President takes 'precedence over all other persons in the State' (Art. 12.1), it was clearly not envisaged as playing an active part in the day-to-day decision-making process. Instead, it seems that de Valera intended the Office of President to be something of a 'reserve power', 'intervening on the people's behalf only if Government or parliament appeared to be threatening to violate the letter or spirit of the Constitution' (Gallagher, 1988: 76; see also: Dáil Debates, vol. 67, 11 May 1937, cols 40, 51). Even so, the discretionary powers afforded to the President 'fall far short of what a President would require if his or her role were genuinely to guard the Constitution or prevent the Government or Oireachtas attempting to set up a dictator' (ibid.). In this respect, the Republic of Ireland is unusual in bequeathing these powers to the judiciary (see Chapter 4).

The constitution enacted in 1937 provides for a Government of not less than seven members and not more than 15 (Art. 28.1). The Government sits at 'the apex of the parliamentary system, fusing legislative and executive power, and is collectively responsible to Dáil Eireann' (O'Leary, 1991: 137). All Government members must be members of Oireachtas, but no more than two members from the Seanad, with the proviso that the Tánaiste and Minister for Finance must be members of the Dáil (Art. 28.7.1). Government is led by the Taoiseach – in practice the leader of the largest party or coalition arrangement in the Dáil. Table 1.2 shows the political leaders of the Republic since 1922.

The Tánaiste is appointed by the Taoiseach and is most typically also leader of the smaller coalition party in government. Whilst it is clear that de Valera's modification of the provisions for government in the Free State Constitution specifically raised the authority of the Taoiseach vis-à-vis the cabinet, it is also true that for the

Table 1.2 *Political Leaders in the Irish Republic since 1922*

Years	Leader	Party
1922	Michael Collins	(CnG)
1922–32	William T. Cosgrave	(CNG)
1932–7	Eamon de Valera	(FF)
1937–48	Eamon de Valera	(FF)
1948–51	John A. Costello	(FG)
1951–4	Eamon de Valera	(FF)
1954–7	John A. Costello	(FG)
1957–9	Eamon de Valera	(FF)
1959–66	Sean Lemass	(FF)
1966–73	Jack Lynch	(FF)
1973–7	Liam Cosgrave	(FG) coalition with Labour
1977–9	Jack Lynch	(FF)
1979–81	Charles Haughey	(FF)
1981–2	Garret FitzGerald	(FG) coalition with Labour
1982	Charles Haughey	(FF)
1982–7	Garret FitzGerald	(FG) coalition with Labour
1987–9	Charles Haughey	(FF)
1989–92	Charles Haughey	(FF) coalition with (PD)
1992	Albert Reynolds	(FF) coalition with (PD)
1993–4	Albert Reynolds	(FF) coalition with Labour
1994–7	John Bruton	(FG) coalition with Labour and Democratic Left
1997–2002 and 2002–7	Bertie Ahern	(FF) coalition with (PD)
2007–8	Bertie Ahern	(FF) coalition with Green party, (PD) and Independents
2008–	Brian Cowen	(FF) coalition with Green party, (PD) and Independents

May 2008: a change of leadership in Fianna Fáil resulted in the replacement of Bertie Ahern with Brian Cowen: the coalition remained in place.
(CNG) Cumann na nGaedheal; (FF) Fianna Fáil; (FG) Fine Gael; (PD) Progressive Democrats.

most part this new constitutional shift in emphasis was only an acknowledgement of what had already occurred in practice – if not under the first Prime Minister, then certainly since (Chubb, 1988: 96).

Referring to the changes in the 1937 constitution, de Valera argued that he was 'only making explicit what was implicit in the past' (Dáil Debates, 14 June 1937, vol. 68, cols 421–3). Nonetheless, some contemporaries were concerned that too much power would be concentrated in the office of the Taoiseach. Intervening in a Dáil debate on the new Irish constitution of 1937, Cosgrave argued that ministerial independence should be protected from too assertive a prime minister claiming that 'in this new constitution, the prime minister has been given pre-eminent power and position' (Dáil Debates, 14 Nov 1937, col. 348). As it turned out, however, de Valera did not flaunt his authority in this regard, forcing only six government resignations or non-reinstatements in 21 years (Farrell, 1971b: 39). Still, the consequence was that for some time comparative scholars tended to view the position of Taoiseach among the strongest heads of government (O'Leary, 1991; King, 1994), though this pre-eminence has been steadily undermined by the normalization of coalition politics in Ireland since 1989.

Devolved government from 1921–72 in Northern Ireland was created via the 1920 Government of Ireland Act, which insisted, in section 75, that the supreme authority of the Westminster Parliament remained unaffected by devolution (Bogdanor, 1999). Similar caveats apply to the modern devolved government in the region, with powers conferred by Westminster, based upon the provisions of the 1998 Northern Ireland Act (which followed the Good Friday Agreement) and further legislation which followed the 2006 St Andrews Agreement. The assertion of Westminster that it remained the ultimate arbiter of what powers can be transferred – and when – is not mere constitutional nit-picking. Although the 1920s to the 1970s were characterized by Westminster disinterest and a 'hands-off' approach, the 1998–2002 phase of unstable devolved government in Northern Ireland was characterized by regular interventions from the Secretary of State to suspend the institutions. The subsequent sustained period of political stability for Northern Ireland has diminished such interventionism.

Political Constraints to Executive Power

The constitution of the Irish Republic provides the Taoiseach with considerable powers of appointment, including the appointment of other members of government (subject to parliamentary approval) (Art.13.1.2); the Attorney General, who has a seat at the cabinet table (Art. 30.2); 11 members of Seanad Éireann; and the junior ministers (ministers of state), who, though legally are appointed by government, practically are appointed by the Taoiseach. To these may be added considerable 'resources of office' (considered below). Still, however, the realpolitik of securing and maintaining government leadership tends to place a number of practical constraints on the Taoiseach's scope for exercising these powers, notably the conventions of coalition and cabinet appointments.

In Northern Ireland, the Executive operates within a semi-autonomous political framework, the boundaries of which are determined at Westminster. It is the UK Parliament which determines how much power is given to Northern Ireland. In an asymmetric devolution model, Northern Ireland stands between Scotland (maximum devolution) and Wales (minimal devolution) in terms of the powers awarded. There are three categories of legislative powers: devolved (those already transferred); reserved (those which could be transferred at some point); and retained (those which are held by Westminster, seemingly in perpetuity). The Northern Ireland executive has considerable powers in the areas of education, culture, regeneration and social transformation, but little fiscal power (it is unable to raise taxation locally) and none in terms of foreign policy.

The authority of the First and Deputy First Minister is subject to major constraint. Both have to be approved by a majority of Assembly members. The 1998 Northern Ireland Act ensures that devolution can only exist if executive places are shared between representatives of the Unionist and nationalist communities. Executive representation is allocated according to the strength of political parties in the Assembly. The D'Hondt formula allocates seats according to parties using the equation: Seats held by a party/(1 + Number of ministries held). Where two parties hold the same number of seats, the party with the higher first preference vote at the election is allocated the next ministry.

Use of the D'Hondt formula allows representation for all four of Northern Ireland's main parties across the sectarian divide and within the Executive, and may thus be seen as laudable. It provides a major check upon First and Deputy First Ministerial power, but, more negatively, may produce party fiefdoms and departmentalism at the expense of collective cabinet government. The ill-fated executive of 1999–2002 was memorably described as little more than a loose holding company of ministers rather than a joined-up government (Laver, 2000). Political parties, not the First or the Deputy First Minister, nominate ministers to run departments, which may become party vehicles. The talent pool and collective commitment across parties may be limited and it is difficult for Assembly members to remove incompetent ministers, requiring cross-community backing that is unlikely to be forthcoming.

Coalition Politics

According to Mitchell (2003a: 220) the history of coalition negotiations 'can be conveniently divided into three periods': before 1973; 1973–89; and after 1989. During the first period, Fianna Fáil's hold on government from 1932 to 1948 entrenched the majoritarian system of government. Throughout the period, Fianna Fáil dominated electoral politics as single-party government, being replaced on only two occasions by diverse coalitions. Not surprisingly, de Valera was a strong proponent of single-party government and often expressed the view that coalitions were inherently weak. In these conditions, the adversarial Westminster-style of government inherited from the British provided 'an ideal template for the continuation of civil war politics in the Dáil', so that together throughout this period the hegemony of Fianna Fáil and the strong leadership style of de Valera meant that 'Dáil Éireann moved even closer to (if not beyond) its Westminster origins, and became a chamber in which the opposition had few parliamentary rights and little opportunity for input into policy-making' (MacCarthaigh, 2005: 68). During this period, 'Fianna Fáil's pivotal position was such that, if the opposition parties refused to combine against it, then no governing alternative existed' (Mitchell, 2003c: 130).

The period between 1973 and 1989 retained the same logic of electoral competition, often characterized as Fianna Fáil versus 'the rest', but 'the rest' were now streamlined into just two parties – Fine Gael and Labour – as opposed to the five parties that were required to oust Fianna Fáil in 1948 (Mitchell, 2000: 130). The simplified politics of coalition bargaining was further facilitated by Labour and Fine Gael moving closer together so as to present a viable alternative government to Fianna Fáil. During this 16-year period, no Irish government served a consecutive term and Fianna Fáil single-party governments alternated with Fine Gael/Labour coalitions after each government resignation (Mitchell, 2003c: 130).

In 1989, the Fianna Fáil Taoiseach and leader of a minority government, Charles Haughey, called a snap election in the hope of winning an overall majority. But this did not happen, and in order to stay in power he was obliged to ditch the Fianna Fáil principle of never entering a coalition, by going into government with the Progressive Democrats (PD) (Mitchell, 2000: 131). The decision to coalesce proved to be a watershed and effectively ended the 'Fianna Fáil versus the rest axis around which political and parliamentary life had revolved since the mid-1920s' (MacCarthaigh, 2005: 85). Even though Fianna Fáil was still the largest party, because of its need for coalition to govern, it was now an 'ordinary party' that needed to 'fish for partners' like any other. This meant that for the first time *all* the parties now had a choice of coalition partners. According to Mitchell (2003c: 131), 'in coalition politics choice is power'.

More generally, the coincidental improvement in public finances helped remove the association of coalition and crisis. Since then, both the growth of the 'Celtic tiger' and the Northern Ireland peace process were overseen by coalition governments arguably securing their reputation as competent instruments of government. Aside from its impact on relative party positions, the convention of coalition government has also served to raise the profile of the Tánaiste (most usually the leader of the main coalition partner) as a rival power at the centre of government, demonstrated by (the leader of the Labour party) Dick Spring's insistence on the creation of the Office of Tánaiste in 1993 as the price for entering into government with Fianna Fáil (Finlay, 1998: 157). As part of his 'broadening democracy' agenda in government (contained in the coalition's joint *Programme for a Partnership Government, 1993–7*), the role and functions of the Office of the Tánaiste were designed to, in the words of the Fianna Fáil leader of the time, Albert Reynolds, 'encompass briefing and advising the Tánaiste generally on all Government policy matters; representing the Government on the new National Economic and Social Forum and thereby ensuring direct liaison through the Minister of State and Chief Whip attached to my Department' (Dáil Debates, vol.426, 17 February 1993). As a result, he received all government papers, not just those dealing with his own ministerial brief (Foreign Affairs). The introduction of *Partnership Programme Managers* to oversee the execution and implementation of the coalition's joint programme, so as to 'overcome bureaucratic and political obstacles to policy delivery' (Mitchell, 2003b: 438), served as a further check upon the Office and powers of the Taoiseach, which were now counter-balanced to some degree by the Office and powers of the Tánaiste (for details, see Farrell, 1993b). Although the office of Tánaiste was later abolished when the 'Rainbow Government' (a three-way coalition between Fine Gael, Labour and Democratic Left, 1994–7) left office, coalition partners are still in a good position to influence the shape and scope of government.

Suggesting that the study of coalition politics should extend beyond 'the traditional focus on government formation and dissolution', Mitchell (1999: 269) argues that coalition arrangements may have a significant impact upon the policies of government in 'the actual life of the coalition'. Junior coalition partners may seek to preserve their 'brand identity' by extracting commitments to policy on key distinguishing issues either in the programme for government or in the arrangements for government. Thus, for example, in the 1993–4 Fianna Fáil/Labour coalition, Labour secured the establishment of a Department of Equality and Law Reform, which began 'a process of reform of family law culminating in the divorce referendum of 1995' (Elgie and Fitzgerald, 2005: 314). In 1997, as a result of the Fianna Fáil/PD coalition, a Department of Public Enterprise was formed from parts of the Departments of Enterprise, Trade and Employment; Transport; Energy; and Communications. In 2002, again in a Fianna Fáil/PD coalition, the brief of Equality and Law Reform was merged into the Department of Justice, in order to 'reflect or … emphasise new priorities in government' (*Irish Times*, 27 June 1997). It was perhaps no coincidence that this change also resulted in a larger cabinet portfolio for key PD Minister, Michael McDowell.

Northern Ireland's devolved government is based upon statutory coalition, set against a backdrop of institutionalized division, in which parallel or weighted majorities of Unionists and nationalists are required for key legislative measures. Coalition may have been more akin to a loveless marriage in its first (1999–2002) phase after the Good Friday Agreement. During this period, Democratic Unionist Party (DUP) ministers undermined the Executive by rotating ministers, refusing to deal with Sinn Féin, boycotting executive meetings and refusing to recognize the North–South Ministerial Council established under Strand Two of the Agreement. For their part, Sinn Féin's ministers refused to recognize the police service of the state they themselves were serving in the Executive. Given that policing and justice were non-devolved matters, the boycott did not affect the Executive directly, but its net effect was to undermine confidence in Sinn Féin's role in government. With Sinn Féin declaring support for policing in 2007, the Executive and Assembly were restored to a seemingly much more secure basis, with participation by all parties in the interlinked institutions of the Northern Ireland executive and assembly, the all-Ireland ministerial council (the North–South dimension) and the British–Irish Council (the East–West dimension).

Cabinet Conventions

'Compared to other established parliamentary democracies, Irish prime ministers have possibly the most limited pool from which to choose their cabinet' (O'Malley, 2006: 319). Managerially, the Taoiseach has to choose some 30 cabinet and junior ministers from a limited pool of perhaps fewer than 90 deputies that support him (O'Leary, 1991: 137). Added to this, the fact that there is little tradition in Ireland of dismissing ministers mid-term, reshuffles are uncommon in Ireland (Budge, 1985). Further, in a small polity where all possible candidates for selection are known personally to the Taoiseach, cabinet choices may easily wield significant influence over governmental or even party political cohesion. Taken together, these, and the fact that many more Irish ministers depend on politics for their livelihood, with no obvious alternative sinecures to offer

(O'Malley, 2006: 319), tend to encourage conservatism in Taoiseach cabinet selection. In other words, Taoisigh are less inclined to take risks in cabinet selection, tending usually to hire a 'safe pair of hands' from the limited pool available to them (O'Malley, 2006). If, as O'Leary (1991: 137) suggests, 'at least half of these deputies will be unsuitable for office on grounds of youth, unwillingness to serve, administrative incompetence, or emergent (or fully-blown) senility', such caution makes practical sense.

Whilst in theory the Taoiseach's powers to nominate 11 members of the Seanad and to appoint up to two cabinet ministers from the Seanad gives significant executive discretion, in practice this is not the case. To date this discretion has been used only three times, most recently in the short-lived Fine Gael/Labour coalition, when the Taoiseach Garret FitzGerald wished to appoint someone to Foreign Affairs who shared his views completely (most significantly in relation to Northern Ireland, during the run-up to the Anglo-Irish Treaty). Most usually, however, the fact that the Seanad is convoked some three months after the Dáil has tended to make this practice unworkable. Moreover, there tends to be a general understanding that 'Ministers should be Dáil people', which is perhaps a more astute appreciation of 'a Taoiseach's political dependence on TDs' (O'Malley, 2006: 324).[1]

Additionally, the choice of government members by Taoisigh may be constrained by other political expediencies such as factionalism and geopolitics. In the case of the former, a prudent Taoiseach may find it wiser to appoint rival ministers into his cabinet, even over his own party faithful, in order to stymie proto-rebellion. Presumably, this logic explains Charles Haughey's appointment of Dessie O'Malley and Martin O'Donoghue, both of whom were later to leave Fianna Fáil to form a new independent party – the Progressive Democrats – under O'Malley's leadership. As to the latter, O'Malley (2006: 329) points to the 'established political wisdom ... that certain areas in Ireland must have a minister' – a rule of thumb that usually places one Cork representative at the cabinet table in most governments.

With Northern Ireland's Executive places being conditional upon the application of D'Hondt there is a reliance upon each political party choosing the best talent available. Choices are necessarily limited. The region's governing political parties muster a total membership of less than 20,000. These same parties do yield the vast bulk of Assembly representatives: 99 of the 108 Assembly members belonged to the Executive parties of the DUP, the Ulster Unionist Party (UUP), Sinn Féin and the Social Democratic and Labour Party (SDLP) after the 2007 election. Nonetheless, the talent pool is shallow in forming an Executive which provides positions for 11 per cent of Assembly members, compared to the mere 3 per cent of MPs in the House of Commons who operate at cabinet level.

Cabinet conventions have yet to develop fully given the infant status of Northern Ireland's Executive. The importance of committee structures is apparent, however, in scrutinizing the role of the Executive and in shaping legislation. Importantly, departmental committees are always chaired by an Assembly member drawn from the opposite community to that of the minister. Thus Sinn Féin's ministers, for example, find themselves dealing with committees chaired by UUP or DUP Assembly members. In common with Executive departmental nominations, proposals for committee chairs are subject to cross-community Assembly approval.

Socio-Economic Constraints to Executive Autonomy

In a small open economy, such as the Republic of Ireland's, it might be expected that the economic environment would act as a considerable constraint to executive autonomy. A survey of senior civil servants and members of the Dáil found that 74 per cent tended to perceive globalization as 'a largely non-negotiable external economic constraint' (Smith and Hay, 2007: 10), with 62.3 per cent seeing European integration as 'a threat to the autonomy of domestic policy-makers' (Smith and Hay, 2007: 14).

Still, Irish governments have worked hard to find ways of mediating international forces. The *Programme for National Recovery* (1987–90), the *Programme for Economic and Social Progress* (1991–3), the *Programme for Competitiveness and Work* (1994–6), *Programme 2000* (1997–2000), *Programme for Prosperity and Fairness* (2000–2), *Programme for Sustaining Progress* (2003–5) and the latest *Towards 2016*, where representatives of employer organizations, trade unions, farmers and – since 1997 – the community and voluntary sector (i.e. the 'Social Partners') work in common institutions[2] with government to deliberate about economic and social policy, are often portrayed as innovative and reflexive governance mechanisms that allow Irish governments to mediate the impact of global forces on a small, open economy (House and McGrath, 2004; O'Donnell, 2008). Moreover, it could easily be argued that since taking responsibility for Social Partnership in 1987, the Office of the Taoiseach has grown in importance by taking specific responsibility for the coordination of partnership agreements and arrangements. The same argument could also be made regarding the impact of EU membership (Laffan and O'Mahoney, 2007: 173).

For Northern Ireland, the main socio-economic constraints upon the Executive are the public sector dependency of the post-Troubles economy and the lack of fiscal autonomy. The Barnett Formula, introduced in 1980, continues to dominate expenditure plans, being based mainly upon population at the expense of the needs of the infrastructure. Whilst tax-varying powers might yet be conceded to the region, such a move would hardly be a panacea; the power has yet to be used in Scotland, given the political difficulties which would accrue to any party introducing a tax increase. The failure of Northern Ireland to attract inward investment pre-dated and post-dated the Troubles, although three decades of violence obviously exacerbated the situation. By the early 1980s, Northern Ireland's special problems rendered it largely immune to the monetarist experiments of Thatcherism. The province's citizens have, from those times, been the largest recipients per head of Treasury public expenditure and have been insulated from any supposed Barnett 'squeeze', or any needs-based formula (Wilson, 1989; Midwinter, 2007). The leaders of the 2007 Northern Ireland Executive negotiated a start-up financial package from the British and Irish governments, but this only marginally alleviated economic pressures.

Impact of EU Membership

The governmental machinery to develop and coordinate Irish policy on EU issues has evolved out of that used before. Formal governmental structures have remained largely unchanged with Ireland's membership of the EU and it is claimed that 'by and large, EU business was grafted onto the pre-existing pattern of public policy making in Ireland through a process of what might be called "internalization"' (Laffan, 2000: 129). 'Internalization' refers to the Irish system of European administration, whereby the majority of EU associated business is carried out by the relevant national departments in any given policy area (Laffan, 2001). Within this system, the so-called 'Holy Trinity', comprising the Departments of Foreign Affairs, Finance and the Taoiseach's Office, maintains overarching responsibility for coordination of policy across different areas (Laffan, 2001: 34). There has been a shift of responsibilities from the Department of Foreign Affairs to the Office of the Taoiseach, which arguably augments the significance and influence of the latter.

Until March 1987, the European Communities Committee was chaired by the Deputy Secretary of Foreign Affairs and serviced by that department. Thereafter, responsibility was transferred to the Taoiseach's Office, when the then Taoiseach, Charles Haughey, designated a portfolio for the coordination of EU policy to be held by the Minister of State in his department. In consequence, it became clear that the Committee was 'no longer a purely administrative committee but spans the administrative/political divide' (Laffan, 1991a: 191). In 1989, this committee became a planning committee, with organizational and logistical responsibilities in the run-up to the 1990 Irish Presidency (Laffan, 2000: 131). At this point, its policy coordination functions were superseded by the establishment, again by Charles Haughey, of a Ministerial Group, though the Ministers and Secretaries Group (MSG) was maintained in order 'to co-ordinate the preparation of a National Plan for Delors I and to negotiate the Community Support Framework' (ibid.). Subsequently, a high-level committee of ministers and senior civil servants was established and the Taoiseach's Office was heavily involved in the establishment of seven regions in 1988 in response to Commission demands for partnership in implementing EU structural funds (Laffan and O'Mahony, 2007: 173). However, the EU's decision to designate the whole of Ireland as a *single region* for funding allocation purposes 'postponed the development of political, representative and administrative structures for regional development in Ireland' (O'Donnell and Walsh, 1995: 225) and arguably contributed further to centralized executive authority (see Chapter 9).

EU membership of Northern Ireland is filtered via a UK prism. The UK Government acts as the representative for Northern Ireland affairs within the EU, although the First and Deputy First Minister's Office and Northern Ireland's three MEPs make representations to the national government on pertinent matters. The main impact of EU membership has been in terms of a 'peace dividend'. The substantial sums provided by the PEACE programmes has allowed a plethora of community and cross-border projects to develop. All-Ireland activity within an EU context is less threatening to Unionists than other forms of 'North-Southery' (Tannam, 1999). The most important cross-border established under the Good Friday Agreement was the Special European Union Programmes Body, which acts as agent for the implementation of PEACE programmes and has the widest remit of any of the post-1998 all-island executive bodies.

Political and Administrative Resources of Office

Notwithstanding the various influences and potential constraints upon their practical political authority, most prime ministers – by virtue of their office – have access to a range of political and administrative resources unavailable to other politicians: directly, in terms of their constitutional position and powers; indirectly, in terms of their national and international political profile, their access to the media and associated perks; and the staffing and administrative resources associated with prime ministerial office.

Head of Government

Articles 13.1.1 and 28.5.1 of the constitution officially designate the Taoiseach as Head of Government. In this capacity, the Taoiseach meets and negotiates with heads of state and heads of government within and outside of the EU in a variety of international contexts. In consequence, amongst the whole of government the Taoiseach easily benefits the most from a high media profile and the 'trappings of office'. According to Chubb (1992: 185), the Taoiseach 'personifies the government, and, from the time of Lemass onwards, the practice of building up the personal image of leaders by assiduous public relations activities has increased their potential to dominate'. The First and Deputy First Minister roles in Northern Ireland are less powerful and more symbolic. This is partly a result of their duopoly status, with neither regarded as superior to the other, but, more importantly, reflecting Northern Ireland's position as just one part of the United Kingdom.

Political Party

With the exception of John A. Costello, 1948–51 and 1954–7, all Taoisigh have been party leaders. Elgie and Fitzgerald (2005: 318) argue that within highly centralized parties (such as Fianna Fáil and Fine Gael) this constitutes a significant source of power. Generally speaking, the position of the Taoiseach is stronger in a unified party than one divided. Some historic leaders, such as Cosgrave, de Valera, Lemass and Haughey, developed a 'cult of leadership'. Chubb (1992: 187) recalls an interview with Lemass on 3 February 1969, in which the latter explained that in the event of a difference of opinion between him and his cabinet, he would say to them: 'Do as I do or get another leader'. Although it is hard to think of any Taoiseach being quite so cavalier in more contemporary politics, there are still examples of Taoisigh who have tried. In 1981, Garret FitzGerald's decision to appoint his trusted confidante and friend, James Dooge, as Minister for Foreign Affairs, whom he had nominated to the Seanad for this very purpose, was subsequently told by the Chair of his parliamentary party that 'TDs were insulted that he thought none of them capable of doing the job and that he had lost their trust' (O'Malley, 2006: 325; see also: O'Byrnes, 1986). In 1993, Albert Reynolds's stubborn refusal to reconsider his decision to appoint Harry Whelehan to the position of Attorney General cost him both the coalition government and the party leadership.

The coalitional nature of the Northern Ireland government and the operation of D'Hondt means that party strengths within the Assembly determine the shape of the Executive. Party leaderships are important in determining executive positions by deciding which party representatives will be nominated for departmental posts. Party leaders consult only with senior colleagues in making these nominations and the process is very much 'top-down'. It is not automatic that party leaders take the key positions. For example, Sinn Féin's President, Gerry Adams, did not take a ministerial position in the post-2007 executive, instead nominating Martin McGuinness for the role of Deputy First Minister and proposing other colleagues for departmental portfolios. Likewise, Mark Durkan, the SDLP leader, did not join the Executive.

Power of Initiation

Above all others in Government, the Taoiseach is best placed to shape the policy prerogatives of government. Despite the constrictions of coalition, the Taoiseach sets the agenda and order of items for cabinet, thereby controlling 'the time given to consideration of each item, who is to speak, and when a decision should be reached – or postponed' (Elgie and Fitzgerald, 2005: 315). Garret FitzGerald (2004: 68) acknowledges that during his own period in office, with respect to Northern Ireland policy, 'the Cabinet knew that I intended to determine both the broad lines of policy and the detail of its application'. And in relation to his other 'pet policy' – development aid – 'neither the Minister for Finance nor the Cabinet expected to be able to change my mind, and did not seek to do so'. In 1996, Farrell (1996: 176) noted that 'in practice, ministers do not challenge a Taoiseach's control of the agenda', and in a large measure this appears still to be the case. Finlay (1998) described how, in 1993, Albert Reynolds pushed provisions for a tax amnesty through cabinet, despite the serious misgivings of many of his cabinet colleagues. More recently, in 2002, Bertie Ahern pushed for a referendum on abortion, 'despite a lack of enthusiasm from his coalition partners' (Murphy, 2003: 16).

The Taoiseach enjoys similar privileges in relation to the legislature, where Article 25 of the Dáil's standing orders allows him or her to determine the order in which government business will be taken each day. Gallagher (1988: 98) notes that 'the Government has a virtual monopoly on proposing legislation, and it is the Government's bills that the Oireachtas considers'. As a result, 'the Dáil is often perceived as one of the least influential legislatures in western Europe, and it is the Taoiseach who is the main beneficiary of this situation' (Elgie and Fitzgerald, 2005: 316).

Within the Northern Ireland Assembly, legislation can be initiated by the Executive, by assembly committees or by assembly members (MLAs). However, the first phase of devolved government of the modern era, from 1999–2002, was marked by reticence on the part of committees or MLAs to act in this manner; only three bills were introduced by these sources during the period, compared to 46 by the Executive

(Wilford 2007: 171). The part-time nature of the Assembly – the chamber sits for only two days per week – means that much of the scrutiny of Executive legislation is done in committees. Most Executive bills are sent to committees for consultation prior to formal introduction and the majority of committee amendments – unlike those tabled by backbench MLAs – are accepted.

Resources of Office

The Department of the Taoiseach comprises 'approximately 300 people in a number of different sections or divisions' (Elgie and Fitzgerald, 2005: 316) charged with responsibilities both for policy formulation and coordination. The Office also includes the Taoiseach's Private Office, the Office of the Chief Whip, the Government Secretariat and the Government Information Service (charged with the preparation of materials for cabinet meetings and the execution of decisions). It is in this capacity that the Secretary General to the Government attends cabinet in a non-voting capacity to take the minutes. More generally, the Secretariat coordinates the work of government as a whole, liaising with government ministers to ensure that decisions are being made and deadlines are being met (Elgie and Fitzgerald, 2005: 317). It has already been noted that the significance and influence of the Department has grown as a consequence of EU membership and its primary responsibility for Social Partnership arrangements. More generally, however, the Department may be used by different Taoisigh to 'incubate' favoured policy areas and 'pet projects' associated with the different governmental programmes.

Thus, for example, in 1983/4 Garret FitzGerald used the Taoiseach's Office to launch and pursue the New Ireland Forum of 1983–4 as well as the Anglo-Irish Agreement of 1985 – the latter despite the reluctance of his cabinet colleagues (O'Leary, 1991: 138). In 1987, Charles Haughey – a Taoiseach 'not slow to exercise his authority' – used the Office to call together representatives of business and trades unions to negotiate a joint approach to the management of Ireland's fiscal and economic crisis, inadvertently initiating the tradition of Irish 'Social partnership' (see Chapter 10).[3] In 1994, under John Bruton's leadership of the 'Rainbow Government', the Office was used to provide political and administrative support parallel to Government initiatives concerning the development of a strategic approach to local government encompassed in the Government White Paper *Better Local Government* (see Chapter 9) and reforms to the civil service encompassed in the Strategic Management Initiative (see Chapter 3).

The First and Deputy First Minister in Northern Ireland have attempted to consolidate their positions as joint 'firsts among equals' within the Executive. This process preceded the arrival of a DUP–Sinn Féin dyarchy at the head of government. The first phase of devolution saw the UUP–SDLP duopoly attempt to strengthen the centre by the appointment of two junior ministers within the Office of the First and Deputy First Minister (OFDFM) (Wilford, 2001). Criticism of dyarchy by the DUP and Sinn Féin melted rapidly when those two parties displaced the UUP and SDLP as the leading community representatives, thus taking the posts of First and Deputy

First Minister. The post-2007 devolution era saw further bolstering of the centre, although a dedicated committee continues to scrutinize the wide range of activities undertaken by the OFDFM. The Office is responsible for overseeing the Executive's Programme for Government, which outlines strategic priorities and departmental budgets. The Programme for Government represents the joined-up government which sits uneasily on the loose consociational foundations upon which the Executive is constructed.

Internal Executive Relations

In the Republic of Ireland, the balance of power within the Executive quite clearly rests with the Taoiseach, vis-à-vis the President and cabinet. Relations between Taoisigh and Presidents have for the most part tended to be cordial if not close, perhaps because of the distance that separate offices of state afford them, but also because constitutionally and politically the Taoiseach clearly holds the upper hand. Liam Cosgrave is reported to have seen President O'Dalaigh only four times in the two years 1974–76 (Elgie and Fitzgerald, 2005: 307) and to have engendered the President's resignation after refusing to demand an apology from his Defence Minister, Patrick Donegan, for calling O'Dalaigh a 'thundering disgrace' following his decision to refer the Emergency Powers bill (giving additional powers to the state in respect of suspected IRA members) to the Supreme Court (which subsequently declared the bill constitutional).

For the most part, however, presidents have steered clear of controversy. Sometimes, governments have requested presidents to refrain from certain activities. In 1991, for example, the Government asked Mary Robinson not to deliver the BBC's annual Dimbleby Lecture in London. The subject of the lecture was to be the position of women and the family in Ireland, which it may be assumed the Government did not wish her to discuss (Morgan, 1999: 261). In 1993, the Government refused Robinson permission to co-chair a commission marking the 50th anniversary of the United Nations and advising on its future reform (Morgan, 1999: 267). On both occasions, the President accepted the Government's requests without confrontation (O'Leary and Burke, 1998: 153, 220–2).

Most Taoisigh have sought to avoid political confrontation whenever possible, since few can afford to lose support needlessly. Even the archetypal 'chief' of Irish politics, de Valera, usually sought unity in cabinet rather than resorting to votes, often arranging agreement by 'force of physical exhaustion' (O'Leary, 1991: 137). In consequence, some of the later de Valera administrations moved very slowly, 'at the pace of the last man to be convinced' (Farrell, 1971a: 39). A cabinet colleague of FitzGerald noted that 'his concern to reach consensus on the issues facing government meant that our Cabinet meetings were much longer than was comfortable' (Hussey, 1993).

Conversely, it might be argued that the widely acknowledged antipathy of Fianna Fáil leader, Albert Reynolds, towards his PD coalition partners ultimately contributed to his premature exit from office, when the latter withdrew their support in 1992 (Farrell, 1993b: 149; O'Halpin, 1997: 79; Connaughton, 2005: 252). The collapse of the following Fianna Fáil coalition with Labour can also be traced to deteriorating coalition relations and Reynolds's insistence on the appointment of Whelehan as Attorney General against the wishes of his partners in government (Finlay, 1998). In consequence, President Robinson let it be known that she was willing to use the discretionary powers afforded to her by Article 13.2.2 of the constitution (enabling the President to refuse to dissolve the Dáil), leading to the formation of the 'Rainbow Coalition' between Fine Gael, Labour and the Democratic Left. Here, however, both the circumstances and the characters involved in this episode of interexecutive relations make this case the exception rather than the rule.

The coalitional nature of the Northern Ireland Executive produced some unlikely political bedfellows. As late as July 2006, the DUP leader was insisting that he would never share power with Sinn Féin shortly before re-entering inclusive government with the republican 'enemy' and with Martin McGuinness, the former IRA member, as Deputy First Minister, only ten months later. The DUP's boycott of Executive meetings from 1999 to 2002 inhibited collective government. The willingness of ministers to act unilaterally was exemplified by Sinn Féin's McGuinness, who, as Education Minister, announced the scrapping of the eleven-plus transfer test and the abolition of school league tables without reference to his Unionist colleagues in the Executive. The 1999–2002 era of devolution was described as little more than 'war by other means' (Wilford and Wilson, 2001: 79), but a more solidified approach to power sharing seemed certain after 2007, as the old issues of violence and the constitutional question diminished in salience.

Indeed the post-2007 Executive proved a much more cohesive body, a feature assisted by the dominance of the DUP and Sinn Féin, who, combined, held eight of the ten departmental ministerial posts in the 2007–11 Executive and all of the four (OFDFM, plus two assistant ministers) ministerial posts at the heart of the Executive. An element of playing to the ethnic gallery nonetheless remained. The Transport Minister, Sinn Féin's Conor Murphy, instructed his civil servants to search for alternatives to the term 'Northern Ireland' as he grappled with serving a state which republicans had long rejected. Nonetheless, the boycotts which had characterized earlier devolved government had been replaced by more cooperative relations and joined-up government. The UUP and SDLP have the option of forming an opposition to the DUP–SF 'rainbow axis', although the disadvantages – loss of ministerial positions and influence – clearly outweigh the advantages of being able to dispense with the shackles of collective responsibility.

Conclusion

In discussing prime ministers in parliamentary democracies, Rose (1991: 19–20) suggests that a four-fold typology of roles is available to prime ministers, depending on the extent to which the constitution centralizes or disperses power in government, and whether or not there is single- or multiparty government. Figure 1.1 extends and adapts the logic of Rose's propositions in consideration of contemporary Irish politics.

Figure 1.1   A Typology of Prime Ministerial Roles

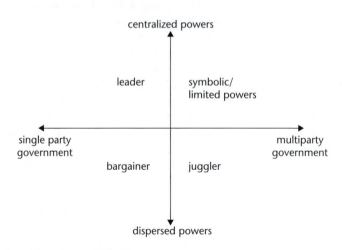

Source: Adapted from Rose, 1991: 19.

Instead of looking for evidence of centralized constitutional authority, we look at the extent to which power may be centralized in the offices of the Head of Government or dispersed within and outside government and the state. Instead of juxtaposing single-party government against multiparty government, we posit a continuum between these two, which may include two-party coalitions comprised of a 'senior' and a 'junior' party (typical in the Republic) or more formulaic and egalitarian consociational coalitions (associated with contemporary Northern Irish politics). The four roles associated with Rose's (1991) typology are still valid, but in our model they should be understood more as tendencies rather than concrete typology.

According to this (modified) model, where a head of government has centralized authority in a unitary state, with a strong majority- or single-party government, he or she has the maximum opportunity to be an effective leader. Under the same conditions, but with power more dispersed between other powerful institutions, the Head of Government is important but not all powerful, and it becomes necessary for him or her to bargain. The more parties involved in government, the less secure is the majority of the Head of Government; or, the stronger the conventions of coalition, the more he or she has to juggle interests to maintain government. The 'juggler' is distinguishable from the 'bargainer' by a necessarily more short-termist approach, since 'under such pressure a prime minister must give first priority to keeping the majority of the moment in play' (Rose, 1991: 19). Finally, where policy authority is equally dispersed between powerful institutions and multiple parties, the more likely it is that the powers held by the Head of Government are more symbolic than substantive.`

In Northern Ireland, the legal requirements for coalition which followed the unlikely consociation are reflected in unusual government arrangements in which no single party can dominate. Insofar as juggling is exercised, it is in terms of the relationship between a minister and a departmental committee in order to achieve that minister's political ambitions. This is not to say that the First and Deputy First Minister are bereft of power. They have three sources of this: firstly, as leaders or very senior figures within their respective parties they can exert some control over their own Assembly members; secondly, there are some powers of leadership associated with the office of OFDFM; thirdly, there is the status associated with being the leaders of the Executive and the country. The sum of these parts, however, is not great and Northern Ireland's coalitional party dispensation allows for a more even interparty struggle than that found in the Taoiseach-led bargaining process to the South.

In the Republic of Ireland, the relative hegemony of Fianna Fáil, encapsulated in its long-time record of single-party government and more recently its status as the 'senior party' in coalition arrangements with the PD and Labour, has tended to placed Irish Taoisigh firmly in the left quadrant of Figure 1.1. The choice of roles between 'leader' and 'bargainer' is epitomized in the Irish literature by Farrell's (1971a) epithet of 'chairman or chief'. More generally, the authority of the Taoiseach depends on how he manages his position. In more contemporary Ireland, broader socio-economic shifts associated with EU membership and management of the economy have circumscribed the macropolicy measures available to the Executive. Still, it would be a misnomer to suggest that as a consequence the Taoiseach has lost power: instead its exercise has become more complex so as to provide a greater challenge to Taoisigh to mediate between a variety of interests.

2

The Legislature

Legislatures (or assemblies, or parliaments) pose perhaps the most fascinating problem of all structures of government, for they have been and continue to be both the most decried and the most revered, the most hoped for and often the least successful institution in contemporary governments.

(Blondel, 1973: 2)

Introduction

Legislatures are ubiquitous: most countries have them; those without them usually find their absence short-lived; and those countries that have never had them may be counted on one hand (Blondel, 1973: 10; Norton, 1990a: 2). In comparative politics, the range of institutional options for democratic states is limited: 'with one exception (Switzerland), every existing democracy today is either presidential (as in the United States), parliamentary (as in most of western Europe), or a semi-presidential hybrid of the two (as in France and Portugal, where there is a directly elected president and a prime minister who must have a majority in the legislature' (Stepan with Skach, 2001: 259). Whilst a presidential regime is characterized by a system of *mutual independence* (whereby the legislative power has a fixed electoral mandate that is its own source of legitimacy and the executive power has a fixed electoral mandate that is its own source of legitimacy), a parliamentary regime is characterized by a system of *mutual dependence*. In other words, the executive power must be supported by a majority in the Legislature and can fall if it receives a vote of no confidence. The executive power (normally in conjunction with the Head of State) has the capacity to dissolve the Legislature and call for elections.

According to this simple typology, the Republic of Ireland is classified as a parliamentary system since, despite constitutional provisions for directly elected presidents, 'political practice is parliamentary' (Duverger, 1980; Lijphart, 1999; Stepan with Skach, 2001). Whilst the legislative system of the Irish Republic has been marked by continuity, Northern Ireland's legislative arrangements have been dysfunctional and prone to fluctuation and uncertainty. In common with the Irish Republic, Northern Ireland is a parliamentary system: its laws have always been made by legislatures and the head of these legislatures, the British monarch, is merely a symbolic presence bereft of real power. The most distinctive feature of the Northern Ireland parliamentary system is that different legislatures have presided within the polity, due to its political instability.

The Status of Legislatures

In the years prior to Irish independence, the very existence of a national legislature had symbolic value for the nation state, such that it 'became the symbol on which nationalist energies were focused, adding a formal stamp of approval to their campaign against Britain' (Arkins, 1990: 91–2). The Sinn Féin candidates who were elected at the general election to the UK parliament in December 1918, and who themselves constituted Dáil Eireánn in January 1919, were members of an independence movement engaged in active struggle (Chubb, 1992: 39). A secret session of these representatives[1] met on 7 January 1919 and convened a group to draw up standing orders and a constitution (Farrell, 1988: 21). In consequence, the first meeting of the First Dáil took place on 21 January 1919 in the Mansion House, Dublin. It was presented with four documents: a Declaration of Independence; a Message to the Free Nations of the World; the constitution; and the Democratic Programme – a statement of social and economic policy lifted from the Labour Party manifesto and never subsequently revisited (Farrell, 1969a). With the exception of one republican Labour representative for Wexford, Richard Corish, the other elected representatives, including the remains of the Irish Party, the Unionists and unionist Labour, all refused to join (Garvin 1996: 39). The Second Dáil of 1921 'was actually not elected at all' and, although sometimes referred to by extreme republicans as 'the last legitimate parliament of the Irish Republic' (ibid.), it was comprised of a limited number of Sinn Féin nominees whose primary task was to mobilize popular support for independent government. Increasing divisions about the form and scope of this independent government led to civil war (Lee, 1989: 56–69).

In these circumstances, Chubb (1992: 39) argued, the Dáil Constitution presented in 1919 'was not seriously intended to meet all the needs of an effectively operating independent state' but was rather 'essentially part of a publicity exercise'. Nevertheless, Farrell (1988: 22) argued that this draft constitution provided the essential link between the institutions of the new Irish state and the structures, processes and values of the British system, ultimately reflecting the 'timidity of the Irish revolution' and confirming the 'innate conservatism of its leaders'. There was, Farrell (1971b: 83) argued, 'never any serious dispute; a familiar and acceptable model – the Westminster model – was available and was simply taken over'.

It was not until after independence, in September 1923, that the first 'remotely normal' Dáil election took place, returning Cosgrave to power (Lee, 1989: 95). Still, the legitimacy of this Third or Free State Dáil was contested by those opposed to the Treaty and further challenged by the fact that neither the First nor the Second Dáil were ever formally dissolved (so that presumably the membership of all three overlapped considerably). The view taken by the Free State Government, that together the vote on the Treaty and the June election both disestablished the Republic and created the Free State, whilst presenting a clear continuity from one to the other, was not universally accepted. This denial of continuity, much encouraged by de Valera, when combined with the primacy of the Executive in the Westminster model, helped to relegate the status of parliament in the new state.

In Northern Ireland, from the foundation of the state, under the Government of Ireland Act in 1920, until 1972, the province was governed by two parliaments. The Westminster parliament oversaw issues affecting the United Kingdom in its entirety, such as defence, foreign policy, taxation and, post-World War II, many general aspects of the welfare state. Northern Ireland's devolved parliament (bicameral, although the lower chamber dominated) controlled the local economy and the local welfare state. The devolved parliament operated with considerable autonomy. British political leaders took little interest in Northern Ireland and the Speaker of the House of Commons at Westminster generally prohibited discussion by MPs of issues in the province which were in the domain of the devolved institution.

Despite the considerable extent of devolution to Northern Ireland, the Westminster legislature remained sovereign. This overarching control was more than a constitutional formality. As conflict developed within the province from 1969 onwards, it was evident that the Northern Ireland parliament could no longer maintain legislative authority. It was suspended in March 1972 by the Westminster government, which imposed direct rule from London. Following this, legislative arrangements for Northern Ireland oscillated between direct rule and episodic attempts to revive devolved government on a non-majoritarian basis, before a more secure implementation of devolved power-sharing in 2007. The first attempt to roll back devolved powers took place in 1974, under the auspices of the Sunningdale Agreement, which created a ruling executive and assembly.

The collapse of the Sunningdale Agreement after five months was followed eight years later by an attempt to gradually restore devolution via a 78-member devolved assembly, designed to acquire power on an incremental basis. The lack of political consensus within the state ensured that the 1982 rolling devolution plan failed to materialize, the potential legislative assembly being denied powers due to a boycott by nationalists. Direct rule from Westminster continued until 1999, when a new 108-member assembly and a governing executive were established within Northern Ireland, as part of the 1998 Good Friday Agreement (GFA). The institutional framework established by the Agreement was based upon a complex multi-stranded legislative architecture, embracing devolved government and power-sharing within Northern Ireland, linked to formalized all-island economic cooperation and continuing British–Irish intergovernmental arrangements.

Although significant functions short of tax-raising were devolved to the post-1998 devolved assembly, Westminster remained dominant. As political consensus proved difficult to obtain within the Assembly and Executive, devolved government was suspended four times between 2000 and 2002, before the 2007 devolution model was implemented. Although direct rule from Westminster remained the default position of the Westminster government in the absence of consensus over the form of devolved government, the post-2007 duopoly of previous 'extremes' of the DUP and

Sinn Féin stabilized Northern Ireland, by allowing full political participation from republicans and Loyalists.

The Representative Capacity of Legislatures

The first Irish parliament in 1919 consisted of a single house since 'the independence movement neither needed nor wanted more' (Chubb, 1992: 196). Yet, when the Treaty was being negotiated, part of the agreement included the establishment of a second house in order to ensure that the unionist minority in the new state could be adequately represented. Though the Irish Free State constitution adopted by the Dáil in December 1922 provided for a senate, no agreement could be found for a formula for its selection (ibid.). This, combined with the strong antipathy of de Valera and Fianna Fáil, led to its abolition in 1936. It was replaced by provisions in the 1937 constitution for a new senate, Seanad Éireann. Of the 60 senators, 43 are elected from five panels (Cultural and Educational, Agricultural, Labour, Industrial and Commercial, and Administrative), 11 are nominated by the Taoiseach and the remaining six are elected by a selection of universities (three by the National University of Ireland and three by the University of Dublin). Despite these early vocationalist principles, in practice the significance of party politics soon outweighed the significance of any collective interest within the panels and, in 2004, the Report on Seanad Reform argued that 'its arcane and outdated system of nomination and election diminishes Senators' legitimacy' and creates a situation whereby 'unless a candidate comes from a political background, he/she has practically no chance of getting elected' (Seanad Éireann, 2004: 26).

The representative capacity of the Dáil is broadly similar to that in many Western European parliaments (Gallagher, 2005b: 212). On average, members of the Dáil (TDs) tend to be middle-aged, middle class and male. Most are in their forties or fifties; almost half have a university degree and professional occupation; and women are significantly under-represented (ibid.). On average, 12 women were elected to each Dáil from 1977 to 1992 (Galligan, 1998: 36). Currently, women hold only 14 per cent of the seats in the Dáil, compared to 17 per cent in the Seanad (O'Connor, 2008: 148). Additionally, however, Irish TDs have very strong local ties: 'nearly all live in their constituency, most were born and raised there, and around three-quarters were members of local government before being elected to the Dáil' (Gallagher, 2005b: 212). The peculiar Irish emphasis on personal and local ties between TDs and their constituents is well documented (Farrell, 1983a; Komito, 1992a; Gallagher and Komito, 1999; Collins and O'Shea, 2003; Gallagher and Komito, 2005) and will be discussed in more detail in the section on assembly member–legislature relations (pp. 45–6). For the moment, however, it serves to note that – just like their counterparts in the Seanad – the great majority of Dáil members are in practice 'full time politicians'.

In Northern Ireland, the parliament established at the formation of the state struggled to achieve universal legitimacy. From its outset it was seen as a 'Protestant parliament for a Protestant people'. Successive prime ministers did little to disabuse the majority or minority populations of this view. There were ongoing tensions within parliament between sectarian populists and other Unionists of a marginally more liberal persuasion, the latter being concerned to consolidate parliament through some form of rapprochement with the disaffected Catholic nationalist majority (Bew, Gibbon and Patterson, 2002). The parliament had an in-built Unionist major-ity, given the population ratio, and electoral processes were designed to preserve Unionist control. Its majoritarian form of decision-making heavily favoured the dominant UUP. The hegemonic position of the UUP within the Northern Ireland parliament was consolidated by the abolition of proportional representation during the 1920s, in contravention of the 1920 Government of Ireland Act. Designed mainly to inhibit fragmentation within unionism, the measure also impacted negatively upon nationalist representation within parliament. At local council level, gerrymandering of electoral boundaries ensured that Unionists controlled almost 20 per cent of coun-cils beyond the 65 per cent expected given the Unionist–nationalist demographic balance (Buckland, 1981).

The inability of the Northern Ireland Legislature to adopt an inclusive representa-tive capacity from 1921 until 1972 constituted a serious representational deficiency. The Unionist party of government made no attempt to appeal outside its ethnic bloc and, as such, intrabloc contests were of much greater importance than debate within the Legislature in shaping political outcomes. Occasional challenges 'from below', most notably from the Northern Ireland Labour Party, were easily quelled. Most of the leadership of the UUP also belonged to the Protestant Orange Order. Such duality of membership was perceived as useful to career advancement and reinforced the perceptions of a legislature in which sectarian politics dominated. The absence of legislative traditions of reform and responsiveness to the minority community proved fatal when nationalists challenged the state through civil rights protests during the late 1960s (Farrell, 1980).

Since the abolition of that form of one-party 'democracy' in 1972, Northern Ireland's legislature and executive has been built upon proportional representation for its two main traditions, conditions built into the legislation which established power-sharing. Since devolved government was established after the Good Friday Agreement, only 15 per cent of Assembly members have been women and the repre-sentative function of the Northern Ireland Legislature is clearly shaped to cater for the ambitions of the two main *ethnic* groups, seemingly at the expense of other iden-tities. The institutional mechanisms for achieving devolved power-sharing have been based upon parallel consent for legislation among Unionist and nationalist political representatives. In the Northern Ireland Assembly created after the Good Friday Agreement, significant legislation required either the support of a majority of Unionists and a majority of nationalists, or at least 40 per cent support from either side (either provision could be operated, according to Assembly wishes). Ethnic bloc identifications were formally recognized via the requirement for Assembly members to be designated as 'Unionist', 'nationalist' or 'other'. 'Others' amounted to an average of only 7 per cent of the Assembly's elected representatives at the first three Assembly elections, in 1998, 2003 and 2007. Although more than one-third of Northern Ireland's electors claim to be neither nationalist nor Unionist, this is not reflected in bloc affiliations or voting procedures within the Legislature (see Northern Ireland Life and Times Surveys (Political Attitudes) 2000–7, at www.ark.ac.uk).

Legislative Powers

The Oireachtas does not draw up and enact legislation, but rather approves of draft legislation placed before it by government (Robinson, 1974: 6). The drafting of legislation is carried out by specialist barristers in the Office of Parliamentary Draftsmen, operating under the auspices of the Attorney General (Donelan, 1992: 3). It is the Attorney General's job to ensure that draft legislation is compatible with the constitution. Assuming that it is, the bill may subsequently be introduced to the Houses of the Oireachtas for discussion (stage one), where Gallagher (2005b: 220) notes that the 'law making procedure is closely based, in the letter and in the spirit, on that of Westminster'. Additionally bills may be introduced via the Seanad or independent TD proposals (private members' bills), providing that they have the support of a group of at least seven deputies.

Following their introduction, bills pass through a further five stages: stage two enables a general debate on the principle of the bill without getting into its details; stage three, the committee stage, where the bill is discussed in detail and where amendments that do not contradict the principle of the bill may be proposed; stage four, the report stage, relays any new revisions or amendments to the text and allows a further opportunity for amendment; and stage five is the formal passing of the bill prior to its discussion in the other house. Finally, when the bill is accepted by both houses of the Oireachtas, it is sent to the President for signing into law. The President may at this point refer the bill to the Supreme Court if there are any doubts regarding its constitutionality.

Given the prevalence of government legislation, generally speaking bills are initiated in the Dáil and passed over to the Seanad for discussion where, in the event of a disagreement, the Dáil has the upper hand. If the Seanad is unhappy with a piece of legislation, the most it can do is delay its passage by 90 days. Thereafter, the Dáil may overrule it. Should this occur, providing that the bill is not a constitutional bill, the Seanad may invoke the 'Article 27 procedure' where a majority of senators *plus* one third of the Dáil may petition the President not to sign the bill and refer it instead to a referendum. To date, this has never happened.

Private members' bills (PMBs) are possible, though rare: in all, 21 have been passed since 1923 (MacCarthaigh, 2005: 110). Five of these occurred between 1951 and 1954, when a multiparty coalition government traded places with a Fianna Fáil minority government; and three occurred in 1996 during the Rainbow Coalition's period in government (MacCarthaigh, 2005: 111). MacCarthaigh (2005: 115) argues that 'the government's control of the parliamentary agenda, which is reflected in standing orders, severely restricts PMBs' and supports the view that in Ireland the legislative agenda is clearly controlled by government. Moreover, it is hard to argue that PMBs reflect the triumph of the Legislature over the Executive, since in reality they are impossible to pass without the support of government parties and back-benchers. In consequence, Gallagher (2005b: 224–5) argues that 'the Dáil cannot be seen as an active participant in the process of making laws' and that its 'chief role is legitimating legislation rather than really making it'.

In Northern Ireland, the absence of devolved government from 1972 until 1999 and again from 2002 until 2006 left the Westminster parliament responsible for enacting virtually all legislation for Northern Ireland (although European Union directives were increasingly influential in shaping that legislation). Westminster MPs support or reject, but cannot amend, legislation steered through parliament by the Secretary of State for Northern Ireland, a severe democratic deficit (Hazleton, 1994). This democratic deficit was far from fully addressed by the slightly improved scrutiny of Northern Ireland affairs at Westminster during the 1990s, via a grand committee and a dedicated select committee. These committees enhanced debate on Northern Ireland issues, but one evaluation suggested that the select committee had 'failed dismally' as an agent of change (Wilford and Elliott, 1999: 39).

Devolved government in Northern Ireland, in its original majoritarian and subsequent consociational forms, has enjoyed considerable nominal power, but has been hindered by considerable financial constraints (Wilson, 1989). The devolved government established under the Good Friday Agreement was a fairly substantial entity. Although devoid of tax-raising powers, the Northern Ireland Assembly assumed responsibility for education, health, social services and local economic development, whilst Westminster retained control of defence and foreign policy, plus overall economic strategy. The Northern Ireland Act 1998 did not devolve powers to the Assembly in respect of policing and justice: these powers would remain with Westminster until such time as sufficient political consensus emerged in Northern Ireland for their transfer.

The legislative process within the Northern Ireland Assembly relied heavily upon input from committees. Of the four stages of consideration of a bill, the committee stage was the most important, involving a clause-by-clause examination of a bill's contents (Tonge, 2005a). Committees are involved in prior consultation with departments before a bill is introduced. The Northern Ireland Assembly merged the best aspects of standing (prelegislative) and select (post-legislative) committees in the Westminster parliamentary model and were the most successful feature of the otherwise non-consensual 1999–2002 Assembly, a case of damning with faint praise given the modest performances of the ten executive departments. Most bills received prelegislative committee scrutiny and the committees tended to improve bills via their amendments.

Opportunities for Scrutiny and Criticism of Government

In the Republic of Ireland, it has already been noted that the Seanad is the weaker of the two legislative chambers. In addition, since almost one senator in five is nominated by the Taoiseach, both 'the Seanad's inclination and capacity to act as an effective check on government is severely limited' (Seanad Éireann, 2004: 26). This leaves the primary responsibility for scrutiny and criticism of government to the Dáil, through the use of parliamentary questions, debates and the various committees. Question Time in the Dáil takes place for an hour and a quarter on Tuesday, Wednesday and Thursday afternoons. This time is divided between questions for the Taoiseach (on Tuesdays and part of Wednesdays) and questions to other members of government. Questions must be indicated in advance in order to give the minister and departmental civil servants time to gather the information sought. In general, ministers respond with written answers, delivered within three working days, though some questions may specifically request an oral answer. Where this is the case, on receipt of the information requested, the deputy asking the question is allowed to submit a 'supplementary question'.

During the lifespan of the Dáil, the average number of questions per year has increased massively – from around 1,200 a year in the mid-1930s to around 4,000 a year in the mid-1960s to some 24,000 a year in the period 2001–03 (Gallagher, 2005b: 228) – but the time allotted for their answers has not. Additionally, there is a strong convention that answers given will be as curt as possible (O'Toole, 1995: 257). Commenting on her own experience as a TD, Joan Burton (*Irish Times* 16 August 2003) suggested that 'these sessions are wholly unsatisfactory ... leaving the minister full scope to trot out dreary departmental answers ... with no scope for further intervention from the deputy raising the question'. This view was further substantiated by the Chair of the long-running Beef Tribunal, when he noted that if questions asked in the Dáil had been answered as fully as they were in the tribunal, the tribunal would not have been necessary (Gallagher, 2005b: 228).

The reputation for Dáil debate is little better. Gallagher (2005b: 222) argues that 'Dáil debates are often dialogues of the deaf, set pieces with a strong element of theatre in which TDs speak for the record or in order to get publicity at local level'. If this is the case, it seems that the tone of Dáil debates is more 'amateur rep' than 'national theatre'. In an opinion piece in the *Irish Times* (18 October 2002), Kathy Sheridan suggested that 'today's Dáil speeches are flat':

> TDs and Ministers rarely stand up to speak without a script in their hands. In most cases, a civil servant or party backroom worker has written the script, and the deputy or Minister is often reading it for the first time when he or she gets on their feet. And it shows.

Whether this is the cause or consequence of much reduced media coverage is not clear. It seems, however, that rather than reporting Dáil debates, contemporary political journalists can themselves often elicit more information from a minister than an opposition politician in the Dáil, 'where the Ceann Comhairle keeps tight control and relishes telling TDs they are "out of order"' (ibid.). Standing orders favour the government, and the neutrality of the Ceann Comhairle (Chair of Dáil Éireann) tends towards the preservation of the status quo rather than enforcing the Dáil's right to act as a check on government (MacCarthaigh, 2005: 137).

It is in this context that parliamentary committees may be seen as the only viable check on government behaviour, though in practice their impact may be limited. With 166 Dáil deputies, 'when one removes from consideration the thirty members of the government, the Cathaoirleach and Leas Cathaoirleach, and major opposition party leaders, there are only about 130 members to sit on committees' (Ward, 1996: 52). Moreover, in terms of their legislative impact, the principle enshrined in the 'committee stage' of the passage of a bill, whereby amendments may be proposed *provided that they do not conflict with the principle of the bill*, significantly curtails the potential impact of Dáil committees. Additionally, the fact that committees only get to examine legislative proposals after they have been discussed in plenary (stage two), decreases the committee's political room for manoeuvre in attempting to edit a bill *after* the political parties have already taken a position (Gallagher, 2005b: 224). Despite this, however, if the capacity for scrutiny and criticism of government is to be found anywhere in the Irish Legislature, the Oireachtas committees probably present the best bet.

Oireachtas committees have a chequered history. Historically, Fianna Fáil has viewed the prospect of an efficient committee system with suspicion, seeing it as a potential threat to the power of the executive (Arkins, 1990: 96). Until 1978, committees were generally used only for the management of Oireachtas business and services and for disciplinary matters (O'Halpin, 1998: 134). The one exception was the Dáil Committee of Public Accounts, and even this was limited in its investigative capacity when the courts ruled in 1971 that its inquiry into the use of public funds during the arms crisis could not compel witnesses to testify (*Irish Times* 10 March 2006).[2] The European Communities (Amendment) Act 1973, which formally recognized the Republic's accession to the EC, necessitated the creation of a Joint Committee on European Community Secondary Legislation (Robinson, 1974: 18–20), but still it was 'clearly hampered in its work by inadequate staffing and services' (Chubb, 1992: 202). It was not until the Fine Gael/Labour coalition of 1982–87 that 'the first efforts to construct a meaningful committee system were made' (O'Halpin, 1998: 135).

Following pre-election promises, the Fine Gael/Labour government increased the number of Oireachtas committees from seven to sixteen. Whilst some of the impetus for the new committees certainly arose as a consequence of the growing legislative workload arising with EU membership (MacCarthaigh, 2005: 138), the sheer variety of topics covered – including women's rights, marriage breakdown, small businesses, cooperation with developing countries, the Irish language and vandalism – is suggestive of both interparty and intraparty pressures (Chubb, 1992: 203). Despite this, however, in 1987 the returning Fianna Fáil government did not re-establish them, limiting its creation of new committees to only three (women's rights, the Irish language and commercial state-sponsored bodies). Chubb (ibid.) argued that:

> A combination of Fianna Fáil's traditional lack of enthusiasm for intrusive committees; the failure of the Dáil to debate more than a few of the reports that they had produced; the reluctance of all but a few of their members to put much effort into them; and the equivocal attitude of Deputies generally, all combined to spell the end of the first – flawed – attempt at grafting a comprehensive committee system on to the procedures of the Oireachtas.

Since 1993, committees have become a permanent feature of the House and have been credited with several important developments (MacCarthaigh, 2005: 139–47). Most notably in 2006, the Supreme Court upheld the right of an Oireachtas committee to inquire into the conduct of Judge Brian Curtin. The judge had been acquitted for possession of child pornography when it was discovered that the warrant under which his computer was seized was out of date (*Irish Times*, 10 March 2006). In consequence, the right of the Oireachtas 'Committee on Article 35.4.1 of the Constitution and section 39 of the Courts of Justice Act 1924' to consider the impeachment of a judge for 'stated misbehaviour' was upheld, creating a significant legal precedent for the removal of judges by the Legislature (*Irish Times*, 18 March 2006).

In Northern Ireland, the requirement for consociational power-sharing has prevented the development of a 'normal' system of government and opposition, and has thus prevented proper scrutiny of executive decisions. There is a lack of formal opposition to a Rainbow Coalition government that, in its early years, failed to develop as the sum of its parts (Wilford, 2001; Aughey, 2005; Tonge 2005a, 2005b). Since the restoration of devolved government, the search for joined-up government has continued as old Unionist–nationalist enmities have been laid aside.

Insofar as scrutiny of ministers existed, this occurred within the Assembly committees, which produced reports on legislation and could table amendments during the passage of bills. Ten departmental committees, standing committees and ad hoc committees provided an extensive network of scrutiny arenas for legislative and procedural decisions within the 1999–2002 Assembly. To ensure that committees have not been too compliant to the demands of ministers, their chairs, allocated under the D'Hondt system according to party strength in the Assembly, have never been drawn from the same party as the minister. Nonetheless, the demands of party loyalty have sometimes outweighed the calls for collective government. For example, in the early years of devolved power-sharing Sinn Féin and DUP ministers joined their Assembly party colleagues in criticizing budget decisions even though, as ministers, they had been responsible for setting the budgets!

Beyond the committees, oral, written and private notice questions offer some scrutiny facilities for Assembly members. Based largely on the Westminster model, two hours per week are set aside for oral questioning of ministers, including the First and Deputy First Minister. Questions are selected randomly by computer, with those unanswered due to lack of time given a written answer by the minister. Written questions may extract more detailed information, but have the disadvantage that they must be submitted to ministers almost two weeks in advance. Private Notice Questions are those submitted at short notice (a minimum of four hours must be given) to ministers by Assembly members, on subjects deemed by the Speaker to be urgent. Questions to ministers from members belonging to the same party tend to be supine, although arguably no more so than those offered in the House of Commons.

Executive–Legislature Relations

Lijphart's (1999) comparative study of government structures in democracies sets out a dichotomous classification of executive–legislature relations, where governments operate under either a 'majoritarian' or a 'consensus' institutional configuration. Using this classification, Lane and Ersson (1998: 216) suggested that the Irish Executive (along with the British and French) is among the most powerful in Europe by virtue of its ability to control the parliamentary agenda, dissolve the parliament at will and declare elections at a time of its own choosing. Commenting on this classification, MacCarthaigh (2005: 45) notes that all of these systems of government are 'associated with strong centralised governments, weak committee systems and little opposition input into government work'. According to O'Halpin (1998: 127), whatever the index of parliamentary vitality used, whether it is 'procedures covering the tabling of questions, successful private members' bills, committee work, substantive amendment of government bills by either house, the number of sitting days each year – the Irish legislature appears conspicuously weak and the executive remarkably strong'.

These facts notwithstanding, Gallagher (2005b: 217) notes that whilst 'it remains true that Irish governments do not routinely fear dismissal by the Dáil', still the Westminster model 'does not adequately capture the reality of the Dáil's role in appointing and dismissing governments'. In his analysis of the period 1948–2002, Gallagher (2005b: 214–5) notes that there are three ways that a government may be agreed following an election. First, where a single party or pre-agreed coalition wins a majority of seats (this has occurred five times since 1948); second, by political parties agreeing a majority coalition after an indeterminate result (this has occurred on seven occasions since 1948); and third, when members of the Dáil agree to a minority coalition. Clearly, it is in the last case that the Dáil has most influence, and Gallagher (2005b: 215–6) notes six instances where the decision of the Dáil has been decisive: four minority Fianna Fáil governments; one minority Fine Gael/Labour government; and one minority Fianna Fáil/PD government. Additionally, there have been eight occasions when the Dáil has effectively terminated governments that have chosen to resign rather than face a vote of no-confidence (1927, 1938, 1944, 1951, 1957, 1982, 1987, 1994) and a further two occasions (1982 and 1992) when a no-confidence vote has been taken and the government has been dismissed (Gallagher, 2005b: 216–7). In this respect, Gallagher (2005b: 212) suggests that 'it is more realistic to see parliament as wielding power *through* the government that it has elected than to see it as seeking to *check* a government that has come into being independently of it'.

In Northern Ireland, the Executive is largely insulated from dismissal or even serious scrutiny from within. In legislative terms, the primary concerns of the British government in implementing the Good Friday Agreement were to achieve proportionality in government with mutual vetoes. The composition of the Executive dominated thoughts at the expense of consideration of how it would execute its duties. Ministerial fiefdoms – rather than joined-up coalition government – became the norm. For example, Sinn Féin's control of the education and health ministries led to strong criticism of policies emanating from those departments by DUP 'colleagues' supposedly working together in government. Whilst Assembly rules allow for the removal of incompetent ministers, this is achievable only through a resolution backed by majorities of Unionist and nationalist Assembly members, a condition unlikely ever to be fulfilled within the lingering sectarianism which underpins structures and attitudes. The First and Deputy First Ministers of the Assembly do not possess the power to dismiss ministers. The loss of confidence among members of one's own party is far more damaging to a minister, as the resignation of Ian Paisley junior in 2008, over alleged lobbying and links to a property developer, indicated.

Political Party–Legislature Relations

In his analysis of political parties in the Republic of Ireland and the development of parliamentary accountability, MacCarthaigh (2005: 52–93) points to three key phases in the relationship between the two: the 1922 constitution and the consolidation of parliamentary politics; the 1937 constitution and the establishment of 'Fianna Fáil versus the rest'; and the end of this period from 1989 onwards, when it became clear that Fianna Fáil could no longer sustain single-party government.

During the first period, the drafters of the 1922 constitution envisaged a political system in which a strong legislature would elect coalition governments, which they assumed to be the inevitable consequence of deploying the single transferable vote system of proportional representation (Chubb, 1992: 23). Ironically, this did not happen: Fianna Fáil's electoral dominance until the late 1980s ensured that 'Dáil Éireann has more closely resembled the model of a weak legislature dominated by a majority party' (MacCarthaigh, 2005: 54). Together, the adversarial system of government and opposition expressed in the Westminster model, and the memory of the civil war which immediately followed independence, led to a very confrontational style of parliamentary politics. For some years, TDs and senators of the Fianna Fáil parliamentary party were under orders not 'to conduct any business with ministers or [government backbench] deputies in the bar or restaurant' and 'fraternization under any circumstances was not permitted' (O'Halpin, 1998: 126). In consequence, little use was made of committees to explore issues, discuss bills in detail or promote cross-party consensus on any matter. In this respect, Arkins (1990: 91) argued that Fianna Fáil's predominance undoubtedly influenced the nature of relations between the Executive and the Legislature.

During the second period, the scope for parliamentary reform was constrained by the attitudes of the two larger parties. In 1971, although a Fianna Fáil government established an informal committee on reform of Dáil procedures, its terms of reference were narrowly interpreted (MacCarthaigh, 2005: 76). The committee's final report proposed amendments to standing orders relating to Oireachtas timetabling, private members' and government bills, as well as recommending a 'wide ranging examination' of 'how effectively the Houses of the Oireachtas are discharging their functions' (Government of Ireland, 1972: 6). Still, Labour remained the only political party with an unambiguous desire for parliamentary reform (Desmond, 1975). It seems clear that Fine Gael, 'despite its anti-Fianna Fáil rhetoric, also saw the role of government and parliament in an adversarial manner, with a view to one day assuming control of the executive function' (MacCarthaigh, 2005: 77). The scale of their electoral defeat in 1977 perhaps helped to shift their attitudes towards parliamentary reform and, in 1980, they produced their own comprehensive set of proposals for Dáil reform.

Between 1981 and 1982 there were three elected governments in Ireland.[3] The last, a Fine Gael/Labour coalition remained in office until 1987, when it was succeeded by a Fianna Fáil government that had only the most tenuous electoral advantage. Given the appalling economic circumstances of the period, Fine Gael agreed to support the government's attempts at economic reform in what became known as the 'Tallaght

Strategy'.[4] It is possible that the political and economic instability throughout this period foreshadowed a change of heart in both larger parties regarding the desirability of Oireachtas reform. In 1990, Fine Gael produced a second set of proposals for Dáil reform and Fianna Fáil began to move towards a less adversarial style of political leadership with the advent of 'government by partnership' evinced in the Programme for National Recovery (see Chapter 10).

In 1989, MacCarthaigh (2005: 84) argues, the decision by Fianna Fáil to coalesce with the PDs – a party dedicated to government transparency and accountability – marks the beginning of the third key phase in Republic of Ireland (ROI) party/parliament relations. By demonstrating both its willingness and ability to agree to coalition government, 'Fianna Fáil effectively undermined the foundation on which the post-war party system had been structured' (Mair, 1993: 171). This decision ended the 'Fianna Fáil versus the rest' axis around which political and parliamentary life had revolved since the mid-1920s (MacCarthaigh, 2005: 89). This new balance of power was perhaps most clearly evidenced by the Dáil's decision in 1994 to approve a new government without an intervening election, replacing the Fianna Fáil/Labour coalition with a new Rainbow Coalition of Fine Gael, Labour and the Democratic Left (Girvin, 1999). The publication of more strident proposals for Oireachtas reform by Fine Gael (2000) and Labour (2003) is further testimony to the changing dynamic between political parties and parliament in the Republic.

In Northern Ireland, relations between parties and the Legislature have varied considerably, reflecting sharp differences in party structure and discipline. For Sinn Féin and the DUP, party unity is invariably a vital consideration, a condition facilitated by top-down leadership structures. For the UUP, chaotic internal structures meant that the party's contribution to the 1999–2002 Assembly was marred by internal dissent, including challenges to the leader's authority within and outside the Legislature.

Since the Good Friday Agreement, four-party politics within Northern Ireland has consolidated into a two-party dominance of the Executive and, to a lesser extent, the Legislature, by the DUP and Sinn Féin, as the principal representatives of their ethnic blocs. Their triumph was not envisaged: the initial post-Agreement orthodoxy assumed a UUP–SDLP coalition as the main axis of power. Internal dissent over the Agreement within the UUP, suspension of the Assembly in 2002 and the substantial electoral realignment to the DUP and Sinn Féin ensured that the mark 2 version of the Assembly was instead based upon a far-reaching Loyalist–republican axis, rather than an alliance of earlier moderates.

Political parties adopted varied perceptions of the political institutions. For Sinn Féin, devolved government in Northern Ireland is merely part of an interlocked set of all-island institutions. Under Strand 2 of the GFA, a North South Ministerial Council (NSMC) linked the Northern Ireland Executive to government ministers in the Irish Republic, who combined with their northern counterparts to preside over cross-border bodies carrying out all-island activity. The suspension of the Northern Ireland Assembly placed the NSMC and cross-border activities on a 'care and maintenance' footing, before restoration on the basis that all executive members, including those drawn from the DUP, would participate. For Unionists, Strand 1 of the GFA was all-important, restoring a devolved legislature to Northern Ireland. There was cross-community consensus over the desirability of some form of Northern legislature, but the DUP and UUP were cautious over establishing an executive with full devolved powers if that body included Sinn Féin. The DUP required Sinn Féin to divest itself of all IRA links prior to entrance into government, although the IRA Army Council, on which sat Sinn Féin members, remained formally in existence even after the restoration of devolved government in 2007. The British–Irish Council established under Strand 3 of the GFA represented the external linkage for the Northern Ireland Assembly desired by Unionists, the UUP viewing a confederal binding of executives throughout Britain and Ireland as a shoring of the Union (Hennessey, 2000).

Assembly Member–Legislature Relations

Article 16.2.2 of the Republic's constitution provides that there must be one member of the Dáil for every 20–30,000 of the population, a very low ratio by international standards (Ward, 1996: 52). Whilst the Proportional Representation-Single Transferable Vote (PR-STV) system is widely acknowledged as producing extremely representative government, if anything the system that grants more constituency representation also leads to far higher expectations of local representatives, so that constituency work forms a very large part of all TD workloads (Chubb, 1963; Farrell, 1983a; Komito, 1992b; Gallagher and Komito, 2005). Members of the Seanad, on the other hand, generally work to more select though less demanding constituency interests, giving them relatively more time to pursue independent policy advocacy. Notwithstanding some notable exceptions, the Seanad has not developed its relative advantage in policy advocacy. This a great pity, since the terms of reference for most members of the lower House tend to work against their developing this dimension of their post. The reasons for this are varied.

Writing in the *Irish Times* (21 April 2006), TD for Limerick East, Willie O'Dea, candidly noted that 'backbenchers spend 80 per cent of their time servicing individual constituents – to the detriment of the national interest'. As a result of this, he argued, 'the garnering of a few dozen medical cards is more vital to political survival than any creative well-researched Dáil speech on health service reform'. Echoing this idea, O'Halpin (1998: 127) argued that 'with the majority of TDs engaged primarily in interventions with national and local bureaucracy on behalf of their constituents', they tend to be 'all but oblivious to their formal constitutional roles as legislators and scrutineers of the actions of the executive'. Moreover, Gallagher (2005b: 232) notes that the relatively small size of the Dáil leads to a high proportion of TDs becoming either cabinet or junior ministers. In consequence, TDs who are willing and able to deal with national issues may reasonably aspire to ministerial status at some point in their careers and the political capital to be gained from sterling committee service is diminished.

As it is, the current institutional set-up does not provide much incentive for TDs to foster specific policy interests. Commenting on his unusual success in having four private members bills enacted out of only 15 since 1937 (all in the area of family law), Fine Gael TD, Alan Shatter, pointed out that the institutional culture of the Dáil actually discourages backbenchers from this important advocacy role:

> Most Ministers resent individual TDs producing legislation. It's not seen as a constructive way of addressing an issue; it's seen as a mechanism for embarrassing a Minister. Most Civil Servants are pissed off by members of the Dáil drafting legislation because they see it as their prerogative. You're standing on the toes of both the bureaucracy and the Minister when you produce legislation. And if you produce legislation when your own party is in government – that is deemed treacherous.
>
> (MacCarthaigh, 2005: 111)

In Northern Ireland, assembly members can be divided into three categories: executive members, who participate in the supposedly cohesive cross-community government and may shape the policy of departmental ministers; frontbench members, who offer assistance to their party's ministers or act as party representatives where the minister was drawn from another party; and backbench MLAs, whose main legislative functions are normally carried out via the committee system. Party whips operate as at Westminster in ensuring that MLAs toe the party line, although disagreement with the leadership in the cases of the DUP and Sinn Féin would probably lead to resignation. In 2007, Gerry McHugh, a Fermanagh and Tyrone MLA, quit Sinn Féin and sat in the Assembly as an independent, after complaining of the party's lack of democracy and arguing that it was merely administering British rule in Ireland.

Aside from the burying of old enmities within a Unionist–nationalist executive coalition, perhaps the most remarkable feature of the Northern Ireland Assembly is its size. In reflecting the GFA's aspiration to be as inclusive as possible, with 108 members the Assembly offers a legislator for every 9,200 electors. The 129 elected members of the Scottish Parliament, with greater powers, represent more than 2.5 times the number of electors. Using a similar population ratio to that of the Northern Ireland Assembly, the Westminster parliament would contain over 4,300 members. Moreover, whatever the formal position that members of the Northern Ireland Assembly represent all constituents, the realpolitik of the ethnic bloc divide suggests otherwise. Within the multimember system, six members are elected to serve each of the 18 constituencies, with the same electoral boundaries used for PR-STV Assembly and single-plurality Westminster contests. At present, however, the appeal of the four main parties in Northern Ireland is communal and none bother to campaign outside their own (Catholic) nationalist or (Protestant) Unionist areas.

Internal and External Constraints

The extent to which Irish legislatures develop and support the most productive engagement of their members is variable. In the Republic, time for Dáil work is brief. The Dáil sits for just 88 days, which is only a little over half the sitting days of its British counterpart (*Irish Times*, 21 April 2006). There are 166 Dáil deputies for a population of some 4 million, giving each TD an average share of 21,239 of population (Ward,

1996: 62). If Britain was proportionately as well represented, there would be more than 3,000 MPs in the House of Commons (*Irish Times*, 21 April 2006). Despite this, however, the concomitant burden of constituency work still leaves many TDs feeling overburdened. Following the Houses of the Oireachtas Commission Act 2003, in 2004 the Houses of the Oireachtas were given 300 extra staff, including 166 personal assistants for TDs, in addition to the Dáil secretary and constituency secretary that they each already had (*Western People*, 10 November 2004; *Sunday Independent*, 25 April 2004). Commenting on the decision, Fine Gael TD, Michael Ring, explained that 'if the people of Ireland want TDs to do the best they can, they need to under-stand that we need this extra back-up. The volume of letters and emails we receive every day is phenomenal and it's very difficult to control when we have to look after the people in our constituency, as well as the party business' (*Western People*, 10 November 2004). In April 2006, a more radical solution to this problem was proposed by the Fianna Fáil Minister for Environment, Noel Dempsey, when he suggested reducing the number of TDs from 166 to 120 and abolishing multiseat constituencies (*Irish Times*, 21 April 2006). Dismissed by Labour and Fine Gael as 'kite flying', the proposals have yet to be given serious consideration by the Government.

Beyond Dáil politics, the STV method of PR has come in for criticism, not only regarding its tendency to elevate local politicking at the expense of national policy making. It is also suggested that the STV method of PR electoral system, by more or less eliminating the concept of a 'safe seat', has tended to 'discourage people of ability who are outside the political party structure from standing for election' (Robinson, 1974: 5). There has, Robinson argued, 'been a certain inbreeding in Irish political life, allowing a seat to pass from father to son or to the political widow in trust for a future generation'. Commenting on Noel Dempsey's proposals for Dáil reform in the *Irish Times* (21 April 2006), Frank McDonald argues that with fewer TDs and a party list system of PR 'there would be a better chance of attracting talented people who currently shun politics because they see it as mere "messenger boy" drudgery'.

It might be expected that consideration of the external constraints to legislature activ-ity would raise the issue of EU membership as an obvious challenge to national assem-blies. In the Irish Republic, however, the EU is generally cast 'on the side of the angels'. Ireland's entry into the European Community in 1973 incurred a series of legal obliga-tions, relating to non-discrimination and equality of pay, which began to challenge atti-tudes to women, the workplace and the family (Adshead, 2005: 172). In consequence, throughout the 1970s and 1980s, many women sought redress in the courts for griev-ances that the Oireachtas had chosen to ignore. Scannell (1988: 132) notes that:

> While the courts in their interpretation of the Constitution were prepared, when given the opportunity, to respond fairly positively in favour of women's rights, the same could not be said of the legislature. There has admittedly been a great deal of legislation on family law and equal rights for women since 1970, but apart from the Succession Act, 1965, it is diffi-cult to identify any major piece of legislation relevant to the rights of women that was not forced on our representatives by the courts, the women's movement or the EC.

Whereas, on the face of it, the decision to 'pool sovereignty' might be viewed as decreasing state autonomy, in the Irish case it resulted in significant revivification of state machinery through the development of a variety of mechanisms for monitoring and evaluating state performance that the state was obliged to implement as a consequence of EU reforms (Adshead, 2008: 68). In noting that 'for a variety of reasons, the Irish system did not have a strong tradition of monitoring and evaluation', O'Donnell (2000: 186) concludes that 'membership of the EU has had significant implications for the auditing of public expenditure'. Since, for all of the reasons discussed above, the Oireachtas has had a very limited role in public policy evaluation, it is hard to argue that membership of the EU has constrained its capacity in this regard. If anything, the mandatory establishment of the Joint Committee on Secondary Legislation of the European Communities necessitated by Ireland's EC accession drew attention to 'the underdeveloped and inhibited nature of the control exercised by the Oireachtas' (Robinson, 1974: 9), paving the way for subsequent development of the Oireachtas committee system. In view of this, it is reasonable to argue that the greatest challenges to Oireachtas accountability have come from political developments within the state.

In terms of policy formulation, Irish governments have a variety of ways of identifying the public interest without consulting the Legislature. Extensive recourse to direct democracy to settle key political issues in the Republic is a unique feature of Irish politics. Since 1937, there have been 25 referenda on issues including: the electoral system (1959, 1968); initial entry into the European Community (1972) and subsequent EU treaty revisions (1987, 1992, 2001, 2008); and the position of the State on 'moral' issues such as the special position of the Catholic Church (1972), abortion within the State (1983), access to abortion information and services outside the State (1992), divorce (1986, 1995), access to bail (1997), removal of the death penalty (2001) and citizenship (2005).

For issues that require more complex consideration, the National Economic and Social Council (NESC) has been described by the *Irish Times* (5 January 1991) as 'the alternative parliament', diminishing even further the authority of the Dáil. Ward (1996: 55) notes that from 1987 'the National Economic and Social Council prepared reports for the government, without reference to the Oireachtas or political parties, which amounted to national plans for economic and tax policy, social reform, welfare, health, education, and much more'. When both Fine Gael and Labour complained of their exclusion from the process, 'they were told by government that there would have been no agreement on the NESC's plan if parties had been involved' (*Irish Times*, 20 January 1991).

Where important (extra parliamentary) political interests cannot be ignored, and for those political issues that require the representation of key economic and social interests, the advent of 'partnership government' presents an innovative way of bypassing the Legislature. Critics such as O'Cinneide (1998) have linked this extension of corporatism and its intensifying influence over the lives of citizens to a diminution of the policy-making role of backbenchers and opposition TDs. Others point out that whilst 'a host of unelected interest groups take their places at the table of partnership ... one of the most painful ironies associated with this development, has been the extravagantly optimistic suggestion that it somehow deepens democracy' (Meade, 2005: 356).

In Northern Ireland, the chief historic impediment upon the Legislature was its perceived lack of legitimacy among the nationalist population inside Northern Ireland and throughout the island. The rejectionism of northern nationalists was encouraged by episodic antipartition campaigns launched by governments in the South. These, allied to the rejection of the legitimacy of the northern state in articles 2 and 3 of the constitution of the Irish Republic and the continued emphasis upon territorial unity within the Southern state, contributed substantially to the siege mentality of Unionists within the Stormont parliament (Kennedy, 1988; Whyte, 1990; Girvin, 2002). The amendments to the constitution of the Irish Republic, which downgraded Irish unity to an aspiration rather than an imperative, removed the exogenous threat (though it was never more than rhetorical) to the institutions of the North. Equally, the support for the Northern Ireland Assembly and Executive offered by the hitherto abstentionist republicans of Sinn Féin means that a devolved assembly enjoys a previously unknown legitimacy.

The main constraints upon a Northern Ireland legislature have thus become technical, rather than ideological. The part-time basis of the Assembly, sitting for a mere two days per week, means that it has limited time to undertake legislative and representative functions. The Assembly's powers are circumscribed, with the significant powers that remain being excepted or reserved by the Westminster parliament, which is the sole body permitted to transfer further powers. The vulnerability of the Assembly to suspension by the Secretary of State has meant that the Assembly failed to embed as a significant autonomous legislative institution in its early years (Hadfield, 2001).

The weak state of the Northern Ireland economy (public sector oriented and reliant upon subvention) has added to the denial of tax-raising powers for the Assembly and maintained a state of dependence upon Westminster. Moreover, EU legislation shapes 80 per cent of the legislative programme of the Northern Ireland Assembly (McQuade and Fagan, 2002). The Executive established a European Policy Coordination Unit to assist in the implementation of EU directives, although Northern Ireland's representative role within the EU was largely filtered through Whitehall (Tonge, 2005b). The Northern Ireland Assembly had relatively little political or allocational influence upon the vast sums of 'peace process money' given to Northern Ireland (and across the island as a whole) under the PEACE programmes, under which local councils and user groups were the main recipients. The constituency role of elected members, so vital in terms of the Dail and House of Commons, does exist, but is partial, as, whatever the protestations to the contrary, the vast majority of MLAs are elected by, and mainly represent, only one section of the community.

Conclusion

The establishment of legislative assemblies both North and South did not go uncontested. In Northern Ireland different forms of legislature have struggled to establish cross-community legitimacy and, as such, the polity has remained dysfunctional. In the Republic, the legitimacy of the Dáil was accepted only after a bitter civil war. Yet in both polities, the important political symbolism attached to an independent legislature obliged the main political parties to acknowledge the sovereignty of the Assembly in order to make the transition to peaceful, democratic politics. Ironically, however, it seems that the more faithful copy of the Westminster model is provided by the Republic, leaving the contemporary Northern Irish state to experiment with more continental forms of consociational parliamentarianism. Consociation is a response to Northern Ireland's devolved parliament failing to represent all the people between 1921 and 1972. Instead, the institution was perceived by the nationalist minority as a partisan unionist entity under which parliamentary norms of government and opposition, balanced legislation and impartial scrutiny, did not apply.

By contrast, in the Republic it seems all but impossible to work up any interest in, or enthusiasm for, Oireachtas reform. The conspicuous shortcomings of the Oireachtas, in representative, legislative or scrutiny capacities, seem apparent to only a few of its own members, and in general their calls for change have been but cries in the dark. No doubt the primary reason for this lies in the broader institutional context of executive–legislature relations, as they have been mediated by the main political parties in the Republic. The irony is that despite significant attempts to shift the Republic's legislative model away from its Westminster prototype (most notably with the introduction of the STV system of PR), the attitude and behaviour of the two main political parties in the post-independence period has cemented the British model of executive dominance.

In summary, both the Northern Irish and Republic's legislatures are weak in relation to the power of their respective executives. They differ, however, in relation to the sources of this weakness. In Northern Ireland, it arises as a consequence of political expediency in institutional design; in the Republic it is a matter of popular acquiescence.

3

The Bureaucracy

It has become a cliché to praise the Irish civil service for its integrity, an attribute it certainly shared with its parent. Indeed, so perfunctory is the genuflection to its integrity by commentators that it is, as often as not, a mere preamble to criticism.

(Kelly, 1993: 73)

Introduction

Commenting on the development of the British civil service in the mid-1990s, Dowding (1995: 2) suggested that 'twenty years ago, writing a book on the civil service was a comparatively easy task. The service had remained largely unchanged for almost a century, acquiring new tasks and departments, rearrangement here and there; but in the main historians of the civil service could stand on the shoulders of their predecessors'. The same could also be said of the Republic's civil service where, according to one retired secretary, prior to the 1960s 'the whole ethos of the civil service was against initiative. You did not stick your neck out' (McNamara, 1990: 78). Zimmerman (1997: 537) noted that the Taoiseach, Sean Lemass, 'was critical of the passive attitude of departments' that sought 'to avoid risks of experimentation and innovation and to confine themselves to vetting and improving proposals brought to them by private interests and individuals, rather than to generate new ideas themselves' (Lemass, 1961: 5).

Throughout the 1970s, these attitudes were challenged not only by domestic discontent but, more significantly, by external socio-economic forces beyond the control of states. Across Western Europe, the experience of economic crisis in the mid-1970s provided the impetus for changes in government styles and policies: 'as the crisis persisted, the countries converged in their approaches, each in turn moving towards austerity, more conflict, and stronger leadership' (Damgaard *et al.*, 1989: 185). Cutting back public expenditure, viewed initially as a pragmatic response to the budgetary challenges faced by modern states, soon developed a political momentum of its own as the 'New Right' began to exert its influence on the governments of Western Europe. The idea that public bureaucracies can and should be run more like private companies called into question traditional procedures, organizational structures and styles of public administration (Heywood and Wright, 1997). Increasing emphasis on the 'three Es' – economy, efficiency and effectiveness – in public policy led to the growth of new public

51

management (NPM) which 'claims to speak on behalf of taxpayers and consumers and against cosy cultures of professional self-regulation' (Bogdanor, 1997). As a result, towards the turn of the century, Rhodes (1997: 87) was able to note that in Britain:

> the past fifteen years were a permanent revolution for the British civil service … Its famed, perhaps notorious, ability to frustrate reform foundered on the energy and commitment of the longest serving government this century … Margaret Thatcher made no secret of her disdain, bordering on outright hostility, towards the civil service.

While the market-oriented reforms of the Thatcher era were viewed with some scepticism in Ireland, management reforms continue to be strongly influenced by the experience in Britain (Boyle *et al.*, 1998/9: 27) and the 1990s 'have seen the Irish public service embrace the new management decisively' (Kelly, 2000/1: 68). Suggesting that there is an element of the zeal of the convert, Kelly (2000/1: 69) notes that the enthusiasm with which the public service seems to have converted to 'new management' orthodoxies is 'exemplified in the tendency (if one might invert the usual metaphor) not merely to rescue the baby but to drink the bath water'. Still, it can be reasonably argued that despite the changing attitudes and significant reforms, 'the fundamentals of the system have remained intact' (Connolly, 2005: 348).

Origins and Influences

O'Halpin (1991: 287–9) argued that senior officials in the new state devoted considerable effort towards the creation of an efficient, impartial and effective civil service. Together, Joseph Brennan, the secretary of the Department of Finance, and C. J. Gregg, an official from the British Board of Inland Revenue on secondment to the Free State authorities until 1924, established the ground rules for the organization of government, drawing heavily on new Treasury practice in Britain. They were supported at the political level by the Provisional Government's creation of the Civil Service Commission in 1923, which effectively put a stop to political and personal patronage in official appointments and, just as importantly, at popular level also. Kissane (2004: 26) notes that 'crucially, the sub-elites in Irish society – the civil servants, the professions, and the clergy – remained committed to democracy after the civil war, whereas in a case like that of the Weimar Republic, they were hostile to democracy from the beginning'. In consequence, Stapleton (1991: 305) noted that 'the Irish Free State, in contrast to the experience of many other post colonial states of the twentieth century, inherited at its foundation a virtually complete apparatus of government, both central and local; and one that, by the standards and requirements of the time, was relatively modern and effective'.

The introduction, in 1924, of the Ministers and Secretaries Act, which effectively made the secretary of the Department of Finance head of the civil service, was designed to centralize all the work of the government in Ireland under 11 government ministers, thereby strengthening government organization. By vesting 'tight central control over resources – financial and human' in the central controlling Department of Finance, the reforms were designed 'to prevent corruption and fraud by making it difficult for any one individual to make financial or policy decisions in isolation' (Byrne *et al.*, 1995: 8). In addition, the introduction of 'ministerial responsibility' – or 'corporation sole' as it is usually referred to in the Republic – reflected the position, both in theory and in law, that the Minister is (with a few stated exceptions) responsible for every single act of his or her department and of all civil servants within it. Consequently, a considerable quantity of detailed business came to be discharged at high levels of the administration, and senior officials, 'instead of being preoccupied with broad questions of policy, became immersed with matters of detail' (Connaughton, 2005: 248). Thus, despite its principled intentions, the doctrine of 'corporation sole' had other unintended consequences: in a managerial sense, civil servants could to a large extent avoid taking personal responsibility for any decision; and in a policy sense, the facility to routinely pass decisions upwards (and the converse difficulty of passing decisions downwards), increased the possibility of routinely avoiding making difficult decisions (Byrne *et al.*, 1995: 8). Arguably, this situation contributed to conceptualizations of the Irish civil service as inherently conservative.

According to Chubb (1992: 219), 'the administrative machinery of the new state did not have to be created: what existed was taken over by nationalist rebels, most of whom were by no means looking to effect great social and political reforms'. Notwithstanding their political impartiality, the 'world view' of many Irish civil servants was distinctly conservative – influenced not only by their conservative Catholic education but by the Department of Finance which, 'following from the Treasury model inherited from the British administrative system, played a dominant role in state policy formation for much of Ireland's post-independence history' (O'Connell and Rottman, 1992: 231). Jacobsen (1994: 61) summed up Lee's (1989: 310–28) thorough and detailed analysis thus: 'The "Finance attitude" was unrelievedly negative, and the mission of the senior civil servants there was to prevent the state from acquiring interventionist capabilities, to protect private property and their own free-market orthodoxy from incursions'. This attitude was most strikingly borne out by the Department's 'principled objection to increases in state expenditure and taxes, and in particular to increased commitments to social expenditure' (O'Connell and Rottman, 1992: 231).

Such misgivings about the exaggerated influence of the Department of Finance are a long-standing feature of contemporary histories of Irish public administration. It is argued that vesting the Department of Finance with control of the state's resources and civil service has led to tensions between it and other departments. The Department of Finance 'can become preoccupied with line by line examination of all spending proposals', giving it effective control over expenditure aggregates but much less influence over policy efficacy or strategic direction (Byrne *et al.*, 1995: 9). Although new and contemporary at the time of its inception, the organization of the Irish civil service changed very little subsequently, so that it could be argued with some truth that 'the civil service model in operation in Ireland is essentially that introduced by reforms of the British civil service in the middle of the nineteenth century' (Byrne *et al.*, 1995: 8). Lee (1989: 93) argued that the British system bequeathed two important legacies to the Irish civil service: it 'contributed significantly to establishing standards of personal integrity among senior civil servants' and it 'enshrined the cult of the amateur in administration'. This preference for an intelligent 'all rounder' as opposed to a more narrowly focused expert reflects the British concept of an impartial administrator that contrasts with the acknowledged partisanship of senior officials in many European systems.

O'Halpin (1991: 291) noted that when, in 1932, Fianna Fáil came into office for the first time, 'there was no clear out of senior officials and no infusion of political appointees to departments, although some people who had been dismissed for refusing to swear allegiance to the Free State in 1922 were re-instated'. Commenting on the series of reforms begun by the Provisional Government and then upheld by Fianna Fáil, O'Halpin (ibid.) argued that 'the apolitical methods of appointing and promoting civil servants insisted on by the founding fathers of the Irish civil service have proved remarkably durable and impermeable to political interference or even to ministerial involvement'. In fact it can easily be argued that, unlike their predecessors who had inherited 'a motley collection of departments, some of them very difficult to control' (O'Halpin, 1991: 293), Fianna Fáil was able to enjoy the fruits of early Free State government reforms. The Ministers and Secretaries Act had created both a 'high degree of administrative centralisation and of political control of the state machine' (O'Halpin, 1991: 295). 'The de Valera government found nothing to complain of in the administrative machine they inherited – indeed they strengthened the rules debarring civil servants from participating in politics – and officials discovered they could work effectively with their new ministers' (O'Halpin, 1991: 291). Still, even where higher civil servants appeared impartial between different governments, a good deal of evidence suggests that they remained loyal to a very particular and conservative view of the state, one where 'state activism – other than in the service of private property – was an anathema' (Jacobsen, 1994: 65).

In the United Kingdom, the civil service established under Northcote-Trevelyan in the 1850s was largely unchanged in terms of structure until the 1990s. Its core features of permanency, neutrality and anonymity were seen as essential in preserving the integrity of the service, and the changes which arrived under the Conservative governments of the 1980s and 1990s owed more to other concerns, namely that the service was too slow and inefficient, lacked a managerial culture and was too large.

In Northern Ireland, although civil service structures mirror those elsewhere in the United Kingdom, and its head attends regular meetings of permanent secretaries in Whitehall, the Northern Ireland Civil Service (NICS) has always operated as a distinct, autonomous entity. This marks it as a different organization from that found in Scotland and Wales, where the civil service has remained part of a single structure despite devolved political arrangements (Gay and Mitchell, 2007). There is no right of transfer from the British civil service to its Northern Ireland counterpart, or vice-versa. The distinctiveness of the NICS may provide an indication of how the unified civil service elsewhere in the UK may become autonomous within a differentiated polity as the implications of devolution become increasingly evident (Carmichael, 2002). The 31,000 members of the NICS form part of an over large, 200,000 strong, public sector in the province, found mainly in the health service, education and local government (Knox and Carmichael, 2007c).

The civil service, during the period when recruitment was undertaken by itself, was bereft of external scrutiny and overseen by Unionist politicians who sat on senior appointment boards, resulting in the NICS being seen as a tool of the Unionist state, rather than as an impartial servant of the Crown. Given the sectarian framework of the state from the 1920s until the 1970s, it was unsurprising that the NICS discriminated against the Catholic population. The NICS was discouraged by its Unionist political 'masters' from employing Catholics, and the catalogue of discrimination was lengthy. The Ministry of Labour altered its recruitment rules to ensure their non-hiring; some ministries boasted of their dearth of Catholic employees; the Orange Order engaged in surveillance of Catholic civil servants; and the wartime Prime Minister, John Andrews, requested a register of such employees, arguing that they could not be trusted (Bew *et al.*, 2002). In such a climate, it was hardly startling that Catholics did not fill any of the most senior positions – those of permanent and assistant secretary – for 40 years of the state's existence.

The British civil service regarded such sectarian malpractice with distaste, arguing for a more meritocratic system, whilst, less overtly, pursuing its own unofficial discrimination based upon social class. However, the disinclination of British government ministers to intervene ensured that overwhelmingly sectarian recruitment patterns survived until the arrival of direct rule in 1972. Initially, direct British rule only diminished the extent of sectarian practice, not its actuality. The British government's Fair Employment Act 1976 outlawed religious discrimination in recruitment, but the investigative body created by that act, the Fair Employment Agency, found in its 1983 inquiry into the NICS that sectarian recruitment was still evident (Dickson and Osborne, 2007). Since then, however, the NICS has 'provided a template for the rest of the public sector to improve practices' (ibid., 153).

Organizational Evolution

According to Chubb (1992: 219), 'it is hard to discern what, if any, were the principles on which new functions as they were assumed were allocated among departments and between departments, local authorities and state-sponsored bodies'. Although the British system of government bequeathed to the Irish administration significant contemporary reforms spearheaded by the Treasury, it also left a rather haphazard mosaic of organizational responsibility. Prior to independence, Ireland was not administered as a single administrative entity, but via a collection of departments, boards and agencies, only a minority of which were under the direct control of the relevant government minister (O'Halpin, 1991: 283–4). Indeed, 'growth and change were handled in a decidedly pragmatic way' (Chubb, 1992: 219) and it was not until the 1950s that any reform took place.[1]

In 1958, publication of the now renowned government paper entitled *Economic Development* (Government of Ireland, 1958), or 'Whitaker Report' (so called after the Secretary of Finance charged with its composition), marked a watershed for the Irish state (Adshead, 2008), heralding a decade of unparalleled growth and rapid change. By the early 1960s, however, there was growing dissatisfaction with both the structure of the administration and the quality of the administrators: increasing governmental responsibility for developing and directing growth laid bare a civil service that was ill-equipped to deal with its new-found responsibilities for policy-making and implementation (NIEC, 1965). A Public Services Organisation Review Group was established, chaired by Liam St John Devlin, 'to examine and report on the organisation of the Departments of State at higher level, including the appropriate distribution of functions as between both departments themselves and departments and other bodies' (Chubb, 1992: 221).

The Devlin Report (1969), as it came to be called, diagnosed five chief problems with the organization of the civil service. It argued that the 1924 Ministers and Secretaries Act had constrained development of the civil service by effectively ensuring that civil servants were not managers; that there was no separation between policy advice and policy executive functions; and that together these combined with a lack of clear organization at higher levels of the civil service. Overall, the report noted a complete lack of planning and a management emphasis on expenditure control rather than expenditure effectiveness. The Report made a total of 130 separate recommendations to be achieved within five years 'after the first years intensive effort' (Devlin, 1969: 199). The essential argument 'that the civil service needed to be more managerial, and that it should be functionally organised, quickly became the conventional wisdom, although precious little was done about it for many years' (O'Halpin, 1991: 297). In addition to the lack of political will to push for reform and the more general resistance of public servants to change (Chubb, 1992: 223), it has been argued that many of the 'proposals were too technical and not widely understood by the target population' (Byrne *et al.*, 1995: 47). In consequence, many changes were not made, with a few only partially implemented. Amongst these, the institution of the Aireacht (literally translated as ministry) and a Department of the Public Service are perhaps the most significant.

At departmental level, the Aireacht, comprising the Minister, the Secretary and the necessary Assistant Secretaries, was intended to form the policy-making and review body for all executive units for which the department held responsibility, including relevant semi-state bodies, which the report stated 'must be effectively integrated in the public sector' (Devlin, 1969: 163). Executive offices under the departmental remit were to have considerable legal autonomy devolved to them so that their directors (as opposed to the departmental minister) could be held accountable for their (in)actions. The Aireacht would exercise its role via four 'co-ordinating systems' – finance, planning, organization and personnel (Devlin, 1969: 157–8). At the level of central administration, the creation of a Department of the Public Service in 1973 was intended as a driver for organizational change. Following the passing of the Ministers and Secretaries (Amendment) Act, 1973, the Department of Finance retained control over finance and planning, but all organization and personnel issues were transferred to the new department.

In fact, the Aireacht concept was only half-heartedly introduced. Seven years after their introduction, Aireachts had been operational in only two departments, and there is little evidence of them having a significant impact (Murray, 1990: 22). The decision of the Dáil (Dáil Éireann, 1974) to implement the structural elements of the Devlin proposals 'after consideration of the experiments on the separation of policy and execution', left the Devlin reforms moribund. The ability of the Department of Public Service to promote change was clearly compromised and, in 1987, its duties were reintegrated into the Department of Finance. Before its final dissolution, however, it did manage to produce a new reform programme in the form of a government White Paper, *Serving the Country Better* (Government of Ireland, 1985).

Serving the Country Better concentrated on improving the management of the public service in terms of clear statements of aims and objectives of departments; of specific results to be achieved; of decentralization from central to line departments and within line departments; of greater responsiveness to citizens' needs with a more efficient, courteous and prompt service to the public (Byrne *et al.*, 1995: 47). Notwithstanding its references to 'public service', the thrust of the White Paper was clearly directed towards the civil service. The proposals for the separation, where suitable, of civil service roles in relation to policy advice and departmental management were clearly a nod at earlier reforms proposed by the Devlin Report. As with its predecessor, the White Paper 'emphasised the need to install management systems based on personal responsibility for results and value for money' (Connaughton, 2006: 263). Still, the concept of 'corporation sole' remained intact (Connolly, 2005: 341) and, by the late 1980s, 'reform became associated with reducing the size of the civil service in the period of fiscal austerity to the detriment of structural and operational improvements' (Connaughton, 2006: 263).

Reform was not back on the agenda until 1994, when the then Taoiseach, Albert Reynolds, invited the ministers and secretaries of government departments to a lunch, where he announced his determination to give the public service a whole new strategic focus (Boyle, 1995: 2). The *Strategic Management Initiative*, as it became known, was intended to deliver excellent service to the customer, maximum contribution to national development and effective use of resources (Murray and Teahon, 1998). Despite a change of government in the same year, the new Rainbow Coalition continued to develop the strategic reorientation of the civil service with the publication of a new White Paper in 1996, *Delivering Better Government* (Government of Ireland, Department of the Taoiseach, 1996). As it states in its own preamble: 'The central thrust of this report is the achievement of an excellent service for the Government and for the public as customers' (Government of Ireland, 1996a). The culmination of these two initiatives was reflected in the Public Service Management Act, 1997, recasting the role of the most senior official in each department – now referred to as the Secretary General – through an amendment of the concept of 'corporation sole' and charging all departments to frame their 'statement of strategy' in relation to established guidelines on 'customer/client interests and needs' (Humphreys, 1998: 33).

In Northern Ireland, direct rule from 1972 did not end the distinctiveness of the NICS within the UK civil service, even if it was customary for it to follow British civil service practices. The NICS continued to be seen as 'an organisation in waiting, ready to serve a future devolved government', even if that wait at the time appeared interminable (Carmichael and Osborne, 2003: 208). Meanwhile, the province was governed by the Secretary of State, junior ministers and the 1,200 members of the

Northern Ireland Office (NIO) recruited mainly from the NICS. The return of devolved government in 2007 was likely to lead to the return of many civil servants to the NICS from their secondment at the NIO.

Although formally a 'civil service apart', the NICS was subject to the same types of internal restructuring evident elsewhere in the UK. The creation of 'Next Steps' executive agencies, separating policy-making civil servants from deliverers in agencies, has been evident in Northern Ireland in recent decades. Elsewhere in the UK, the separation has been criticized as unsatisfactory and at times unworkable. The creation of agencies has been seen as a device by which ministers could hive off responsibility for policy blunders to chief executives, even though several 'executive' failures, such as those of the Child Support Agency or Prison Service, owed much to injudicious policy decisions by politicians (Campbell and Wilson, 1995; Giddings, 1995; Tonge, 2000). More than 70 per cent of Northern Ireland's civil servants now work in executive agencies, which administer some of the functions associated with local government elsewhere in the UK. The NICS also followed the UK model in the creation of a senior civil service (in 1996), covering the four highest tiers of posts within the organization. The consequence has been that the NICS nowadays is less of a monolith than previously, with a differentiated upper tier to which appointments are based on open competition rather than internal promotion, whilst overseen by civil service commissioners.

The modern demands upon the NICS were outlined in the *Fit for Purpose* document issued in 2004 (Department of Finance and Personnel, 2004). It contained the themes of, firstly, efficiency via sensitivity to the public and reduced size; secondly, increased professionalism through leadership and management training; and thirdly, wholesale adoption of the acceptance of diversity explicit in the GFA (Birrell, 2007). Whilst an assessment of the civil service was welcome, the hints at reductions in size mirrored the proposals for pruning outlined in the 2004 Gershon review of the public sector elsewhere in Britain, at a time when the formation of a fragile new executive suggested that a strong and stable civil service was needed. The challenge for the senior ranks of the NICS was to assist inexperienced ministers of variable competence in developing coherent, joined-up government.

Civil Service Accountability and Monitoring

The governance structure of civil service management in Ireland changed significantly during the 1980s and 1990s with the establishment of the Office of the Ombudsman in 1984, the introduction of a value for money remit for the Comptroller and Auditor General (Amendment) Act, 1993, and the Public Service Management Act, 1997. Additionally, the Data Protection Act, 1989, the Ethics in Public Office Act, 1995,[2] the Freedom of Information Act, 1997,[3] the Committees of the Houses of the Oireachtas (Compellability, Privileges and Immunities of Witnesses) Act, 1997,[4] all represented a significant alteration in governance arrangements that began to challenge the traditional 'cult of secrecy' (Doyle, 1996–7: 64–8) in Irish administration and helped introduce a more contemporary service ethos. Together, with other more general changes in the public service, such as the wider development and deployment of IT, financial management systems and the Strategic Management Initiative, these have led to a tighter focus on accountability and the way that it is exercised in the civil service (Boyle, 1998: 6–7).

Established in January 1984, the Office of the Ombudsman has the task of investigating complaints by members of the public regarding their treatment by public bodies. In doing so, the Ombudsman has the power to demand any information, document or file, or official, from a public body in order to gain details about the complaint (Hogan and Morgan, 1998: 337–93). During 1998–2002, 2,400 valid cases were received, plus another 1,400 that fell outside the Office's remit. Of the valid complaints, 47 per cent related to the civil service, 32 per cent to local government, 18 per cent to health boards, and 3 per cent to *An Post* remit (Gallagher and Komito, 2005: 260). Since the Office of Ombudsman began work, its investigations have found both individual cases of unfairness and/or maladministration, as well as systemic problems within the public service as a whole: significant anomalies in the pensions regulations being a case in point (Connolly, 2005: 345).

Until the Comptroller and Auditor General (Amendment) Act, 1993, despite a number of attempts by successive comptroller and auditor generals to broaden their role, their powers have remained limited by the original provisions for their office established by the British Exchequer and Audit Act of 1866 (O'Halpin, 1985: 506). During the late 1980s, however, under the chairmanship of Fine Gael TD, Jim Mitchell, the Dáil Committee of Public Accounts sought to remedy this problem (Connolly, 2005: 346). The 1993 Act empowered the Comptroller and Auditor General to carry out 'value for money' audits and comparative studies across the public sector, which served both to draw attention to problems where they existed and to promote best practice across the public sector more generally (Connolly, 2005: 347).

By providing for the transfer of responsibility downwards in the civil service hierarchy and outlining the respective roles and responsibilities of ministers vis-à-vis secretary generals and special advisors, the Public Service Management Act, 1997, 'implies that individuals know and recognise the extent of their responsibility and the ways in which they are answerable' (Connaughton, 2006: 264). Managerial responsibility for the department is assigned to the Secretary General, whilst the Minister retains overall responsibility for the political direction and performance of its functions. Under this act, ministerial responsibility is not removed, but its exercise is greatly clarified. Ministers retain overall responsibility for government departments and offices. Members of government are collectively responsible to Dáil Éireann for departments of state administered by them, and ministers have a duty to inform and explain their actions to the Oireachtas (Boyle, 1998: 14). Within the revised framework, however, ministers are increasingly likely to redirect responsibility, 'either through referring queries to agency heads or heads of independent units, or through instructing civil servants allocated responsibility for specific functions under the Public Service Management Act to deal in the first place with a query' (Boyle, 1998: 15).

Given its – and Northern Ireland's – contentious history and the plethora of fair employment legislation that resulted, the NICS is perhaps the most scrutinized civil service in the Western world. By the end of the twentieth century, the service had eradicated religious imbalances within its ranks to the point where the religious background of civil servants (where this was evident) – of 58.6 per cent Protestant and 41.4 per cent Roman Catholic – closely reflected that of the population as a whole (Northern Ireland Civil Service, 2000). During the 1990s, Roman Catholic representation rose by 3 per cent, reflecting, variously, the growth in the Catholic population, the end of sectarian recruitment patterns and the willingness of Catholics to serve the northern state. The gender imbalance, which had been even more acute, had been virtually eradicated by a 6 per cent increase in the percentage of women employees from 1989 to 1999, bringing the proportion of women in the NICS to 48 per cent.

The conduct of Northern Ireland's civil servants is conditioned by the NICS Code of Ethics, which sets out the desired values, standards of behaviour, rights and responsibilities of civil servants. 'Integrity, honesty, objectivity and impartiality' are the four core expectations (Northern Ireland Civil Service, 1999). Civil servants fearful that they are required to compromise such standards are entitled to raise the issue with their department or agency without being penalized for so doing. Under direct rule, the NICS was largely insulated from scrutiny, partly because it merely implemented decisions taken in London, not Belfast. The arrival of devolved government has raised the profile – and level of examination – of the service, as the implementation of the will of local political leaders has come to form an integral part of the devolved settlement. The public accountability mechanisms of the Citizen's Charter, introduced by John Major's Conservative government of the 1990s, had already impacted upon the NICS in producing a more responsive service, with targets set in, for example, responding to letters or telephone calls from the public. The issue of who is accountable at senior levels of government and civil service remains contentious. The tendency at Westminster for ministers to shift blame to civil servants heading agencies – as seen in the cases of the Child Support Agency, the Prison Service and the Rural Payments Agency – may be replicated under devolved government in Northern Ireland in respect of departmental ministers and the NICS.

Relations between Civil Servants and Politicians

The 'Westminster model' is based on a number of assumptions that create a particular set of relationships between ministers and civil servants (Kavanagh *et al.*, 2006: 221). These assumptions are that parliament is sovereign; ministers are accountable to parliament; civil servants are neutral and loyal to ministers; decision-making power is located in the executive; government is legitimized by a public service ethos; and the system of decision-making is secret. Within this framework, 'ministers decide' and 'civil servants advise'. The underpinning assumption is that senior officials are apolitical, without personal, political or policy preferences. In reality, however, relations between ministers and civil servants are more likely to be characterized by interdependence. Officials bring expertise, experience and knowledge of the bureaucratic process; ministers bring authority, policy and direction to the policy process. A department can draft policy, but only a minister can make it, push it through government and turn it into law. A department that lacks an effective minister is effectively rendered impotent, in much the same way as is a minister without the support of his or her department.

In this respect, Connaughton (2006: 263) suggests that the Irish civil service system is best understood by way of Peters's (1987) 'village life' model, that is one where both public servants and their political masters share relatively similar values and goals so that relationships between the two 'are those of mutually cooperative elites with a primary interest in maintaining the state and promoting its efficient and appropriate functioning in the interests of the public'. This view is substantiated by Zimmerman's (1997) study of relations between ministers and senior civil servants, which he found, by and large, to be 'very cooperative' and seems to be shared by senior Irish civil servants. In their review of administrative practice and reform of the Irish civil service, 11 senior civil servants suggested that in the Irish case 'there is general agreement that the operation of the government and the departments it controls should be guided by an overall strategy reflecting the goals of society' (Byrne *et al.*, 1995: 9). Presumably the fact that this is possible reflects the high degree of consensus particularistic of Irish politics (Murphy, 2008).

Still, however, the practice of appointing outside advisers to give ministerial advice is a long-standing one. Eamon de Valera retained the services of Professor Timothy A. Smiddy, of University College Cork, on an ad hoc basis primarily for advice on issues relating to economic policy (Fanning, 1978: 457). Jack Lynch took advice from a professor of economics at Trinity College Dublin, Martin O'Donoghue, on much the same basis (Lee, 1989: 487). Possibly as a result of this experience, prior to entering coalition with Fianna Fáil, the Labour party demanded the appointment of 'programme managers' as a means of ensuring that their coalition agreement 'would be subject to informed and detailed tracking, fine-tuning and review by trusted officials' (O'Halpin, 1997: 80) These programme managers were not resented by the civil servants (the fact that many Fianna Fáil ministers chose to second higher level civil servants to this task may have contributed to their integration). 'Several secretaries commented that ministerial advisors are helpful in solving problems' and 'function well as a conduit between the secretary and the minister', particularly since programme managers – because of their functional remit – are often in a better position to cross-check and/or sound out corresponding action in other departments (Zimmerman, 1997: 539).

The return of devolved government to Northern Ireland in 1998 saw civil servants required to adapt to rule by local ministers for the first time in a quarter of a century. This required immediate structural adaptation, as the NICS had to be reorganized to service the OFDFM, as well as ten departments, replacing the previous six-department structure (Carmichael, 2003).

Amid the chaos of the 1999–2002 devolved administration, civil servants found themselves servicing some executive politicians determined to bring down the institutions, or others still linked to a paramilitary organization desirous of the armed destruction of the state. There was much concern over how civil servants would deal with Sinn Féin ministers, including a prominent former member of the IRA, Martin McGuinness. Nonetheless, relations were mainly cordial from the outset and deficiencies in executive legislation owed more to divisions over the Executive's 'agreed' Programmes for Government within the coalitional executive than to civil service obstruction.

The use of special advisers by Northern Ireland ministers aped that by UK government ministers and contained the seeds of friction between neutral civil servants and the political partisans sometimes employed by ministers. Relations between civil servants and assembly committees have sometimes been tense, not helped by an initial tendency of committee members to blame failings upon the civil service (Carmichael and Osborne, 2003). For example, despite the Assembly lying idle from 2002 until 2007, due to the failure of politicians to work together, MLAs nonetheless saw no irony in criticizing civil service absenteeism as 'unacceptable'. It was revealed that one-third of civil servants had been sick for at least one day during 2006–7, with 12 per cent on long-term sickness, the total annual cost amounting to £25 million (O'Loan, 2007).

Europeanization and Relations with the EU

In relation to the Republic of Ireland, Cromien (2000: 152–3) notes that membership of the EU has impinged on Irish civil servants in a number of ways, but possibly most significantly in terms of the organizational and cultural shift that it provoked through opportunities for foreign travel and interchange with other public servants in Continental Europe. When the twin burdens of work and travel began to take their toll on senior civil servants, 'the work to be done in routine Community committees was quickly delegated from senior officials to their colleagues at middle management or lower' (Cromien, 2000: 152). This began to challenge existing organizational norms and hierarchies, so that in conjunction with other pressures for change elsewhere in the system, in a few years the Irish civil service changed from something that would not have looked out of place in a Dickensian novel to a much more modern and outward looking organization (ibid.).

At the administrative level, the European Communities Committee, which predates EU membership, is the main institutional device for formulating national positions and resolving interdepartmental conflict. Formerly, it met at Secretary level, but now it meets at Assistant Secretary level, where representatives of the Departments of Foreign Affairs, Agriculture, Finance, Industry and Commerce, Labour, and the Taoiseach's Office all attend. Until March, 1987, it was chaired by the Deputy Secretary of Foreign Affairs and serviced by his or her department. Thereafter, responsibility was transferred to the Taoiseach's Office, when the then Taoiseach, Charles Haughey, designated a portfolio for the coordination of EU policy to be held by the Minister of State in his department. At this point it became clear that the Committee was 'no longer a purely administrative committee but spans the administrative/political divide' (Laffan, 1991a: 191). In 1989, this committee became a planning committee, with organizational and logistical responsibilities in the run-up to the 1990 Irish Presidency (Laffan, 2000: 131). At this point, its policy coordination functions were superseded by the establishment, again by Charles Haughey, of a Ministerial Group, though the Ministers and Secretaries Group (MSG) was maintained in order 'to co-ordinate the preparation of a National Plan for Delors I and to negotiate the Community Support Framework' (ibid.). Perhaps surprisingly, the Ministerial Group reached the end of its lifespan with the end of the Irish presidency. In 1992, it was revived briefly by the then Taoiseach, Albert Reynolds, but was later superseded by the Ministers and Secretaries Group, which regained responsibility for planning for the Irish presidency in 1994–5. To date, the MSG remains the central Irish government EU coordinating mechanism. Serviced by a group of senior officials, it meets approximately once a month, augmented by a small number of interdepartmental groups dealing with key cross-departmental issues (Laffan, 2000: 132).

In Brussels, Ireland's permanent representation is accorded a high status in the domestic policy process. A period working in the unit is perceived as useful from a career point of view. The permanent representative and his or her deputy are always career diplomats from the Department of Foreign Affairs, which also supplies the lion share of remaining officials, usually around 45 per cent (Laffan, 1991a: 192). The rest come from various domestic departments with relevant expertise. By and large, the preparation of dossiers and administrative coordination remains the prerogative of the domestic civil service, though the permanent representation in Brussels provides invaluable information regarding the attitudes of other delegations to particular issues and possible negotiating scenarios. The status of the permanent representative also ensures that his or her views are listened to and carry consider-able weight in the formation of national policy responses (Laffan, 1991a: 192).

However, because of the relatively small size of the Irish polity, 'even the people who operate very minor programmes that are EU funded, and who then go over to network communications in Brussels, tend to be influential policy-makers because of the small numbers of people involved'.[5] As a result, the Irish system of policy formation on EU issues is much less institutionalized than in other member states; there are far fewer coordinating committees and those that exist meet less frequently than their counterparts. The small size of the bureaucracy leads to a less formal approach to policy-making; civil servants working in the Community know their counterparts in other government departments and deal with many issues over the telephone (Laffan, 1991a: 193; Adshead, 1996a: 593–601). On the one hand, it may be argued that the small size of Irish bureaucracy, which easily facilitates pragmatic and ad hoc responses to EU policy, leads to 'clear sight over short distances' (Laffan, 1991: 193). On the other hand, policy-makers argue that the fact that many Irish bureaucrats are by necessity generalists rather than specialists has facilitated a good deal of creativity in Irish policy towards the EU, plus the ready transfer of new ideas between different parts of government.[6] This is because, as Laffan (2000: 127) notes, 'in the EU "the devil is in the detail" as it is the nitty-gritty of legislation that matters during the implementation phase'. Here, creative Irish administrative responses, based on much less formal ways of doing business, have led to significant policy innovations (Adshead, 2005: 167).

Whitehall, rather than Stormont, continues to be the key player in respect of Northern Ireland's relations with the European Union. The main dealings with the EU lie within the European Policy and Coordination Unit (EPCU), created within the OFDFM. The unit contains civil servants advising local ministers on the impact of

EU policy on legislation affecting Northern Ireland and represents the province within the Foreign and Commonwealth Office and the European Secretariat of the Cabinet Office. The EPCU liaises with the Office of the Northern Ireland Executive in Brussels. In terms of bilateral EU–NICS dealings, rather than those filtered via a Whitehall prism, the key role of the EPCU lies in its administration of EU PEACE programmes.

Cross-Border Cooperation

The 1985 Anglo-Irish Agreement established a permanent secretariat of civil servants from the Irish Republic and the UK. Despite this, the extent of cross-border cooperation was modest (Tannam, 1998). Part of the reason lay in the resentment towards the manner in which the Anglo-Irish Agreement was created, with, extraordinarily, the Head of the NICS, Sir Kenneth Bloomfield, not being consulted (Carmichael, 2003; Bloomfield, 2007). Despite the scepticism of Unionists and civil servants, the limited nature of all-island bureaucratic links nonetheless emphasized the consultative rather than executive basis of the Agreement, despite the 'sell-out' protestations of Unionists (Tonge, 2002).

From 1998, under the GFA, Anglo-Irish institutional arrangements were replaced by a British–Irish Intergovernmental Council. This, and the accompanying NSMC and British–Irish Council (BIC), amounted (eventually) to far more consensual all-Ireland institutional architecture than the 1985 offerings. Civil servants from both jurisdictions staff the permanent secretariat of the NSMC in Armagh, which extended what was already a 'well-established bureaucratic apparatus' for the development of cross-border EU programmes (Laffan and Payne, 2002: 82). This apparatus involves the bringing together of civil servants from the Irish Republic's Department of Finance and Northern Ireland's Department of Finance and Personnel. These civil servants play a crucial role in determining the projects deemed suitable for approval and financing under the European programmes for cross-border cooperation (the Interreg peace programmes) and service the all-island bodies, such as the Special European Union Programmes Body (SEUPB), facilitated by the GFA within the orbit of the NSMC.

Since the GFA, all-island activity has been coordinated in the Irish Republic by civil servants within the Department of Foreign Affairs. Sectoral all-island cooperation has increased, resulting in an ever-growing number of meetings between civil servants from either side of the border. For example, by 2006, officials from the Department of Tourism, Sport and Recreation in the Irish Republic met their counterparts from the Department of Enterprise, Trade and Investment in Northern Ireland six times per year (Henderson and Teague, 2006). However, there remains asymmetry in the promotion of all-island activity. As the numbers of civil servants involved in cross-border activity has grown, the principal remaining barrier is the reluctance of departments in Northern Ireland to establish North–South units, unlike their counterparts in the Irish Republic (Tannam, 2004).

Civil servants from devolved administrations and from the British and Irish governments provide support for the BIC. Given the 'ceremonial air' of meetings of the BIC, it was unclear initially whether civil servants would be engaged in serious policy work (Trench, 2004: 180). However, the restoration of devolved government to Northern Ireland in 2007 bolstered the BIC, which began to engage in functional work and policy development across all the involved administrations, a development which may necessitate a more permanent secondment from the civil servants involved.

Conclusions: Characterizing the Civil Service

In relation to the Republic's administrative system, it is clear that the small size of the bureaucracy leads to a less formal approach to policy-making, as 'in so compact a society it is possible within political, business and academic circles for everyone to know everyone else' (Jacobsen, 1994: 43). Additionally, many policy-makers argue that the relatively small number of Irish bureaucrats means that many are *by necessity* generalists rather than specialists, and that this has facilitated a good deal of creativity in Irish policy-making, plus the ready transfer of new ideas between different parts of government (Adshead, 2005: 167–8). This aspect of Irish policy-making has been especially noticeable in relation to Ireland's policy within and towards the EU. Civil servants working in the EU generally know their counterparts in other government departments and deal with many issues over the telephone (Laffan, 1991a: 193; Adshead, 1996a: 593–601). It is not clear to what extent this prevalence of informal operating procedures and ways of doing business is either a cause or a consequence of the limited impact of a series of broader civil service reform initiatives (detailed above). As it stands, there is little research into the operating rationale and behaviour of the Irish civil service, though clearly – in view of the key role that the bureaucracy plays in implementing large swathes of government action – it is an area that warrants further research.

In Northern Ireland, the problem of size is the opposite of that encountered south of the border. The civil service appears too large, whilst the public sector in its entirety accounts for the occupations of one in five of Northern Ireland's working adults. The Review of Public Administration in the province in 2006 offered the opportunity for substantial pruning, yet the civil service escaped virtually unscathed, other than the merger of some executive agencies and the transfer of functions between agencies. Since 1979, Conservative and Labour governments have reduced the size of the civil service in Britain, but the NICS has remained immune to such cuts, whilst being subject to the internal restructuring – the separation of policy-making and delivery responsibilities in the UK civil service – evident from the 1990s onwards. Aside from the issue of size, the NICS is continuing to adjust to local devolved coalition government, a process of transition unlikely to be completed until there is final agreement over the extent of powers to be transferred to Northern Ireland.

4

The Judiciary

In view of the crucial role that law plays in regulating social behaviour, no one can doubt that it has immense political significance.

(Heywood, 2002: 303)

Introduction

There are two general types of legal systems: the common-law tradition and the civil-law tradition. Most European states belong to the latter, which originated within the Continental tradition of 'Roman' law that has since been transformed into a comprehensive system of legal codes. Within Europe, only Britain, Ireland and Malta are classifiable as common-law systems. Gallagher *et al.* (1992: 60) notes that 'the fundamental difference between the two is that common law systems rely much less on "laws", seen as acts of parliament, and much more on "the law", seen as the accumulated weight of precedent set by the decisions, definitions, and interpretations made by judges'. In common-law systems, then, judges do not only *apply* the law as it is set out by parliamentary legislation and other legal documents, they also play a part in *making* the law by virtue of the fact that their judgements and pronouncements may themselves later be used as precedents for other cases.

Sources of Law

In the Republic of Ireland, Irish law derives from six sources: common law; statute law; delegated or secondary legislation; the constitution; European law; and international conventions. *Common law* is 'judge made law' deriving from the pronouncements and precedents set by judicial decisions on the basis of evidence presented in court proceedings. *Statute law* is laid down by acts of the Oireachtas (see pp. 37–8), and, in the case of the Republic, also includes a number of laws passed by the British legislature prior to 1922. *Delegated* or *secondary legislation* comprises orders or regulations (known as 'statutory instruments') which are made by a minister in order to comply with an original act, where the exact steps necessary to achieve the ambition of the act are not specified within it. The use of statutory instruments is particularly common in relation to the transposition of EU directives into domestic Irish law, and arises in part from a Supreme Court decision in 1994, which found that 'the sheer number of EU directives necessitated their implementation by means of statutory instruments rather than by Act of the Oireachtas' (Hughes *et al.*, 2007: 318; see also Laffan and Tonra, 2005: 442).

The Irish constitution, Bunreacht na hÉireann, drafted by de Valera and passed by the Dáil in June 1937, was put before the people in a referendum on 1 July 1937 – the same day as the general election – in order to mark a symbolic 'new beginning' for the independent state of Ireland (Gallagher, 2005a: 75). As such, the constitution provides the basic law of the state, since no other laws can be in conflict with it. In this respect the Republic of Ireland is unusual in that any and all constitutional amendments require the consent of the people via a referendum, this following a proposal to amend the constitution having being passed by both houses of the Oireachtas (Constitution of Ireland, Art. 46; see also O'Neill, 2000).

European law derives from the decision by the Irish people to join what is now known as the European Union (but was then the European Economic Community or EEC) via a constitutional referendum on accession in 1972 (see pp. 212–14). In order to prevent a conflict of interest between the competing supremacies of the Irish Supreme Court and the European Court of Justice, the 1972 referendum on accession amended the constitution with the addition of Article 29.4.3, which provides that 'no provision of this constitution invalidates laws enacted, acts done or measures adopted by the State necessitated by the obligations of membership of the Communities'. To date, Ireland's membership of the EU has been responsible for seven constitutional referenda: on joining in May 1972; on the signing of the Single European Act in May 1987, the Draft (Maastricht) Treaty on European Union in June 1992, and the Amsterdam Treaty in May 1998; twice on the ratification of the Nice Treaty (in June 2001, when it was rejected, and again in October 2002, when it was passed) and on the EU constitution rejected in June 2008. The obligations of EU membership comprise regulations, directives and decisions. Regulations are binding on member states exactly as issued. Directives bind member states to conform to them in their own fashion by introducing legislation via national parliaments. Decisions relate either to specific enterprises or specific member states and are binding exactly as issued (Stone Sweet and Weiler, 1998).

Finally, Ireland's signature to international conventions may also impose legal obligations on the state. The European Convention on Human Rights, for example, allows Irish citizens to vindicate their rights through the European Court of Human Rights in Strasbourg or, following the incorporation of the convention into Irish law, directly through the Irish courts. The International Labour Organization (ILO), based in Geneva, is responsible for a number of conventions relating to standards for workers and related employer/employee rights. It should be noted, however, that whilst such conventions might be quite persuasive in the interpretation of domestic law and associated rights and responsibilities they are not in themselves *part of domestic law* in the same way, for example, that the EU treaties are (Morgan, 1985: 196). This situation arises as a consequence of Article 29.6 of the constitution, which establishes the principle that 'no international agreement shall be part of the domestic law of the State save as may be determined by the Oireachtas'. In practice this means that such conventions are not enforceable directly through domestic Irish courts but only via international judicial arenas, such as the European Commission of Human Rights or, in the last resort, the European Court of Human Rights.

Most of the laws pertaining to Northern Ireland are determined at Westminster, which remains the sovereign parliament, although devolution is reshaping this. Indeed the British and Irish governments insisted that the creation of devolved institutions, including those linked to the Irish Republic, did not involve any derogation of sovereignty in their respective states nor affect the ability of the Westminster Parliament to enact legislation for Northern Ireland. The 1920 Government of Ireland Act allowed Northern Ireland's parliament to legislate on all non-excepted and non-reserved powers, but Section 75 of that act confirmed that sovereignty resided at Westminster (Connolly, 1990), features replicated in the 1998 Northern Ireland Act.

Most laws affecting Northern Ireland are similar to those elsewhere in the United Kingdom, reflecting the prolonged periods of direct rule from Westminster from 1972 until 2007. There are, however, occasional important legal exceptions, created under devolved government, which survived London ministerial decree. For example, the 1967 Abortion Act, liberalizing abortion law, was never extended to the region, given local religious sensibilities. Greater variance from Westminster law can now be expected under a sustained period of devolution. Moreover, the Northern Ireland Human Rights Commission, among other bodies, is encouraging the British Government to devise a Bill of Rights specifically for Northern Ireland (Dickson, 2007). Similarly to the Irish Republic, the EU has been an increasing source of law affecting Northern Ireland. Westminster and Stormont legislation has to be EU-compliant and the majority of legislation passing before both parliaments is affected by this requirement.

Separation of Powers

Article 6.1 of the constitution of Ireland stipulates a separation of powers between the Executive, the Legislature and the Judiciary (Morgan, 1985: 33–45; Doolan, 1994: 28–36). The Judiciary is independent of the Executive, and judicial decisions are not subject to scrutiny by the Legislature (Byrne, 2007). The Judiciary is also strictly separated from other branches of government in terms of personnel. Judges are specifically barred from being members of either house of the Oireachtas and may not hold 'any other office or position of emolument' (Hughes *et al.*, 2007: 69). In some cases, they may be appointed to another office and remain a judge, so long as no extra remuneration is involved (Casey, 2000: 305). In addition, the doctrine of non-justiciability outlines those issues over which it is deemed inappropriate for judges to make decisions, since 'such an adjudication would be an infringement by the court on the role which the Constitution has conferred on it' (McDermott, 2000: 280). Given that the doctrine of non-justiciability is itself determined via the pronouncements and precedents of other legal judgements, there are no concrete rules about its application. In this respect, however, Irish judges have on the whole tended not to meddle in political matters if they can help it – an attitude neatly summed up by Judge McCarthy in *Slattery* v. *An Taoiseach* [1993] 1 IR 286 at 301:

> As the courts are jealous of their constitutional role and will repel any attempt by legislature to interfere in the judicial domain, so must the courts be jealous of what lies wholly within the domain of the legislature, the executive and the People.

In this respect, McDermott (2000) outlines a number of areas where judges have claimed non-justiciability in respect of separation of powers. These include the conduct of foreign relations (see *Crotty* v. *An Taoiseach* [1987] IR 713; and *Maher* v. *An Taoiseach* [1984]), the Northern Ireland peace process (McDermott, 2000: 298–9), and governmental appointments (*Riordan* v. *An Taoiseach, the Government of Ireland, the Minister for Finance and the Attorney General*, High Court, 12 June 2000; see also *Irish Times*, 3 June 2000).

Courts have also traditionally been reluctant to get involved in questions about how the state allocates public money. In *O'Reilly* v. *Limerick Corporation*, the plaintiffs were members of the traveller community, living in considerable poverty and destitution in the Limerick city area. They sought a mandatory injunction directing the corporation to provide them with adequately serviced halting sites and damages in respect of the poor conditions that had endured. Ruling in the High Court, however, Judge Costello 'decisively rejected the contention that the courts could with constitutional propriety adjudicate on an allegation that the organs of Government responsible for the distribution of the nation's wealth had improperly exercised their powers' (McDermott, 2000: 282–3). This logic was upheld in *MacMathuna* v. *Attorney General* [1995] 1 IR 484, when Judge Finlay pronounced that the ways in which the state chooses to provide financial assistance to its citizens 'are peculiarly matters within the field of national policy, to be decided by a combination of the executive and the legislature, that cannot be adjudicated upon by the courts'.

The area of litigation that has provoked the most declarations of non-justiciability in Irish courts, however, is in relation to referenda. Here the courts have consistently refused to become involved in disputes over the wording of proposed amendments, whilst insisting that their task is to interpret the constitution as it stands, or as it is amended. So, for example, in *Riordan* v. *An Taoiseach* the applicant claimed that the fifteenth amendment to the constitution, which had lifted the constitutional ban on divorce, was itself unconstitutional (High Court, 14 November 1997). Judge Costello, however, held that 'the courts had no jurisdiction to consider the validity of a constitutional provision' (McDermott, 2000: 293), concluding that 'the courts can have no power to judicially review any question of national policy, which has finally been determined by the people, including amendments the people make in the constitution' (High Court, 14 November 1997, pp. 5–6 of the judgement).

Northern Ireland operates within a UK system, based upon formal separation of the Executive, Legislature and Judiciary. The separation of powers is not absolute; the Lord Chancellor is a political appointment, yet he or she administers justice in Northern Ireland and is responsible for senior judicial appointments. Responsibility for the justice system in Northern Ireland remains at Westminster, although this may change subject to local political agreement being reached.

The Court System

Article 34 of the constitution, which deals broadly with the court structure, establishes 'a three-tiered edifice': at the top is the Court of Final Appeal – the Supreme Court; below this is the High Court; and at the bottom are the 'Courts of local and limited jurisdiction' – the Circuit and District Courts (Morgan, 1985: 190). Under the Courts Service Act 1998, responsibility for the management of the courts system is conferred on the Courts Service, established in 1999 (see www.justice.ie/en/JELR). The Courts Policy Division discharges ministerial functions in relation to the courts, including all constitutional and legislative matters related to judicial appointments and salaries; the making of Rules of Court; and the preparation of material in relation to the Minister's accountability to the Dáil on court issues. The division also ensures that the Courts Service is appropriately resourced and that necessary reporting systems are in place to enable the Minister to discharge his or her responsibility in regard to the Service.

The legal profession is divided between solicitors (who concentrate on client work) and barristers (who specialize in advocacy and litigation). The majority of solicitors work is in private practice, offering legal services in areas such as buying and selling property, commercial transactions, family law and drafting wills. Solicitors also provide legal advice and represent clients in the District and Circuit Courts. They are regulated by statute and represented by the Incorporated Law Society of Ireland. Barristers are usually independent 'sole traders' (though a few are employed by companies or the state). Their primary activities are the drafting of legal opinions and the preparing of court documents, and negotiating settlements and representing clients in the High Court or Supreme Court. Barristers may only take on work that is referred to them by solicitors and must, if available and requested to work on a case, give their services to clients on a first come first served basis. This ensures that all clients have equal access to the courts. Barristers are all members of the Law Library, sharing its facilities in the Four Courts, Dublin. They are regulated by the Bar Council.

Attorney General

In the Republic of Ireland, the Attorney General is the government's adviser in matters of law and represents the state in important legal proceedings (Chubb, 1992: 172). According to the constitution, the Attorney General is allowed to attend cabinet meetings, though he or she may not be a member of the Government and need not be a member of the Oireachtas. If, however, the Attorney General is a member of either the Dáil or the Seanad (Upper House of Parliament), he or she holds the right to be heard in either house. In the cabinet, the Attorney General advises the Government on the constitutional and legal issues that arise, especially in terms of whether proposed legislation complies with the provisions of the constitution and acts and treaties of the EU or other international agreements to which the state is a party. It is, for example, the Attorney General who defends the constitutionality of bills referred to the Supreme Court under Article 26 of the constitution. The Attorney

General holds overall responsibility for the Office of Attorney General (containing the advisory council to the Attorney General), the Office of the Parliamentary Counsel to Government (responsible for drafting legislation), and the Office of the Chief State Solicitor and the Statute Law Revision Unit (responsible for law reform). Finally, the Attorney General is the representative of the public in all legal proceedings in relation to law enforcement and the protection of rights.

District and Circuit Courts

Characterized by the constitution as courts of 'local and limited jurisdiction' (Morgan, 1985: 191), there is formally only one District Court and one Circuit Court, though in practice they are regionally dispersed. The District Court is divided into 23 District Court areas that are presided over by the President of the District Court and 54 District Court judges (Hughes *et al.*, 2007: 59). The District Court is intended to be used for minor criminal offences (the maximum sentence from the District Court is one year) and for civil cases where the claim or award sought does not exceed €6,348 (ibid.). It usually adopts the title of 'Children's Court' when dealing with cases involving children. Circuit Courts are divided into eight Circuit Court areas and sit with a judge and jury. They have jurisdiction to hear the most serious offences, excepting cases of murder, rape, aggravated sexual assault, treason and piracy, which must be heard in the High Court. Civil cases in the Circuit Court do not require a jury and are restricted to cases where the damages or compensation sought does not exceed €38,092 (ibid.).

High Court/Central Criminal Court

Article 34.3.1 of the constitution grants the High Court 'full original jurisdiction and power to determine all matters and questions, whether of law or fact, civil or criminal'. In consequence, the High Court has always had very wide jurisdiction in civil and criminal cases (Morgan, 1985: 192). The Court plays an important role in providing judicial review of decisions of the lower courts (often in relation to the determination of points of law raised in the lower cases before lower courts). In general, civil cases before the High Court involve substantial sums of compensation or damages, since there is no limit to the awards that may be made by the Court. When presiding over criminal matters, the Court is usually referred to as the Central Criminal Court, trying those cases that are exempted from the lower courts' jurisdiction.

Supreme Court

Established under Article 34 of the constitution, the Supreme Court consists of the Chief Justice, the President of the High Court (who normally sits in the High Court) and four or (if one of them is a member of the Law Reform Commission) five ordinary judges, and is the court of final appeal (Morgan, 1985: 194). The Supreme Court holds the authority to hear appeals from all decisions of the High Court and from the Court of Criminal Appeal (the court designated to hear appeals against convictions from the Circuit and Criminal Court up to 1995, when the Court Officers Act 1995 transferred this authority to the Supreme Court – a measure which has yet to be implemented). Additionally, the Supreme Court has the power to decide on the constitutionality of any bill passed by both Houses of the Oireachtas and referred to it by the President (see p. 16). Should the bill be declared unconstitutional, it cannot be passed into law.

Special Criminal Court

Outside the normal court system, the Special Criminal Court provides for judges to preside over criminal cases without a jury in areas of serious crime, where it is believed that the 'ordinary courts' are inadequate to secure effective administration of justice or preservation of public peace (Hughes *et al.*, 2007: 60). This is most usually the case with terrorist or gangland related crimes, where witness and/or jury intimidation is considered likely.

European Court of Justice

In most cases, domestic Irish courts have jurisdiction over actions involving EU law but, in order to avoid EU law being interpreted differently in different member states, Article 177 of the EEC Treaty (which is part of Irish law, by virtue of the 1972 constitutional amendment) provides for the European Court of Justice (ECJ) to give preliminary rulings to member-state courts concerning the interpretation of the Treaty, the validity and interpretation of acts of the institutions of the EU, and the interpretation of the statutes provided by relevant EU institutions. In consequence, the Irish courts retain the authority to determine questions of fact and Irish law, whilst EU law is settled by the European Court which holds the authority to make a final interpretation. In practice, this means that in cases where EU law might apply, the case is suspended at a hearing before the Irish court, pending a judgement from the ECJ. Following from this, the Irish court passes judgement by applying the European Court ruling, plus any other relevant Irish law to the facts of the case.

Court structures in Northern Ireland do not vary markedly from those in the Irish Republic, and the position of the courts in the North is identical in relation to the ECJ. At the head of the system in Northern Ireland lies the House of Lords, with the Law Lords acting as the final court of appeal. Below this lies the Court of Appeal and the High Court; and below these the Crown courts deal with major criminal cases, whilst more minor cases and preliminary hearings for Crown Court referrals are dealt within magistrates' courts. Civil cases are normally dealt with by county courts or small claims courts. The Court Service, which is part of the civil service, presides over the operational efficiency of the court system, provides training for the judiciary and implements local decisions.

In Northern Ireland, the courts system was one of the most controversial features of the conflict, even though disputes over police tactics and lack of accountability were more prominent (McGarry and O'Leary, 1999). Following the recommendation of a commission headed by Lord Diplock in 1972, juryless courts were introduced for trials involving terrorism. The establishment of 'Diplock' courts, in which three judges determined the outcome of trials, was justified by the British Government due to fears of intimidation of jurors. Diplock courts had an above average rate of conviction compared to 'normal' courts, raising issues of bias, a problem exacerbated by the admissibility of 'confessions' of terrorist suspects. Given that the British Government was criticized for 'inhumane and degrading treatment' of terrorist suspects by the European Convention of Human Rights, the extraction of these confessions and use in courts was problematic.

The problem of an absence of trial by jury was further compounded by the use of so-called 'supergrasses' during the 1980s, terrorists whose evidence against their erstwhile colleagues was used to achieve convictions en masse. The mass processing of cases deploying 'supergrasses' was viewed as a system of 'show-trials' which 'did considerable damage to the criminal justice system' (Kennedy-Pipe, 1997: 115). However, trials of terrorist cases linked to Northern Ireland but held in England, which did involve juries, did not always fare better, the wrongful convictions of individuals for the IRA's bombings of pubs in Birmingham and Guildford during the 1970s being prime examples. Amid the breakdown of a conventional system of justice, paramilitary groups 'policed' their own areas during the conflict, and judges presiding over terrorist cases became targets for the IRA. Local community justice schemes remain, but these now have official sanction in the form of restorative justice projects, in which neighbourhood organizations (often containing former paramilitary prisoners) discourage anti-social activity and rehabilitate offenders via legitimate means, open to scrutiny by the Criminal Justice Inspectorate (McEvoy, 2006).

During the conflict, the courts operated within a legal framework designed more to cope with the stringencies of the conflict than with the protection of human rights. The Prevention of Terrorism and Emergency Powers Acts passed during the 1970s gave the security forces wide-ranging powers, with the result that the courts could not act as a restraint upon excess. Indeed the courts were constrained by the ever-burgeoning anti-terrorist legislative apparatus. The Criminal Evidence (Northern Ireland) Order Act 1988 allowed the courts 'in certain carefully defined circumstances to draw such inferences as would be proper from an accused's silence' (House of Commons Debates, vol. 140, col., 183, 8 November 1988; Cunningham, 2001: 61). The Patten Commission on Policing recommended the dismantling of the emergency legislative framework over which judges presided, although this aspect of 'normalisation' is incomplete (Independent Commission on Policing, 1999).

Judicial Appointment, Conduct and Ethics

In the Republic of Ireland, Article 35 of the constitution provides that 'all judges shall be independent in the exercise of their judicial functions and subject only to this constitution and the law'. Article 35.1 states that the judges of the Supreme Court, the High Court and the Circuit and District Courts shall be appointed by the President (who carries out this function on the advice of the Government). In effect, then, the Government controls the appointment of judges (Byrne and McCutcheon, 2001: 121) and, it has been suggested, that in practice 'it does appear that a political affiliation can help those wishing to pursue a judicial career' (Hughes *et al.*, 2007: 71). A report in the *Sunday Tribune* (15 August 2004) noted that in the Supreme Court, four judges have a Fianna Fáil background, with one PD, one Fine Gael and one Labour. In the High Court, 15 judges have a Fianna Fáil background, six Fine Gael, two PD, one Labour and six non-party (ibid.). At the very least, political affiliation does not seem to harm the possibility for judicial appointment.

In 1995, the then Taoiseach (Prime Minister), Albert Reynolds, insistence on appointing his Attorney General to the post of 'President of the High Court', despite revelations that during his tenure as Attorney General there had been a nine month delay in processing a warrant for the extradition of a suspected paedophile, led not only to the collapse of the Fianna Fáil/Labour coalition but also, ultimately, to the establishment of formal procedures governing appointments to the Judiciary. The Courts and Courts Officers Act, 1995, established a Judicial Appointments Advisory Board (JAAB) comprising the Chief Justice; the Presidents of the High Court, Circuit Court and District Court; the Attorney General; a practising barrister nominated by the chair of the Bar Council; and a practising solicitor nominated by the President of the Law Society. Provision was also made for the Government to stipulate up to three nominees with appropriate or relevant experience.

The JAAB's task is to provide a shortlist of seven nominations for appointment to a vacant judicial office. Though its recommendations are not binding, they are a matter of public record, and to date the Government has made all appointments from the list of names submitted (Hughes *et al.*, 2007: 70). While the 1995 Act went some way to creating greater transparency in the appointment of the Judiciary, its impact is limited in that it functions only in relation to *new* judicial appointments. In relation to the appointment of Chief Justice, or the presidents of the High Court, Circuit Court or District Court, the Government is obliged to consider the qualifications and suitability of *serving* judges. In consequence it is rare for the JAAB to have any influence over the appointment of Supreme Court judges, who are almost always serving judges already sitting in other courts. 'As such, the government has a largely free hand in the selection of candidates for the most influential judicial positions' (Hughes *et al.*, 2007: 71).

Concerns have been raised that a disproportionate number of individuals closely associated with the Government are recommended for appointment and that appointments are made on a political basis (Byrne, 2007). In the period 1998–2000, for example, the Minister for Justice received 45 representations in respect of judicial appointments to the District and Circuit Courts. Information released under Freedom of Information legislation disclosed that many of these representations were from members of the party in government, including half the cabinet, as well as the Taoiseach, raising 'serious questions about the level of political control over who gets a job on the Bench and who does not' (*Sunday Independent*, 17 September 2000).

Concerns that the appointment of the Judiciary may be politically compromised are all the more significant since the circumstances in which judges may be dismissed remain unclear (Byrne, 2007). Whilst Article 35.4 of the constitution provides that judges may not be dismissed 'except for stated misbehaviour or incapacity and then only on a majority vote in each House of the Oireachtas', it gives no explicit direction as to what 'stated misbehaviour and incapacity' might reasonably constitute; and thus far neither has been judicially interpreted. This eventuality was averted in 1999 and 2006 by the respective resignations of Supreme Court Judge Hugh O'Flaherty and Circuit Court Judge Brian Curtin.

In April 1999, it became apparent that Philip Sheedy, a man convicted and sentenced to four years in prison following a case involving the death of a woman by dangerous driving, had been released from prison, a year before the original review date for his sentence. The Chief Justice, Liam Hamilton, investigating what became known as 'the Sheedy affair', found that Justice O'Flaherty had approached the Registrar of Dublin Circuit Court, as a result of informal queries on the defendant's behalf, in order to have the case relisted. Following this, Circuit Court Judge Cyril Kelly suspended the remaining term of sentence and Sheedy was released from prison. Hamilton concluded that the actions of both judges had compromised the administration of justice (Hogan and Whyte, 2003). The then Minister for Justice told the Dáil that he had written to both judges informing them that the Government intended, under Article 35.4 of the constitution, to seek their removal from office (*RTE News*, 20 April 1999). This would certainly have been the outcome 'had they not reluctantly resigned within four days of the government making its views known' (Gallagher, 2005a: 89). One month later, answering questions in the Dáil, the Taoiseach, Bertie Ahern, acknowledged that he should 'have found some way of putting the information about his involvement before the Dáil', when it transpired that he had responded 'in a routine manner' to representations from the jailed architect's father concerning day release to work in the community (*RTE News*, 5 May 1999). Arguing that he 'did no more than any TD would', he said that he had 'made no representations to the judiciary and did not seek early release for Philip Sheedy' (*The Examiner*, 4 May 1999; *RTE News*, 5 May 1999).

In 2003, Circuit Court Judge Brian Curtin was acquitted on the charge of possessing child pornography because the search warrant issued during the investigation was out of date. The Oireachtas subsequently set up a committee to inquire into the judge's alleged misbehaviour (see pp. 40–1). The constitutionality of the Oireachtas impeachment process was unsuccessfully challenged by Judge Curtin in the High Court and Supreme Court. Before the process could begin, Judge Curtin resigned on the grounds of ill health (Byrne, 2007).

The idea of monitoring judges' behaviour has in practice proven difficult to implement (Gallagher, 2005a: 89). In 1999 an all-party Oireachtas committee recommended amending the constitution to make provision for a 'judicial council' to review judicial conduct. In June 2001, however, government proposals for a referendum as a consequence of this were withdrawn when the opposition parties indicated that they were unhappy with some of the details (*Irish Times*, 4 May 2001). More generally, the cases referred to above are considered to be much 'more the exception than the rule', and the most recent 'democratic audit' of Ireland was able to note that 'the theoretical and practical independence of the Irish judiciary is well-established' (Hughes *et al.*, 2007: 69). However, as with many of their European counterparts, Irish judges tend to come from relatively privileged backgrounds (Gallagher, 2005a: 90). A Seanad debate of 29 April 1999 noted that of the then 32 judges presiding over the Supreme and High Courts, all had attended one of seven select (all male, private, fee-paying, Catholic-run) secondary schools, with 22 from one single school (Hughes *et al.*, 2007: 75). Not surprisingly, this contrasts sharply with the socio-economic background of the majority of those appearing before the courts, who tend to be from the lowest socio-economic classes, with a disproportionate number from the traveller community (Hughes *et al.*, 2007: 76). Such stark class divisions help explain why the judiciary as a whole tends to be 'characterised by moderation and attachment to regime norms' (Jacob, 1996: 390, quoted in Gallagher, 2005a: 90), 'imposing its own social mores and economic beliefs on the population at large' (Hogan, 2001: 197), with a record of being 'over-cautious' and 'prudent' in relation to the separation of powers doctrine (McDermott, 2000: 303).

In Northern Ireland, the GFA established a Review of Criminal Justice, which was completed in 2000. The Criminal Justice Review Group comprised a mixture of civil servants and independent experts. It engaged in a wide-ranging review of the structures, implementation and fairness of the existing system of criminal justice. One of the key recommendations among its 294 proposals, most of which were accepted by the British Government, was that, in the event of the devolution of responsibility for criminal justice matters to the Northern Ireland Executive, judicial appointments, presently made by the Lord Chancellor's Department on the recommendation of Northern Ireland's Lord Chief Justice, should be made primarily by a Judicial Appointments Commission, comprising representatives from both of the main communities. This development would not remove the claims of 'political' appointments entirely, given that the First and Deputy First Minister would be responsible for appointments to the Commission, which would be chaired by the Lord Chief Justice (McQuade and Fagan, 2002). A Judicial Appointments Unit was set up within the Northern Ireland Court Service to assist the Commission.

In the same manner that the Patten Commission attempted to create a police force for all, so the review of criminal justice was designed to establish a judicial system which would command the support of both communities. Supportive of the devolution of justice responsibilities to Northern Ireland being on a par with those given to Scotland, with the proviso that legislative acts were to be subject to cross-community support, the Review attempted to 'de-partisanise' and 'promote confidence in the criminal justice system' (Criminal Justice Review Group, 2000: 401). Among its recommendations (all of which were adopted) were the prohibition of displays of royal coats of arms within courts (although the coat of arms could still be displayed outside and the Union flag could still be flown from court buildings). 'God Save the Queen' was not to be uttered by members of the judiciary on entry to court, and judicial oaths of allegiance to the Sovereign were removed. A non-political office of Attorney General would act as the main Law Officer for Northern Ireland, with the powers of the current (political) Attorney General at Westminster confined to responsibility for non-devolved areas. A new, independent Public Prosecution Service for Northern Ireland would be established, as was an Independent Criminal Justice Inspectorate, which would provide annual reports on its inspections of the prosecution service.

The overhaul of the judicial system did not meet with unanimous approval. The DUP accused the British Government of attempting to 'decimate' the criminal justice system (House of Commons, 2002: 17) and Unionists generally were more cautious over the transfer of judicial responsibilities to the Northern Ireland Executive. Issues pertaining to victims of the conflict remained unresolved and the Criminal Justice Review Group said little regarding the removal of emergency legislation beyond recommending the establishment of a Law Commission to examine the issue (Criminal Justice Review Group, 2000: 433). Nonetheless, there was overwhelming consensus at Westminster on the need for change to the judicial system, and the Justice (Northern Ireland) Acts of 2002 and 2004 gave legislative effect to the proposals outlined in the review.

Judicial Activism

Notwithstanding the doctrine of non-justiciability and the traditional reticence of Irish judges to challenge the Executive, the interpretive role of judges in the common law legal system has meant that 'the development of common law has been, in the main, the work of judges and not legislatures' (Keane, 2004: 1). It should come as no surprise, then, that occasionally the Judiciary has used its authority to nudge the political system in one direction or another. In the Irish courts, the first significant case of 'judicial activism' is possibly the 1963 case of *Ryan* v. *the Attorney General* [1965] IR 294 (HC & SC), where Justice Kenny held that the 'personal rights' of the citizen, guaranteed by Article 40 of the constitution, were not confined to the rights specified in that and other articles of the constitution. He said that there were unspecified personal rights of the citizen, which followed from what he described as 'the Christian and democratic nature of the State' ([1965] IR 294 at 312 (HC)).

In *Ryan* v. *the Attorney General*, the plaintiff claimed that a local authority scheme for the mass fluoridation of the municipal water supply (intended to protect dental health) violated her constitutional rights, by subjecting her and her family to a form of medication that they had not sought. In his conclusion, Justice Kenny found that Ryan did enjoy a constitutional right of 'bodily integrity', which was not specified in the constitution, and that it followed that an act of the Oireachtas could not impose upon her any process that was dangerous or harmful to her life or health. Nevertheless, after a consideration of the evidence, Justice Kenny also determined that in this case Ryan had not established, as a matter of probability, that her 'bodily integrity' would be compromised by the fluoridation scheme. His decision was upheld on appeal by the Supreme Court, which also endorsed his finding that the rights guaranteed by the constitution were not confined to those to which the document extended express recognition [1965] IR 294 at 312 (HC). Though Ryan's case failed, the precedent set by its conclusion that the constitution of Ireland implicitly imbued Irish citizens with a range of rights – even if they were not specified within it – was later deployed to develop quite different rights in other notable cases.

In *McGee* v. *the Attorney General* [1974] IR 284 (SC), the plaintiff was a married woman who, in agreement with her husband, wished for medical reasons to avoid another pregnancy. Ms McGee issued proceedings claiming that the prohibition on her importing contraceptives to use for that purpose was a violation of her marital privacy. This claim failed in the High Court but was upheld, following appeal, by a majority in the Supreme Court. Of the majority of four, three treated the right to marital privacy as one of the personal rights not specified in the constitution in accordance with the approach adopted in *Ryan* v. *the Attorney General*, with Justice Budd expressly recognizing the existence of a *general* right of privacy. Alone in the majority, Justice Walsh did not ground his judgment on an unspecified right of privacy but rather on the right of parents to decide the number of their offspring, this being an essential feature of the protection afforded to the institution of marriage under Article 41 of the constitution (Keane, 2004: 12).

In *Norris* v. *Attorney General* [1984] IR 36 (HC & SC), however (where the constitutional validity of laws criminalizing homosexual behaviour was in issue), the Supreme Court also established limits to the unspecified rights bequeathed by the Irish constitution. In this case, although a majority of judges accepted the proposition that the 'right to privacy' uncovered by the McGee case might be more wide-ranging than the 'right to marital privacy', all bar one ([1984] IR 36 at 71 (SC)) agreed that this did not justify what, in summing up, Justice O'Higgins CJ described as a 'no go area'.

The constitutional right of privacy was subsequently successfully invoked in a case where two journalists claimed that the tapping by the state of their telephones infringed their right of privacy (*Kennedy* v. *Ireland* [1987] IR 587 (HC)). It was further developed in *Re a Ward of Court (No. 2)* [1996] 2 IR 79 (HC & SC), when the High Court gave permission to a family for the withdrawal of nutrition through a tube from a family member who had been for many years in a permanent vegetative state, although she retained a minimal cognitive capacity. It was held that a patient with a sound mind, who was terminally ill, was entitled to elect not to accept treatment; and that it followed that, in the case of a patient with a non-sound mind, the court, applying the test of what was in the best interests of the ward, could make a similar decision on her behalf.

In 1999, the decision of Justice Kelly, to order the Minister for Health 'to provide funding and do all things necessary for the building, opening and maintenance' of a high support unit to accommodate a young offender requiring such treatment, was seen as clear evidence of a much more robust judicial approach to the powers of the Executive (McDermott, 2000: 286–8). In justifying his extension of legal authority, Justice Kelly argued that the courts had been put in an 'impossible position' insofar as they had been asked to make orders in respect of children who required secure containment where no such facilities were available (*DB* v. *Minister for Justice*, [1999] 1 IR 29). Moreover, he claimed that he 'was not making or interfering with governmental policy' but rather 'simply ensuring that the policy which the Executive had formulated to protect the children was implemented in a timely fashion' (McDermott, 2000: 287).

In 2008, the gay friend of a lesbian couple, who donated his sperm to one of them (resulting in the birth of a boy in 2006), lost his bid for guardianship of the child and was also refused access. The decision of Justice Hedigan on the case concluded that 'where a lesbian couple lived together in a long-term committed relationship, they could be regarded as constituting a de facto family enjoying family rights under article 8 of the European Convention on Human Rights', which did not conflict with Irish law (*Irish Times*, 17 April 2008). The judge further noted that the absence of any provisions in Irish law taking account of the existence of same-sex couples 'seems something that calls for urgent consideration by the legislature' (*Irish Times*, 17 April 2008).

In general, however, there is as much evidence for the contraction of rights in consequence of judicial activism as there is for rights expansion. In 2001, the Supreme Court's decision in the case of *Michael F. Murphy* v. *G.M.* [2001] 4 IR 113 (SC), on the constitutionality of a statute enabling the state to seize all proceeds of crime, was upheld when challenged, even though it meant that the owners of any such property would suffer loss without criminal proceedings or prosecution and, by extension, without being afforded the presumption of innocence and the right to a trial by jury. In the language of lawyers, the action was brought not *in personam*, because of some wrong which the owner of the property was alleged to have committed, but *in rem*, because of the tainted nature of the property itself (Keane, 2004: 3). In 2002, in the High Court case of *Foy* v. *The Registrar General and the A.G.* [2002] IEHC 116, 9 July 2002, Justice McKechnie supported the constitutional interpretation of marriage given by his fellow Justice Costello (in *B.* v. *R* [1995] 1 ILRM 491), who himself had used a case from the mid-nineteenth century (*Hyde* v. *Hyde* [1866] LR 1 P & D 130) as a basis for defining the interpretation of marriage in the constitution. Summing up, Justice McKechnie's view that 'marriage as understood by the constitution, by statute and by case law refers to the union of a biological man with a biological woman' was used to prevent a lesbian couple from marrying in Ireland ([2002] IEHC 116, 9 July 2002; see also ICCL, 2006). The issue of women's rights and the law in the Republic, given its historically conservative culture, is too vast to be dealt with here, but a summary is provided in Box 4.1.

Judicial Oversight and Tribunals of Inquiry

In the Republic of Ireland, Byrne (2007) notes that the Judiciary are a key part of Ireland's 'National Integrity System', which in recent years has even fulfilled some of the traditional scrutinizing duties of the Legislature. Tribunals of Inquiry remain the principal instrument for investigating allegations of political corruption. Established by the Houses of the Oireachtas on the recommendation of the Government, and usually chaired by a member of the Judiciary or a retired judge, tribunals are independent of the Executive and Legislature. They can compel the attendance of witnesses, present their findings to parliament and refer matters to courts for legal action. Since the 1990s there have been eight judicial tribunals of inquiry, investigating allegations of malpractice and corruption in public life (ibid.).

BOX 4.1

Women's Rights and the Law in the Republic of Ireland

Throughout the 1970s, individual women began to challenge the constitutionality of laws that discriminated against them, seeking redress in the courts for grievances that the Oireachtas had chosen to ignore. In doing so, they frequently employed a young woman barrister, Senator Mary Robinson, who was counsel in most of the constitutional cases where women's rights were vindicated (Scannell, 1988: 131). Between 1971 and 1987, there were 45 major challenges relating to sex discrimination and equal rights, and a definite move on behalf of the Judiciary to let the courts play a key role in outlining the scope of constitutional rights. Most importantly, the judges used the case of *Gladys Ryan* v. *the Attorney General* (1965 IR 294) as a basis for the view that the constitutional rights of Irish citizens included those that were *implied* by Article 40 in consideration of the fundamental character of the society envisaged by the constitution itself. Finally, in 1988, the High Court held that the dependent domicile rule, like all other appendages of female servitude, did not survive the enactment of the Constituion (Scannell 1988:132). This, combined with the emergence of Irish feminism and a belated acknowledgement from the Government that action needed to be taken, led to a significant shift in attitudes and values.

In 1974, the High Court invalidated a case of sex discrimination for being in violation of Article 40.1, by declaring that section 5 of the 1974 Adoption Act (preventing widowers, but not widows, from adopting in certain cases), because is was 'founded on an idea of difference in capacity between men and women which has no foundation in fact' (Scannell, 1988: 132–3). In 1981, the Family Law Act ensured that court actions for criminal conversation, enticement and harbouring a spouse (based on the notion that a woman was the property of her husband) were abolished. The Family Law Acts of 1976 (Maintenance of Spouses and Children) and 1981 (Protection of Spouses and Children) outlawed (legal) discrimination against the children of unmarried mothers. Restricted rights to free legal aid in family law cases were granted – but only after they had been pursued in the European Court of Human Rights by Josie Airey (Shatter, 1997: 60–70). In 1986, The Domicile and Recognition of Foreign Divorces Act, 1986 gave married women the right to a separate domicile from their husbands. Finally in 1995 divorce was made available in the Republic on a 'no-fault' basis.

The Beef Tribunal (1991–4) investigated the alarmingly close relations between certain government officials and particular agricultural interests in relation to Irish beef exports to Iraq (O'Toole, 1995). The McCracken Tribunal (1997) investigated payments from leading business man, Ben Dunne, to politicians, including the former Taoiseach, Charles Haughey. The Finlay Tribunal (1996–7) began an investigation into contaminated blood products that was later pursued more fully by the Lindsay Tribunal (Dáil Debates, 3 March 1998, vol. 488). The Moriarty Tribunal (1997–) continues to investigate illegal offshore accounts held by politicians and business people in order to evade tax payments. The Flood (now Mahon) Tribunal (1997–) is investigating political interference in the planning process, including alleged payments by property developers to politicians for 'favourable' planning decisions. The Lindsay Tribunal (1999–2002) investigated practices of the Blood

Transfusion Service that resulted in contaminated blood transfusions infecting patients with HIV and Hepatitis C. The Barr Tribunal (2000–6) investigated the facts and circumstances surrounding the fatal shooting of John Carthy at Abbylara, Co. Longford, on 20 April 2000 (see www.barrtribunal.ie). Finally, the Morris Tribunal (2002–) is investigating complaints concerning Garda behaviour and procedures in the Donegal division.

Much of the work of the tribunals has been frustrated and constrained by the outdated structures, and the persistent non-cooperation of key witnesses has been time-consuming and disruptive to the processes (Transparency International, Global Corruption Report, 2006: 173). By 2005, for example, eight legal challenges had been filed against the Mahon Tribunal alone (ibid.). In an attempt to redress this, Judge Mahon's decision to grant costs to witnesses, who, though involved in corruption, had chosen to cooperate with the Tribunal, was interpreted by many as a would-be 'whistleblower's charter' (*Irish Times*, 1 July 2004). As it stands, however, the Judiciary is dependent upon the Director of Public Prosecutions (DPP) to negotiate immunity with potential witnesses in return for their evidence.

In partial response to this, the Tribunals of Inquiry Bill, 2005 seeks to consolidate, reform and replace existing tribunals' legislation and 'implements in large part the recommendations contained in The Law Reform Commission final report on Public Inquiries including Tribunals of Inquiry, published in May 2005' (Minister for Justice, Equality and Law Reform, 29 November 2005). Paralleling tribunals, 'Commissions of Investigation' will have powers to compel witnesses to give evidence, search premises and remove documents. Still, it is hoped that these Commissions of Investigation will encourage cooperation by moving away from the adversarial approach that applies in courts and tribunals, making recourse to legal representation less likely and the associated costs of inquiries less prohibitive.

Judicial activism and inquiry in Northern Ireland has, inevitably, been concerned with aspects of the conflict. Arguably the most notable and certainly the most expensive was the Saville inquiry into Bloody Sunday, when the British Army shot dead 14 Catholics in January 1972. Conducted by an international tribunal of judges headed by Lord Saville, acting under the Tribunal of Inquiry (Evidence) Act, the Saville inquiry, which ran from 1998 until 2007, was established to examine evidence not available to the previous inquiry, chaired by Lord Widgery, which largely exonerated the conduct of the British Army. By its conclusion, the Saville Inquiry had become extremely time-consuming and costly, taking evidence from 2,500 individuals and costing £172 million, a deterrent to further major inquiries into controversies during the conflict. Nonetheless, the number of such controversies and the extent to which they engendered debate meant that further inquiries into killings were inevitable. In 2004, the British Government conceded four more inquiries into contested events, in these cases the killings of Rosemary Nelson, Robert Hamill, Billy Wright and Pat Finucane, all cases in which collusions between the security forces and paramilitaries were alleged.

Beyond the legacy of conflict, judicial activity has been limited. Interpretation of the Northern Ireland Act, 1998, which provided the legislation arising from the GFA, has not always been easy, and the early post-Agreement years saw the courts used by the UUP for the party's own interpretation of the deal and by the DUP as a means of undermining the Agreement. The First Minister, David Trimble, was deemed by Mr Justice Brian Kerr to have acted unlawfully in deliberately excluding Sinn Féin ministers from meetings of the North–South Ministerial Council. Trimble banned the Sinn Féin representatives as part of an attempt to pressure the IRA into the decommissioning of weapons. The High Court ruling acknowledged the right of the First Minister to engage in selection, but this had to be done in agreement with the Deputy First Minister: prohibitions based upon political motivations were contrary to the Northern Ireland Act, 1998.

The DUP's most prominent challenge was that of *Robinson v. Secretary of State for Northern Ireland* 2002, when the DUP Deputy Leader, Peter Robinson, argued that the Secretary of State, John Reid, had acted unlawfully in permitting the re-election of David Trimble as First Minister in November 2001, given that Trimble's election was delayed (he failed to be elected at the first attempt) beyond the maximum six weeks since the Assembly had last sat, as stated in the Northern Ireland Act, 1998. The Law Lords backed the Secretary of State by a margin of 3 to 2, arguing that it was his prerogative when such an election could be held, a decision which appeared to contradict the Act. Such 'flexibility' was to prove useful in sustaining the Assembly for another year, but the resort to the Law Lords indicated the fragility of the initial phase of power-sharing (Tonge, 2005a).

Conclusion

Although the judicial system is usually viewed as being 'above politics', in recent years across Europe the judicial system has become – intentionally and unintentionally – increasingly politicized. On the one hand, the trend of seeking redress to a growing number of political disputes in court has increased, so that judges have found themselves having to make decisions that have political ramifications. Moreover, 'as the numbers of highly educated citizens and of single-issue pressure groups have grown', there has been a tendency to see judicial action as much more immediate than parliamentary action, which often seems 'too slow-moving if not ineffective' (Gallagher *et al.*, 1992: 59). On the other hand, there has also been a steady increase in judges willing to take political action (Waltman and Holland, 1988), so that the process of 'judicial review' has as a result become a central fact of life in many European states (Holland, 1991).

In the Republic of Ireland, it is perhaps more apt to refer to the 'judicialization of politics' rather than the 'politicization of the judiciary'. Though Irish courts have made decisions on personal rights, which have inevitably had some political ramifications, the tendency has been for Irish judges to provide judgements that are well within more broadly established socio-cultural norms. In the realm of personal rights and freedoms, then, Irish judges have tended to follow popular political norms and values rather than form them. In the broader realm of political corruption, however, they have been much more forthright. Even the sternest critics of the tribunals acknowledge their catalytic role in exposing and changing attitudes towards corruption since they began in 1997 (Byrne, 2007). In truth we will only know the full extent of this alleged change after the conclusion of current high-profile tribunals such as Morris, Mahon and Moriarty.

In Northern Ireland, the judiciary was long seen by the nationalist community as a non-neutral body, too closely aligned with the defence of the state rather than the impartial upholding of law. Much has changed since the GFA, with a wide-ranging review and overhaul of the criminal justice system having been undertaken. The willingness of republicans to sign up to the new dispensation in terms of policing and justice is indicative of the progress of reform. Much of the focus has been upon the creation of a new police force, whereas of even greater importance is the judicial framework within which policing operates. There is now far greater transparency in terms of judicial appointments, and the courts preside over a legal system in which human rights carry greater importance than was hitherto the case. The transfer of responsibilities for policing and justice to a Northern Ireland-based Department of Justice will indicate a further huge shift from a contested judicial system towards one based upon consensus.

Part 2

Political Behaviour

5

Political Parties and the Party System

If the analysis of parties and party systems today seems rather complex because of the variety of approaches deployed by political scientists, it is made both more interesting and rather more complicated by changes that may be occurring in party politics itself.

(Ware, 1996: 12)

Introduction

'Comparative political research has tended to overlook the Irish case because it seems that the Irish party system doesn't fit into the more widely applicable models of party systems' (Mair, 2003: 119). As Lipset and Rokkan's (1967) ground-breaking work was applied to case studies throughout Europe, most studies were happy either to leave out the Republic of Ireland case, or to conclude that 'the Irish party system does not appear to be easily explicable in terms of the cleavage analysis formulated by Lipset and Rokkan' (1967), since in Ireland 'electoral behaviour is exceptionally unstructured' (Carty, 1976: 195). It was argued that 'in many cases, Irish politics are maverick to Western Europe' (Henig and Pinder, 1969: 503). Academics were happy to take the view that Ireland could be 'disregarded because of its size and small industrial base or treated as a special case for historical reasons' (Epstein, 1967: 138). Views about the uniqueness of the Irish case were typically accompanied by the opinion that Irish political parties were 'more or less indistinguishable' (Carty, 1976: 195) and it was even proposed that 'in no other European polity does such a small number of programmatically indistinguishable parties, each commanding heterogeneous electoral support, constitute an entire party system' (Carty, 1981: 85). For some time this remained the 'conventional wisdom', when, throughout the 1970s and 1980s, a small number of Irish academics began to question this assumption.

During the 1970s, Garvin's (1974, 1976, 1978) work (discussed in more detail below) argued that even though political parties in the Republic cannot be fitted easily into a conventional left–right framework, Lipset and Rokkan's centre–periphery concept is crucial to explanations of Fianna Fáil's electoral success as a populist catch-all party, organized from grass-roots political activism. In the 1980s, Sinnott's work called into question the view that no significant differences exist between Irish political parties (Sinnott, 1984: 217) and went so far as to suggest that the Irish party system is 'the product of roughly the same major processes of social and political change that have, in different ways, shaped party systems in many other countries' (Sinnott, 1986: 305). More recently, the work of Gilland-Lutz (2003) has further contributed to the view that Irish political parties occupy distinct political spaces that *are* relatively distinct from one another on a range of issues. Still, the gaps between Irish political parties are not as great as they might be and are often popularly perceived to be even less so.

Since its inception, Northern Ireland's political system has been based upon a binary divide and inter-ethnic bloc political rivalries, constructed upon the constitutional question (Buckland, 1981; Whyte, 1990; Tonge, 2002). Unionist-British parties, whose support base has been almost entirely grounded among Protestants, support Northern Ireland's retention within the United Kingdom, whilst Nationalist-Irish parties, arguing for a united independent Ireland, have been supported almost exclusively by Catholics. The 'centre ground', straddling this ethno-national fault line and religious linkage, has been small, reflected in modest support for the Northern Ireland Labour Party from the 1940s until the 1970s and, since then, for the Alliance Party. Indeed the political centre has been described, perhaps exaggeratedly, as almost mythical (Jeffery and Arthur, 1996).

The rigidity of division and religious exclusivity of party-support bases produces sterility within the Northern Ireland party system, although intrabloc dynamics have been of interest, especially since the 1998 GFA. Although identity (British or Irish) and religion (Protestant or Catholic) are key determinants of party choice, the impact of social class is far from negligible (Evans and Duffy, 1997). However, the severity of fracture on the constitutional question has ensured that Northern Ireland has never enjoyed a system of 'normal' democratic competition, embracing government and opposition. One-party Unionist government from 1920 until 1972 was accompanied by persistent nationalist abstention from parliamentary institutions, whilst British direct rule from 1972 to 1998 removed the region's political parties from structures of government. Consociation from 1999 to 2002 and again from 2007 has produced a power-sharing coalition in which leading Unionist and nationalist parties share power in a government insulated from an official opposition.

Political Parties and Party Systems

A country's party system is the more or less stable configuration of political parties that normally compete in national elections (Bale, 2005: 105). Typically, party systems are characterized by the number of effective political parties, their relative strengths and their respective positions on a range of issues. According to Sartori (1976), party systems may be classified across two dimensions: first according to the number of political parties present in parliament – or the degree of fragmentation; and second, according to the ideological distance between these parties – or the degree of polarization. Using this framework enables us to infer a number of generalized tendencies in relation to party systems and party competition. For example, a system with few parties and a narrow range of ideological differences will tend to foster 'centripetal competition' – in other words, parties that campaign in the centre ground as opposed to extremes. Under conditions of more polarized multipartyism, however, the tendency will be for more 'centrifugal competition', where a larger number of parties will each occupy specific niches across a broader spectrum of political beliefs.

The alternative types of party that may inhabit these various political spaces have been subject to examination by political scientists for some time, so much so that we now have a distinct vocabulary to characterize alternative party types. *Cadre* parties (Duverger, 1954) are parties that are developed and clearly controlled by a small or elite group, with perhaps the later addition of a national organization aimed largely at supporting the centre. *Mass* parties (ibid.) typically evolved from those outside power, adopting a branched membership structure so that party leaders tend to enjoy rather less autonomy than their cadre counterparts. *Catch-all* parties was the term coined by Kirchheimer (1966) to describe those parties that seek to shore up their traditional support with that from floating voters and interest groups. As a result they tend to be more pragmatic than ideological, often ceding control to the leadership in their desire to become 'professional electoral competitors' (Panebianco, 1988). *Cartel* parties (Katz and Mair, 1995) refer to professionalized parties that have become less attached to their (largely symbolic) membership and more a part of 'the system', using an effective leadership to compete for the balance of power and, more often than not, distancing themselves from grass-roots activism.

Notwithstanding the diversity, it has long been argued that nearly all contemporary political parties may trace their roots to the outcome of key political and socioeconomic transformations that prompted political mobilization (Lipset and Rokkan, 1967). In their path-breaking analysis of European political development, Lipset and Rokkan (1967) argued that the political alignments that structure contemporary European politics are founded on four major cleavages: the centre–periphery cleavage; the Church–state cleavage; the urban–rural cleavage; and the class cleavage.

The centre–periphery cleavage derives from the era when the boundaries of modern political states were being drawn. A clash emerged between those who were typically at the centre of the political system – attempting to modernize and standardize laws, markets and cultures – and those who were generally on the periphery of these new states, seeking to preserve their independence and autonomy. This same process is also responsible for the Church–state cleavage, epitomized by the conflict between secular modernizers and traditional sources of power and patronage supported by the Church. The debate – essentially over rights and powers – typically concerned issues of public morality and education and whether or not the Church or the state should be the final arbiter on related policy issues.

The rural–urban cleavage between traditionally dominant rural interests and newly constituted commercial and industrial interests came to prominence with the Industrial Revolution (though it had already developed earlier in the medieval period). In Britain and in much of continental Europe, this conflict (cleavage) did not last, or was resolved by, the advance of industrialized societies and the predominance of urban/dominant cultures. In Scandinavia and parts of eastern Europe, however, it was much more significant. Sustained rural opposition to the urban elites led eventually to the creation of powerful agrarian parties.

Finally, the class cleavage is often regarded as the most important cleavage to emerge from the Industrial Revolution, because it facilitated the constitution of new and expanding groups of owners of capital (with their established allies amidst elites) and workers (represented by the development of trade unions and trade union movements).

Not only are these cleavages central to understanding the emergence of contemporary parties, but, according to Lipset and Rokkan's (1967: 52) so-called 'freezing hypothesis', their significance endures because these parties are now embedded into national party systems and unlikely to change without the injection of a significant new voter cohort into the system. Whilst Inglehart's (1977) post-materialist thesis argued that this was possible, as a consequence of widespread attitudinal shifts and value change (Kitschelt, 1994; Dalton, 2000), it is nevertheless hard to argue that the significance of cleavages is lost. In 1996, for example, Ware (1996: 213) was able to note that 'of the twenty-three established, independent liberal democracies in the late 1950s, only four had a radically different party system thirty years later at the end of the 1980s'.

Explaining the Emergence of Irish Party Systems

In the Republic of Ireland case, the Representation of the People Act, 1918 brought about the greatest single extension of the electorate in Irish history. Estimates vary as to the extent of this enfranchisement: Sinnott (1984: 301) suggested that between the elections of 1910 and 1918 the Irish electorate more than doubled; whereas Farrell (1971a: 45–7) claimed that during the same period the electorate may even have tripled in size. More significantly, Garvin (1974: 309) argued that the election of 1918 marked the mobilization of the last major element in Irish society. Before 1918, a rate-payer franchise system existed, which meant that the poor and the young were, in effect, disenfranchised. Only a decade later and the transition to a stable democratic system was largely complete; a development that was due in no small part to the creation of Fianna Fáil, led by Eamon de Valera and comprising almost exclusively of anti-Treaty supporters (Prager, 1986: 195). By walking gingerly between Republican conceptions and Free State institutions, Fianna Fáil proved that the newly established democratic structures could be used to represent the interests of pro- and anti-Treaty supporters alike (Prager, 1986: 197). Whilst Cumann na nGaedheal was supported predominantly by business leaders, prosperous farmers and the Catholic Church (Moss, 1968: 136), Fianna Fáil appealed precisely to those groups who, up to then, had refused to identify with Free State politics (Prager, 1986: 196). The party gained in political strength because of its disproportionate attraction to the poorer, less anglicized and peripheral sections of the nation (Garvin, 1978: 333).

Of all the four cleavage structures identified by Lipset and Rokkan, the centre–periphery cleavage has been most prominent in discussions regarding the comparability, or otherwise, of the Irish party system. Two propositions concerning its relevance stand out. Both relate the significance of the centre–periphery cleavage to the broader political context of the nationalist struggle, yet come to quite different conclusions. The first, associated with the work of Garvin (1974, 1977, 1978, 1981), points to the ironic status of the Irish case as a 'periphery dominated centre'. The second, associated primarily with Sinnott (1984), focuses specifically on the notion of an 'internal centre–periphery conflict' (see also Whyte, 1974: 647–8).

Garvin's (1974: 309–10) application of the centre–periphery cleavage focuses on the persistent success of Fianna Fáil as a grass-roots political mobilizer, which in many ways was able to trade on its 'extra-parliamentary' status when compared with the Fine Gael party that was organized around a pre-existing parliamentary group. Manning (1972: 18) described Cumann na nGaedheal, Fine Gael's immediate prede-cessor, as a party that enjoyed the support of the propertied classes and which was strongest in the urban, eastern and midland areas, and weaker in the rural small-farm areas of the west coast. Fianna Fáil, by contrast, started in the 1920s by inheriting a core of west coast ultra-nationalist rural Republican support and spread rapidly east-ward toward Dublin, helped on by a classic leaders-local activists-grassroots system of organizational linkages that contrasted with the 'local notables' character of Fine Gael (Garvin, 1974: 308).

Before the entry of Fianna Fáil into Dáil politics, approximately 50 per cent of Irish citizens – particularly in the west and rural areas – did not vote (Garvin, 1977: 169). Between 1923 and 1927, voter turnout increased by approximately 10 per cent throughout the country and was as high as 76 per cent by 1932 (Garvin, 1977: 173). Reinforcing the significance of this increased electoral college, Garvin (1974: 309) noted that, although Cumann na nGaedheal won 40,000 more votes in 1932 than in 1923, still their total share of the vote declined by 4 per cent. Overall, electoral turnout in the new state increased from 61 per cent of the population to 77 per cent between 1923 and 1932 (ibid.). Most significantly during this period, Fianna Fáil's vote increased by around a quarter of a million, most of which was concentrated in the western part of the state (ibid.). Relating the electoral success of the Fianna Fáil directly to their organizational monopoly of the western periphery, and to their ability to mobilize the newly enfranchised western electorate, Garvin's (1974: 307) central argument is that the Republic provides an example of 'a polity in which the political concerns and style of the rural periphery came to "invade" and dominate the urban centre'.

Critics of this 'periphery dominated centre' interpretation of the Irish case point to the fact that Fianna Fáil's electoral advance was a national as opposed to a purely regional phenomenon: moreover, support for Cumann na nGaedheal was spread across the state in such a way that they could not be regarded as a party of the centre (Carty, 1976, 1981). Instead of rejecting the relevance of Lipset and Rokkan's cleav-age model, however, others have argued that it is perhaps more appropriately applied in an alternative way. Following on from Whyte (1974: 647–8), Sinnott's (1984) application of the Lipset-Rokkan (1967) model to the Irish case begins with the assumption that the social foundations for the centre–periphery cleavage lie in the period prior to Irish independence and the 1918 Representation of the People Act. Citing Farrell's (1970) earlier analysis of the minority status of the Labour party, Sinnott (1984: 302) argued that the 1918 election was singularly focused upon the tensions between periphery and centre – the 'us' versus 'them' reflected in 'peripheral Ireland versus metropolitan Britain'. Moreover, he suggests that if it is accepted that the 1918 election was a mobilizing election, it is no surprise that 'this nationalist consensus did not cease to exist when secession occurred'. Thus he argues that:

> As of 1918 at any rate, Irish politics could be seen as a textbook example of the process Lipset and Rokkan were talking about: the setting or freezing of party alternatives and electoral alignments around one or more of the four fundamental cleavage lines they had postulated.
> (Sinnott, 1984: 302)

The primary role played by the centre–periphery cleavage goes a long way to explaining the initial political success of Fianna Fáil as a mass party. Still, the relationship of the other three cleavages to the centre–periphery cleavage were equally significant in the manner in which they also helped assure Fianna Fáil a primary position as the leading 'catch-all' party in the evolving party system. The first point, which follows from Farrell's (1970) analysis, is that the owner–worker (or class) cleavage was almost completely subordinated by the centre–periphery issue – a development that was further accentuated by Labour's withdrawal from the 1918 election. The second point, is that throughout the early post-independence period the Church–state and urban–rural cleavages were aligned 'almost to the point of coincidence' with the centre–periphery cleavage (Sinnott, 1984: 302). 'The periphery was overwhelmingly Roman Catholic and the representatives of that tradition had been in constant conflict with the authorities at the centre throughout the nineteenth century' (ibid.). Similarly, the effect of secession of the 26 southern counties of Ireland from the remainder of the United Kingdom (which included the six Northern Irish counties) effectively resolved the urban–rural cleavage. As Whyte (1974: 647) noted, the new state resolved any would-be urban–rural tensions 'in an unusually absolute way: the agrarian sector broke off to found its own state'.

As a consequence of the prevailing cleavage structure, it could be said that Fianna Fáil's early electoral success was 'over-determined', both by the freezing of the party system and by the subsuming of other cleavage tensions by the centre–periphery cleavage. In the first case, Fianna Fáil was able to argue most effectively that it was *the* national party, leaving the other parties to explain why they were somehow 'less nationally minded'. The ability of Fianna Fáil to compete for office in a state that it largely professed to reject was certainly a winning electoral ruse: once the electoral competition was focused on 'the national question', the other parties were clearly outclassed by this masterful stroke of political manoeuvring. In the second case, the subordination of the class cleavage and the coincident alignment of the urban–rural and Church–state cleavages allowed Fianna Fáil to present itself as a populist, republican and catch-all party, which was able to foster a view of itself as the party most able to deliver an 'enduring societal vision' for post-independent Ireland.

Fianna Fáil's meteoric rise is, however, but one half of this story: the other half lies in the failure of the Irish Left and the continued inability of political alternatives to present robust opposition. Much has been made of the Labour party's decision in 1918 not to contest the election. Farrell (1970: 487) argued that it marked a 'major turning point in the history of these islands' and may even be regarded as the 'real foundation of contemporary Irish politics' (Farrell, 1969b: 501). Crucially, it is argued, Labour's withdrawal from the contest enabled the lines of political representation to be completely defined in relation to the 'national question'.

In Northern Ireland, the party system emerged on pro- versus anti-state lines which were broadly coterminous with a religious cleavage, one based on Protestant–Catholic rivalry rather than Church versus secular grounds. The UUP dominated Northern Ireland politics from the 1920s until the advent of direct Westminster rule in the early 1970s, its solitary governance of the province seen by supporters as natural. The abolition of PR-STV for local and regional elections during the 1920s consolidated UUP dominance and diminished the risk of intrabloc fragmentation. In acting more as a movement than a party organization, the UUP represented Unionists across the social classes and also embraced the Protestant Orange Order in a mainly uncontentious alliance (Patterson and Kaufmann, 2007a). Apart from a brief rise in fortunes for the cross-community Northern Ireland Labour Party during the early 1960s, the UUP governed without undue electoral threat, with neither electoral nor political challenge being offered by the mainly abstentionist Nationalist Party. Governance was one-party; an official opposition was not created until 1965, and the politics of the region were sterile and partisan (Farrell, 1980; Buckland, 1981; Tonge, 2002). Direct Westminster rule saw the onset of intrabloc Unionist rivalry between the UUP and the DUP, whilst the formation of the SDLP in 1970, and the entry of Sinn Féin into the electoral arena in 1982, greatly enlivened nationalist politics. Since the 1980s, there have been effectively two competitive party systems in Northern Ireland; one Unionist, the other nationalist, in which the dominant party in each has altered since the GFA, with the rise of the DUP and Sinn Féin.

Party Families in the Republic of Ireland

In the unique position of being the only European colony, it is not surprising that the evolution of Irish political parties should be both marked by this distinction and differentiated from the mainstream European experience as a consequence. For the Republic of Ireland, the consequence was that despite a degree of fragmentation, reflected in the divergent political desires and ambitions of the new political parties emerging in the Free State, the ideological distance between them, and hence the degree of party polarization, was limited. The reason for this is no mystery, since nearly all political parties (with the exception of the Labour Party) established in the post-independence period emerged, one way or another, from the struggle for independence. Granddaddy to them all was Sinn Féin.

The name 'Sinn Féin', meaning 'Ourselves', was coined in 1904 by Máire Butler and adopted by Arthur Griffiths as the encapsulation of his policy of national self-reliance (Coakley, 1980: 173) that he had been pursuing via a number of different organizations and groups, including Cumann na nGaedheal, which he founded with others in 1900 (Gallagher, 1985: 94). The political party Sinn Féin was subsequently founded in 1905 as a broad grouping of nationalists favouring total separation from Britain

(Lee, 1989: 7). By and large, the history of Sinn Féin reveals an enduring tendency to split between pragmatists and idealists (Pyne, 1969; Manning, 1972: 90; Gallagher, 1985: 94). Following independence, Coakley (2005b: 21) notes that the core of the new state's political elite was made up of pro-Treaty members of Sinn Féin, who reorganized in 1923 under the banner of Cumann na nGaedheal (and again in 1933 as Fine Gael). By April 1926, the remainder of the party was split into two nearly equal factions, divided over their willingness to accept the legitimacy of the Free State Dáil. At the party's 1926 ard-fheis, de Valera's proposal that Dáil abstention should become an issue of policy, not of principle, led ultimately to he and his supporters leaving the party to form a new republican party, Fianna Fáil. By the June election of 1927, those favouring abstention from the Dáil had won five seats and the newly formed Fianna Fáil 44, resulting in a massive haemorrhaging of non-abstentionist Sinn Féin support to Fianna Fáil. Sinn Féin lost all their seats and did not compete again until 1957, when they contested 19 constituencies, winning four seats, which they still refused to take (Gallagher, 1985: 95). By the election of 1961, their electoral support had halved and they were unable to win any seats.

The fact that the two major parties in the Republic, Fianna Fáil ('Soldiers of Destiny') and Fine Gael ('Tribe of the Gaels'), share a common ancestry, and are distinguished chiefly according to the side they took in the civil war following independence, goes a good way to explaining the lack of party polarization in Republic of Ireland politics. Although it is possible to discern some policy traits that distinguish these parties according to more usual socio-economic cleavages, as the significance of civil war politics has receded both parties have moved closer to the 'middle ground', a trend further facilitated by the Irish electoral system. Since 1987, the need of all Irish parties to obtain office in coalition has cemented the prioritization of 'office, votes, and then policy' (Marsh and Mitchell, 1999) in a manner which further mitigates against significant ideological differentiation. In the remainder of this section, we will outline how the main party groupings in the Republic of Ireland reflect this view of party competition, both historically and contemporarily.

Agrarian and Centre Parties

Founded by Captain Willie Redmond in September 1926, the National League represented a (failed) attempt to break out of the civil war domination of Irish politics in the 1920s (Manning, 1972: 93). It was formally dissolved in January 1931, and subsequently Redmond issued a statement saying that he could no longer ignore Cosgrave's appeals to support his government (Gallagher, 1985: 102). The Farmers' Party, by contrast, was able to resist and contested every election from 1922 to 1932, making it the only minor party to survive ten years of Cosgrave government. Essentially the political wing of the Farmers' Union, it was concerned almost exclusively with interests of agricultural community and – despite tending to support the Cosgrave government of 1923–27 – fell short of combining with Cumann na nGaedheal, which although mooted was never successfully adopted. With the entry of Fianna Fáil into the Dáil, however, political competition crystallized between those who supported and those who opposed the Treaty. In consequence, the support base for the Farmers' Party diminished and, by 1932, those members that remained in the Dáil went on to help found the National Centre Party.

The National Centre Party aimed to avoid civil war politics and protect agricultural interests, but it was designed to foster broader support than had been the case with the Farmers' Party (which tended to garner most support from larger farmers). Led by Frank MacDermot, the party fielded 26 candidates, solely in rural constituencies, in 1933. Despite attempting to be a middle course between Cumann na nGaedheal and Fianna Fáil, during de Valera's economic war with Britain, the party found itself entirely in agreement with Cumann na nGaedheal. Though initially reluctant, following the banning of the Blueshirts (the colloquial reference to the National Guard – see below) in August 1933, political negotiations for a merger led to the creation of Fine Gael in 1933.

Clann na Talmhan was founded by Michael Donnellan in 1938 following his dissatisfaction with Fianna Fáil's treatment of farming interests and the demise of other agricultural parties. Although the party was quite adept at parliamentary politics, winning ten seats in the 1943 election, it never saw itself as more than a sectional representative. Clann na Talmhan joined the interparty governments of 1948 and 1954 but never attempted to become a major party, and, by 1965, it had faded away.

Conservative Parties

Formally launched on 27 April 1923, Cumann na nGaedheal was formed from the pro-Treaty wing of Sinn Féin, which had been running the country since the split in the party. In consequence, the building of the new state and its institutions was in the hands of a group of people who supported the political and economic status quo, either through conviction or out of political realism (Coakley, 2005b: 21). They were a group of strong political figures of a broadly conservative disposition, which was reflected in the new close relationship with the Catholic Church. Moss (1933: 135–6) described the support base of Cumann na nGaedheal in the early 1930s as being the 'local business leaders, the priests and the prosperous farmers' (see also Manning, 1972: 18; Garvin, 1974: 308). It continued in power until 1932, when it was defeated by Fianna Fáil. Following a further defeat in 1933, Cumann na nGaedheal merged with the Centre Party and the National Guard to form Fine Gael in September 1933.

The National Party was a splinter group of nine Cumann na nGaedheal TDs, led by the then Minister for Industry and Commerce, Joseph McGrath. The party came into existence as a result of the army mutiny of 1924, when a small group of TDs were dissatisfied with the government's handling of the crisis and impatient for progress towards a 32-county state (Manning, 1972: 88). When their dispute failed and they were refused readmission to the party they resigned en bloc from the Dáil, precipitating a national election that marked the end of the party.

The creation of Clann Éireann was also the result of a split in Cumann na nGaedheal, when three TDs resigned over the failure of the 1925 Boundary Commission to reduce the size of Northern Ireland and so provide a basis for ending partition. Led by

Professor William Magennis of University College Dublin, though they contested the next election of 1926 with seven candidates, none were elected and the party disappeared.

By 1933, the creation of Fine Gael marked the primary distinction between the two major parties in the Republic for much of the post-independence period:

> The pro-Treaty party which stood for peace and ordered government won the support of the conservative, propertied class in the country: the large farmers, the leaders in industry and commerce, and the well-established professional men. The anti-Treaty party relied chiefly on the small farmers, the shop-keepers, and sections of the artisan and labourer classes.
>
> (McCracken, 1958: 128)

Gallagher (1985: 43) noted that in relation to social and economic policies, Fine Gael bore out O'Higgins's comment that 'we were probably the most conservative-minded revolutionaries ever to put through a revolution' (White, 1948: 2). Added to this, their predecessors in the Dáil seemed to lack the political acumen necessary to build broad support. In 1924, the Finance Minister, Ernest Blythe, cut the old age pension from ten to nine shillings a week (Fanning, 1978: 110–1) and, in the same year, the Minister for Industry and Commerce, Patrick Quilligan, went so far as to suggest that people might have to die of starvation as a consequence of government expenditure cuts (Dáil Debates, 30 October 1924, 9: 561–2). Fine Gael's close association with the National Guard seemed only to augment this view.

The National Guard was a reorganization of the Army Comrades Association (ACA), which had been created in 1932 as a rallying point for ex-service men and pro-Treatyites. By 1933, under the leadership of the former police commissioner Eoin O'Duffy, the organization had been transformed into the National Guard. It adopted a uniform that included a distinctive blue shirt and styled itself as an Irish, Christian organization, which would admit no foreigners, no Jews and was opposed to political parties and trade unions. De Valera reacted decisively to the movement by proposing a bill to prohibit the wearing of uniforms in public, echoing similar anti-fascist measures in other European states at the time. Cosgrave's opposition to the bill was vociferous. Arguing against it in the Dáil, he claimed that 'the Blackshirts were victorious in Italy and the Hitler Shirts were victorious in Germany, as, assuredly, in spite of this bill and in spite of the Public Safety Act, the Blueshirts will be victorious in the Irish Free State' (Aldous, 2007: 85). When the bill was passed and 'the Blueshirts' were banned, they responded by merging with Cumann na nGaedheal and the Centre Party to form Fine Gael, under the leadership of Eoin O'Duffy. Despite a deliberate and decisive repositioning of the party further to the left under the leadership of Garret FitzGerald in the 1980s (Girvin, 1987; Sharp, 1989), it is still a common colloquialism in contemporary Irish politics to refer to Fine Gael as 'the Blueshirts'.

Fianna Fáil: A National Movement or a National Party?

Whilst Cumann na nGaedheal was supported predominantly by business leaders, prosperous farmers and the Catholic Church (Moss, 1968: 136), Fianna Fáil appealed to those groups who, up to then, had refused to identify with Free State politics (Prager, 1986: 196). Established in 1926, following de Valera's withdrawal from Sinn Féin, the party gained in political strength because of its disproportionate attraction to the poorer, less anglicized and peripheral sections of the nation (Garvin, 1978: 333).

For many Fianna Fáil voters, 'the Sinn Féin war had represented a battle against the whole existing order and its multitude of abuses' (Moss, 1933: 135) and it could be argued that initially a good proportion of support for Fianna Fáil was not simply because they were against the Treaty but because they stood in opposition to Fine Gael (who were for the Treaty). In their analysis of economic growth in the post-independence period, Neary and O'Grada (1991: 255) argued that Fianna Fáil managed to maintain significant support from the urban working class as a conse-quence of increasing prosperity in the towns, which led to 'cheap food and better job prospects' for many, despite the continuing agricultural war that was adversely affecting the farmers. In this regard, however, the association of Fine Gael with larger farmers and the more prosperous ensured that Fianna Fáil could maintain the support of 'the smaller (and poorer) farmers, the small shopkeepers, the urban and rural petit bourgeoisie and even, in some measure, the urban working class' (Bew and Patterson, 1982: 3). The result was that Fianna Fáil gained the support of voters who, in another political environment, might have voted for a social democratic or labour alternative.

The trend has been an enduring one amongst politicians and voters alike. In his memoirs, the left-wing radical, Noel Browne (who himself was briefly a member of Fianna Fáil), was able to report that 'all my life I have enjoyed the company of the rank and file of Fianna Fáil: they are refreshing, mildly iconoclastic and independent, and given any chance at all would be first class material for a properly developed society' (Browne, 1986: 222). In later years, Fianna Fáil Taoiseach, Bertie Ahern, was proudly declaring himself a socialist and expounding the glories of 'community' in a positive critique of Robert Putnam's (1993, 2000) work on social capital (An Taoiseach Bertie Ahern, *Village:* 9-12 September, 2005:10). In terms of voter support, although as a catch-all party, Fianna Fáil's great success has been to win almost equal shares of support from all classes. Its notable achievement has been in cultivating traditional support bases amongst the working class, so that 'Fianna Fáil won the support of Labour's natural constituency' (Allen, 1997: 2). In her history of the Irish Labour Party, Puirséil (2007: 309) notes an inverse relation between the Labour party's fortunes and those of Fianna Fáil, concluding that 'Fianna Fáil had charisma and a singleness of purpose that Labour lacked. It styled itself not as a party but as a national movement' (see Walsh, 1986).

Parties of the Left

The Irish Labour Party was established in 1912 as the political wing of the Irish Trades Union Congress (ITUC). Referring to Labour's decision not to contest the 1918 election, Farrell (1970: 502) suggested that, whatever their reasoning, 'as the great drama of modern Irish state-building began', it seems that the Labour leaders 'confused the prompter's stool with a place on the stage'. The rationale for Labour's electoral abstention has been variously ascribed. According to O'Donnell (1963: 16):

> Labour leaders could not make up their minds what road to take. They were a bothered lot of men who gave themselves one task above every other, to hold the branches of the trade unions together in a period of controversy.

Labour were not particularly radical and had not been an active force in the civil war: in fact they did not really offer anything that was not available already from a more dynamic Fianna Fáil. Quoting Lemass's view that 'members of that Party desire to be respectable above everything else', Puirséil (2007: 29) concludes that Fianna Fáil did not so much steal Labour clothes but rather that the Irish Labour party never really felt comfortable flaunting radical style. Sandwiched between the nationalist republicanism of De Valera's Fianna Fáil and the vitriolic disdain for all things left espoused by the Catholic Church, the Labour party struggled to find support. The consequence was a tendency to lurch leftwards or rightwards depending on the political exigencies, but always returning to 'a dull equilibrium before long' (Puirséil, 2007: 82). In the absence of a clear Labour niche, Fianna Fáil gained ground – eventually at Labour's expense – when in 1944 it became clear that they could hold office alone without need of Labour support.

Jostling for position with Fianna Fáil in the political ground just left of centre has been an enduring problem for the Labour party. In the years when Fianna Fáil was able to hold office alone, if it wanted office at all, Labour was obliged to join in coalition with Fine Gael. This job was perhaps easiest under Garret FitzGerald's leadership, but it became more problematic when John Bruton succeeded him as Fine Gael party leader. In the general election of 1992, following the so-called 'Spring tide' (when, under Dick Spring's leadership, Labour achieved their best electoral result ever), relations between the two leaders deteriorated to such an extent that a coalition between their parties became impossible (Collins, 1993: 197; Finlay, 1998: 134). Under the leadership of Albert Reynolds, Fianna Fáil responded with an offer of 'partnership government' with Labour, producing a programme for government that more or less mimicked much of the Labour manifesto (Finlay, 1998: 138; Kavanagh, 2001: 122). The Fianna Fáil/Labour coalition that resulted was short-lived and replaced in 1994 by the 'Rainbow Coalition' with Fine Gael and the Democratic Left. Despite a creditable period in office, however, it seems that Labour's prior decision to coalesce with Fianna Fáil was not appreciated by voters (who, in the election of 1997, reversed Labour's gains from 33 to 17 Dáil deputies) and marked the beginning of a lasting split in the parliamentary party between pro- and anti-Fianna Fáil TDs (Kavanagh, 2001: 124).

The Labour Party's enduring electoral dilemma represents the 'catch 22' of Irish politics: if Labour joins forces with Fine Gael, it loses its claim to be left; if it joins forces with Fianna Fáil, it loses its claim to be in opposition. Its inability to solve effectively this riddle has possibly contributed to the 'conventional wisdom' that in the Republic of Ireland support for parties of the left has consistently been much weaker than in any other European democracy (Coakley, 1993a: 40, 2005a: 61) – a view that only holds so long as Fianna Fáil's left leanings are ignored. In their analysis of Irish Social and Political Attitudes Survey (ISPAS) data from 2002, for example, Kennedy and Sinnott (2006: 89) note that although there is 'still little evidence of a single "left–right" socio-economic cleavage … Irish society leans to the "left" on economy'. The failure of conventional parties of 'the left' seems to be as much a reflection of poor strategy as poor support. It is noteworthy, for example, that small left parties regularly emerge from the Republic's political terrain and, even though a cynic might argue that they tend to wilt and die just as regularly, the fact is that even against the odds such parties continue to form.

Clann na Poblachta was founded in 1946 by Sean MacBride, son of Maud Gonne and John MacBride (executed in 1916). It gathered support from Fianna Fáil members, who were disillusioned by empty republican rhetoric, as well as former IRA volunteers from the 1930s who were now willing to try constitutional politics. In addition to its republican ideals, the party was equally ambitious for social reform, attracting Dr Noel Browne and Jack McQuillan. In autumn 1947 the party won two out of three by-elections and elected MacBride to the Dáil. Fielding 90 candidates in the election of 1948 – many of whom were without political experience – the party gained ten TDs and was thus able to dislodge Fianna Fáil's overall majority. The party joined the interparty coalition (of 1948), supplying two of the most controversial ministers – Noel Browne as Minister for Health and Sean MacBride for External Affairs (an appointment that certainly influenced the declaration of the Republic in 1949). The circumstances surrounding the disintegration of the Government and Noel Browne's clash with the bishops is legendary. Subsequent political revival proved difficult, and the party failed to gain any seats in 1961, disbanding shortly after the election of 1965. In the end, its performance in office and especially its decision to ally with Fine Gael led many members to revert to their original affiliations. Two in particular, Noel Browne and Jack McQuillan, left to form the National Progressive Democrats in 1958. Placing itself to the left of Labour, the party made little progress and was, according to Gallagher (1985: 114), 'never anything more than a collective name for them and their supporters'. Its existence was short-lived when, in 1963, Browne and McQuillan joined the Labour party and declared the party disbanded.

The Workers' Party, by contrast, was much longer in duration and originates from a split within Sinn Féin in 1970, when the party leadership moved to end the policy of abstention from the Dáil. Following this, the then leadership became known as 'official Sinn Féin' (though party members never referred to themselves as such) and continued to develop along the Marxist lines begun in the 1960s (Dunphy and Hopkins, 1992). Those who disputed the decision and tended towards a more traditional conservative republicanism went on to reorganize the Irish Republican Army (IRA) by setting up a 'provisional' IRA army council, which soon came to be referred to as 'Provisional Sinn Féin'. In 1977 'official' Sinn Féin became 'Sinn Féin: The Workers Party' and, by 1982, dropped Sinn Féin from their party title altogether. A decade later, and following a failed attempt at major organizational restructuring and renewal, the leader of the party, Proinsias De Rossa, led six of the seven TDs, the MEP and most of its members out of the Workers' Party in order to form a new party (Holmes, 1994: 148). Provisionally titled 'New Agenda', it was renamed

'Democratic Left' at its founding conference in Dublin in March 1992. In 1994, it joined the Rainbow Coalition (with the Labour Party and Fine Gael) and held office until 1997. In 1999, after a merger with the Labour Party, De Rossa became the Labour Party's first president (Dunphy, 1998).

The most recent party to emerge on the left of the political spectrum is the Greens. The party emerged following a meeting held in the Central Hotel Dublin on 3 December 1981. Originally known as the Ecology Party of Ireland (EOI), following a structural reorganization emphasizing more bottom-up democratic activities, the party changed its name to the 'Comhaontas Glas' or 'Green Alliance'. In 1986, a minor split in the party left the majority convinced of the primacy of electoral campaigning, which the party has pursued with increasing success ever since. The year 2007 marked the political apotheosis of this strategy when they entered a coalition government with Fianna Fáil and independents.

Minor Parties and Independents

Last, but certainly never least in Irish politics, are the small number of independent TDs and minor political parties that, given the STV system of PR, are often able to wield power wildly disproportionate to their size in the Irish electoral system. In 1997, the Fianna Fáil/PD coalition could not command a majority of Dáil support and therefore sought the support of three independent TDs. In separate discussions with these three, Mildred Fox (Wicklow), Jackie Healy Rae (Kerry South) and Harry Blaney (Donegal North East), the Government was reported to have made deals costing millions of pounds (*Irish Times*, 27 June 1997). After four meetings with government representatives, Fox claimed to have secured five specific pledges of benefit to her constituents, including the provision of a new secondary school in Kilcoole; upgrading of the main roadway (N81) between Blessington and Carlow; £80,000 towards the cost of a CAT scan for Loughlinstown Hospital; provision of a suboffice of Wicklow county council in Blessington; and a new District Veterinary Office in the county (ibid.). Refusing to elaborate on the deal that he had made, Jackie Healy Rae claimed only to have got what he was looking for, in an arrangement that was 'between him and the people of South Kerry'.

In 2007, a €2.5million package of support for a hospital in his Dublin North Central constituency was the price of independent TD Finian McGrath's support for the government coalition arrangement between Fianna Fáil, the Greens and the PDs (*Irish Times*, 31 December 2007). Other projects that formed part of the deal included €1,165,485 towards a disabled housing project in Coolock; €200,000 for the Stardust victim's committee; €108,377 in extra funding for schools; and €30,000 for a community centre for Artane-Beaumont; plus 117 new jobs in frontline health services in his constituency and 110 extra staff at the Beaumont Hospital (ibid.). Details of the deals made with other independents Jackie Healy Rae and Michael Lowry (Tipperary North) were not available.

Perhaps the best example of disproportionate influence over government, however, is the PDs. With never more than 14 TDs in the Dáil, they have taken part in five of the seven governing coalitions (see Chapter 6) since their formation. In 1985, subsequent to his expulsion from Fianna Fáil due to a dispute over Charles Haughey's leadership and the party's policy on Northern Ireland, Dessie O'Malley went on to form the PDs together with Mary Harney, also from Fianna Fáil, and Michael McDowell, a disaffected Fine Gael supporter (Collins, 2005: 5–39). Although it is claimed that the PDs 'broke the mould of Irish politics' because they were not a civil war party but mobilized instead around contemporary political issues (Mair and Weeks, 2005: 149; Collins, 2005), as we have already seen, this is in fact neither unique nor unusual. What is more remarkable is their decision to develop as an increasingly right of centre political entity. Although feted as Ireland's neo-liberals by academics and the media (Murphy, G., 2006), this is a political trajectory that ultimately lost them support, and the PDs disbanded in 2008.

Party Families in Northern Ireland

Sinn Féin provides the linkage between the party systems north and south of the border, being the only party to attract significant support in both polities. In its modern guise (as post-1970 Provisional Sinn Féin) the party began contesting elections in 1982 and, Westminster apart, relegated the supposed principle of abstention from political institutions to a mere tactic, initially in respect of Dáil Éireann (recognized in 1986) and 12 years later regarding the Northern Ireland Assembly (Lynn, 2002; English, 2003; Murray and Tonge, 2005). Upon contesting elections in the North in 1982, Sinn Féin immediately captured the support of one-third of Catholic voters, a figure which also proved a ceiling amid ongoing IRA violence, for which the party offered backing. Following the IRA's 1994 ceasefire, support for Sinn Féin began to rise rapidly and the party now enjoys the support of over 60 per cent of Catholic voters.

Part of Sinn Féin's support since the 1980s has been a reward for its community work, encouraging working-class Catholics to benefit from local state facilities and welfare; the party also retains the flavour of a movement in its core support bases in urban Belfast (Cassidy, 2005). Gradually, party began to displace 'army' (the IRA) as the latter's activities became perceived as a barrier to electoral growth. Irish republicanism, as represented by Sinn Féin and the IRA, converted into a less isolated, but more diluted, Irish pan-nationalism, embracing all the nationalist parties on the island in an attempt to seek consensus around the principle of Irish self-determination, not necessarily reunification. Sinn Féin has moved from the tactics it used to employ – of support for armed struggle, abstention from 'partitionist' representative institutions, rejection of the police and courts in the North and demands for rapid British withdrawal from the region – in a retreat by instalments, which, according to critics, has not been masked by the Sinn Féin leadership's obfuscations and evasions (e.g. McIntyre, 1995, 2001; Moloney, 2003). For its part, the leadership has heralded each U-turn optimistically as 'another phase in the struggle' (e.g. Adams, 2007). Utterly dominant among working-class Catholics and extending its reach into the middle-class, Sinn Féin's changed agenda has reaped success in mobilizing young voters and former non-voters (McAllister, 2004).

As the one-time natural party of government in Northern Ireland, the UUP has struggled to adjust to its modern reduced circumstances (Walker, 2004). It fell from being the largest-supported party to the fourth-largest party in a mere ten years, from 1997 to 2007, abandoned by Unionists across the social classes, deserted by some of its elected representatives and forsaken by the Orange Order, whose affiliation expired in 2005. Always more of a loose movement than a party, the UUP struggled to adjust to the need for tight party discipline amid the controversy of its support for the GFA. The party's demise followed the collapse in support for the Agreement by 2002, with Unionist voters blaming the UUP, and either abandoning the party or, as happened to a significant extent, abstaining from voting. Whilst the UUP of old could rely upon deference and loyalty as sustenance, this is no longer true of newer generations, more rebellious in nature (Patterson and Kaufmann, 2007b). Since the reintroduction of PR-STV for most elections from 1973 onwards, after its abolition by the UUP in the 1920s, the UUP risked being outflanked by a party to which Unionists felt more instrumentally aligned as the defender of their interests. Until 1998, this was prevented by Unionist unity on most political issues, notably the Anglo-Irish Agreement, but this dissipated for a short, fateful time after the GFA.

The DUP emerged as a political party based around the politics and religion of Ian Paisley. 'Paisleyism' began to emerge as a serious entity as a political and anti-ecumenical movement in 1966, opposing a minor revival of republicanism evident in that year's fiftieth anniversary commemorations of the Easter Rising (O'Callaghan and O'Donnell, 2006). From this, Paisleyism began to become more organized in the form of the Protestant Unionist Party, which mobilized against the civil rights movement and the launch of the DUP in 1971. Avowedly left of centre on economic issues, but right wing on constitutional matters, it has been the latter which have been of greater interest and relevance to the party (Tonge, 2005a). The party was traditionally on the Loyalist side of the Ulster–British and Ulster–Loyalist typology, in terms of its conditional loyalty to political institutions, its primary loyalty to Ulster and the Crown rather than to Westminster and its hostility to perceived enemies of Ulster (Todd, 1987).

Despite the presence of many of its senior figures within the Free Presbyterian Church, the DUP's religious dimension has tended to be played down in favour of political pragmatism (Southern, 2005), a distinction increased by the replacement of Paisley as leader by Peter Robinson in 2008. In garnering the votes of rural evangelical Protestants and many working-class Loyalists, the DUP has proved adept at fusing hardline constitutional politics with a traditional moral outlook (Bruce, 1986). In common with its Unionist counterpart, it took on more of the appearance of a movement than a normal political party, but one in which the leader's remit was much stronger compared to the internal arcane and chaotic organizational structures which allowed UUP leaders to be undermined from the 1970s onwards.

Following its emergence in 1970 from the civil rights campaigns, the SDLP offered a more participatory, mildly leftist and secular form of politics which sharply distinguished the party from the clerical influences and abstentionism of the Nationalist Party (Farrell, 1980; Staunton, 2001). Despite its socialist leanings, the SDLP failed to attract Protestants to the party, 96 per cent of members being Catholic, and its nationalism has generally outweighed other ideological inputs to the party (Murray, 1998; Evans *et al.*, 2000; Murray and Tonge, 2005). Nonetheless, the SDLP's nationalism and approach to Irish unity adopted less of the traditional territorial form, being based upon a more people-based formula for Irish unity, an 'agreed Ireland'. Under the format of the party leader, from 1979 until 2001, John Hume, the SDLP did much to devise a formula for Irish self-determination (in reality, codetermination, North and South) which would not merely force Unionists into a territorially and politically indivisible polity. Indeed this essentially SDLP idea formed the basis of the Downing Street Declaration and the GFA.

Despite Hume's desire for agreement rather than coercion between non-reconciled traditions, there is continuing debate between those viewing 'Humespeak' as essentially nuanced language designed to steer Unionists towards Irish unity, amid the admittedly sometimes vague concept of an 'agreed Ireland' (e.g. Cunningham, 1997), and those who suggest Hume's commitment to social and economic parity within the North was at least as strong as his advocacy of territorial and political unification (e.g. Loughlin, 2006). Despite its strongly pro-European stance, the party is not post-nationalist in other aspects, and is often unclear whether it regards Unionists and nationalists as two traditions, or nations, or states, on the island of Ireland. Nonetheless the SDLP has always been adamant that Irish unity cannot be enforced (Tonge, 2008).

Beyond the 'bloc four' lies the Alliance Party, whose formation in 1970 was designed to represent the non-aligned political centre. However, the party was Unionist in constitutional terms from the outset and was supported and joined mainly by Protestants (McGarry and O'Leary, 1995). The Alliance does nonetheless attract support from both sides of the divide and Catholics provide approximately 20 per cent of its members and voters. Its support base, low at around 5 per cent but never negligible, is predominantly middle class. The Alliance rejects the institutionalization of the communal divide it claims is apparent in the Unionist–nationalist division of spoils within political institutions. The Northern Ireland Women's Coalition emerged briefly in the 'centre ground' and was elected to the 1998–2002 Assembly, having strongly backed the GFA, but its candidates were not returned in 2003 and the party folded soon afterwards. The under-representation of women (averaging only 15 per cent of Assembly members) remains a problem (Cowell-Meyers, 2003; Ward, 2006).

Not all the political fringe is centrist. The politics of Loyalist paramilitarism have been severely underdeveloped compared to its republican counterpart, but have nonetheless been important, perhaps most notably via the emergence of a 'new Loyalism' which backed the GFA, in marked contrast to how Loyalists regarded the Sunningdale Agreement during the 1970s (McAuley, 2005). The Progressive Unionist Party (PUP), associated with the Ulster Volunteer Force, has enjoyed representation within the Northern Ireland Assembly. Enjoying support mainly in East Belfast, the PUP fuses socialist politics with a strong defence of the constitutional position (Edwards, 2007). Attempts at sustaining a political party associated with the Ulster Defence Association (UDA) have failed. Nonetheless, the UDA has episodically offered significant political contributions, most notably via its *Common Sense* document in 1987 (Bruce, 1994). *Common Sense* advocated power-sharing and proportionality in government over a decade before its realization in the GFA.

Political Dynamics in Northern Ireland

Electoral competition in Northern Ireland occurs within hermetically sealed blocs. The key period of competition within these blocs came immediately after the GFA, with the switch of Unionist and nationalist electors to the DUP and Sinn Féin, respectively. Elections within Northern Ireland are 'not just about representing opinion; they are intrinsically about acquiring bargaining strength to be deployed during government formation' (Mitchell, 2007: 122).

With Unionist and nationalist blocs guaranteed places in government in Northern Ireland, there is little incentive for the parties within those blocs to campaign for votes beyond their own bloc. With six Assembly members elected from each constituency, the threshold required for election is a mere 14 per cent. Use of the alternative vote system, requiring parties to obtain an outright majority of votes through second preferences, might encourage greater cross-communal party appeals, although, in religiously homogeneous areas, ethnic party appeals would not need to be diluted.

The consociational political dispensation and application of the d'Hondt mechanism of allocation of government seats (based upon the number of Assembly seats held by each party) ensure that two separate party competitions take place, within each community, solidifying communalism. The vast majority of lower preference transfers, surplus or terminal, remain within the respective ethnic blocs.

The Unionist–nationalist Executive formation was established as a bridge across a huge electoral chasm. Whatever the faults of consociational power-sharing, no one can doubt its ambition: if parties had waited for electoral or political healing of the communal divide among voters or party members, partnership in government would never have occurred (Tonge and Evans, 2002). Whilst ostensibly democratic, party structures tend to be dominated by the leadership, the notable exception being the UUP, although even here there has been a tightening of hitherto chaotic organization. Whilst there is some evidence of a willingness of UUP and SDLP voters to transfer across the divide, the partnership axis of the DUP and Sinn Féin in government is hardly replicated at electoral level, where the odds of a terminal transfer vote heading from one of those parties to the other stood at 477:1 in 2007, the year the leaders of those two parties came to share power at the head of the Executive. The bipolarity recognized at representative level, via designations of Assembly members as 'Unionist', 'Nationalist' or 'Other' reflects – and arguably consolidates – an acute communal fault line among the electorate (Wilford and Wilson, 2003).

Northern Ireland's main political parties operate as 'catch-us' rather than 'catch-all' organizations. However, the assumption offered by anti-consociationalists, that the institutional arrangements which followed the GFA encouraged the growth of centrifugal forces, is not borne out by evidence. A growth of 'extremism' which followed the GFA was supposedly evidenced by the electoral rise of Sinn Féin and the DUP, at the expense of the SDLP and UUP, respectively. This interpretation failed to be cognizant of the growth in moderation in the DUP and Sinn Féin, even if party rhetoric sometimes obscured this underlying trend.

In explaining how electorates support apparently militant parties, which are engaged in centripetalism despite some of their communal rhetoric, Mitchell *et al.*,

Table 5.1   *Correlations between Party Vote and Turnout, Northern Ireland: Westminster and Assembly Elections, 2005–7*

2005 Westminster election			2007 Assembly election		
UUP	−.55	p < .05	UUP	−.61	p < .01
DUP	−.75	p < .001	DUP	−.70	p < .01
SDLP	.47	p < .05	SDLP	.48	p < .05
SF	.83	p < .001	SF	.78	p < .01

(2008) have developed the useful concept of parties as ethnic tribunes: organizations which act as strong voices for their communities but not in a rejectionist manner. The DUP and Sinn Féin continue to portray themselves as leaders of their respective groups. Their increasingly unchallenged positions in this role allow these parties to 'do business' on behalf of their ethnic groups. Whilst Sinn Féin promoted the GFA as part of an onward march for nationalists, the DUP was required to delegitimize the UUP for having signed up to a deal on inadequate terms which 'betrayed' Protestants, before claiming the credit for a renegotiated arrangement from 2007 onwards (see Ganiel, 2007).

One final aspect of the Northern Ireland party system is worthy of note. Turnout levels are asymmetric across the divide (see Table 5.1), with nationalists more likely to vote than Unionists, an indication of how much more willing they are to participate in the Northern Irish polity than in previous generations. This is the reverse of the situation that pertained up to the 1970s, when Protestants, with much higher regard for the state and more benefits from it, were far more likely to vote. Despite the rapid growth of the DUP since the GFA, there is a negative relationship between the DUP vote and turnout, indicating that apathy and disenchantment are evident among sections of the Unionist electorate.

Conclusion

In the Republic of Ireland, the fact that the two main Irish political parties are divided by the stances they took in relation to the conclusion of the civil war is traditionally highlighted as the chief peculiarity of Irish party politics. This is significant. First, because it marks the failure to develop an explicit 'left–right' political spectrum in Irish politics (although arguably a centrist–left fault line exists); second, because it marks the birth of one of Western Europe's most successful political parties. Notwithstanding its disappointments in recent elections, 'Fianna Fáil is now, relatively speaking, Europe's most consistently successful vote-getter' (Coakley, 2003: 239). Still, there are signs of change. Since the 1980s, both the vote and seat share of independent candidates has surged. In the 2002 election, all together, independents won nearly 10 per cent of the vote and 8 per cent of the seats (Mair and Weeks,

2005: 156), which was all the more significant since the election marked the lowest turnout since the 1920s (Lyons and Sinnott, 2003). This, combined with the PR-STV electoral system, suggests that perhaps the most contemporary peculiarity of Irish politics is the potential influence of minor parties and independents.

In the 2007 election, once again it was the independent TDs who held the winning cards. Fianna Fáil's loss of three seats (more had been predicted) meant that they had to work even harder to lead a government – one that now necessitated a coalition with the Greens *and* the PDs, *plus* the support of three independents. The PDs seem to have paid the highest price for the improvement in Fine Gael's fortunes. Labour's failure to make comparable progress, however, ensured that even though a number of independents lost their seats, decreasing their overall share of the vote to 7 per cent (Suiter, 2008: 107), still their presence was critical to the composition of government.

Northern Ireland's political system reflects an acute communal divide which has not lessened in electoral terms, despite the emergence of an elite-level power-sharing consociation. There are few incentives for parties to campaign beyond their ethnic support group and the electoral performance of avowedly non-communal parties, such as Alliance, has been modest (Evans and Tonge, 2003). Whilst a substantial section of the electorate, around 30 per cent according to successive Northern Ireland Life and Times surveys, rejects the label of either Unionist or nationalist, this is not reflected in voting patterns. Distinctive polities have required specific messages, and, although Sinn Féin's all-island status offers advantage in terms of potential growth, the perception of the party as a predominantly northern entity has inhibited full development in the Irish Republic, despite the party having long divested itself of the electoral albatross of IRA linkages. Should Fianna Fáil decide to stand in elections, in addition to organizing, in Northern Ireland, it will be confronted with Sinn Féin's problems in reverse, for it possesses a 32-county organization, but one even more heavily skewed towards one polity within those 32 counties. Fianna Fáil's possible entry into the northern arena has been justified by the party as a mark of the unthreatening modern Irish discourse on Northern Ireland, a territory to which the Irish Government no longer lays claim (Hayward, 2004). The presence of two all-Ireland parties potentially competing for votes would strengthen the representational dimension to the assertion contained in the GFA that any citizen born on the island of Ireland can consider themselves Irish.

Intrabloc realignment has provided the dynamic within Northern Ireland politics, amid a largely static intercommunal rivalry, marked only by modest growth of the nationalist bloc. The DUP and Sinn Féin's success was built upon their perceived positions as the better defenders of bloc interests in a post-Agreement polity. For the DUP, this meant revising the terms (slightly) of the GFA, whilst Sinn Féin was entrusted as a custodian of the original deal.

6

The Electoral System and Voting Behaviour

Voting is less unequal than other forms of political participation, but it is far from unbiased.

(Lijphart, 1996: 1)

Introduction

The use of the single transferable vote (STV) system of proportional representation (PR) in Ireland – North and South – provides rare examples of regular deployment of the system. Whilst PR is very common in Europe, it is usually based upon electoral choices made from predetermined party lists. Within Europe, only Ireland (North and South) and Malta utilize PR-STV for their lower chambers (Mitchell and Gillespie, 1999). Although candidate-based PR-STV is thus associated with Ireland, it might be considered part of the British legacy there. Developed during the 1850s (simultaneously by Carl Andrae in Denmark and Thomas Hare in England), the STV system of PR was strongly advocated by contemporary electoral reform campaigners in Britain (Sinnott, 2005: 107). Moreover, given British concerns regarding the representation of minorities in the event of Home Rule for Ireland, the STV system of PR seemed particularly apposite (in 1912, an element of STV-PR was inserted into the abortive Home Rule bill). Perhaps not surprisingly, the views of contemporary Irish political reformers were 'substantially influenced by the current thinking in Britain' (ibid.). The founder of Sinn Féin, Arthur Griffiths, was also one of the founding members of the Proportional Representation Society of Ireland.

Following its introduction in Ireland for the local election of Sligo Corporation in 1919, the British government introduced the system for all local elections in the country in 1920. By 1921, the national election held under the Government of Ireland Act saw the STV system of PR introduced and even supported by a considerable portion of the nationalist movement. As Sinnott (ibid.) argues, 'it is not surprising, therefore, that when independence negotiations were under way and the issue of representation of minorities was being considered, the desirability of PR was common ground'.

Following Irish independence, provision for a PR system of electoral competition was inserted into the 1922 constitution and, though the STV method was not specifically

107

prescribed, this was the system specified in the Electoral Act of 1923. In his subsequent redrafting of the 1937 constitution, de Valera – arguing that the electoral system was 'too important to be left to the vagaries of party warfare' – gave a constitutional guarantee to the continued use of the STV system of PR in the Republic of Ireland. Despite reform proposals by prominent political interests (see below), the STV system of PR maintains a high level of support throughout the ROI to this day.

For Northern Ireland, the Government of Ireland Act, 1920 paved the way for the use of PR-STV in elections to councils and to the regional parliament governing the province. Deployment of the system was seen as ensuring fair representation for the nationalist minority, but, as part of a flagrant abuse of power and to protect Unionist bloc unity, PR-STV was abolished from the Northern Irish polity by 1929. Its reappearance in the 1970s formed part of the reform drive of the British Government under direct rule. Westminster parliamentary elections are still based upon the first-past-the-post single plurality, but all other contests now utilize PR-STV. A majority of the multimember Assembly constituencies return Unionist and nationalist representatives. By the 2003 Assembly election, only 2 per cent of non-voters claimed that 'there was no point in voting in my constituency because it was obvious who would win' (Electoral Commission, 2004: 98). At the 2007 Assembly election only one constituency (West Belfast) returned exclusively nationalist representatives; four constituencies were bereft of nationalist representatives. It is the Westminster single plurality method that is now sometimes seen as anachronistic and subject to demands for change (McGarry and O'Leary, 2004). However, to operate PR-STV exclusively for Northern Ireland within a Westminster election would create problems of constituency redesign and of how to achieve fair Unionist–nationalist representation.

Proportional Representation and the Single Transferable Vote

The PR-STV system is based upon multimember constituencies, the assumption being that each elected representative can adequately represent the area. The Westminster first-past-the-post system yields a single parliamentary representative, from which stem claims concerning the special relationship between the MP and constituents. STV is intended to create as close a relationship as possible between the proportion of votes and seats won by each party in order to produce a national parliament that is truly representative of the division of political opinion in the country. Under this system, candidates' names are listed on the ballot sheet in alphabetical order. The voter places a number one beside their first preference candidate, a number two beside their second, and so on. In order to be elected, candidates must reach a predetermined quota, calculated by adding one to the sum reached by dividing the total number of valid votes by the total number of seats plus one:

$$\text{Quota} = \left(\frac{\text{Total number of valid votes}}{\text{Number of seats} + 1} \right) + 1$$

A candidate who reaches this quota is automatically elected. Where a candidate regis-
ters more than the necessary quota, the 'surplus vote' is reallocated to the other candidates according to voter preferences. This ensures that the ballot is not merely a crude
choice of one candidate, but that the ranking of candidates is taken into account.
Moreover, vote transfers ensure that surplus votes for candidates are not wasted. If no
candidate reaches the quota at the 'first count', the candidate with the least votes is
eliminated from the poll and their second preference votes are transferred to the
remaining candidates in the 'second count'. These counts continue until enough
candidates meet the necessary quota to be elected. The timing of transfers of surpluses
or elimination of low polling candidates is conditional upon whether a surplus is of
sufficient size as to potentially alter the ranking of candidates. If yes, the surplus is
transferred; if no, the bottom candidate is eliminated (see Mitchell and Gillespie,
1999: 78). If, after all transfers have been allocated, there is still no candidate with the
required amount of votes, the candidate remaining with the most votes takes the seat
(Sinnott, 2005: 112–16 provides a number of practical examples of this process).

Two further aspects of the system are noteworthy, in relation to the distribution of
preferences and the distribution of seats. Regarding the former, under STV, when
someone is elected at the first count, *all* of his or her votes are examined to determine second preferences. If, however, a candidate is elected at any count other than
the first, only those votes received *at the count of election* (or 'round' of counting)
are examined for subsequent preferences (Borooah, 2003: 158). This latter convention
may give a misleading impression of voter preferences because the votes received at
earlier counts (or rounds) are ignored for the purpose of transferring votes. Thus, for
example, a candidate from *party X* may be elected at the third count and pass on his
or her surplus, but if the transfers to elect that candidate came from an eliminated
candidate of *party Y*, then the destination of the surplus will reflect the preferences
of party Y voters and not party X.

In relation to the distribution of seats under PR-STV, the larger the district (or
constituency) size the more proportionate is the electoral result. In the Republic of
Ireland, this means that larger districts with five seats generally deliver more proportionate results than smaller districts with three. Generally speaking, three-seat
constituencies tend to favour the larger parties, whereas smaller parties often do best
in five-seat constituencies where the vote is most proportionate. To illustrate this
point, Fine Gael have on four occasions won less seats than their percentage of the
vote, and in 18 of the 25 elections during 1923–97 Labour obtained a smaller share
of seats than its share of first preference votes (Sinnott, 1999: 144, 2005: 117–18).
Still, 'with such a small district magnitude, no electoral system could be expected to
have delivered more proportionality than STV in Ireland' (Gallagher, 1987: 29) and
the degree of proportionality achieved is a major accomplishment given the small
district magnitudes (Chubb, 1992: 146).

In Northern Ireland Assembly elections, six members are returned for each of the
18 constituencies. This large number ensures a low level of disproportionality in
terms of votes cast and seats won. In the 2007 Assembly election, for example, the
DUP won 33.3 per cent of the seats with 30.1 per cent of the vote; Sinn Féin won
25.9 per cent of seats with 26.1 per cent of the vote; the SDLP won 14.8 per cent of

the seats with 15.2 per cent of the vote; and the UUP won 16.7 per cent of seats with 14.9 per cent of the vote. Whilst there is clearly disproportionality, evidenced, for example, by the UUP's superior haul of seats relative to vote, and despite that party's lower poll share than that of the SDLP, the overall picture is one of high proportionality. In terms of those elected, PR-STV is not a system in which first preference candidates are frequently overhauled due to transfers to ostensibly less popular candidates. In the 2007 Assembly election, for example, of the 108 candidates across the 18 constituencies attaining a top six placing according to first preference votes, only five failed to be eventually elected. Admittedly, the figure was higher in 2003, at 15, but the 'jostling' through of lower preference transfers usually involves (with notable exceptions) only the final seat.

The large number of local councillors (582) elected from Northern Ireland's councils also assists in terms of proportionality at district elections. Thus, in 2005, for example, the difference between overall first preference percentage vote share and the total percentage of council seats obtained across Northern Ireland did not exceed 1.8 per cent for any of the four main parties. In contrast, European elections produce a much higher level of disproportionality, as Northern Ireland is treated as a single constituency, yielding three elected representatives. Given that there are four large parties trying to fill three places, with a higher threshold for election, it is inevitable that one party will suffer a large number of wasted votes. In 2004, for example, the 'victims' were SDLP voters, who despite registering 87,559 first preference votes (16 per cent of the poll) found themselves without an elected representative from their first-choice party.

The persistence of first-past-the-post in Northern Ireland for elections to the Westminster parliament reflects wider caution over change for general elections within the UK polity. During the 1990s, after years in opposition, the Labour Party promised a referendum on the question of electoral reform, but this vanished in 1997 with the arrival of the party in government, with a 179 majority, under the single plurality system. In Northern Ireland, as elsewhere, the system exaggerates success. For decades, this benefited the UUP, who gained sufficient votes to benefit from a winner-takes-all situation in numerous Unionist constituencies. More recent times have seen the advantage switch to the DUP. In the 2005 Westminster election, for example, the DUP won 50 per cent of the 18 parliamentary seats with 33 per cent of the vote.

Impact on Voting Behaviour

By law, a general election to the Dáil must be held at least once every five years. There are 166 TDs (or members of the Dáil), representing the 41 electoral constituencies into which the state is divided. No constituency may return less than three members, and larger constituencies may be represented by up to five. Since, however, 'the primary focus of PR-STV is on the choice of individual representatives' (Sinnott, 2005: 106), in the Republic of Ireland there is an obvious resonance with the old cliché that 'all politics is local'. Ireland's STV method of PR, which allows voters to mark as many preferences as there are candidates in multiple seat constituencies, not only obliges candidates of the same party to compete against each other, but also offers the opportunity for voters to switch between parties, according to their preferences. The result is a highly personalized and localized electoral competition, where issues of national policy often take second place (or may be considered equally important) to issues of local concern.

Just as significant is the way in which the electoral system tends to refract national policy issues into local politics. Thus, for example, in the election of 2002, most of the 14 independent seats went to those candidates 'characteristically arguing that the constituency or even one part of it, had not received its fair share of government spending' (Gallagher, 2003: 102). Three had distinctive health-related platforms. Paudge Connolly (Cavan-Monaghan) stood as the 'hospital action' candidate, with both Jerry Cowley (Mayo) and Liam Twomey (Wexford) seeking improved, dedicated health services (ibid.). In Sligo, Marian Harkin campaigned for a better share of infrastructural investment for her constituency (Gallagher, 2003: 103). In another electoral system hospital closures and specialized care, as well as national infrastructure, might be considered issues of national policy rather than issues of specific local concern. Moreover, it could be argued that by allowing local constituencies to vent their concerns via the election of independents, the larger parties were able to treat these as local issues and avoid making them the subject of national political debate. This need not be the case. In the 2007 election, the Fine Gael/Labour coalition of opposition against the incumbent Fianna Fáil/PD Government made health one of their primary campaign issues. In the STV-PR electoral system, political parties may choose whether to contest the election on local or national issues.

Notwithstanding the significance of localism in Irish politics, Laver (2005: 191) notes that even if the STV-PR electoral system does reinforce a high level of personalism, it is still the case that Irish governments are formed and run by political parties, and so it is worth examining the relationships between voters and parties. Using data from the Irish National Election Study (INES) of 2002, Laver (2005: 193) concludes that 'on the matter of whether voters choose candidates or parties ... about 40 per cent seem to be candidate voters, about 40 per cent party voters, with the remaining 20 per cent balancing the two motivations'. In addition, older people are more likely to be committed party supporters than younger people and the influence of familial political background is still significant (Laver, 2005: 197). Older voters (in their 40s and over) tend to vote more for Fianna Fáil, Fine Gael, PD and Labour; whereas voters for Sinn Féin and the Greens tend on average to be a decade or so younger (ibid.). Whilst the gender breakdown of support for the mainstream parties is not significant, Sinn Féin has more male supporters (58 per cent) and the Greens have more female (55 per cent) (Laver, 2005: 197–8). Finally, where voters live seems to be a strong determinant of voting behaviour, with a strong positive correlation between the degree of urbanization and modernization, suggesting a growing urban–rural divide in Irish politics (Laver, 2005: 198).

In the six-member Northern Ireland Assembly constituencies, the low quota required to attain election – a mere 14.3 per cent – ensures that candidates can normally rely upon votes from their own 'ethnic pool' to be elected. The impact upon voting behaviour is therefore that electors are faced with choices from parties operating in an almost sealed ethnic bloc, in which those with the greater communal appeal – as distinct from universal pitch – are likely to succeed. The ethnic parties of Sinn Féin, SDLP, DUP and UUP make no serious attempts to operate as 'catch-all' parties, instead operating within a system of electoral apartheid as 'catch-us' organizations. Sinn Féin's electoral pitch since 1998 has been as the stouter defender of nationalist gains under the GFA (Maillot, 2004; Murray and Tonge, 2005). The DUP's position was to oppose the 'concessions' of the Agreement and demand further movement from republicans, until such time as the party achieved dominance within the Unionist community, after which a more pragmatic approach was evident (Aughey, 2005).

Impact on Politicians

The prevalence of both inter- and intraparty competition at local level makes it perfectly rational for politicians seeking to maximize their votes to develop a consensus relating to macropolicy issues (in order to avail themselves of vote transfers from candidates from a variety of parties), whilst differentiating themselves in relation to local issues. This trend was further encouraged by a number of developments within the party system throughout the late 1980s: first, as Labour and Fine Gael moved closer together, so as to present a viable alternative government to Fianna Fáil (Mitchell, 2003b: 130); later in Fine Gael's agreement to support the economic reforms proposed by the minority Fianna Fáil Government (the 'Tallaght Strategy'); and, finally, by Fianna Fáil's decision to ditch the 'principle' of never entering a coalition by going into government with the PDs (Mitchell, 2000: 131). These twin rationalities, which in many ways support and augment each other, have important consequences for political behaviour in the Republic of Ireland.

At local level, the exaggerated significance of local politicking has been highlighted by a number of seminal articles on Irish politics. The first major work that tended towards this perspective is probably Chubb's (1963) article 'Going about Persecuting Civil Servants'. The title, which was coined from an interview by Chubb with an experienced politician, drew attention to widely shared views between both constituents and their representatives regarding the role of a TD. Chubb recorded that key words such as 'service', 'availability' and 'representation' were used to describe the relations between constituents and their TDs. According to Farrell (1983a), this insight 'captured a perception of reality familiar to most political practitioners, commonly assumed in journalistic analyses and comment, reinforced by academic studies, and criticised by those committed to parliamentary reform'. It was a view that other writers have concurred with, laying great emphasis on personal and local ties between public representatives and their constituents (Bax, 1970, 1975, 1976; Sack, 1976; Carty, 1981). Whilst critics in the media have gone so far as to label this behaviour clientelist (*Irish Times*, 3 June 1997, 13 April 2002, 21 April 2006), most academic research suggests that brokerage rather than clientelism is what happens in Ireland (Komito, 1984, 1989, 1992a,1992b; Gallagher and Komito, 1993; Collins and O'Shea, 2003).

In fact, politicians are most usually telling constituents about what they are entitled to already, or intervening in relation to the delivery, or speeding up, of a service to which the constituent is already entitled (Gallagher and Komito, 1993; Collins and O'Shea, 2003). No doubt this mode of political activity makes the constituency work of TDs disproportionately burdensome, leading Farrell (1985: 14) to note an 'evident consensus among deputies that the competition in constituency service has got out of hand' – a point that has been confirmed by a number of politicians from a variety of political parties since (Boland, 1991; FitzGerald, 1991, 2003; Martin, 1991; Hussey, 1993; Dempsey 2006 (see McDonald, 2006).

At national level, the emphasis on the local constituency work arguably detracts politicians from focusing on national political issues. Local constituency work is not only extremely time consuming, but its significance serves to diminish the importance of other TD roles. Writing in the *Sunday Independent* (8 August 2006), TD for Limerick East, Willie O'Dea, candidly noted that 'backbenchers spend 80 per cent of their time servicing individual constituents – to the detriment of the national interest'. As a result of this, he argued, 'the garnering of a few dozen medical cards is more vital to political survival than any creative well-researched Dáil speech on health service reform' (*Irish Times*, 21 April 2006).

Within this context, the local constituency skills needed to be a successful politician in Ireland may not be the most desirable in terms of national politics. In their attempts to achieve electoral popularity, Irish politicians may tend to follow public opinion, rather than lead it. It is argued that this leads to a notable level of 'cautiousness' amongst our politicians that has a significant impact on policy outcomes (Murphy, 2008). In Irish politics, it is often the case that where public opinion is most divided, politicians will be most reticent in advancing their own opinions. Perhaps the most conspicuous example of this is the unwillingness of Irish governments (or legislature) to put forward legislation on abortion (Bacik, 2004: 106–31). Another more recent example follows the Government's decision in the 2005 budget to grant all parents €1,000 for each child under the age of six, in order to contribute to the costs of childcare – rather than spending this money on building childcare facilities, training child carers or tackling a range of anomalies in early years care and education provision (Adshead and Neylon, 2008). Any of these measures might have antagonized a significant rump of conservative voters who think that mothers should stay at home to care for children. On the one hand, this kind of behaviour can be seen to contribute to the consensual style of politics that is prevalent in Ireland (O'Donnell *et al.*, 2007), whilst, on the other hand, it also explains the almost complete absence of more radical political positions and/or parties in the Republic.

In Northern Ireland, given that over 90 per cent of Assembly and local council elected representatives are drawn from one of the two main ethnic blocs, it appears that, for most of Northern Ireland's politicians, winning in a PR-STV electoral system requires two key attributes: personal appeal and, more importantly, ethnic appeal. There is a surprising dearth of analysis of the relative importance of these two attributes. Personal appeal is grounded in the ability to represent district wards or assembly constituencies; given the limited powers of district councils, the impact of a local councillor can only be minimal, but it may be more relevant at the level of the regional assembly. Ethnic appeal is based upon the appeal of the candidate's party to more broadly represent the interests of the Protestant–Unionist or Catholic–nationalist bloc in what is still often perceived as zero-sum game politics. Given the growing ability of parties to manage the first preference vote levels of their candidates, it seems that party-ethnic appeal has greater importance than personal-representative attributes.

Upon election, it is common for successful candidates to claim that they will represent all their constituents irrespective of their community of origin. In formal terms this claim is true, but it is somewhat undermined by the disinterest in soliciting support from the 'rival' community. Of course, some candidates claim to entirely eschew the Unionist–nationalist rivalry. The only sizeable non-bloc organization to survive the pervasiveness of ethnic alignment is the Alliance Party, the majority of whose elected representatives owe their success to Unionist lower-preference transfer additions to their first preference scores. Whilst Alliance candidates indeed reject 'sectarian' labelling, their claims are somewhat negated by analysis of where their victories are located. After three post-GFA assembly elections held during 1998–2007, Alliance had still to win a single seat in any of the seven constituencies where Catholics formed a majority. Indeed, beyond middle-class South Belfast, Alliance's seats are in overwhelmingly Protestant areas. When Alliance candidates are eliminated in PR-STV counts, a higher percentage of their transferred votes go to 'moderate' Unionist candidates than 'moderate' nationalists. For example, in 2007, the UUP received 40 per cent of such transfers, compared to 31 per cent for the SDLP (the DUP and Sinn Féin received 5 per cent and 3 per cent, respectively).

Impact on the Party System

The classic argument against PR is that it leads to political instability because it encourages the proliferation of political parties. According to Sartori (1986: 64), 'PR formulas facilitate multi-partyism and are, conversely, hardly conducive to two-partyism'. The implied criticism here stems from the view that multipartyism makes it more difficult for a single party to gain an overall majority, with a consequent tendency towards coalition governments, which are often viewed as being inherently more unstable than single party governments. Taking this line of argument further, it is argued that the STV system of PR is – in terms of supporting united and cohesive parties – the most damaging of all (Taagepera and Shugart, 1989: 28). The underlying assumption is that 'where intra-party choice is allowed, parliamentary parties will tend to be disunited' (Katz, 1980: 34) and that 'the single transferable vote, like preferential voting in general, is detrimental to the development of a responsible party system' (Blais, 1991: 248). If these are the 'rules', however, the Irish case seems to be the exception. Whilst Ireland has maintained the same electoral system since the foundation of the state, the number of political parties has varied quite considerably:

> broadly speaking, the number of parties has fluctuated from six, plus a large group of independents, in June 1927, down to three plus independents in 1938, back up to six in 1948, down to three with almost no independents in 1965 and back up to five in 1987.
>
> (Sinnott, 1995: 91)

At the conclusion of the 2007 general election, the number of parties stood at six, with five independents. The election result was a close one: out of the 165 seats Fianna Fáil took 77; with Fine Gael and Labour (who had campaigned together to offer an alternative government) taking 51 and 20, respectively. Of the smaller parties, the Greens took 6, Sinn Féin 4 and the PDs 2. In the end, Fianna Fáil formed a coalition government with the Greens and the PDs, plus the support of three of the five independent TDs elected (*Irish Times*, 15 June 2007). Not for the first time, the support of independent, non-affiliated TDs had a considerable influence over the shape of government.

During the 1920s and 1930s, a considerable number of independent deputies were elected to the Dáil, representing a range of opinions (including Unionism and nationalism), before their support base was largely 'mopped up' by the larger parties as they were established (Coakley, 1993b: 18; 1999: 22). Table 6.1 shows that it was not until de Valera's government of 1933 that any political party leading the government enjoyed a majority of Dáil support; thereafter, only ten out of 27 governments achieved 51 per cent or over. The so-called 'Independents' who support minority governments have been characterized by Chubb (1957: 134) as 'independent farmers, business candidates, party dissidents and political oddities'. It is not unusual, however, for deputies calling themselves independent to be 'camp followers' or members of small parties (Chubb, 1992: 169) and, because of this, they are often willing to offer their support to minority governments on favourable terms.

As Table 6.1 illustrates, following the 1977 general election, none of the subsequent six elections produced a clear winner, so that on each occasion government formation was not straightforward (Gallagher, 1993: 127–9). After the 1981 election, though Fine Gael and Labour had agreed to a coalition, with only 80 of the 166 seats, the Government was only able to hold on with on the support of independents. After the February 1982 election, Fianna Fáil attempted to form a minority government with support from the Workers' Party and independents. In 1987, both Fianna Fáil and the opposition parties ranged against them managed to secure 82 deputies each: Charles Haughey was able to lead a minority government only following Tony Gregory's abstention from the vote, enabling the Ceann Comhairle (Chair of Dáil Éireann) to pass a casting vote in favour of Fianna Fáil.

The role played by independents is particularly significant in the Irish system, and one which is quite clearly facilitated by the STV system of PR:

> by focusing on individual candidates, by encouraging competition between deputies and candidates in the provision of local constituency service and, through the mechanism of multi-seat constituency, by lowering the threshold of representation to a point at which it is within the reach of non-party candidates.
>
> (Sinnott, 2005: 120)

The persistent presence of up to half a dozen independent TDs in the Dáil does not necessarily mean that minority governments will be unstable (indeed it could be argued that they provide a degree of stability through their negotiated support for government), but it does raise questions about the transparency of government negotiations

Table 6.1 *The Composition of Governments in the Republic of Ireland, 1922–2008*

Date	Party/coalition (leader)	Dáil support (%)
Jan 1922	Cumann na nGaedheal (Collins) provisional government	49.0
Aug 1922	Cumann na nGaedheal (Cosgrave) provisional government	49.0
Sep 1922	Cumann na nGaedheal (Cosgrave) provisional government	45.3
Dec 1922	Cumann na nGaedheal (Cosgrave) minority government	45.3
Sep 1923	Cumann na nGaedheal (Cosgrave) minority government	41.2
June 1927	Cumann na nGaedheal (Cosgrave) minority government	30.7
Oct 1927	Cumann na nGaedheal (Cosgrave) minority government	40.5
April 1930	Cumann na nGaedheal (Cosgrave) minority government	40.5
Mar 1932	Fianna Fáil (de Valera) minority government	47.1
Feb 1933	Fianna Fáil (de Valera)	50.3
July 1937	Fianna Fáil (de Valera) government with no absolute majority	50.0
June 1938	Fianna Fáil (de Valera)	55.8
July 1943	Fianna Fáil (de Valera)	48.5
June 1944	Fianna Fáil (de Valera)	55.1
Feb 1948	Fine Gael/Labour/Clann na Talmhan, National Labour (Costello)	45.6
June 1951	Fianna Fáil (de Valera) minority government	46.9
June 1954	Fine Gael*/Labour/Clann na Talmhan (Costello*)	50.3
Mar 1957	Fianna Fáil (de Valera)	53.1
June 1959	Fianna Fáil (Lemass)	53.1
Oct 1961	Fianna Fáil (Lemass) minority government	48.6
April 1965	Fianna Fáil (Lemass)	50.0
Nov 1966	Fianna Fáil (Lynch)	50.0
July 1969	Fianna Fáil (Lynch)	52.1
Mar 1973	Fine Gael*/Labour coalition (Cosgrave*)	50.7
July 1977	Fianna Fáil (Lynch)	56.8
Dec 1979	Fianna Fáil (Haughey)	56.8
June 1981	Fine Gael (FitzGerald) minority government	48.2
Mar 1982	Fianna Fáil (Haughey) minority government	48.8
Dec 1982	Fine Gael*/Labour coalition (FitzGerald*)	51.8
Mar 1987	Fianna Fáil (Haughey) minority government	48.8
July 1989	Fianna Fáil/PD coalition (Haughey)	50.0
Feb 1992	Fianna Fáil/PD coalition (Reynolds)	50.0
Jan 1993	Fianna Fáil/Labour coalition (Reynolds)	60.8
Dec 1994	Fine Gael*/Labour/Democratic Left (Rainbow) coalition (Bruton*)	50.6
June 1997	Fianna Fáil*/PD coalition (Ahern*) + support of 4 inds	48.8
June 2002	Fianna Fáil*/PD coalition (Ahern*) + support of 3 inds	53.6
June 2007	Fianna Fáil*/Green/PD coalition (Ahern*) + support of 3 inds	53.0
May 2008	Fianna Fáil*/Green/PD coalition (Cowen*) + support of 3 inds	53.0

* denotes coalition and party leader.

Source: adapted from Coakley and Gallagher, 2005: 475.

Table 6.2 *Surplus Vote Transfers to the Same Bloc, Northern Ireland Assembly Elections, 1998–2007 (% of Votes Available for Transfer)*

	1998 surplus staying within same bloc	2003 surplus staying within same bloc	2007 surplus staying within same bloc
DUP	97.8	93.1	94.3
UUP	90.5	91.2	n/a
SF	88.4	95.7	87.2
SDLP	95.1	92.4	92.9

Table 6.3 *Terminal Vote Transfers to 'Other Bloc' Parties, Northern Ireland Assembly Elections, 1998–2007 (% of Votes Available for Transfer)*

	1998 transfers	1998 available transfers	1998 (%)	2003 transfers	2003 available transfers	2003 (%)	2007 transfers	2007 Available transfers	2007 (%)
UUP-SDLP	0	0	–	4246	5931	40.9	1773	6734	26.3
UUP-SF	0	0	–	42	4466	0.9	191	5808	3.3
DUP-SDLP	397	4512	8.8	366	3126	11.7	0	0	–
DUP-SF	41	5512	0.7	0	91	0.0	–	–	–
SDLP-UUP	868	8600	10.1	429	1399	30.7	757	8345	9.1
SDLP-DUP	87	7006	1.2	8	1399	0.6	139	6345	2.2
SF-UUP	24	9291	0.3	54	5015	1.1	109	5886	1.9
SF-DUP	23	9291	0.2	7	3253	0.2	15	6286	0.2

and the price that would-be governments might be willing to pay for independent support.

PR-STV in Northern Ireland may be seen as reinforcing communalism, in that votes transfer within rather than beyond ethnic blocs. Surplus votes, as might be expected, overwhelmingly remain within the same bloc (Table 6.2). More strikingly, however, even when all candidates from the voter's ethnic bloc have been elected or eliminated, there is reluctance to transfer votes to the rival bloc (Table 6.3).

A sizeable minority of UUP and SDLP first preference voters are prepared to transfer across the divide when 'own side' options are exhausted. There are also terminal transfers to the centrist Alliance Party. In 2007, there were no terminal transfers available from Unionist parties for Alliance to collect, and only two such cases from nationalist parties. In those cases, Alliance accumulated 42 per cent of SDLP terminal transfers.

Intrabloc competition is thus what matters, at the expense of interbloc rivalry or the dissolution of the blocs; but to blame PR-STV for the perpetuation of sectarian electoral politics is to ignore the perpetuation of such divisions under exclusively single plurality systems from the late 1920s until the early 1970s. As an explicitly

Table 6.4   *Vote Transfers to and from Sinn Féin, Republic of Ireland General Election, 2007*

	Number of transfers	Possible such transfers	(%) of transfers
FF to SF	4604	65865	7.0
SF to FF	20777	79274	26.2
FG to SF	2294	29372	7.8
SF to FG	16688	77978	21.4
LAB to SF	645	5048	12.8
SF to LAB	14395	55062	26.1
GP to SF	3619	22635	16.0
SF to GP	5368	22084	24.3
PD to SF	143	5439	2.6
SF to PD	951	20364	4.7

sectarian-headcount construct, Northern Ireland is vulnerable to ethnic bloc politics which can, at best, only be mitigated, not ameliorated, by electoral design.

Moreover, PR-STV can be useful in facilitating the moderation of a party's stance. This has been most notable in the case of Sinn Féin, which, pre-peace process, found itself largely bereft of lower preference transfers from SDLP voters, but has since been rewarded for its movement from support for violence into constitutional politics, not only by increased first preference votes but also through becoming easily the most favoured second choice of SDLP first-preference voters (O'Leary, 2001; Murray and Tonge, 2005). In the Irish Republic, Sinn Féin is still seen as too extreme and suffers from a lack of reciprocity in terms of vote transfer. Sinn Féin voters transfer lower preference votes to other parties, but do not receive anywhere near the same percentages in return, as Table 6.4 indicates. In the largely sealed dual bloc system of Northern Ireland, strong antipathy from a sizeable section of the electorate can be ignored as irrelevant if outside the party's own bloc.

Reform Initiatives

Some 20 years after insisting on the insertion of the STV system of PR into the constitution, de Valera's enthusiasm for it began to wane. Although Fianna Fáil had been in power for 21 out of the 27 years since the enactment of the 1937 constitution, they had won an overall majority of seats only four times (Sinnott, 2005: 108). On the eve of his retirement, it seemed to de Valera that, without his leadership of the party, Fianna Fáil minority governments might prove much more common. In consequence, he proposed the abolition of PR altogether and its replacement by the plurality system. Arguing that PR led to a multiplicity of parties and, by extension, an increasing probability of electoral instability, de Valera suggested that the electorate would be better served by having a clear choice between two competing alternative governments. In this way, the decision on government formation would clearly rest with the people, as opposed to political negotiators of would-be coalition parties. Fine Gael and Labour – reasonably pointing out that it would perpetuate Fianna Fáil rule indefinitely and undermine parliamentary opposition – rallied against the proposal (FitzGerald, 1959). In June 1959, the ensuing constitutional referendum, proposing to replace proportional representation with the plurality system, was defeated by 51.8 per cent to 48.2 per cent (Sinnott, 2005: 108).

In addition to the parliamentary opposition, all of the national newspapers (except the Fianna Fáil-aligned *Irish Press*) were against the proposal, as were the Workers Union of Ireland, the Irish Congress of Trades Unions and Dublin Corporation (Sinnott, 1995: 222). Additionally, when a civic group, *Tuairim*, published a pamphlet on the pros and cons of the STV-PR system, they concluded that it should only be changed if a better alternative were put in its stead. The group proposed the establishment of an independent commission to look at the options. Even this 'objective' analysis seems to suggest that the Government's proposal was flawed. Still, the narrow margin of defeat for the proposal seems to have convinced Fianna Fáil that it was worth trying again.

Following the conclusion of the 1965 general election, which returned a second consecutive minority Fianna Fáil government, the then Taoiseach, Sean Lemass – perhaps mindful of the unpopularity of the plurality system of voting proposed in the previous referendum – argued that 'there are probably many methods of reducing the disadvantage of the present system of electing Dáil deputies other than those put forward in 1959, and there is an obligation on all of us to do some thinking about them' (O'Leary, 1979: 66, quoted in Sinnott, 1995: 223). Rising to the challenge, Garret FitzGerald published two newspaper articles arguing in favour of the alternative vote (*Irish Times*, 16 and 18 April 1965). During the same period, however, an all-party Committee of the Dáil, established to carry out a Constitutional Review, failed to reach agreement on what the best alternative to STV-PR might be. In partial consequence, when another Fianna Fáil government proposed a second constitutional referendum on the abolition of the STV system of PR in 1968, they used exactly the same format as 1959, suggesting its substitution by the plurality system.

A second proposition designed to ensure, as far as possible, that the ratio of population to members of the Dáil remained comparable in all constituencies was also added. Designed ostensibly to take cognizance of changing demographics, 'it did not go unnoticed that the areas that would benefit from such a change tended to be areas in which Fianna Fáil had widespread and stable support' (Sinnott, 1995: 224). This referendum, as with the one in 1959, marshalled much the same range of opposition forces, though in this instance the result was more decisive. From an overall turnout of 65.8 per cent, 39.2 per cent were in favour of the Government proposal, with 60.8 per cent against (ibid.). Instead of provoking more debate, the two referenda tended instead to copper-fasten the popular as well as constitutional legitimacy of the STV-PR system in the Republic. Electoral reform would not appear on the political agenda again for another three decades.

In 1996, the Constitutional Review Group (1996: 60) concluded that 'the present PR-STV system has had popular support and should not be changed without careful advance assessment of the possible effects'. It went on to note that 'if there were to be change, a list system of proportional representation or a dual system that combines proportional representation and non-proportional components would "satisfy" more of the relevant criteria than a move to a non-PR system' (ibid.). This type of method, sometimes referred to as the 'additional member system' (AMS) is currently used in Germany, Italy, New Zealand, Scotland and Wales. In this system, a proportion of seats (half in Germany, but more in other states) are filled using a simple plurality (first-past-the-post) system. The remainder of the seats are filled using the party list system, whereby parties compile lists of candidates, to place before voters. Voters then vote for parties, not individuals, using any method of PR. The key element in this system is that parties control the order of candidate prefer-ences, not voters. It is argued that, in this way, the system retains an element of indi-vidualized constituency representation (via the simple plurality vote), but also encourages voters to think of the election along national party-political lines.

In 1997, when the Fianna Fáil/PD coalition government appointed Noel Dempsey, a renowned advocate of electoral reform, as Minister for Environment, Heritage and Local Government (including responsibility for conduct of elections), it was inter-preted as a sign that Fianna Fáil were still interested in electoral reform (Sinnott, 2005: 121). It was not, however, until 2006 that the Minister moved on this issue and proposed reducing the number of TDs from 166 to 120 (*Irish Times*, 21 April 2006). The opposition dismissed his proposals 'as an exercise in kite-flying', and once more Fianna Fáil was accused of trying to 'rig the electoral system to its own advantage' (ibid.). The proposals, which came to nothing, failed to fire up a debate and only reinforced the view that the STV system of PR looks likely to remain the preferred electoral system for some time to come.

In Northern Ireland, there was one dalliance with an alternative electoral system. In 1996, the Northern Ireland Forum elections were designed to produce negotiating teams for peace talks. The British Government was anxious that as many parties as possible were represented at these talks, and it crafted an electoral system to achieve this. The 18 Westminster constituencies each returned five elected representatives, but using a party list system. In addition, the ten best performing parties across the entire region, in terms of percentage share of the vote, were each awarded two seats in the Forum. This 'top-up' method, although highly disproportionate and allowing parties with miniscule vote-shares to win seats, achieved its purpose of ensuring that fringe parties linked to Loyalist paramilitaries attained representation.

Apart from the 1996 one-off experiment, PR-STV is solidly embedded as Northern Ireland's main electoral system, for several reasons. Firstly, the need for coalitions produced by its proportional outcomes is hardly a problem in a polity in which coalitional power sharing is a statutory requirement. Majoritarian first-past-the-post systems have been proved palpably unsuitable for divided societies, such as Northern Ireland, where adequate minority representation is essential to the consen-sual functioning of the state. Secondly, the PR-STV system allows voters to express internal bloc preferences, with Sinn Féin voters, for example, reinforcing nationalist solidarity by transferring lower preferences to SDLP candidates. Thirdly, parties have become accustomed to operating PR-STV, allowing them to diminish the potentially destabilizing effects of a candidate-centred system. The risk of a region-wide party list system, as used as an add-on in the 1996 Forum elections, is that it encourages more parties to compete: better to have 'mavericks' within the main party tents (see McGarry and O'Leary, 2004) than party fragmentation and the risk of political insta-bility. The use of 'preference-spreading' among a party's candidates has become more marked in recent years (see Farrell *et al.*, 1996 for an overview of the differ-ences between 'spread-the-preferences' and 'plump-for-one' strategies). For example, Sinn Féin's Gerry Adams received 75 per cent of all votes cast in West Belfast in the 2005 Westminster single plurality election. In the 2007 Assembly election, however, Sinn Féin's workers toured the constituency urging first preference votes for differ-ent Sinn Féin candidates in certain areas, to ensure that Adams did not pile up a need-lessly high surplus. The outcome was that the highest percentage of first preferences received by a Sinn Féin candidate – Adams with 17.9 per cent – exceeded that of the 'least' popular Sinn Féin candidate by a mere 5.4 per cent. Moreover, only 1.5 per cent covered the difference in first preference votes between the other four Sinn Féin candidates, all of whom were elected.

Finally, in terms of legitimacy, PR-STV passes the 'understanding' test, in that only 1 per cent of non-voters claim their reason for not voting is that the 'voting system is too confusing' – a lowly twelfth place in the list of reasons for abstentions – with only 1.5 per cent of ballots spoiled under the system (Electoral Commission, 2004: 98). The main reasons for ballots being spoiled are first preferences for more than one candidate (43 per cent) or no first preference indicated (42 per cent) (ibid.). PR-STV also appears to pass the 'turnout test', in that electoral turnouts are fairly healthy for all electoral contests in Northern Ireland. Variation appears greater according to the institution under election rather than the system. The optimistic view is that 'multi-level voting raises the prospect of a sophisticated electorate making rational electoral choices and appreciating the variable geometry of modern government structures' (MacGinty, 2001: 3). This, more than the popularity and beguiling simplicity of single plurality, may explain why Westminster elections remain the most popular. Table 6.5 shows average turnout figures for region-wide elections since Sinn Féin's entry into the electoral arena in 1982, since when the 'big four' parties have contested all elections.

Table 6.5 *Average Election Turnout in Northern Ireland by Type of Contest and System, 1982–2007 (%)*

Election	Voting system	Number of contests	Average turnout (%)
Westminster	First-past-the-post	6	67.1
Assembly	PR-STV	4*	64.4
Council	PR-STV	6	59.0
European	PR-STV	5	55.7
Forum	PR-party list + top-up	1	64.7

* The 1982 Assembly election is included here; nationalists boycotted the institution, which was wound up in 1986.

The above assets notwithstanding, PR-STV has been criticized for reinforcing communal divisions (Wilford and Wilson, 2006). There are no inducements to parties to campaign across the sectarian divide, and the rigidity of interbloc division is such that intrabloc ethnic outbidding is the norm. The alternative vote, with single member constituencies, has been put forward as a better system in encouraging cross-ethnic appeals (Horowitz, 2001). Yet, the alternative vote would probably worsen matters. The system relies upon a party obtaining overall support (via first and second preferences; the preference system is limited to two choices) and exceeding 50 per cent to ensure its candidate is elected in a single member constituency. This threshold, much higher than that required under PR-STV, ought to encourage parties to seek support beyond their ethnic pool. This, however, would not happen, given the sectarian demography of the province. In West Belfast, for example, Sinn Féin would not need a single vote beyond its ethnic pool to take the seat under an alternative vote: the seat comprises 83 per cent Catholics. The same applies to the DUP in East Belfast: a seat in which 85 per cent of the population is Protestant, according to the 2001 census. Only four constituencies – Belfast North and South; Fermanagh; South Tyrone; and Upper Bann – appear sufficiently religiously mixed to encourage appeals beyond the divide; even here, however, a much more likely scenario is of intrabloc Unionist and nationalist transfers. The patchwork-quilt nature of these religiously mixed constituencies may contribute to strong sectarian animosities in working-class areas, making electoral thawing more unlikely than usual. Whilst Northern Ireland's politics may indeed be fractured, demands for electoral outreach by the bloc parties carry the somewhat elitist assumption that either the parties or electorate are innately sectarian. That voters might choose – on a voluntary basis – parties advocating Irish unity or Northern Ireland's place in the United Kingdom, as a central part of their agenda, is somehow seen as retarded and unwelcome.

One of the original Lijphartian requirements for the successful operation of consociational systems was strong bloc leadership to enable implementation of a deal (Lijphart, 1977). In this respect, PR-STV did not assist during the early post-GFA years, when a party list system might have assisted internal party management within the UUP. The candidate-oriented system proved troublesome for the UUP leader, David Trimble, as pro- and anti-Agreement candidates contested elections, with the latter tending to attract the votes of electors. The presence of such 'mavericks' was, however, less a condemnation of PR-STV than it was testimony to the anarchic structure of the UUP and the depth of tactical divisions within the party, which would not have been suppressed whatever electoral system was operationalized (Tonge and Evans, 2001; Walker, 2004). A closed party list would have the advantage of eliminating the 'alphabetical bias' under which a disproportiately high number of candidates with surnames beginning with a letter high in the alphabet are returned, as a consequence of voter response to ballot ordering. This has not, however, been an issue in Northern Ireland, and the party list system has little to commend it otherwise when compared to candidate-based PR-STV. This is not to claim that PR-STV is free of imperfections. Its claims to proportionality were undermined at the first post-GFA Assembly election, when the UUP obtained four more seats – and took the post of First Minister – despite being outpolled on first preference votes by the SDLP. A further enduring, if less important, criticism is the length of the count. In the 2003 Assembly election, for example, the average time for the count to be completed in a constituency was 18.2 hours.

Conclusion

It is certainly the case that the STV system of PR is capable of achieving a high degree of proportionality in electoral outcomes, which it is argued is 'virtually as high as that produced by electoral systems that have the achievement of proportionality as their sole aim' (Gallagher, 1996: 519). On the one hand, the high level of competition between candidates obliges them to set their record of achievements before the electorate and avoids the election of 'faceless' party members who are not known to voters. Moreover, the availability of more than one member per district allows voters a choice of representative: if they have a problem, there may be more than one representative to provide a solution. On the other hand, it is clear that the degree of proportionality varies between constituencies, and it is fair to say that the larger parties have tended to benefit more from this anomaly. Additionally, the intraparty competition created by multiseat constituencies may be divisive for parties, and the emphasis on local politics may come at the price of national policy and strategy.

Whatever the disadvantages of STV-PR, voters throughout Ireland appear to accept the system, if high turnout can be regarded as a major indicator of legitimacy. Certainly PR-STV contributes to the political character of politics in both polities. In the Irish Republic, it helps maintain significant elements of personalism and localism and sustains the pragmatic non-ideological basis of Irish party politics (Farrell, 1973: 218; Kissane, 2004: 16; Adshead, 2008), which it may be argued is becoming even more consensus driven since the late 1980s.

In the North, where coalition government is a statutory requirement, the proportional outcomes of PR-STV facilitate bloc representation in line with the electorate's wishes. The lack of lower preference transfers across the ethnic blocs means that PR-STV does very little to dismantle that divide, but it is doubtful whether any electoral system would improve the position. Intrabloc competition is what matters and the parties have become increasingly sophisticated in the management of voter preferences to prevent their most popular candidates accumulating over-large surpluses. In Northern Ireland, personalities are important, but party and, above all, ethnic bloc, are paramount.

As coalition politics has become the contemporary norm in the Irish Republic, it is clear that Irish voters do not elect governments: they elect local representatives (usually from national parties) who engage in negotiations for government. Whilst, in theory, effective government may have come at the price of democratic accountability, in practice it means that Irish voters are already well acquainted with the notion of elite level negotiation of government priorities and programmes. This, in addition to other 'corporatist leaning' tendencies in governance, such as the Labour Court, the National Economic and Social Council, the National Economic and Social Forum, the original vocational basis of the Seanad, and previous 'National Understandings' between government, trades unions and employer organizations in 1979 and 1981 (O'Donnell *et al.*, 2007), might help explain the particular receptiveness of the Irish polity to current Social Partnership arrangements (see Chapter 10). Ironically, then, the political behaviour generated by the STV system of PR, which is widely regarded as contributing to political instability, may play some part in the success of contemporary Irish 'government by partnership', which was widely credited for creating governmental stability and underpinning the 'Celtic tiger'.

7

Civil Society, Interest Groups and Pressure Politics

It is one of the more remarkable phenomena of recent years that right across Europe and in the wider global community there is a renewed interest in the question of the nature of civil society and its health.

(Dermot McCarthy, Address to Community
Workers' Cooperative Conference, 2006)

Introduction

As the evolution of modern welfare states increased the scope and depth of government activities, there was a consequent impact upon political behaviour. Citizens became more politicized and governments became more dependent on an array of groups for cooperation and compliance (Kavanagh *et al.*, 2006: 422). The study of groups and group behaviour became an important part of political science (Latham, 1952; Finer, 1958; Eckstein, 1963; Castles, 1967; Olson, 1971) and it was widely acknowledged that 'civil society' – that is the 'space' of organized activity that is not undertaken by either the Government or private business – is an important part of all healthy democracies (Putnam, 1993, 2000; Edwards, 2004). Although distinct definitions of civil society vary, they usually include formal and informal associations, such as philanthropic organizations; informal citizen groups and social movements; voluntary and community groups; trade unions; professional and business associations; faith-based organizations; and cooperatives and mutuals. Participation in or membership of such organizations is voluntary in nature. Taken together, these organizations are sometimes referred to as 'the third sector' (RIA, 2006; see also Acheson *et al.*, 2004).

In the Republic of Ireland, civic activism takes place via a wide range of organizations, covering every area of social, cultural and economic life. The subsector that has seen the greatest growth in recent years is that concerned with ethnic minorities, refugees and asylum seekers (Hughes *et al.*, 2007: 448) – a subgroup that itself makes up a significant proportion of volunteers across a range of voluntary groups (perhaps a partial result of the under-employment of some ethnic minorities and the non-eligibility for work of asylum seekers). Taking all voluntarist sectors together,

'Ireland shows higher levels of engagement in informal social networks and community activism than the UK, higher rates of involvement in membership organisations, and a greater confidence that ordinary people can make a difference to public decision making' (Hughes *et al.*, 2007: 440). That this level of voluntarism is clearly perceived to be a positive social resource is reflected in Taoiseach Bertie Ahern's references to social capital as 'a kind of glue that holds society together' and 'the exact opposite of social exclusion' (2003).

The Northern Ireland peace process was characterized by several developments within civil society. Firstly, there was increased contact between groups across the ethnic divide. Secondly, conflict transformation initiatives were developed at grassroots level, partly by former prisoners, but also embracing a wider range of actors (McAuley, 2008; Bloomer, 2008). Thirdly, some organizations which had developed within civil society on the republican side were co-opted by the state, blurring distinctions between the state and civil society (Bean, 2008). Although these three developments might be seen ameliorating the obvious fracture within civil society, there is a disjuncture between a consociational political framework which legitimizes a polity based upon the ready acceptance and endorsement of bipolar identity, culture and aspiration and the model of a united, single, civil society which a more integrationist approach might produce (Little, 2004). Whilst a plethora of grassroots organizations may exist, this may represent a society less civil than communal, one in which the articulation of the particular interests of a section of society dominate.

Classifying Interest Groups

Academic interest in pressure group activity and organization is long-standing, and though there have been a number of attempts to create a typology of groups, most draw attention to a central dichotomy between two main types of groups: first, those representing a shared or sectional interest, economic or otherwise; and, second, those formed on the basis of a shared attitude or cause. For the former, membership is limited to those who share that particular interest, and, for the latter, membership is usually open to anyone willing to support the issue in question. So, for example, in relation to healthcare, sectional interests may be represented by professional medical associations (such as the Irish Medical Association in the Irish Republic or the British Medical Association in Northern Ireland) and nursing unions (such as the Irish Nurses' Organisation in the Irish Republic and in Northern Ireland), but attitudinal or cause groups – such as the campaigns to save local hospitals, or to gain access to specialized services – may spring up over any health-related interest with a much more broad-ranging membership. In addition to this, more recent considerations of group activities in politics have pointed to the significant difference between 'insider' and 'outsider' status groups (Marsh and Rhodes, 1992; Grant, 2000; Richardson, 2000). Whilst insider groups enjoy legitimacy from government and are consulted on a regular basis, outsider groups do not have this consultative role with government (either because they do not wish or are not offered it). The insider/outsider status of some groups versus others is particularly important in the Republic of Ireland, where 'insider' status is most usually bequeathed to those participating in the national Social Partnership agreements and also alleged to accrue to some groups more than others (Adshead and Millar, 2008; Adshead and McInerney, 2008a, 2008b).

It is also possible to think of different groups according to the nature and duration of their particular activities as well as their organizational structure (Maguire, 1976). In relation to the former, it could be argued, for example, that the most appropriate ambition for any pressure group is to become redundant by achieving its objectives. In this sense, groups with relatively limited aims may be better placed than those with wider ambitions: it is often easier to retain an active membership when they perceive clear organizational targets that have a good chance of being met – in other words, when a group has an exclusive interest in a particular issue. By contrast, groups with broader and more long-standing organizational objectives, which may include service delivery, information and advocacy work, often run the risk of losing membership interest or public support and, in consequence, maintaining the membership (which has its own costs in terms of time, resources and efforts) becomes an important organizational goal in its own right. If this is the case, then pressure group politics may no longer be the exclusive activity of the association, but one of a number of broader organizational remits, as well as a range of initiatives to maintain membership. Where this is the case, it is possible to think of 'pressure group politics' as being only a partial concern, alongside other organizational objectives.

In terms of organizational structure, the difference between associational and institutional group organizations is that associational groups tend to operate with formal membership, organizational structures and functional specialization; whereas the institutional groups are often those formal or informal institutions of society, which on occasion act as pressure groups, such as the churches, educational institutions, trade unions and so on. In this respect, the existence of some groups is continuous, whereas for others it reflects an ad hoc decision to organize around a particular issue. Whereas it might be assumed that larger groups stand a better chance of making a political impact than smaller groups, this is not always the case since 'the larger groups, with membership numbers required for political impact, must devote much of their efforts to organisational maintenance' (Regan and Wilson, 1986: 409). It is with these considerations in mind, that we review the range of groups operating in Ireland at the moment.

Employers' Associations

Irish employers were traditionally represented by two national organizations, the Federation of Irish Employers (FIE) and the Confederation of Irish Industry (CII). Traditionally the two entities were distinguished by the CII's interest in 'business issues' versus the FIE's somewhat broader focus on industrial relations, pay and social policy. However, they had considerable overlap in membership and closely coordinated their activities. Their decision to merge organizations in 1992 arose from a joint recognition that 'because there were two business organisations [in the social partnership negotiations], neither was as strong as if there was one cohesive voice'.[1] It was also the view that 'if you had two organisations it was easier to play one off against the other'. Their amalgamation in 1993 to form the Irish Business and Employers' Confederation (IBEC) was a significant development as it meant that there was a now more unified 'voice' for business in social partnership. In the leadership's view, this has increased their capacity to formulate and pursue a longer-term, more strategically focused, business agenda. While IBEC is the dominant employers' association, and is the prime negotiating party in national wage agreements, other significant associations are the Chambers of Commerce of Ireland (CCI) and the Construction Industry Federation (CIF). Both are represented on the NESC. In relation to the latter, the long-standing importance of the construction industry to the Irish economy has accorded it a concomitant political significance. Figures from the Standards in Public Office Commission show that property developers and construction-related companies are the largest declared source of donations to Ireland's political parties and the main source of declared donations for Fianna Fáil (Hughes *et al.*, 2007: 399).

As elsewhere in the United Kingdom, the Confederation of British Industry (CBI) is the main employers' organization in Northern Ireland, the province representing one of the 13 regions covered by the organization. The CBI has been described as 'politically conservative' and it supported the restrictions upon trade union activity imposed by the Thatcher and Major Conservative governments during the 1980s and 1990s (Cradden and Erridge, 1990). Although strongly opposed to sectarian discrimination, regarding it as economically dysfunctional, the CBI in Northern Ireland has been critical of some fair employment legislation as unnecessarily burdensome upon businesses.

Trades Unions

In the Republic of Ireland, the Irish Congress of Trade Unions (ICTU) is the peak labour association, representing some 435,000 workers and accounting for approximately 90 per cent of all trade unionists in the country (O'Donnell *et al.*, 2007: 8). However, commentaries on Irish trade unionism tend always to refer to its fragmented base (Roche, 1992; O'Donnell *et al.*, 2007) which, according to Hardiman (1992: 342), 'meant that the capacity of the ICTU to articulate "class-wide" interests and to devise collective strategies was always limited'. In fact, there are only a small number of Irish trade unions affiliated to the Irish Labour party, and for the most part Irish trades unions 'have always attempted to maintain that independence' so that they might deal with any government or grouping, depending on the issue.[2] It is in this respect that commentators refer to the pragmatic attitude taken by Irish trade unions to politics and policy (Hardiman, 1992: 342; Cradden, 1999). It is perhaps because of this that despite its fragmented organizational structure, the Irish trade union movement has displayed a capacity to act in a concerted manner and to pursue policies that are in significant respects class oriented (O'Donnell *et al.*, 2007: 9). Similarly, while the ICTU's influence and authority within the labour movement has been enhanced during the period of social partnership, this reflects both its success at operating within the national political domain since 1987 and its moral authority premised on internal democratic mechanisms, rather than any formal centralization of decision-making power (ibid.).

Strong all-island trade union linkages have always existed, despite the political sensitivities involved. The ICTU operates on both sides of the border, with its Northern Ireland Committee (NIC) acting on behalf of trade unionists in the north. The NIC enjoys considerable autonomy from its parent organization, running a Belfast office and holding its own annual conference at which officials are elected. At 244,000, trade union membership amounts to 37 per cent of employees, 10 per cent higher than the UK average, a reflection partly of the large extent of public sector employment, which has greater union density, although overall only a minority of employers recognize trade unions (Black, 2004).

In attempting to represent both traditions in the North, the NIC has avoided taking overt stances on constitutional issues. Instead, Northern Ireland's trade unions have regularly embarked on anti-sectarian initiatives. Nonetheless, sharp internal divisions were also apparent during the conflict. The Loyalist Association of Workers (LAW), strong in Belfast shipyards during the 1970s, offered a strong base for working-class anti-republicanism during that time. The LAW claimed a membership of 100,000 at its peak (Elliott and Flackes, 1999) and mobilized workers against the IRA and in favour of tougher security policies. It was the fusion of Protestant labourism with paramilitarism, which defeated the 1974 Sunningdale power-sharing experiment, when LAW joined the Ulster Workers Council strike. Having overcome this period of division, the northern trade unions have played a significant role in straddling the bloc divide, although the movement faces the more universal problem of marginalization and irrelevance amid growing non-unionization.

Agricultural and Rural Interests

Since the state's foundation, the agricultural sector in Ireland has been accorded a special status, both for its own strategic importance and as a key industry for the promotion of economic growth. The long-standing significance attached to agriculture in the Republic, together with a relatively high proportion of the state's labour force employed in agriculture, might easily lead us to expect agricultural and rural associations to be deep-seated and powerful. In fact, however, the structure of the farming industry and the diversity of interests among farmers precluded them from becoming a significant political force until the 1960s (Adshead, 1996a: 590). From the mid-1960s, however, the National Farmers' Association, founded in 1955, emerged as the major umbrella organization. As well as a membership of some 150,000, the Association maintains a staff of 50 plus and, with the value of agriculture to the national economy set to double to €40billion by 2030 (*Irish Times*, 31 May 2008), it remains a significant sectoral interest. It owns an influential weekly newspaper, the *Farmers' Journal* (circulation 75,000), provides accountancy and taxation services, has a subsidiary company, Farm Business Development, and is engaged in other business activities such as insurance (Adshead, 1996a: 607). It also holds a Brussels office and a large headquarters and conference centre (The Irish

Farm Centre) in Dublin, making it one of the state's most effective pressure groups. Together with the Irish Creamery Milk Suppliers Association, founded in 1950, and the Irish Co-operative Organisation Society, which acts as the coordinating body of the agricultural cooperative movement in Ireland, these organizations comprise the 'inner circle' of agricultural interests enjoying good relations with government. To a large extent this is possible because of the European Union's primary responsibility for agricultural policy, which enables both Irish government representatives and agricultural interests to view Brussels-based policy negotiations as a more positive-sum arrangement than would be the case if agricultural policy were entirely made and funded at the domestic policy level (Scharpf, 1988).

In Northern Ireland, the Ulster Farmers' Union (UFU) enjoyed very close relations with the dominant UUP, to the extent that it was 'fostered as a means of extending the hegemonic party's control over as much of society and economy as possible' (Greer, 1994: 17). The replacement of Unionist government by direct rule ended the symbiotic government–union relationship, and the UFU, ignored by some nationalist farmers, went into decline, although its influence remains substantial (Greer, 1996). The UFU is more closely connected to the National Farmers' Unions in England, Scotland and Wales than to its counterparts in the Irish Republic (Hainsworth, 1990). In common with these NFUs, the UFU, after the introduction of direct rule, wielded considerable influence upon the Ministry of Agriculture, Food and Fisheries (MAFF), although the closeness of that relationship was lessening even prior to MAFF's move into the broader Department for Environment, Food and Rural Affairs in 2001. The UFU is systematically consulted by the Department of Agriculture and Rural Development (DARD) within the Northern Ireland Executive, and relations between ministry and union are cooperative. Within a year of the restoration of devolved government in 2007, the UFU had made 12 formal submissions on agricultural policy to DARD and UFU proposals – such as a voluntary ban on livestock imports from areas affected by blue tongue disease – were agenda-setting and welcomed by the Agriculture Minister.

Mutual Associations and Cooperatives

Established in 1960 as an all-Ireland body, the Irish League of Credit Unions (ILCU) is the leading trade and representative association for credit unions in Ireland, representing the interests of more than 500 of these, of which 104 are in Northern Ireland and 426 are in the Republic (O'Dwyer, 2006). Credit unions are principally community-based financial cooperatives, established by the communities they serve and operating on a not-for-profit basis. Any profits made are returned to members of the association or used for additional services to members and their communities (Briscoe and Ward, 2000). In this way, credit unions are a significant source of 'social finance', lending money to people already in debt or in poor financial circumstances to plan their way out of debt.

Credit unions and cooperatives came into being in response to the failure of the market to provide quality goods and services universally (Carnegie Trust, 2007: 11). Following the development of a British cooperative movement in the mid-nineteenth century, the Irish cooperative movement which emerged during the 1890s (Bolger,

1977; Tucker, 1983) was dedicated to establishing cooperative creameries; cooperative societies, which jointly bought agricultural necessities and sold their produce; and credit societies, providing small loans to farmers. A century later and the Republic's agricultural cooperatives catered for some 200,000 large and small scale farmer members in rural areas, with some half a million people involved in credit unions, so that by any yardstick cooperatives are an important feature of both rural and urban life in Ireland (Briscoe, 1982: 11). More recently, the development of new rural credit unions in the context of increasing service rationalization in rural areas has focused attention on their capacity to act as important drivers for local and community development initiatives (Byrne *et al.*, 2004; see also Lee, 2003). Still, whilst some of the more familiar (and often rural) cooperative organizations have been the subject of study (Devereux, 1993; O'Cearbhaill and Varley, 1996; Curtin and Varley, 2002; Powell and Geoghegan, 2004), the important contribution of others, such as the Community Workers Co-operative (CWC) and the Community Platform (set up in 1996 as a representative fora for 28 national networks and organizations engaged in combating poverty and social exclusion in the community, so that they might be better represented in social partnership negotiations) have been largely ignored by mainstream Irish academia, so that information on the political contribution and activities of cooperatives in Ireland is limited.

Although enjoying less penetration than in the Irish Republic, credit unions are more prominent in Northern Ireland than elsewhere in the United Kingdom, and they operate on a separate legislative framework. Of these unions, 72 have been created in the region since their inception in 1958, containing 336,000 members (Goth *et al.*, 2006). The greater salience of credit unions in Northern Ireland (one adult in every four is a member) owes much to their backing from a diverse range of organizations, from the Orange Order to the Catholic Church, although this diversity reflects a sectarian divide in terms of usage of certain unions. Regulated credit unions also formed an important community service during the conflict, when paramilitary groups tended to operate, on a much smaller scale, 'social finance' and mutuality schemes. Credit unions remain an important source of working-class borrowing and finance.

Faith-Based Organizations

Faith-based organizations have long played a key role in civil society: as both repositories and transmitters of social values, and also as organizations that are often embedded in communities that are otherwise hard to reach (Carnegie Trust, 2007: 9). It is in this context that the Republic of Ireland attracts attention 'simply because it has stayed so Catholic for so long' (Fahey, 1992: 246). In relation to the 'transmission of social values', the influence of the Catholic Church can be traced in the content of public policy on marriage, divorce, contraception, health services, and also in the degree to which the Church has been embedded in the system of social services that has developed in post-independence Ireland (Adshead *et al.*, 2008: 8–9). The distinctiveness of the Irish school system, for example, is not so much the denominational character of schools supported by the state but rather the denominational control exercised by the clergy and religious orders as opposed to lay representative bodies (Fahey, 1992: 252). In relation to health, Wren (2003: 124) notes that:

> During the 1990s, the Catholic Church sought: to prevent liberal legislation in areas affecting sexuality, despite concerns about the threat of AIDS and the consequences of unplanned pregnancies; to prevent abortion in any circumstances; and to influence legislation on bioethics.

It took three legislative attempts in the early 1990s before the sale of condoms ceased to be restricted, and, due to the dominance of Catholic voluntary hospitals (religious owned, but state funded) in Dublin throughout the 1980s and early 1990s, it remained more difficult to obtain female sterilizations in Dublin than in the regions, where major hospitals were publicly owned (Commission on the Status of Women, 1993: 345). Still, it was clear that by the 1990s governments no longer feared to challenge the Church, and the Church was more distracted with its own policy issues, such as clerical abuse and associated compensations to victims, to mount a concerted campaign against increasing liberalization (Wren, 2003: 124–36).

In relation to community and outreach work carried out by religious organizations, there is a long history of faith-based activities around issues of social justice in support organizations such as Cairde, Simon, Saint Vincent de Paul and others. However, in the Republic of Ireland context, the faith-based and Catholic organizations are largely synonymous. The significant contribution made by the Catholic religious to volunteerism and community development was more formally recognized by the creation of the Conference of Religions of Ireland (CORI). With a membership of over 80 religious congregations and a membership of some 10,000 men and women (www.cori.ei/aboutus), CORI has become a long-standing member of the Republic's social partnership arrangements, with a place on the council of the NESC and the NESF.

In Northern Ireland, approximately two-fifths of the population describe their participation in church activities as 'very' or 'quite' important (Heenan, 2004). Religious practice has a major role in community construction, with worshippers engaging in events which fuse religious approaches with social activity, such as choir practice, prayer groups, community politics, sporting contests, youth clubs and charity work (Mitchell, 2006). These events are common across faiths, although patterns differ according to whether the church is Protestant or Catholic. Churchgoing itself adopts the form of social ritual and opportunity for meeting, in addition to its religious importance (O'Connor, 1993).

With 40,000 members, the Protestant Orange Order remains one of the largest organizations in Northern Ireland (Jarman, 1997). Although lodges operate independently of local Protestant churches – they contain Protestants of different shades, including non-churchgoers – and attempt a multiplicity of functions, the Order remains anxious to stress its religious function (Storey, 2002; McAuley and Tonge, 2007; Tonge and McAuley, 2008). The Order continues to provide considerable social capital, particularly in rural areas.

Women's Groups

Women's groups and political activism have a long though largely unacknowledged history in Ireland. Some trace their origins to nationalist political activities in the pre-independence period. These include the Ladies Land League, a much more radical version of the (men's) Land League, which operated in its stead when Parnell and other leaders of the Land League were imprisoned; Inghinnidhe na hEireann (Daughters of Erin), a Gaelic revival association led by Maud Gonne as a consequence of her frustration that women were excluded from membership of contemporary nationalist associations; and Cumann na mBan, a support organization to the Irish Volunteers which, in addition to first aid, stretcher bearing and field signalling, provided a great deal of fund raising in support of the volunteers (Ward, 1983). Others operated during much the same period, but with more universalist concerns (Murphy, 1989). The Irish Women's Suffrage and Local Government Association, the Irish Catholic Women's Suffrage Association, the Irish Women's Franchaise League, the Church League for Women's Suffrage, the Irish Women's Reform League Movement, and the Irish Women's Suffrage Federation all sought votes for women – their attitude is summed up by Hanna Sheehy Skeffington:

> Home Rule or no Home Rule, Westminster or College Green, there is a new spirit abroad among women: whether the vote is reluctantly granted by a Liberal government or wrested from an Irish Parliament, to women in the end it matters but little.
>
> (*Irish Citizen*, 8 June 1912)

Following independence, as de Valera's vision of 'comely maidens' became encrypted into the 1937 constitution (see p.12), women's groups tended to clearly reflect these alternative political orientations. The development of organizations such as the Irish Country Women's Association, with over 1,000 locally based guilds providing educational, community and self-help groups, supported a more traditional, rural view of Irish women. However, the development of Irish feminist associations, such as the Irish Women's Liberation Movement (IWLM), were concerned with the establishment of women's rights, anti-discrimination measures and the equality of opportunity (Galligan, 1998: 51–60; Connolly, 2003: 111–29). Established in 1971 by a small group of professional politicians, writers, journalists and activists (Levine, 1985), the IWLM (in)famously campaigned for access to contraceptives (McCafferty, 1984) and later split into a series of issue-specific women's support organizations, including AIM (Action, Information, Motivation) – a campaign of law reform in a series of areas related to women (especially marital separation) – ADAPT – established as a support group for single parents – and Women's Aid – providing centres of refuge for battered wives.

In 1970, the Government appointed a Commission for the Status of Women designed 'to examine and report on the status of women in Irish society' (Commission on the Status of Women, 1972: 7). Following up on one of its recommendations, the Council for the Status of Women was established in 1972, changing its name to the National Women's Council of Ireland (NWCI) in 1995. With over 100 membership organizations, the NWCI quickly assumed an important representative role. However, it has had mixed relations with government. Although the organization is widely acknowledged for its success in representing women's interests and views to government (Galligan, 1998: 50), it has also been willing to withdraw from government circles in pursuit of its principles. In 2002, for example, the National Women's Council and the Community Platform (an umbrella group representing 28 community and voluntary organizations in social partnership negotiations) both publicly withdrew from the negotiations for the national partnership agreement, Sustaining Progress 2003–5, shortly before its conclusion, expressing concern that it did little to promote social inclusion and arguing that agreements made in the preceding programme remained to be implemented (CWC, 2003; NWCI, 2003). They subsequently rejoined the partnership process in 2006.

Women's groups in Northern Ireland have struggled to articulate their interests within a conservative political and social culture and amid underrepresentation in political institutions. A proliferation of women's groups occurred from the mid-1970s onwards to articulate women's interests, although such groups were themselves often divided on the national question (Connolly, 1999). The culture in which women's primary role was child-rearing is changing rapidly, evidenced by the 29 per cent rise in the number of economically active women from 1984 to 2002 and the large number of women's groups that have developed in association with gender, rights, quality and childcare issues (Fearon and Rebouche, 2006). With 35 per cent of nominations to statutory bodies coming from political parties, which remain male bastions at the levels of leadership and elected representatives (but not at ordinary membership level), it is unsurprising that the presence of women remains low within the polity (Ward, 2006, 2007). The problem has been exacerbated by the concentration upon equalization in terms of the Unionist–nationalist divide, rather than gender imbalance.

Since the GFA, state recognition of women's groups situated in civil society has improved, notwithstanding the political demise of the Women's Coalition after the failure of its two Assembly representatives to be re-elected in 2003. The actions of the Women's Coalition, combined with other female MLAs, ensured that £1 million of emergency funding was provided for women's groups in financial trouble as devolved government went into temporary crisis in 2002 (Taillon and McCann, 2002; Ward, 2007). The number of women's groups is considerable; 383 were reported to be in existence in 2001, containing 6,000 members (Ward, 2007). The motivation for involvement for many women is a 'frustration with the deadlocked and blinkered approach of "big P" politics' (Ward, 2006). The Civic Forum established under the GFA offered a bridge between women's groups and formal institutional representation, with 38 per cent of the initial members of the Forum being women, drawn mainly from the voluntary and community sectors (Fearon and Rebouche, 2006). Overall, women's groups have been moderately successful in their ability to transcend ethno-sectarian division (Coulter, 1999a,b).

The Community and Voluntary Sectors

Although often considered together, in recent years the distinction between the community sector on the one hand and the voluntary sector on the other has been made more concrete by changes in the nature of voluntary action (Daly, 2007: 3). Where once voluntary action was primarily conceived as charitable work associated with traditional, largely religious and service-providing organizations, the emphasis has now shifted towards an increasing emphasis on community empowerment and rights (Donoghue, 1998: 4). This shift, which has gained broad acceptance in policy circles, is reflected in contemporary notions of the voluntary sector – as being more service-oriented, forming part of the non-profit sector that is often viewed as part of the 'shadow state' (Donoghue *et al.*, 1999; Deakin, 2001) – and the community sector – as being much more clearly focused on local development, empowerment and attempts to foster social inclusion (Lee, 2003).

Notwithstanding government attempts to recognize this diversity (DSCFA, 2000), it has proven problematic and has effectively acted as a considerable constraint on the capacity of the community and voluntary sector *as a whole* to influence government. This is particularly so in relation to the incorporation of the community and voluntary sectors (since 1996) into national social partnership agreements. Superficially, the community and voluntary pillar looks much the same as the trade union pillar, comprising a cluster of representative groups bound together by common interest in social inclusion in what appears to be much the same way that the trade union pillar comprises a cluster of representative groups bound together by a common interest in improved pay and conditions (Adshead, 2006). In practice, however, with a larger, more unwieldy membership comprising radically diversified interests, the community and voluntary pillar's inclusion presented a challenge to established arrangements (Murphy, 2002; Meade, 2005). As Adshead and McInerney (2008b) note:

> Compared to the other social partners, the composition of the community and voluntary sector remains expansive, fluid and diverse – a feature that prevents it from coalescing easily with the other social partners, or even within its own ranks. In consequence, the sector as a whole is unable to act strategically. This inability to prioritise action areas often means that in practical terms, the sector is failing to realise its collective representative weight.

In Northern Ireland, since the arrival of devolved power-sharing, the concept of the polity as a pluralist, pressure group democracy has, for the first time, gained credence, but the rise of voluntary associations and pressure groups, numerically at least, preceded devolution. By 2000 there were over 5,000 voluntary organizations appearing on the Northern Ireland Council for Voluntary Action database, compared to only 500 in 1975 (Birrell and Murie, 1980; Knox, 2001; Morison, 2006). The financial turnover of these groups is considerable, reaching nearly £700million by 2001 (Cochrane, 2006).

Civil society was expanding during the conflict, but its existence was at times in nationalist areas a part of an 'anti-state', in which communities organized on semi-autonomous lines. The failure of national representative institutions and the weaknesses of local authorities created space for community self-help. Non-governmental organizations have proliferated, and although they have often developed as another means of community 'defence', modern funding regulations often require them to cooperate with equivalents across the sectarian divide.

State–Civil Society Relations

In the Republic, although the early years of the Irish state witnessed the growth of a proliferation of community and voluntary organizations (Acheson *et al.*, 2005), resources for social policy were limited, and expectations of government support for social action were low during this period with no natural channel for the organization of state support (Harvey, 2008: 3). More recently, attention to the relationship between the state and civil society has increased, particularly in terms of recognizing the important role that civil society plays in promoting a variety of state goals, such as local service delivery and community development, and the prevention of anti-social behaviour and attempts to foster social inclusion. It is in this context that the concept of 'social capital' has become increasingly significant and that 'civil society' has been recognized as an important source of social capital. Social capital 'consists of those features of social organisation – such as networks of secondary associations, high levels of inter-personal trust and norms of mutual aid and reciprocity – which act as resources for individuals and facilitate collective action' (Lochner *et al.*, 1999: 260). In both the Republic and Northern Ireland, a variety of state initiatives may be viewed as attempts by the state to acknowledge the importance of, and foster the growth of, social capital.

In the Republic, although commitments to develop a formal policy for voluntary and community activity were made in 1976, 1981 and 1990, it was not until 2000 that the government White Paper, *Supporting Voluntary Activity* (DSCFA, 2000), was produced. Welcomed by the community and voluntary sector as a whole, the Paper not only acknowledged and endorsed the important role played by the sector in relation to social policy but also confirmed their pivotal role in supporting and voicing social inclusion interests. In recognition of this, the White Paper proposed the creation of Voluntary Activity Units in every government department, the introduction of multi-annual funding and guidelines governing the relationship between funder and funded, as well as a significant injection of funds for national networks and federations, training and research (ibid.). In 1992, however, the re-election of the same coalition government (Fianna Fáil/PD) under a different leadership (Reynolds not Haughey) brought about a complete change of attitude. Indeed, 'although *Supporting Voluntary Activity* formally remained government policy, its key provisions were renounced, the funding scheme reduced (and in the case of research scrapped) and the independence of the sector sharply restricted' (Harvey, 2008: 6, see also 2003).

Although the reasons for this abrupt change of heart remain unclear, it is possible that as 'the growing interaction between the state and the voluntary sector has become increasingly formalised through the social partnership process at national level, and via area-based partnerships at the local level' (Hughes *et al.*, 2007: 440–1), governments may feel that they no longer need to cultivate their relations with the sector outside of social partnership. This is unfortunate. Although Social Partnership has received international recognition as 'a unique set of institutional innovations for creative, dynamic, and self-reflexive governance' (House and McGrath, 2004: 30; Sabel, 1996) and is strongly supported by the 'traditional social partners' (agricultural, business and trade union representatives), in practice, if not always in political rhetoric, the experience of the community and voluntary pillar has been much more uneven. Taken together, the variable organizational dynamics of different *community* and *voluntary* organizations (referred to above), plus the different attitudes and ideas that they may hold about the nature and process of pact agreements, leads to quite different participatory styles and approaches:

> For some, achieving the principle of participation was the outcome, which led to the view that it was paramount to stay participating, even if there were no tangible benefits. For others, more concerned with achieving practical outcomes, there was a greater inclination to come and go from the process – depending on the degree to which they felt it was worthwhile participating (I: 2) … The aims and ambitions of some members, such as CORI, are clearly more long term. They believed that by adopting a series of long term tactics, by way of target setting over a series of agreements, then they were beginning to develop a framework within which to work. (I: 5)[3]

The history of participation of other pillar members, such as the National Women's Council and the Community Platform, reveals quite a different attitude. Commenting on their participation in the Programme for Prosperity and Fairness 2000–2, one representative from this section argued that 'there was no real negotiation with the community and voluntary pillar, there was no opportunity to discuss policy outcomes, to discuss things that could actually deliver for people, so it was a sham'.[4] It was during this period that the relationship between government and organizations within the community and voluntary pillar became particularly strained (Hughes *et al.*, 2007: 447)

In 2002, the public withdrawal of 16 members of the community and voluntary pillar from the national agreement, Sustaining Progress 2003–5, resulted in these organizations losing their place in the partnership arrangements (the Government appointed other community representatives) as well as on a range of other national consultative fora and negotiating bodies (Acheson *et al.*, 2004). One of these organizations, the CWC, a national anti-poverty network, had its funding withdrawn, despite a range of evaluations attesting to its exceptional efficacy in addressing poverty and social exclusion (Hughes *et al.*, 2007: 448; see also *Irish Times*, 25 January 2005). The CWC chair concluded that

> The CWC is clearly being punished for its role in bringing the critical voice of disadvantaged communities together and allowing it to be heard. The right to have this independent voice and the role of the government in ensuring that such a voice exists is central to a healthy democracy. By making this decision this government is saying to disadvantaged communities throughout Ireland – 'we will support you as long as you do not question our policies'.
> (CWC, 2005)

Increasing state recognition of civil society actors and associated attempts to formalize state–civil society relations come at the price of complete organizational autonomy. The state currently provides around 60 per cent of funding to the non-profit sector, private donations comprise around 10 per cent, fees around 15 per cent and corporate donations a little under 1.5 per cent (Donoghue *et al.*, 2006: 47). Anecdotal suggestions that this level of dependency on state funding has led to a degree of 'self-censorship' in order not to jeopardize funding, or the state's regard more generally, seem borne out by the experience of those groups that have openly criticized state policies.

In Northern Ireland, for the first five decades of the state's existence, the UUP, operating as a movement, attempted to cater for sectional Unionist interests. There were few intermediate actors, as state and party had a symbiotic relationship. The pressure upon the UUP during the late 1960s came less from organized pressure groups and more from a broader social movement in the form of the civil rights campaign. With the advent of the Troubles, paramilitaries were seen as more import-ant than pressure groups for several decades. Nonetheless, pressure groups prolifer-ated and a variety of groups developed to exert pressure for continuing change, to monitor the extent of progress or to assist in the delivery of local services.

Northern Ireland civil society remains at the margins of influence upon decision-making, in terms of the national (Stormont) and local (council) arenas (Shirlow and Murtagh, 2006). Institutional recognition of the potential role of civil society arrived via the creation in the GFA of the Civic Forum, an idea promoted particularly strongly by the Women's Coalition during the GFA negotiations. Its 60 members are drawn from a wide variety of interests. The Forum is a 'notable institution' for the breadth of its members (McEvoy, 2008). However, it has no legislative powers and has been criticized as a talking shop for the unelected and unelectable. The Forum is supposed to respond to government consultations, analyse social, cultural and economic issues and contribute ideas in terms of economic efficiency (McQuade and Fagan, 2002).

A review of the role of the Civic Forum was promised by the devolved adminis-tration, following the revival of devolution in 2007. The First and Deputy First Minister select the areas of civil society to be represented and also have six 'personal' appointments. Almost one-third (18) are drawn from the community and voluntary sectors. Business and trade union representatives enjoy equal representa-tion (seven each). The churches (five), culture (four), arts and sports (four), agricul-ture and fisheries (three), victims (two), community relations (two) and education (two) are also represented. The importance of the voluntary and community sectors was also acknowledged at the time of the GFA by the announcement of a compact between government and community, although the promise of 'real partnership' has yet to be fully realized (Department of Health and Social Security, 1998).

Post-conflict Northern Ireland has witnessed a rapprochement between those aspects of civil society which appeared in response to perceived national state failures. Perhaps the most striking example has been the state's willingness to harness commu-nity restorative justice programmes. These were developed by local communities, dominated by armed groups, as a non-violent alternative to paramilitary punishment beatings and shootings. Despite their non-violence, such schemes were nonetheless initially still community-based, but they have subsequently received state sanction, despite the involvement of large numbers of former members of paramilitary groups. Voluntary organizations and community groups, ranging from local welfare associations to former prisoners' groups, have received recognition and financing by the state, a process aided also by the EU's peace programmes, the latter often making cross-community contact a condition of funding.

Conclusion

The Republic's tradition of self-help 'evidenced in an active, large-scale and widespread voluntary sector and in large numbers of community development initiatives, local credit unions and co-operatives' (Adshead, 2002: 125–6) is a long-standing one. Still, it is argued that recent economic success has led to the rediscovery of civil society (Daly, 2007: 1). This is evidenced in government attempts to more formally structure the nature of government–society relations via the White Papers *Supporting Voluntary Activity* (DSCFA, 2000) and *Delivering Better Government* (Department of the Taoiseach, 1996); the incorporation of a community and voluntary pillar into national Social Partnership agreements; as well as the Taskforce on Active Citizenship (http://www.activecitizen.ie) and an associated interest in the introduction of citizenship studies at school level (Tormey, 2006).

Still, the multiple roles and expectations that are now held out for civil society actors and interest groups produce new tensions and dilemmas (Kenny, 2001). They must operate in an environment where the tensions between civil society advocacy work and service provision remain unresolved at the level of policy formulation or implementation. Moreover, the increasing administrative and bureaucratic burden of more formalized relations with government and social partnership takes away from time spent on the ground, either in social advocacy or delivering services. The consequent and inevitable 'professionalization' of civil society actors in a range of organizational contexts may itself begin to challenge the authenticity of representation, creating new tensions between paid workers and volunteers. Finally and perhaps most significantly, the tension between the desire for recognition from government and influence over policy versus organizational autonomy and independence suggests that in the Republic of Ireland, at least, increasing government recognition represents something of a 'poisoned chalice' to those without traditional clout and influence.

The nature and input of Northern Ireland's civil society has been conditioned by the political circumstances of the era, and different phases of this might be identified. From the 1920s until the 1970s, civil society was under-represented in terms of policy-making or delivery. The UUP purportedly embodied the interests of 'the people' and 'representation' was confined to select groups, most notably the Orange Order and groups essential to the economy, such as farmers' groups. Following this, direct rule from Westminster allowed civil society to develop in terms of action over the local delivery of state services determined elsewhere, but civil society was also severely fractured amid conflict. Nationalist civil society was constructed out of opposition to many national state activities and became partially an anti-state

communal self-help phenomenon. The current phase of improved political relationships and devolved government is witnessing the emergence of more universal
groups within civil society, although representational strength remains slight and
there persist two civil societies due to the acute ethno-religious divide. The ability of
civil society to yield groups which breach the sectarian divide is an indicator of
progress towards long-standing political stability (Wolff, 2002). Given existing religious and sporting distinctions, educational apartheid, partially separate media, low
rates of intercommunal activity and rare intermarriage, it would be unrealistic to
expect community-specific representation to rapidly evaporate. Nonetheless, growing
cooperation between groups in civil society across the divide, on the basis of mutual
support, is reducing the existing chasm.

8

Political Culture

Much of politics takes place in our heads: that is, it is shaped by our ideas, values and assumptions about how society should be organized, and our expectations, hopes and fears about government. At the end of the day, what we believe about the society in which we live may be more important than the reality of its power structure and the actual distribution of resources and opportunities within it.

(Heywood, 2002: 199)

Introduction

The idea that the political orientations, beliefs and values prevailing among a population constitute a crucial determinant of the type of political system by which that population is governed is not new. The view that the social organization of a population may predispose it to one view of government over another, and that en masse these beliefs render some political systems acceptable or legitimate, was first proposed by Aristotle (1984 [c. 350 BC]) in his treatment of Greek city states; later by Montesquieu (1949 [1748]), when he argued that the nation might operate as a tyranny, a monarchy or a republic, depending on the prevalence of servile, honest or egalitarian dispositions; and later still by Tocqueville (1947 [1856]), when he argued that democracy flourished in the United States because of the liberal, egalitarian and participatory orientations of the American people. Similarly, the belief that democracy thrives where the majority of the people share values and attitudes that support the operation of democracy has been put forward by a number of more contemporary authors such as Lasswell (1951), Lipset (1959), Almond and Verba (1963) and Eckstein (1966).

Following this chain of thought, Linz and Stepan's (1996: 7) comparative study of democratic transition and consolidation across southern Europe, South America and post-communist Europe suggested that 'consolidated democracies need to have in place five interacting arenas to reinforce one another in order for such consolidation to exist'. First, the conditions must exist for the development of a free and lively civil society whose primary influence is on the development of interests and values as the major generators of political society (Linz and Stepan, 1996: 14). Second, there must be a relatively autonomous and valued political society which supports 'those core

141

institutions of a democratic political society' (Linz and Stepan, 1996: 8). Third, there must be a rule of law to ensure legal guarantees for citizens' freedoms and independent associational life. Fourth, there must be a state bureaucracy in order that a democratic government may be able 'to exercise effectively its claim to a monopoly of the legitimate use of force in the territory', provide basic services and collect appropriate taxes (Linz and Stepan, 1996: 11). Fifth, there must be an institutionalized economic society mediating between the state and the market via 'a set of socio-politically crafted and socio-politically accepted norms, institutions, and regulations' (ibid.). The remainder of this chapter gives consideration to these five arenas of democracy in relation to the Republic and Northern Ireland.

Political Culture and Civil Society

Until very recently, accounts of the political culture in the Republic of Ireland were prone to noting that the post-independence state was characterized by an unusually high degree of political and social conservatism, arising from the persistence of rural and peasant culture in Ireland, the relative failure of left politics, and Ireland's relative isolation from Continental European political movements and influences.

Without doubt, the preservation and maintenance of conservative values and attitudes in Ireland can be attributed to the predominance of 'rural culture' in Ireland. The outlook on life of the farming community, dubbed by Commins (1986: 52) as 'rural fundamentalism', nourished conservative and authoritarian values in Ireland. Deference – to males and the elderly, to the Church and the school system – was a marked feature of Irish society (Chubb, 1992: 17). Even now, despite increasing urbanization, it is still a misconception to assume that the values and attitudes of town people are very different to those from the country. At least half of the population of Dublin have moved from the country (many still travel 'home' at the weekends); and there is continuous movement from the countryside to the town. In some senses, to try and divide Irish people between urban and rural cultures is to miss the significance of the great number of those Irish people who are somewhere in-between (Chubb, 1992: 3–13). The conservative nature of Irish society was further reinforced geographically, by Ireland's peripheral existence at the edge of Europe (see Chapter 11); politically, by the relative failure of socialism to take off in Ireland (see Chapter 5); and last, but by no means least, socially, by the hegemonic influence of the Catholic Church.

Cut off from Continental influence, the Industrial Revolution and the plight of the urban working classes were entirely foreign to Irish society. Little interest was shown in the efforts of Continental social reformers, and in Ireland the phrase 'social question' meant for most people the rural problem and not the urban problem as it did elsewhere (MacMahon, 1981: 264). Prior to independence, the six northern counties comprised the industrial heartland of the country (O'Connor, 1992). Following partition, as few as 5 per cent of the population in the rest of Ireland was engaged in manufacturing (McLaughlin, 1993: 208). As a consequence, it was the economic interests of the conservative farming classes that initially took precedence in the new state and the labour movement failed to achieve a leading role (see pp. 97–100). In addition, the idea was promulgated that because British rule and the Protestant establishment had been overthrown, Ireland was somehow a classless society (McLaughlin, 1993: 209). The theme of Ireland as a classless society became a 'well-established social and political doctrine' (Farrell, 1970: 486). The fact that this is not true (see O'Leary, 1990) is less important than the fact that so many believed it to be true, and as a consequence in Ireland *social* class did not translate into class *politics* (Mair, 1992: 389). This attitude is borne out by 'the striking electoral debility of *class*-based, left-wing parties' in Ireland and the fact 'there is no other single country in western Europe that even approaches the weak position of the Irish left' (Mair, 1992: 384–5).

Whilst the overwhelming majority of Catholics in the state ensures that Catholicism is an integral part of Irish society, since the 1970s there has been a recognizable separation between Church and state. Developments towards the end of the 1960s marked the beginning of this transition. The process of *aggiornamento*, initiated by Pope John XXIII and the Second Vatican Council (1962–65), broached issues such as the liturgy, relations between the clergy and the laity, marriage, divorce, contraception, attitudes to other religions and the role of the state – issues that heretofore were 'beyond discussion' for many Irish. Although initially it failed to produce the intellectual ferment that was caused in other Catholic countries, by the late 1960s increasing numbers of younger clergy and a few seniors began to acknowledge that some change was inevitable. These developments within the Church coincided with other liberalizing trends outside of it and they began to challenge traditional conceptions of Irish Catholicism.

Social trends associated with demographic change and urbanization contributed both to the process of separation between Church and state and also to a reinvention of Irish identity – one where the influence of the Church is important, but no longer hegemonic. To date, the introduction of legislation dealing with availability of contraceptives, abortion information, the decriminalization of homosexuality and the relinquishing of the constitutional ban on divorce all attest to this view. This trend towards secularization in Irish society is reflected in the attitudes of the major political parties. The 1995 referendum on divorce was notable insofar as it heralded the emergence of an all-party consensus *in favour* of divorce (Adshead, 1996b: 140). Moreover, it also appears to be strongly reflected in the attitudes of ordinary Irish people.

The election of Mary Robinson as President of the Republic of Ireland in 1990 confirmed this view. Remarkable as a professional *woman* holding the highest office in the state, Robinson ascended to this height as a practising Catholic, married to a Protestant, with a CV which also included independent membership of the Seanad, a law professorship at Trinity College Dublin, and extensive experience as a practising constitutional lawyer. As well as taking a number of cases to advance women's rights, Mary Robinson was also involved in seeking to liberalize contraceptive laws, decriminalize homosexuality and she opposed the insertion of an anti-abortion clause into the constitution in 1983. She supported the unsuccessful attempt to remove the constitutional ban on divorce in 1986, as well as the successful action taken in 1995. Elected with 77 per cent of the vote, a level of support that she more than maintained throughout her presidential office, the widespread and enthusiastic support for Mary Robinson was widely associated with the creation of a new self-image in Ireland: that of a modernizing state, which is beginning to acknowledge diversity of tradition, religion and values across the island (Adshead, 1996b: 141).

Data from the 1999–2000 European Values Survey and the 2002 census showed that the Republic of Ireland is still predominantly Catholic, with 88 per cent of the population professing to be Roman Catholics, while the main Protestant churches (Church of Ireland, Presbyterian and Methodist) accounted for 3 per cent, leaving 9 per cent with no declared denominational affiliation (Fahey *et al.*, 2006: 35). Catholicism is still an important part of Irish identity, but it appears that its significance is in decline. In 1995 82 per cent of the population still attended Mass at least once a week (Sinnott, 1995: 9), a figure that has been consistently in decline since, falling below 60 per cent in 1999–2000 and down to 50 per cent in 2003 (Fahey *et al.*, 2006: 41). Moreover, still relatively high levels of formal religious practice do not necessarily translate into positive attitudes towards the Church. Across the island of Ireland, Catholics in the Republic stand out as having the lowest levels of confidence in their church (Fahey *et al.*, 2006: 47). Although decreasing confidence in the Catholic Church is often attributed to its involvement in a series of sex scandals during the 1990s, survey evidence suggests that in fact these events 'did not so much engender a radical new loss of confidence in the church as carry forward a downward momentum that had begun up to two decades earlier (Fahey *et al.*, 2006: 49). From this it seems that the significance of the Catholic Church in Ireland should no longer be confused with its influence. Irish Catholics have become more individualistic and diverse, whilst the younger and more educated, living in towns and cities, have become less willing to conform to traditional values.

In common with the Irish Republic and Western Europe more broadly, there has been a drift away from religious identification in Northern Ireland. The link between religion and political decision-making was less overt and the polity did not adopt bans, constitutional or otherwise, in areas such as divorce (where UK-wide laws were followed) or contraception. Nonetheless, the 'special position' of the Orange Order within the Ulster Unionist governing 'family', and the exclusion of Catholics from decision-making, ensured a political culture which was endowed with a sectarian flavour.

The shift away from religious identification has been slight and religion remains perhaps the most significant societal marker, one which dominates official discourse. In the 2001 census, 40.3 per cent of the population identified themselves as Catholics (although the census estimated the true figure as 43.8 per cent, due to the use of the 'community of origin' ascribing technique), whilst 45.6 per cent are labelled as Protestant, drawn mainly from the Presbyterian and Church of Ireland denominations. Of the respondents, 13.9 per cent replied 'none' to the religious identification question or declined to answer, an increase of 2.9 per cent on the 1991 figure. Only 0.3 per cent of the population are members of religions other than Protestantism and Catholicism, and the binary divide still dominates.

There is a high level of religious worship in Northern Ireland, with over half (51 per cent) attending church services at least twice per month (see the Northern Ireland

Life and Times Survey 2002 at www.ark.ac.uk/nilt). Boal *et al.*, (1996: 1) found among Catholics 'a very active churchgoing population, loyal to the sacraments, prayer and other devotional practices', although Heenan (2004) has found that a higher percentage of Protestants than Catholics felt churchgoing to be 'very' or 'quite' important. Attendance at Sunday Mass is a religious obligation for Catholics, and there is a strong Sabbatarian tradition among Protestants. Women are significantly more likely to attend church regularly than are men.

The high levels of religious identification and observation impact upon civil society. Most obviously it is fractured, with the division between the two main religions affecting various aspects of life. From the age of five most Catholics and Protestants are educated separately until they reach higher education. Whilst teenage years and adulthood may involve many shared experiences and social events across the divide, these are less common among working-class children, as they are more likely to live apart from the 'other' community. Some important cultural institutions in Northern Ireland society are associated exclusively with one section of the community. Although the Gaelic Athletic Association relaxed its prohibition on members of the British security forces joining at the end of the 1990s, Protestant membership is negligible, whilst the Orange Order, which fuses culture, religion and politics, prohibits its members from marrying Catholics. As Mitchell (2006: 140) argues, 'secularisation has not yet made a huge impact on current communal relations in Northern Ireland because most people have been socialised into some form of religious belief and activity'.

Legislation in Northern Ireland has also been affected by a conservative religious culture, although a combination of EU law, political pragmatism, secularism and demands from young people, in particular, have loosened the religiously oriented legislative framework. The lingering illustration of the exceptionalism of Northern Ireland, compared to elsewhere in the UK, is seen in its abortion law. The provisions of the 1967 Abortion Act legalizing abortion have not been extended to the region. In other respects, ranging from Sunday opening of leisure amenities and shops to gay civil partnerships, religious objections have been ignored.

Political Culture and Political Society

Essentially, the Irish model of government follows the British 'Westminster model' (reflected in Irish parliamentarianism and the organization of the civil service). Although de Valera's redrafting of the constitution in 1937 suffused the state with more US-style checks and balances (through the creation of the Office of the President and the requirement for popular consent to every constitutional amendment), it is the British influence that is most significant; directly in terms of the laws, offices, organization and attitudes to government, and indirectly in the 'backlash' against these influences epitomized in the state's attempt to reclaim its Irish identity (through the Gaelic revival, the 1937 constitution, detachment from the Commonwealth and ultimately the active pursuit of European integration).

According to Jacobsen (1994: 45; see also Fanning, 1986), 'although Irish scholars are correcting a traditional inclination to blame all woes on perfidious Albion, the impact of colonial domination – for better or worse – was powerful'. Despite evidence to the contrary, the more popular (or populist) view is that 'for Irish people, the significant context is their history of colonialism and the relative economic and political underdevelopment that existed from it' (Shirlow, 1995: 97). The argument, put forward most cogently by Crotty (1986: 16), is that, in common with 'all the countries of the underdeveloped Third World in the Caribbean, Latin America, Africa and Asia', Ireland was subject to 'an alien, individualistic, capitalist culture' that 'superimposed [itself] forcefully on an indigenous, collectivist, non-capitalist society of food producers', with the generalized consequence in every case of 'persistent underdevelopment'. Hindsight, of course, affords us all 20-20 vision and it is now easy to dismiss this view, but even before the 'Celtic Tiger' boom years, some of Crotty's contemporaries were unhappy with this analysis.

Internationally, cross-national research has confirmed the relation between colonial status in the British empire and later democratization (Bollen, 1979, 1983; Bollen and Jackman, 1985), whilst prominent Irish scholars have been quick to point to the 'often mentioned advantage of having taken over bodily the British legal system, the revenue and the general administrative apparatus, most of which organisations were staffed by native Irishmen and had been for a generation' (Garvin, 1996: 24). MacMahon (1981: 280) was perhaps too scathing when he suggested that 'the national pastime of attributing social and economic evils to English influence provided observers with an easy explanation and an excuse for not analysing the situation at a deeper level'; yet he had – albeit inadvertently – captured one of the more fundamental impacts of post-colonialism in Ireland, namely, the significant impact that post-colonial status had upon values and attitudes in post-independence Ireland (Fanon, 1963; Kirby, 1988).

In this respect, a much larger measure of agreement exists regarding the impact of colonialism. At the elite level, O'Connell and Rottman (1992: 231) argued that 'the most important part of the post-colonial legacy can be seen in the policy stance of the state itself. The Department of Finance, which, following the Treasury model inherited from the British administrative system played a dominant role in state policy formation for much of Ireland's post independence history, was opposed in principle to increases in state expenditure and taxes, and in particular to increased commitments to social welfare'. This view is reflected by Cousins (1997: 228) who argued that 'the development of the welfare state in Ireland was directly affected by colonial inheritances and institutional legacies, such as the imposition of early welfare measures by the United Kingdom parliament', which, though subsequently reformed in Britain, were never fully addressed after Irish independence (see Chapter 11). Thus it was that the natural social conservatism of Irish elites and policy-makers was augmented with a robust neo-classical economic orthodoxy inherited from the British.

As well as the direct legacies to Irish governmental attitudes and organization, the indirect impact of colonial ties with Britain are perhaps best seen in the state's various attempts at developing a national consciousness and identity that was distinctly Irish, the ultimate result being the development of *holistic* as opposed to *liberal* nationalism in the Republic – an unusual juxtaposition that is not normally found in democratic states. Whereas liberal nationalism is concerned with establishing national values and rights (usually in the context of values of tolerance and pluralism), holistic nationalism is usually based on an ethnic conception of the nation that stresses the conversion, or the expulsion, or possibly worse, of the 'other' in defence of a traditional conception of community (Mudde, 1996). The importance of nationalist mythologies in the creation (and recreation) of Irish identity has already been noted elsewhere (McBride, 1999; Whelan, 2001; Ni Eigearthaigh, 2007).

In this respect, Fanning (2002: 31) notes that throughout the nineteenth century profound shifts occurred within Irish nationalism whereby one hegemonic construction of Irishness, which emphasized the Irishness of the minority Protestant elite, was gradually displaced by a new Catholic 'Irish-Ireland' nationalist hegemony. The comparatively early development of mass political organizations in Ireland (Garvin, 1987) long preceded a belated industrialization and this fostered a religious–ethnic conceptualization of nation bound up with kinship ties and peasant tribalisms as opposed to one shaped by class politics and secular modernization (see also Hutchinson and Smith, 1992: 114). Coakley (1993a: 37) noted that 'while observers are agreed that Irish people by and large accept the principles of liberal democratic government, they have also pointed to certain features of Irish political culture that are of questionable compatibility with democracy'. The importance of authoritarianism, conformism, anti-intellectualism and loyalty has traditionally been identified as distinctive elements in Irish political culture (Chubb, 1970: 43–60; 1992: 3–20).

The contested perception of what constitutes liberal democracy in Northern Ireland has dogged the state from inception. The region has never enjoyed a normal functioning democracy, based upon the ideals of a system of government and opposition and rotation of power, and this void has not been rectified by the displacement of majoritarianism with coalition government. From the 1920s until the early 1970s, the prevailing political culture was one in which state institutions were held exclusively by the UUP, which claimed to embody the interests of 'the (Unionist) people'. Direct rule from Westminster ended that position, and devolution since 1998 has seen the creation of a new political culture based upon the concept of parity of esteem and representation for Unionists and nationalists.

Embryonic civic nationalism and Unionism have emerged, based upon a repudiation of historical communal excesses and a desire to work across the ethnic divide for the common good; but these new ideological constructions are fragile and tentative The desire of the immediate post-GFA First Minister, David Trimble, to create a 'pluralist parliament for a pluralist people', amounted to a clear eschewing of much of the ethnic partisanship which had passed for political life in Northern Ireland. The key tenets of the previous dispensation were a constant siege mentality among Unionists over the dissident minority in the province and an abject rejection of state institutions by nationalists. Two insecure communities did not cooperate and they looked to their parent nations to advance their communal cause (Boyce, 1990). Bereft of dialogue, the political culture was mutually exclusive, based upon the aspiration of a victory for British-Unionist nationalism over its rival. For many Unionists, nationalists amounted to the enemy within, a minority entirely disloyal to the state. For many nationalists, the northern state was a vestige of British colonialism, with

Unionists and Loyalists acting as neo-colonial settlers propped up by their British masters and subjugating an Irish minority regarded as an inferior people. Within this ethnic polity, class politics – or any other alternative identities – failed to develop.

Since the GFA, the political culture has changed towards one of mutual acceptance and inclusivity, displacing the previous characteristics of hostility and exclusion. Several sets of relationships which shape Northern Ireland's political culture have been improved. Intergovernmental relations between the British and Irish governments have improved markedly (O'Kane, 2007). Institutional cooperation between Unionists and nationalists has displaced much of the old internal enmity among political elites. At the local level mutual respect has been established between many former combatants through bridge-building work undertaken by grassroots conflict-resolution organizations (Cochrane, 2001; Shirlow and McEvoy, 2008). Civil society remains dysfunctional, evidenced by the extent of territorial separation of Protestant and Catholic working-class communities; but there is the prospect of the erosion of such physical division in the future. A common civil culture is being created around a shared, uncontroversial 'northern Irishness', although this may not dissipate the rival national allegiances and contested constitutional preferences retained by citizens.

Political Culture and the Rule of Law

Kissane (2002: 17) quotes the description by Kevin O'Higgins of the Provisional Government that took over from the British, when he suggested that it comprised:

> Simply eight young men in the City Hall ... standing amidst the ruins of one administration, with the foundations of another not yet laid, and with wild men screaming through the keyhole. No police force was functioning through the country, no system of justice was operating, the wheels of administration hung idle, battered out of recognition by rival jurisdictions'.

The Provisional Government quickly set about establishing a new judicial system and police force and began to tackle state revenue, customs and excise systems (Garvin, 1996: 92–3). Notwithstanding the obvious challenges to government presented by civil war and the conviction by a substantial minority of the state's illegitimacy, the real problem for the nascent state was the 'increasing uncontrollability of the IRA during late 1921 and early 1922' (Garvin, 1996: 55). The Government response was swift and determined yet, as Garvin (1996: 102) noted, contemporaneous accounts indicate that the 'silent majority' supported the state's efforts in the imposition of law and order. An eye-witness account from the *Irish Times* of the siege of Four Courts in July 1922 claimed that 'for the first time in our history a Government using force to put down an insurrection has had the overwhelming support of the common people' (ibid.). The tendency to characterize Irish political culture as authoritarian during that time (Garvin, 1996: 179; Kissane, 2002: 25) and since (Lee, 1989: 659; Chubb, 1992: 17; Coakley, 2005a: 39) is marked.

If the early years of the state were marked by authoritarian attitudes and measures designed to combat terrorism, the IRA's killing of the British Ambassador,

Christopher Ewart Biggs, in July 1976, proved the catalyst for even tougher measures (ICCL, 2006b: 11). Recalled for an emergency sitting, the Dáil voted in favour of a substantial increase in the powers of the state, in its anti-subversive struggle, with the introduction of the Emergency Powers Act, which provided for seven-day detention without charges (ibid.). Since that time, the state has been equally willing to consider other strong measures against crime and subversive activity, without encountering any great public controversy.

Though the act was not renewed the following year, in 1995, following a number of gangland killings that ended ultimately with the murder of crime journalist Veronica Guerin, the seven-day detention legislation was reintroduced. In 1996, a referendum proposal to permit the refusal of a right to bail on the advice of the Garda was passed by 78.2 per cent (Coakley and Gallagher, 2005: 471). In 2001, legislation enabling the state to seize all proceeds of crime, even if this meant that property owners might suffer without criminal proceedings or prosecution (and by extension, without being afforded the presumption of innocence and the right to a trial by jury), was challenged in the Supreme Court and upheld (see p. 79). Subsequently, the Criminal Justice Bill, 2007 included proposals to restrict the right to silence as well as broadening out the categories of offences in relation to which suspects may be held in Garda custody for up to seven days (*Irish Independent*, 14 March 2007). Other innovations in the Bill included granting judges the authority to impose electronic monitoring as a condition of bail and to issue 'post-release crime prevention orders' (similar to the ASBO or anti-social behaviour orders in Britain).

As a consequence of these developments and others, in 2007 a published posthumous letter from Mr Justice Sean O'Leary sought to draw attention to 'a harsh, populist approach to those persons who stand accused of socially unacceptable crimes', and suggested that recent developments pointed to 'a failure by the courts, up to and including in particular the Supreme Court, to vindicate the legal rights of the morally undesirable or socially unacceptable' (*Irish Times*, 3 January 2007). In a political culture so clearly circumscribed by Catholic traditionalism and holistic nationalism (as detailed above), ideas about what is or who is 'socially unacceptable' may be uncomfortably broad.

Despite a raft of legislation dealing with marital breakdown, divorce (and by extension the right to remarry) was not available in the Republic until 1995. Until the late 1980s, on paper at least, the Republic 'easily had the worst legal regime for lesbians and gay men in Western Europe' (ICCL, 2006b: 19). There was no recognition or protection of any sort and gay men faced a total ban on any type of sexual activity. In 1988, a landmark judgement by the European Court of Human Rights, in the case of *Norris* v. *Ireland*, held that sexual privacy and intimate association were fundamental human rights, leading ultimately to the decriminalization of homosexual acts in 1993 and a recognizable shift in public policy embodied in the Prohibition of Incitement to Hatred Act, 1989, the Employment Equality Act, 1998, the Equal Status Act, 2000 and the Equality Act, 2004.

The Prohibition of Incitement to Hatred Act, 1989 makes it an offence to incite hatred against any group of persons in the state or elsewhere on account of their race, colour, nationality, religion, ethnic or national origins, or membership of the Traveller community. Though the act has resulted in very few convictions, leading to concerns about its effectiveness, it is hard to draw any firm conclusions as there is a lack of accurate data (Ní Shé *et al.*, 2007: 49; see also NCCRI, 2001). The Employment Equality Act, 1998 and the Equal Status Act, 2000 provide for a range of protections that prohibit discrimination in the workplace, and in the provision of goods and services, on nine grounds. These grounds are gender, marital status, family status, sexual orientation, religion, age, disability, race and membership of the Traveller community.

In relation to government services, however, only some services are explicitly recognized under the Equal Status Act (such as education), whereas others, such as the Garda, have been excluded. Moreover, those areas covered by the act may have significant exemptions. In the case of education, for example, schools are allowed to refuse admission to those of alternative religion in order to maintain the 'religious ethos' of the school (Equal Status Act, section 7(3)9(c)). This has led to allegations of racist behaviour in some areas of high immigrant population where large numbers of black children have been excluded (*Irish Times*, 15 April 2008). In order to ensure the implementation of these protections and provide easy access to redress in cases of discrimination or victimization, the equality legislation also provided for the establishment of the Equality Authority and the Equality Tribunal (see www.equalitytribunal.ie).

The 2004 Equality Act gave effect to more recent developments at the European Union level in the area of equality protection, including the Race Directive (2000/43/EC), the Framework Employment Directive (2000/78/EC) and the Gender Employment Equality Directive (2002/73/EC), as well as tidying up and improving its implementation by transferring the jurisdiction in discriminatory dismissal cases from the Labour Court to the Equality Tribunal. This provides additional cohesion in the hearing of claims for redress under the 1998 Employment Equality Act (Ní Shé *et al.*, 2007: 49). These legislative developments, together with the creation of the Irish Human Rights Commission in 2001 (as one of the conditions of the Belfast Agreement) and an independent Garda Siochana Ombudsman Commission in 2004, make it plausible to argue that in the Republic government attitudes towards the protection of human rights have become robust.

Establishing the rule of law has been exceptionally difficult in Northern Ireland, where the legal and policing systems were rejected for decades by nationalists as simply an extension of Unionist political control, with the dominant community policing the other (McGarry and O'Leary, 1999). According to one critic of the former police force, the Royal Ulster Constabulary (RUC), it was the autonomy granted to the police force by the Unionist Government and the police service's lack of accountability that were the real problems, with the police believing they could 'act with impunity' (Smyth, 1999: 119). The legislative apparatus designed to combat violence was considerable, even during peaceful periods. The Special Powers Act survived in various forms from the 1920s until the 1970s, replaced by the Emergency Provisions Act in 1973. The state's response to the most concerted campaign of violence in Western Europe since World War II was to regularly breach human rights. Such infringements included detention without trial; abolition of trial by jury; police harassment; collusion with Loyalist paramilitaries; the use of dubious 'supergrass' trials; intimidation of lawyer and partial abolition of the right to silence for defendants (Hillyard, 1997).

During the conflict, substates existed, as paramilitary control of working-class areas was rife, justified by such groups as a form of communal 'defence', even if such claims were grandiose. Although the IRA's direct control of 'no-go' areas was ended by the British Government's Operation Motorman in 1972, the organization dominated its areas of core support until its standing down in 2005. The UDA was formed as an amalgamation of existing community 'defence' organizations and controlled many working-class Protestant areas, whilst the Ulster Volunteer Force, although smaller and much less visible, did likewise in similar areas not controlled by the UDA (McAuley, 2004; McDonald and Cusack, 2005; Wood, 2006; Spencer, 2008). Within these states within a state, it was paramilitary groups, rather than the RUC, whose writ held sway, responsible for thousands of punishment attacks on those they deemed guilty of wrongdoing.

The changes to policing wrought by the Patten Commission Report (1999) were allied to a broader downgrading of security, as the British Army's 37-year Operation Banner ended and troop numbers were reduced to 5,000. The advent of 50:50 Catholic and non-Catholic recruitment to the police force, its renaming as the Police Service of Northern Ireland (PSNI) and the promise of a new type of policing, less political with a new culture and ethos, all contributed to the decision of Sinn Féin to back state policing from January 2007. Given the previous republican rejection of a Six County Police Force, the decision was seismic, contributing greatly to a normalized Northern Ireland as paramilitarism finally receded. In the years immediately prior to the endorsement of the PSNI, there had been 'transitional arrangements' in which republican paramilitaries had established quasi-legal forms of community restorative justice which removed the violent previous treatment of offenders (Jarman, 2008). Republican support for policing did not, however, greatly alter the legal framework. The provisions of the 1973 Emergency Provisions Act were updated in UK-wide Terrorism Acts almost three decades later.

Political Culture and State Apparatus

In 1996, Doyle (1996–7: 64) suggested that 'control of official information is still seen by government and senior civil servants as essential to the proper functioning of government'; and there is still much evidence to sustain this view of contemporary politics in the Republic. Following independence, the Civil War divisions, the Second World War Emergency Censorship Act, the Broadcasting Act (1960, section 31) and the outbreak of the Troubles all conspired to ensure the Irish state remained centralized and secretive (Felle and Adshead, 2009). In 1932, the Department of the President of the Executive Council laid down that 'cabinet documents not likely to be required again can be burned ... personally by the private secretary [to the minister]' (Farrell, 1993a: 97). This approach was further enshrined with the 1963 Official Secrets Act, prohibiting the release of all 'official' information unless explicitly permitted (Doyle, 1996–7: 65). This attitude was further exemplified in 1991 when a senior civil servant in the Department of the Taoiseach petitioned the Supreme Court to prevent disclosure of civil service files on the grounds that the maintenance of secrecy was 'in the interests of good government and the efficient running of the public service' (ibid.). Although the petition was lost, for much of government administration the attitude prevails.

In 1997, following increasing pressure for explanations of government decisions that were based on policy 'guide-lines and circulars that were not made public' (Ellis, 1994), and in the wake of controversy over the Beef Tribunal and associated efforts to extract information from government (see p. 39 and pp. 79–81), a political consensus emerged, spearheaded by the Labour Party, on the need for freedom of information legislation. Following the collapse of the Fianna Fáil/Labour coalition Government committed to freedom-of-information legislation, John Bruton, leader of Fine Gael and the incoming Rainbow Coalition between Fine Gael, Labour and the Democratic Left, famously announced that he was 'going to open up the shutters' and that his government would be 'government through a pane of glass' (Felle and Adshead, 2009). The 1997 Freedom of Information (FOI) Act, led by junior Labour Minister Eithne Fitzgerald, covered all government departments, state organizations, universities, hospitals, agencies and local government institutions. Instead of a government presumption of secrecy, the act was intended to allow for access to all government documents, with a few exceptions for commercially sensitive material, documents relating to criminal cases, security and defence, issues concerning international relations of the state and cabinet documents.

Following its introduction some government departments – such as the departments of Defence; Finance; Enterprise, Trade and Employment; and Foreign Affairs – were extremely efficient and took to the 'spirit of the Act' in their approach (ibid.). Another extremely positive example is the Courts Service, which routinely does not even bother going through the motions of the FOI and releases documents directly on request to journalists. Similarly, after a couple of years of FOI requests, the Department of Finance decided to publish the entire Tax Strategy Group portfolio of documents after each annual budget, a measure that they also used in relation to decentralization (ibid.).

Other departments, such as Justice and Health, acted to the 'letter of the law' and were much more cautious about what they released. Commenting on his experience with the Department of Justice, one senior official suggested that 'the worst thing you can do is send an email to the Department of Justice. They don't want emails, they don't want letters, they want verbals, preferably on a park bench somewhere' (Felle and Adshead, 2009:13). In this respect there is a widespread view that the FOI may have engendered a new bureaucratic culture, but not necessarily a more open one. One senior political commentator observed that in his experience with freedom-of-information requests, one of the key problems lay with the use of 'Post-it' notes stuck to official records, but with no official status:

> I've got FOI requests back where you can see the little line of shade and you know there was a post-it there but you can't prove it nor can you say 'I've just received FOI documentation

that has been tampered with' which would be illegal, because all you've got is a photocopy but having absolutely no doubt whatsoever that it has been done.

(Felle and Adshead, 2009: 10)

In 2003, an amendment to the FOI was introduced by the Fianna Fáil/ PD coalition, which significantly broadened the interpretation of 'cabinet' within the act and thus removed FOI access to high-level government documents, including all correspondence between ministers. A parallel broadening of the scope of 'government' to include 'any meeting of civil servants, or non civil servants, about any government decision' was described as 'constitutionally dubious' by the former FOI Commissioner (Information Commissioner, 2005). This, together with an introduction of fees ranging from €15 for a request to €150 for an appeal to the Information Commissioner following the refusal of a request (even if the appeal was upheld), represented a significant rolling back of the alleged change of attitude in government.

Unaccustomed to power, Northern Ireland's politicians are still establishing appropriate modes of legislation, scrutiny and accountability within devolved institutions. The first local ministerial casualty of the need for transparency in political dealings, Ian Paisley junior, resigned his position in 2008, despite being cleared of wrongdoing by the Northern Ireland ombudsman. The ombudsman is the most important figure in terms of citizens' complaints of maladministration against government departments and local councils, with other ombudsmen existing for complaints against bodies such as the health service or for dealing with policing issues. Transparency of Executive business is also assisted by the FOI, introduced in 2000 and overseen by the Ministry of Justice in London, which permits citizens to request information on decisions, subject to certain exemptions. Across the UK, an average of 8,000 requests for information have been made per quarter: 4,000 to government bodies and 4,000 to other monitored bodies, of which 60 per cent elicited full disclosure. Requests to the Northern Ireland Office were substantially less likely to be rewarded with full disclosure, only 42 per cent of the 378 requests in 2006 and 2007 being fully granted. A major test for the devolved Executive is whether it can end the culture of non-accountability and secrecy long associated with the Northern Ireland Office under direct rule.

Political Culture and Economic Society

Whilst contemporary accounts of the Irish polity and economic society are often prone to bemoaning the advance of neo-liberalism at the cost of social solidarity and equity (Allen, 2000: 13–5; Kirby, 2002: 160–3; Connolly, 2007), these critiques are misguided on two counts. First, there is much to support the view that in the early years of the state Irish politicians and bureaucrats (especially in the Department of Finance) had a committed attachment to free market economics. Second, the state's latter-day development of 'social partnership' is more reflective of a move *away* from the British-style 'pendulum politics' of left versus right and *towards* the more Continental European model of social consensus and quasi-corporatist economic relations.

Characterizing the post-independence policy regime as essentially fiscal liberal, Kirby (2007: 2) notes that during this period 'the role of the state was to keep out of the way of private enterprise, and keep taxation as low as possible and therefore, at least in the short-term, social services as meagre as possible'. Certainly, Cumman na nGaedheal's attitudes to government were conservative (Lee, 1989: 127; Ferriter, 2004: 318). Notwithstanding the national developmental desires of Fianna Fáil and even the interventionist enthusiasms of Lemass, the early attitudes of Fianna Fáil throughout the 1930s, 1940s and 1950s were little different. Jacobsen (1994: 64) noted that:

> More characteristic of Fianna Fáil's attitudes and expressive of key interests in the party was Sean MacEntee's decree that it was only natural that a pool of unemployed people serve the whims of the marketplace, and that the state need only ensure 'the operation of the free play of forces' in the market.

The 'finance attitude' was, according to Lee (1989: 310–28), 'unrelievedly negative', and the ambition of senior civil servants there was to ensure that the state did not acquire interventionist capabilities, 'to protect private property and their own free-market orthodoxy from incursions' (Jacobsen, 1994: 61). This attitude was most strikingly borne out by the Department's 'principled objection to increases in state expenditure and taxes, and in particular to increased commitments to social expenditure' (O'Connell and Rottman, 1992: 231).

More recently, the move towards quasi-corporatist forms of economic management, with the advent of social partnership in the late 1980s, is alleged to reflect changing government approaches to both political and economic management of the state, which arise as a consequence of both the direct and indirect impact of EU membership (Adshead, 2005). It is argued that both the trade union movement and the business community greatly benefited from the stimulus provided by other European models of behaviour (J. Fitzgerald, 2000: 33) and that the successful growth of social partnership owes an intellectual debt to the experiences of countries such as the Netherlands and Germany, rather than to the more traditional channels of influence from the UK (Sexton and O'Connell, 1996). Although there is much debate about the precise characterization of Irish social partnership and the extent to which it may or may not represent a new mode of governance (Ó'Riáin, 2006), a review of the literature on social partnership seems to suggest that 'basically you can characterise the Irish state in any way that you want, so long as you include some reference to corporatism' (Adshead, 2006: 321).

Crucially, it is the advent of social partnership that probably marks the most significant cultural shift in terms of political management of economic society – for it is in this respect that the 'politics of partnership' have become side-lined from mainstream debates between Irish political parties and voters and shunted into a constantly evolving policy arena all of their own. To date, Ireland has experienced seven social pacts (see Chapter 10) and all of the main political parties have been involved at one stage or another of the partnership process. Pointing to the quasi-institutionalization of the partnership process, in a series of interviews with government, business and union representatives, all acknowledged 'the cultural shift' to partnership governance (O'Donnell *et al.*, 2007). When asked to characterize the precise terms of this shift and enunciate the conditions necessary for successful social pacts, the answers from government, employer and union officials were all but identical, illustrating a unique consensus about the terms and conditions for economic policy-making in the Irish state. In many respects, debates about economic management have become depoliticized, or at least divorced from association with any mainstream Irish political parties. Economic management, it seems, is now a technical activity that has become, if not completely depoliticized, at least separated from association with any mainstream Irish political parties. Whether in the longer term this is a positive or negative development, for either the economy or democracy, is as yet unclear.

Northern Ireland's dependency culture is, along with the sectarian divide, its biggest difficulty within a post-conflict polity. Having relied upon a combination of British, United States and EU financial aid, the region is obliged to confront its problems of a lack of productivity and excessive dependence upon the state sector. Northern Ireland's Unionist political leaders have urged the British Government to heed lessons from the Irish Republic in terms of the need to lower business taxes, but such pleas have been ignored, highlighting the impotence of local politicians in shaping fiscal policies. Economic management of Northern Ireland continues to lie mainly in London, and the Northern Ireland Executive has insufficient resources or responsibilities to alter its unfavourable private sector–public sector mix or to reorientate the labour market. Northern Ireland's working-age employment rate remains the lowest of all the UK regions (DETI, 2008). The Labour governments under Tony Blair from 1997 until 2007 presided over the most benign period of industrial relations in UK history, not due to any formal social partnership, but instead as a consequence of continuous economic growth, previous legislative restrictions imposed upon trade unions, diminished union membership and the changing nature of work. In Northern Ireland, the average number of working days lost through strikes among employees became the highest in the UK by 2004. Public sector disputes have become more common across the UK than within the private sector and the skewed balance of Northern Ireland's workforce means that the province has become more vulnerable to disputes. Between 2004 and 2007 alone, there were strikes involving civil servants, classroom assistants and further education lecturers.

Conclusion

Garvin (1991: 42) suggested that in the Republic, Irish democracy was the product of two 'strange foster parents' competing from the start 'with the overwhelming might of the centralised British imperial state and, more subtly, with the rival authority system of the Catholic Church'. The consequence, he argued, is both a pervasive populism, reflected in a political system where political leaders and the general public are unusually vulnerable to each other's influence – and a weakness of secular political institutions. With regard to the former, he concludes that the 'the populist syndrome of mutual availability of elites and masses to each other has gradually eroded the autonomy of many Irish social institutions and prevented the application of rational criteria in policy-making' (Garvin, 1991: 53). The public assurance given to the Irish Farmers Association (IFA) by the Taoiseach, Brian Cowen, in June 2008 to veto any EU agreement to a World Trade Organization (WTO) deal (as it was then constructed) is a perfect illustration of this. The farming lobby had threatened to vote 'No' to the EU Lisbon Treaty if assurances were not given that the Government would safeguard their interests in the WTO negotiations. 'After hours of behind-the-scenes negotiations', which included a two-hour meeting between the Taoiseach and the IFA president, Pádraig Walshe, 'Mr Walshe said he was in no doubt that without the commitment from Mr Cowen, the executive would have recommended a No vote'. As a result of the successful negotiations, however, 'the IFA would be writing to all its members urging them and their families to come out and vote Yes' (*Irish Times*, 4 June 2008). That political support could be traded in such a way, over a referendum issue that – with the exception of Sinn Féin – held all-party agreement, suggests that the political culture in the Republic of Ireland is one where political principles may be discarded in favour of political consensus.

Northern Ireland retains two cultures, which arguably have been ossified by a GFA which acknowledges the bi-polarity of political, religious and cultural division, but which aspires to their placement in a non-hostile context. Its citizens have common patterns and equal status in terms of residence, work and leisure, but these are often conducted in separate spaces. The region shares the conservative inheritance of the state to the South, but has not been immune from the forces of secularism and liberalism. Greater liberalization and declining religious practice have not altered Northern Ireland's status as an ethnically divided polity. The most important components of ethnicity may be changing from religious-cultural to cultural-political, but Northern Ireland's societal divide remains.

Part 3

Public Policy

9

Territorial Administration and Subnational Government

The answer is not to go back to the old model of councils trying to plan and run most services. Instead councils should focus on their roles as leaders of local communities by developing a clear vision for their localities, organising and supporting partnerships and guaranteeing quality services for all.

(Tony Blair, 1998: 1)

Introduction

The Irish Republic and the UK are states where the institutions and organization of local government are not constitutionally protected. Central government plays the most significant role in determining the form and structure of local government, whose powers are limited to those defined by central government statute. In the Republic, central government approaches to subnational government have been characterized by pragmatism. This is reflected most recently in the government policies of regionalization and decentralization as well as much longer established expediencies, such as the institution of the managerial system for local government and a range of responses to localized problems, evidenced in the massive growth of state-sponsored bodies and different organizations and agencies created by central government. Despite the proliferation of regional agencies, plus a little tinkering with the organization of local government, there has been no substantive reform of subnational government. Instead an 'administrative jungle' has grown and thrived as a result of central government's relatively short-term approach to the organization of subnational government.

In contrast to Ireland, British central governments have shown a much greater enthusiasm for reform of subnational government, albeit equally short-term and non-strategic. The reorganization of British local governance throughout the 1980s has been variously characterized as 'an end in itself' (R. Leach, 1994: 345), or as a 'classic example of policy drift' (S. Leach, 1993, 1994a, 1994b), emerging 'as much through accident as by design – a by-product of the Thatcherite conflict with local government in the 1980s' (Williams, 1993: 96). In Northern Ireland, local government has undergone several revisions, and major reform has been on the political agenda in recent years.

Origins and Influences

When the Irish state was established, it inherited the British system of local government, which pre-dated the state's birth. Under local government reform acts, the
local franchise was extended to such an extent that local government soon became
the basis for a developing national struggle for independence.[1]

Between 1898 and independence, local government was dominated by national
political issues and movements. It is even argued that the Local Government of
Ireland Act of 1898 was – unintentionally – 'the legislative father of the Irish Free
State' (Horgan, 1926: 535). County councils in particular became centres of nationalism (Chubb, 1992: 269). This intermeshing of national politics with local politics
created the first instance of an unusual paradox in Irish subnational government – the
existence of strong local influence in a highly centralized state (Farrell, 1983a;
Komito, 1989, 1992a).

After independence, despite the drafting of an extremely prescriptive constitution
(see Farrell, 1988), no constitutional provision was made for local government. The
Irish state developed a highly centralized system of government not only because the
majority of its political institutions and administrative bureaucracy were inherited
from Britain – an unequivocally unitary state – but also because the manner in which
they were placed under Irish control was the ultimate act of political consolidation.
Barrington (1987: 136) argued that the state established in 1922 was consciously and
deliberately a centralized one:

> The revolutionary government that took over was determined to show itself fully in control
> of the system of government and to establish its willingness and capacity to rule, faced as
> it was with: a bitter civil war with former comrades; well developed public institutions fully
> staffed by public servants transferred from British rule whose loyalty to the new order they
> naturally, if wrongly, distrusted; a major post-war slump; the general consciousness of the
> smallness and poverty of the whole; a 'business-like' determination to keep things simple,
> solvent and, so far as possible, depoliticized.

The Irish government's desire for centralized power was, however, concerned less
with political principle and more with finding immediate and pragmatic solutions to
the problems of government in the aftermath of war. The preference for functional
efficiency, even at the expense of democratic accountability, is a trait that has characterized local government in Ireland since its foundation and which is, perhaps, best
exemplified by the 'managerial system' of local administration.

The basic principle of the managerial system is a 'legal dichotomy of reserved
powers of councils and executive functions of managers', each provided for by
central government legislation (Bromage, 1954: 93). The main functions reserved for
elected members include the adoption of the annual estimate of expenses; the fixing
of annual rates and amounts to be borrowed to meet these expenses; the making of
development plans and by-laws; house-building programmes; and assisting other
local bodies in providing services and amenities. These various functions can be
exercised only on the passing of a resolution. Executive functions, which are the
responsibility of the county/city manager, include arrangements made by the

manager in relation to staff; acceptance of tenders; making contracts; fixing rents; making lettings; and deciding on applications for planning permissions. Following the Local Government (Planning and Development) Act of 1963, the increasing emphasis on local development through planning, zoning, acquisition of land and site assemblage, and urban renewal initiatives, resulted in managers playing an ever larger role – often taking a leading part in the development of their areas (Bannon, 1991: 44; Chubb, 1992: 278).

City and county managers are appointed by the local authority on the recommendation of the Local Appointments Commission (a three-person body set up in 1926 to select and recommend to local authorities persons for appointment to principal offices). Though internal promotions to the post of manager are not permitted, nearly all managers have had previous service with local authorities and it is exceptional when a person outside the local authority service succeeds in being recommended by the commission (Dooney and O'Toole, 1992: 138–40). As permanent, professional and salaried officials, the manager and his or her staff are often in a stronger position to influence policy formulation and implementation when compared to the unpaid, part-time and perhaps transient elected councillors to whom they give their service.

Local government in Northern Ireland has had a chequered history. For over 50 years, local councils were associated with some of the worst instances of institutional sectarianism. Nationalist councils were far from innocent, but the greater number of councils under Unionist control ensured that local government was much more readily associated with Unionist malpractice. From the outset, local councils were used as either nationalist sites of resistance to the state, or as vehicles for Unionist consolidation of the spoils of partition. In order to extend local Unionist control, the Unionist government used the 1922 Local Government Ireland Act (Northern Ireland) to abolish PR in elections to local authorities. This move, combined with the gerrymandering of electoral boundaries undertaken by the Electoral Commission headed by Sir John Leech during the same year, ensured that Unionists would from hereon enjoy dominance of local councils beyond even their population 'entitlement'. To the injustices of gerrymandering could be added the imbalances caused by the 'ratepayer' qualification required to be a local elector. Those not owning their own homes were not entitled to vote in local elections, a restriction which disproportionately adversely affected Catholics, even though much of the Protestant working class was also disenfranchised. The outcome of these fixes and prohibitions was that, although amounting to only 66 per cent of the population, Unionists controlled 85 per cent of councils (Buckland, 1981). Major councils such as Omagh and Derry, with nationalist populations, became dominated by Unionists (Farrell, 1980).

The fear of Unionist intrabloc fragmentation provided one motivation for the abolition of PR. The perceived threat from the 21 nationalist councils refusing to recognize the state and attempting to secede from its jurisdiction provided the major 'justification' (Aughey, 1996). The fixing of electoral boundaries was then justified by the electoral commission on the grounds of the non-participation by nationalists in its deliberations. The abolition of PR at local level was followed by its scrapping for Stormont parliamentary elections in 1929. Unionist control of the parliamentary and local levels of the state was secure. Far from being seen as relatively neutral service-delivers, local councils were perceived as sectarian entities, with councillors deliberately favouring 'their' community. Undoubtedly the depth of discrimination in some fields was exaggerated (Whyte, 1983; Wilson, 1989). Housing allocations, for example, were, with some notable exceptions, not consistently made in favour of Protestants on Unionist councils. Equally, however, in terms of public appointments, councils operated in a nakedly sectarian manner. Measures to address inequities in terms of the franchise were introduced by Northern Ireland's Prime Minister, Terrence O'Neil, during the late 1960s, as pressure mounted from the growing civil rights campaigns. Nonetheless, it was only following the collapse of the Stormont Government in 1972, and the introduction of a plethora of fair employment measures under direct rule, that the sectarian allocations of local authorities began to evaporate.

Territorial Organization

For local government purposes the Irish state is divided into 29 county and five county borough (city) areas of equivalent status, each with a separate elected council. The five county borough corporations represent large urban populations (in Dublin, Cork, Waterford and Limerick) existing within their respective county boundaries. Below this tier of local government is a lower tier of representative authorities in the smaller urban areas of counties and county boroughs: there are five borough corporations, 49 urban district councils and 26 town commissioners (Government of Ireland, 1996a: 97). There were originally a set of rural district councils too, but these were abolished and their powers transferred to the county councils in the 1920s (Sinnott, 1995: 254).

Although the counties and county boroughs have equivalent legal status as the main units of local government in rural and urban areas respectively, some functions are carried out by county councils throughout the entire county, including the urban areas represented by county boroughs (these include motor taxation, library services, fire, building control, emergency planning, national and regional roads, and most aspects of pollution control). Similarly, at subcounty level some functions that are legally vested in urban authorities are exercised on their behalf by the county council as a consequence of local agreements (Government of Ireland, 1996a). Though the county is the most important unit of local government, its range of functions is limited, relating primarily to physical infrastructure and public recreation facilities (Sinnott, 1995: 255). These include the provision and organization of public housing, local road networks, water supply, waste management and sewerage, the maintenance of public amenities and a limited role in environmental protection. County councils also have some secondary functions in the areas of education, health and welfare, though in these areas they are subordinate to the specialized state-sponsored bodies responsible for each of these areas.

State-sponsored bodies are 'autonomous public bodies, other than universities, neither temporary in character nor purely advisory in function' (IPA, 1997: 128). There are five types of state-sponsored bodies: commercial, developmental, health, cultural and regulatory/advisory. The creation of numerous state-sponsored bodies and the transfer of functions to them that might otherwise be the responsibility of local government typifies Irish government attitudes to policy delivery, whereby practical problems are often solved at the expense of democratic accountability. In consequence, despite the lack of any formal institutional reorganization of subnational government, over time the need to develop policy delivery mechanisms led to the creation of several types of organization operating at subnational level (Chubb, 1992: 262).

On the one hand, there are a number of authorities responsible for the administration of some services, whose governing bodies consist both of members of the local authority and interested associations or groups in the region, such as the eight Area Health Boards, or the eight Regional Tourism Organizations. On the other hand, some central authorities have themselves decentralized their business to regional level for administrative, managerial or customer convenience. These include state-sponsored bodies such as the Electricity Supply Board, the Industrial Development Authority and certain government departments. The authorities with devolved powers and those with decentralized administrations all operate boundaries to suit themselves and so the regional areas thus far created do not coincide. Chubb (1992: 263) noted that since there is also an underlying network of local authorities, 'the result is a jungle of administrative areas that is both impenetrable to the ordinary citizen and frequently inconvenient for any kind of business that involves more than one authority or regional organization'.

By the early 1990s, there was a growing consensus that local government was ripe for reform (Adshead and Quinn, 1998). Typically, this view did not stem from any radical desire for change, but rather from a realistic appreciation that after years of ad hoc responses, the plethora of agencies operating at subnational level had become an 'administrative jungle' (Chubb, 1992: 263). Coupled with the acceptance of the need to improve subnational structures was an enormous increase in development activities at this level – exemplified by the variety of local activists from different organizational backgrounds – much of it driven by EU initiatives. Although these initiatives have varying aims and objectives, it is possible to identify common approaches. There has been an emphasis on the creation of partnerships that have fostered innovation, bringing together actors from statutory, voluntary, public and private sectors in a manner that has gained international recognition (Sabel, 1996).

New approaches to local development have resulted in local authorities acquiring new functions: instead of operating as administrative agents of central government, with responsibility for a limited number of services, they now act as central coordinators for the ever-widening arena of actors in subnational development. The 1994 Programme for Government stated that 'the local authority must become the focus for working through local partnerships involving local community-based groupings, voluntary bodies, the private sector, and public agencies' (Government of Ireland, 1994: 70). In this regard, the Operational Programme for Local Urban and Rural Development, 1994–99 supported this new view of local authorities and provided significant evidence of their taking a new approach to partnership initiatives at local level. These ambitions for increasing local partnership approaches to policy delivery were further developed with the creation of Strategic Policy Committees and County Development Boards as a consequence of reforms laid out in the Government White Paper *Better Local Government*. Without supporting institutional reorganization, it is not clear how permanent or meaningful these changes might be.

The most recent reform proposals, proposed by the Minister for the Environment, John Gormley, in April 2008, were designed to 'begin the process of reshaping local government in a way that will provide a greater role for local, democratic leadership' (Government of Ireland, 2008). The proposals – which included proposals for new ethics legislation for councillors, a cap on council election spending of €5,000 per candidate, a new system of funding for local government, plus a change in the role of county managers versus elected representatives and a mayor for Dublin city – were widely considered to be a triumph of style over substance. In the absence of significant financial reorganization (see the following section) it is hard to envisage how local government might effectively change its organizational and operational remit (*Irish Times*, 23 April 2008).

Northern Ireland remains overgoverned and, although the problem is less acute than it was in the first five decades of the state's existence, it is apparent that a lack of consensus for change has led to a continuation of an excess of councils and elected representatives. From the 1920s until 1972, Northern Ireland was governed by a 52-member parliament at Stormont, under which lay a vastly overcomplex system of 74 local councils. These comprised two county boroughs, of Belfast and Derry, which covered most services; an 'upper tier' of 16 borough and county councils; and a 'lower tier' of 56 urban and rural district councils. This complicated arrangement was ended by the Local Government Act (Northern Ireland), 1972, which replaced the different tiers with a solitary one of 26 district councils, comprising five city councils (Belfast, Derry, Armagh, Lisburn and Newry) and 21 district or borough councils (McQuade and Fagan, 2002). The reform of local government in Northern Ireland coincided with that undertaken elsewhere in the UK, but was based upon a separate review, headed by Sir Patrick Macrory. Northern Ireland remains distinctive in only holding elections to its councils every four years, whereas under the 'English' model many councils stage elections annually (sometimes with a fallow fourth year), with one-third of council seats being contested.

The primary advantage of the Macrory proposals lay in their reduction of the Byzantine local council network. A major disadvantage, however, was that the powers of local authorities were substantially reduced, although, given their sectarian histories, this was not necessarily seen by those beyond the councils as a negative aspect. Macrory's proposals did not bolster local democracy, but led to education, libraries and health being administered by predominantly non-elected boards. A second important disadvantage was that the size of councils varied considerably, from tiny Moyle, with an electorate of a mere 10,500, to Belfast, with 210,000. Such imbalances discouraged meaningful horizontal cooperation between councils. The Macrory pruning still left Northern Ireland with over 500 councillors, with the figure eventually rising to 582 and, almost 30 years after the Macrory reforms, a further review of public administration in the region commenced.

Financial Organization

There are two aspects to the funding of Irish local authorities: capital and revenue expenditure. Capital expenditure is normally financed by borrowing from the Local Loans Fund, operated by the Department of Finance. Commissioners of Public Works, acting on the behalf of the Department of Finance, sanction loans if the project applied for is deemed satisfactory and within the remit of the local authority. As a consequence of increasing financial rectitude, local capital expenditure (taken as a proportion of the Public Capital Programme) decreased from around one-quarter in 1977 to less than one-fifth in 1992 (McManus, 1993: 37). This trend has continued with the Irish Government's financial commitments to Economic and Monetary Union.

Revenue, or current expenditure, is met from three main sources: rates, government grants and miscellaneous receipts from property and other charges. As a consequence of a Fianna Fáil election promise in 1977, domestic rates were abolished and replaced by a state grant in compensation for lost revenue. The Government initially agreed to provide a 100 per cent recoupment of the lost revenue to local authorities but, in 1983, this was amended to a fixed annual total and local authorities were empowered to levy local service charges. Despite elaborate waiver provisions made for the less well-off, service charges proved extremely unpopular and were strenuously resisted. Few local authority areas were able to introduce them and those that did had great difficulty enforcing them. Although a popular national vote-catcher, the decision to abolish rates on domestic property meant that the financial dependence of local authorities upon central government was greatly increased: local revenues were, on average, diminished by half (Chubb, 1992: 274).

The determination of central government to decide the maximum increases in the rates that remained not only hit local revenues but also severely curbed local government autonomy. The abolition of domestic rates was the final major transfer of decision-making power to central government (Hederman O'Brien, 1989: 341). The chair of the Government appointed Commission on Taxation (1980–5) reported that 'it might have been expected that such a transfer would have been marked by a recognition of its implications, some policy or plan for the new situation. The apparatus of local machinery was left in place and no significant change was made to its structure' (Hederman O'Brien, 1989: 342). The fact that the abolition of domestic rates was carried out initially without legislation only underlined the power of central government vis-à-vis local authorities. This power has been further increased by the centralized nature of the grants system now in operation (McManus, 1993: 39).

As a result of abolishing domestic rates, state grants form a larger part of local revenue, at around 44 per cent (Dooney and O'Toole, 1992: 147). Several government departments are responsible for different types of grant to local government, including agricultural grants given to replace 'lost rates' from agricultural producers, housing subsidy grants to meet loan repayments on local housing schemes, road grants, and some subsidies towards sanitary services such as water supplies or sewerage schemes. A further category of general grant, known as the rate support grant, may be used at the authority's discretion. These grants are allocated to individual authorities by the Minister of Environment (responsible for local government), on the basis of proposals from them, the level of need in each area and the state of on-going works in the locality.

The last category of revenue, miscellaneous receipts, arises as a consequence of charges for the provision of goods and services, the biggest earner being housing in the form of either rents or payments of house loans. Attempts in 1983 to reintroduce some local fiscal flexibility, allowing local service charges (for water, sewerage, refuse collection, etc.), were for the most part a failure: in many instances local authorities refused to accept such a 'political hot potato', whilst other authorities with members in favour of such a move found that they could not pass such a reso-lution at local level.

By 1994, it was evident that local government was financially hamstrung and if, as the government had promised, it wished to develop its role as a key player amidst the ever widening arena of subnational actors some financial reform was necessary. In 1995, the Rainbow Coalition introduced an income tax allowance in respect of local authority charges. Since, however, the 1977 rates removal applied only to domestic properties, businesses increasingly felt that they were bearing a dispropor-tionate burden of local government finance. During the period 1984–94, rates on businesses increased by 102 per cent, whilst the consumer price index increased by only 33 per cent. Business representatives argued that they were being unfairly burdened with the cost of local service charges because they had little electoral influ-ence when compared to the mass of domestic voters who did not wish to pay local charges. In 1997, the Local Government (Financial Provisions) Act enabled local authorities to claim the revenues from road taxes and from certain duties and fees charged under other enactments. This was widely perceived as a stop-gap measure until more comprehensive arrangements could be made as a consequence of the central government sponsored review of local government finance. There have been no other reforms as yet, and although the Green Paper entitled *Stronger Local Democracy: Options for Change* (Government of Ireland, 2008) raised the issue of local government funding, it fell far short of proposing a funding mechanism. Although a report on local government funding by Indecom consultants in 2006 esti-mated that 'local authorities would need an extra €1.5billion a year between them to meet the cost of "existing and emerging demands" for their services within four years', the issue was largely avoided by its referral to (another) Commission on Taxation (*Irish Times*, 23 April 2008).

In Northern Ireland, the limited powers of service-delivery accruing to local government means that it spends little money: less than 4 per cent of public expendi-ture is accounted for by local councils, which employ only 9,000 citizens. The services provided by local government amount to more than the 'bins and burials' with which local authorities are associated – but not much more. The main responsi-bilities of local councils are licensing and regulation, in terms of environmental health and refuse collection; and entertainment, leisure and births, marriages and deaths. Local authorities are also involved in limited local economic development, including cooperative projects with other authorities in local strategy partnerships developed under the EU's PEACE programmes. Community relations projects are also under-taken by local councils. The major local powers are now held at regional level, mainly by the Assembly, although the housing executive operates as a regional tier, or within the non-elected sector of local government (the area health and education boards).

Despite the modest financial burden of local government, it was not immune to the UK-wide changes introduced by the Thatcher governments of 1979–90 and which have continued in various forms since. Local authorities were required to contract out services to the private sector and to retreat from being service providers to service regulators. The softer tone of 'Best Value' under the post-1997 Labour Government required local authorities to challenge existing modes of service delivery; to consult with the public; and to compare service provision with other councils and facilitate competition with the private sector, to allow pragmatic choices to be made over whether public authorities or private organizations could provide more efficient services. Given the low level of service provision already offered by councils in Northern Ireland, the impact of contracting out was less marked than elsewhere in the UK, but the region's councils still operated within that broad ideological framework. However, when the Northern Ireland Executive's Environmental Minister introduced Best Value legislation in 2001, replicating the measures contained in the Local Government Act, 1999 introduced for England and Wales, it was rejected.

Northern Ireland was exempted from the poll tax, or community charge, the flat rate tax introduced disastrously by the Conservative Government in 1989 in Scotland and one year later in England and Wales. Given the ongoing Troubles at the time, the poll tax could have been impossible to collect in parts of Northern Ireland, being difficult enough to garner amid protests elsewhere in the UK. The ill-fated tax was soon replaced by the more consensual council tax, with its banded property valuations; but, again, Northern Ireland remained exceptional, as rates were maintained as the main source of locally raised revenue for local councils.

Reform Initiatives and Key Drivers for Change

The Republic of Ireland is almost unique among her European neighbours in not having implemented any major reform of local government throughout the post-war period (Coyle, 1994: 25). Whilst there have been several proposals for reform, such changes as have occurred have been ad hoc, functionally expedient and minimalist. The Cork City Management Act in 1929 – the consequence of lobbying by businesses and professionals for a more accountable system of local government – marked the introduction of the 'managerial system' already discussed. It was followed by a series of local Acts for various cities, culminating in the County Management Act of 1940, which extended the system and operationalized it throughout the state by 1942.[2] Under this system, the provision of all local services fell under the direction of a single individual – the city or county manager – answerable to the council but with a statutory position and statutory powers. The consequence of this was virtually a single administration in each county area (Chubb, 1992: 271).

Over time, subcounty districts faced the problem of how to provide an increasing range of public services with a relative scarcity of technical, administrative and financial resources when compared to larger county units. As a result, many gave up some of their functions to county level. Counties and county boroughs (the major cities that have county status) increasingly began to dominate subnational government and 'local government in Ireland became and is now primarily county council government' (ibid.). Added to this, the small number of elected authorities at subcounty level (represented by boroughs, urban districts and town commissioners) means that by the standards of comparable small states there are very few locally elected councils (Barrington, 1980: 43). Over the years, despite numerous reports and policy studies instigated by central government, no major changes occurred (Adshead and Quinn, 1998: 212–15). With the exception of a little tinkering to the system here and there, it could reasonably be argued that Irish local government has changed very little since the foundation of the state.[3] Indeed, it was not until the early 1990s that the first steps towards the long-awaited reform were introduced.

In 1991, the area covered by Dublin county council and Dun Laoghaire corporation was redivided into four county authorities: Dublin County Council was reduced and three new county boundaries were created in Fingal, South Dublin and Dun Laoghaire/ Rathdown. The 1991 Local Government Act 'substantially relaxed' the *ultra vires* restriction upon local government by introducing broad powers of general competence for local authorities to act in the interests of local communities (Government of Ireland, 1996a: 8). Although local authorities' continued dependence upon central government for financial and technical resources meant that in practice this freedom was limited, it was taken as a sign of the Government's commitment to local government reform. As part of a review of public sector management, the Government commissioned a report on the financing of local government (KMPG, 1991).

In 1993, following provisions made in the 1991 Local Government Act, eight Regional Authorities were set up in order to coordinate public service provision and to act as review bodies to advise on the deployment of EU Structural and Cohesion Funds in their regions. This might have been another ad hoc response to demands for more efficient policy delivery, but in 1994 a new Rainbow Coalition took over government and pledged to 'build on the reforms of recent years by the adoption of a strategic approach to the renewal of local government' (Government of Ireland, 1996a: 10). In July 1995, the Rainbow Government established the Devolution Commission, charged with investigating all aspects of decentralization. In 1996, the Interim Report of the Commission noted that 'Irish local government is in a particularly weak position as regards its status and role in society and in the overall framework of government' (Government of Ireland, 1996b: 33).

In December of the same year, the publication of the *Better Local Government* White Paper (Government of Ireland, 1996a) sought to address concerns that 'through lack of resources and inability to respond to problems which transcend their traditional functions, local authorities have tended to be by-passed by the growth of new forms of community development organisations, many of which are attracting State and EU support' (Government of Ireland, 1996a: 6). Building on the recommendations of the first interim report of the Devolution Commission, the White Paper proposed changes in local social partnership arrangements in two specific directions – via the introduction of Strategic Policy Committees and County Development Boards.

Strategic Policy Committees (SPCs) were established for all major service areas in each local authority and were intended to strengthen the role of councillors in the policy- and decision-making processes within local authorities. Together, the chairs of the SPCs and of the local council would form a Corporate Policy Group, which was intended to further strengthen the role of elected representatives in the policy- and decision-making process and act as a democratic counter-balance to the executive local authority manager. In addition to placing the role of strategic development more concretely within the aegis of local government, the introduction of the SPCs was also accompanied by a decision to reserve one-third of the available places for relevant sectoral interest groups – thereby bringing an institutionalized social partnership process into all local authorities for the first time and mirroring national partnership formulas (Government of Ireland, 1996a). Significantly, however, different social partners were to select their representatives in different ways (Adshead and McInerney, 2008b). Trade unions, business and farming interests were allowed to nominate their local representatives via their national peak organizations, while the community and voluntary sectors were obliged to undertake a local process of selection. This led to the creation in most areas of broadly based Community and Voluntary Fora. In a small number of instances specific community platforms have been established with a distinct social-inclusion focus (Harvey, 2003).

Alongside the enhancement of the role of local councillors via the SPCs, County/City Development Boards (CDBs) were established as part of a broader effort to widen the influence of local government within the local development process. This is considered to have been a response to the Devolution Commission report, which emphasized the need to integrate local government and local development systems as well as increasing the role of local government as a local development actor. Composition of the CDBs reflects a further use of a standardized partnership formula, closely resembling those already in place (Adshead and McInerney, 2008a). Membership of the CDBs is drawn from the local authority, state agencies and the various civil society interests represented in national social partnership. One of the key functions of this local partnership structure is to enhance coordination, cooperation and integration of effort amongst existing bodies, largely through the production of a ten-year development strategy. The allocation of the CDB chairperson function and the employment of CDB staff under the local authority aegis serves to enhance the role of the local authority in the local development process. The government's intention that CDBs should act as a locus for local development is illustrated by the fact that many of the existing area-based partnership structures, as well as a number of independent state-funded civil society organizations, are expected to present work plans to the CDBs for 'endorsement', though more recently this has been softened towards an information-sharing function.

The perception that Northern Ireland is overgoverned was exacerbated by the arrival of devolved government following the GFA. A country of 1.6 million people was now governed by the Westminster parliament, containing 18 MPs representing Northern Ireland; a 108-member Assembly; 582 councillors across 26 local authorities and a plethora of boards and agencies. These included province-wide housing and executive agencies and area health and education boards, on which councillors sat, but whose membership comprised mainly government appointees.

There was considerable personnel overlap between Assembly and council members during the early post-GFA years, an unsurprising feature given the uncertainty which dogged the early years of power-sharing devolved from the Executive. However, the Government and then the Executive, as devolution revived, agreed to end 'double-jobbing'.

By the early part of this century, there were several drivers for another fundamental reform of the structures of local government. Prior to its 2002–7 suspension, the Executive had embarked on a wide-ranging review of public administration, covering issues of responsibility, service provision, efficiency, effectiveness and accountability. The Review was maintained under direct rule, yet implementation of its findings was delayed by the restored Executive in 2007.

The Review of Public Administration aspired to clear relationships between regional and local government; to establish coterminous boundaries between local councils and service provision boards; to foster strong local government and a positive impact upon community relations. The focus tended to rest more strongly upon elected councils than upon area boards (Knox and Carmichael, 2006). Insofar as the Review examined area boards, its proposals were more concerned with quantity than quality, arguing for reductions in the number of subregional boards. Most notably, the 18 health and social services trusts would be consolidated into a mere five remaining bodies.

The most radical proposal in the Review was for a reduction in the number of councils to 7 from 26. This would produce better coterminosity with subregional education and health boards, allowing greater clarity for the public in terms of who provided their services. Under the 26 council model and patchwork quilt of area boards, an individual could straddle several different geopolitical units according to the service used. The Review proposed a limited transfer of functions from quangos to councils, facilitating a reduction of almost one-third of the number of non-elected state service providers. The UK government strongly backed the seven county model, at the expense of the 11 or 15 council alternatives discussed in the Review (Review of Public Administration, 2006).

The proposed reduction in the number of councils to seven was opposed by all parties except Sinn Féin, which believed it could become the leading party in a majority of the councils and enhance its influence within stronger local authorities. Critics of the proposals also feared consolidation of a growing nationalist west versus Unionist east polarization (with an evenly balanced Belfast) via the construction of the new 'super-councils' which would 'balkanise' the region (Knox and Carmichael, 2007a: 11, 2007b: 9). There was, however, scant evidence to support the sectarian demography argument; and 'sectarian demography' – if this term is to be used – is the basis of Northern Ireland's existence, explicitly so in the terms of the GFA. With a majority of them having served in local government, Assembly members were reluctant to see reductions in the number of their former and – in many cases, pending legislation – current council colleagues. The Executive's decision to suspend implementation of the Review of Public Administration reflected such emotional commitments rather more than a practical defence of good local governance for Northern Ireland. The Government's arguments that evenness of size and rating base, allied to more efficient service delivery, appeared to justify a substantial reduction of councils (Hanson, 2007).

There were, however, valid arguments against some of the Review's arguments. The most obvious was that council boundaries were not coterminous with the health and social service boards, undermining a key requirement of the reforms. In reducing the number of councils by 19, the Government risked overcorrecting the excess of previous governance. Northern Ireland would now have fewer councillors per citizen than Scotland or Wales, the obvious places of comparison. Eventually, in 2008, the Executive decided upon a compromise between the status quo and the huge reductions supported by the local government review and the UK government, opting for an 11 council model, with the first elections to the new authorities to take place in 2011.

Central–Local Relations

In the Republic, local government is governed by the doctrine, inherited from Britain, of *ultra vires*, which is understood to mean that 'local authorities have no powers, save those that are defined by statute'. In other words, the Dáil and central government are ultimately responsible for control of local government. Although the *ultra vires* principle was relaxed by the 1991 Local Government Act, giving local authorities broad powers of local competence to act 'in the interests of local communities', continued dependence on central government for financial and technical resources means that, in practice, this freedom is limited. Together, the *ultra vires* doctrine, financial dependence on central government, plus the tradition of mixing national and local politics and, until recently, of dual mandates, confirmed local government's dependent status vis-à-vis central government. As a result, in the Republic, local government is more often seen as another forum for national politics, rather than as a political and civic space in its own right. Irish government proposals for regionalization and decentralization bear witness to the view.

In July 1997, the European Commission published *Agenda 2000*, the EU blueprint for the future strategic direction of the European Union (CEC, 1997). Informing the document were two important factors: first, the need to make financial provision for the envisioned enlargement of the EU; and second, the need to address calls from substantial net contributors to the EU budget to reduce their contributions. For Ireland, this news was compounded by its remarkably successful rate of economic growth since 1993, which meant that the state's GDP per capita, expressed as a proportion of the EU average, had now breached the 75 per cent ceiling set for regions to qualify for full Objective One status in the allocation of EU Structural Funds. The Irish Government was anxious that the areas covered by at least some of the recently established eight Regional Authorities might still qualify for funding. According to the geographical scales which Eurostat (the EU's research office for census and survey data) uses for statistical purposes, the eight regional authorities were classified at NUTS III level (the acronym NUTS is derived from 'Nomenclature of Territorial Statistical Units' used by Eurostat). At least three of these regions, the Border, Midlands and West (the BMW group), had GDP per capita below the 75 per cent Structural Funds' threshold (O'Leary, 1999).

Brazening out significant opposition from political parties, long-time campaigners for devolution, would-be members of the new regions and a very cynical European Commission, in November 1998 the Government divided Ireland into two NUTS II regions for statistical purposes: the BMW group qualifying for Objective One status; and the remaining Southern and Eastern Region qualifying as an Objective One area in transition (Boyle, 2000). The rationale for this 'overnight conversion' to regionalization was clearly enounced by the Minister for Finance, Charlie McCreevy, when he explained that 'the government's objective in this round of Structural Funds will be to secure for Ireland the optimum level of funding' (Dáil Debates, 29 April 1998). Perhaps in order not to further confuse the already extremely complex mosaic of organizations and institutions operating at subnational level, the new regions were given no governmental powers or functions. Giving a detailed exposition of the events and arguments surrounding this move, Boyle (2000: 767) argues that, though the EU was in a prime position to influence the outcome of regional debates in Ireland during this time, for a variety of reasons, the European Commission lacked either the will or the capacity to follow through with their objections to Irish government actions. The conclusion is a familiar one, suggesting that where national governments are determined to resist unwanted domestic outcomes from developments at EU level, they are able to play a 'gatekeeper' role throughout the policy process in order to advance their own preferred policy outcomes (Bache, 1998).

In December 2003, the Minister for Finance announced the Government's commitment to 'voluntary decentralisation' of over 10,300 posts in civil service departments, offices and agencies to over 50 locations across the state (Humphreys and O'Donnell, 2006). In defence of the plan, the Tánaiste of the time, Mary Harney, suggested that 'the Irish government could not expect business to locate in all parts of Ireland, if the government itself was unwilling to do so' (*Irish Times,* 6 June 2006). Were it to be completely fulfilled, the decentralization initiative would result in eight departmental headquarters, plus the majority of civil and public service posts being held outside Dublin (Humphreys and O'Donnell, 2006: xi). To date, however, the implementation of this initiative has been extremely slow with 'very few of the decentralisation vacancies being filled by people from Dublin' (www.rte.ie/news/2008/0509/decentralisation.html). In summer 2007, a landmark Labour Court ruling, effectively prohibiting state agencies from making promotions conditional upon staff being prepared to move, did nothing to push progress on decentralization (*Irish Times*, 12 May 2008). Outlining a series of difficulties associated with moving senior civil servants out of the capital, the union representing senior civil service grades called for an urgent review of the decentralization scheme (*Irish Times*, 10 May 2008), suggesting that there will be no significant change for some time to come.

In Northern Ireland, the 'centre' with which local government worked during direct rule was multi-institutional, comprising the UK Government, Whitehall, the Westminster Parliament, the Northern Ireland Office and the Northern Ireland Civil

Service. Devolved government means that 'central–local' relations now refer primarily to the position of local councils in respect of the Northern Ireland Assembly.

Relations between councils and the old Stormont parliament of 1921–72 varied according to the composition of the council. Nationalist councils ended their attempted secession from the state in favour of a moribund non-recognition of the legitimacy of the Northern Ireland parliament. Unionist Party dominance of most councils was not absolute, given the sizeable number of independents and the credible performances of the Northern Ireland Labour Party. Moreover, relationships between Unionists at Stormont and on local authorities were not always bereft of friction. Nonetheless, there was sufficient cordiality and consensus to make central–local relations during this era largely unproblematic.

The Macrory revisions of local government during the 1970s were strongly opposed by many councillors, given their diminution of local powers. The main central–local conflict during the era of direct rule followed the 1985 Anglo-Irish Agreement. Unionist councils postponed some council decision-making and refused to set rates, as part of an unsuccessful attempt to bring down the deal. The UK Government comfortably faced down the protest, appointing commissioners to fix rates and the protest dwindled (the UK Government used a similar tactic in respect of Liverpool city council's ideological protests against the Thatcher Government during the same period). The brief era of Unionist unity evident at the commencement of the protest eventually evaporated.

Meanwhile, the election of Sinn Féin candidates to local councils from 1983 onwards created much tension within the council chamber. The party viewed local councils as 'another site of republican struggle', arguing that 'by no means are their [local councils'] duties confined to bins and burials – a myth convenient both to Unionists and the British government' (*An Phoblacht*, 9 May 1985). Ultimately, Sinn Féin's growing contact with the local state was to contribute towards the party's shift towards constitutional politics. During the 1980s, however, Sinn Féin's elected representatives were instructed by their party's ard – fheis to provide unconditional support for the IRA's armed struggle. Some councillors retained their role within the IRA, whose critics found themselves demoted within Sinn Féin. By the end of the decade, however, the need for the IRA cheerleader role was downgraded. The British Government introduced the Election Authorities (Northern Ireland) Act, which prohibited election candidates from advocacy of political violence. Sinn Féin began to urge inward investment to the areas where they were electorally strong and the party recognized the vote ceiling created by the IRA's actions. One Sinn Féin councillor, Martin O'Muilleor, declared that the continuing IRA campaign was 'political suicide' (Moloney, 2003: 299). Sinn Féin's growing presence on councils, becoming, for example, the largest party on Belfast City Council by 2001, did not lead to heightened central–local conflict, however, as once might have been anticipated, the party instead coming to operate within existing rules (Tonge, 2006a,b).

The impact of Sinn Féin's arrival in local government was to increase inter- and intrabloc rivalries and to further diminish the number of independents elected at local level. Party politics now dominate, in a trend which mirrors that elsewhere in the UK. The sharpness of contests assists turnout; the average turnout for local elections in Northern Ireland from 1973 until 2005 was 61 per cent; the comparable figure for Great Britain is 40 per cent (Rallings *et al.*, 1996; Elliott and Flackes, 1999; House of Commons, 1999; see also www.cain.ulst.ac.uk).

Conclusion

In the Republic of Ireland, although the county is the most important unit of local government, its range of functions is limited, relating primarily to physical infrastructure and public recreation facilities. These functions include the provision and organization of public housing, local road networks, the water supply, waste management and sewerage, the maintenance of public amenities, and a limited role in environmental protection. County/city councils are responsible for motor taxation, library services, fire, building control, emergency planning, aspects of national and regional roads, and most aspects of pollution control. There are some secondary functions in the areas of education, health and welfare, though in these areas they are subordinate to the specialized state-sponsored body responsible (VEC and Regional Health Boards). The virtual non-existence of a local revenue base, and the prescriptive nature of the relationship between local authorities and the Department of the Environment and Local Government at national level, results in a low level of local autonomy that might easily justify the Irish local government's more accurate depiction of it as local administration. Despite this, or perhaps because of it, local authorities have developed the role of local facilitators between a range of other subnational actors, in many cases becoming lynchpins for local development. Still, within this context it is clear that the balance of decision-making power between the executive manager and elected representatives rests firmly with the former.

Local government in Northern Ireland has reflected the problems of the state. For 50 years, local councils operated on a basis of sectarian majoritarianism. There is agreement upon a need to end over-governance, and the reduction in the number of councils from 26 to 11 will greatly alleviate the problem, but the lack of coterminosity with other service delivery boards remains a problem. Local councils have largely eradicated their internal sectarian methodologies and a majority now operate power-sharing arrangements between Unionists and nationalists. These vary in nature according to local circumstance, but generally involve rotating the post of mayor and allocating or electing committee chairs according to party proportions within the council chamber. The erosion of local government power endured during the 1970s and exacerbated by the contracting-out of services in the latter part of the last century will not be reversed. Instead, the focus is upon streamlining local government, helping it to work more effectively alongside the key 'quangoized' repositories of local power below Assembly level, contained in area boards.

10

Economic Management

If private foreign investment is needed to provide the new jobs that are required in Ireland and if it is not permitted or if it is discouraged, Irish people will still have to work with capital that is not owned by Irishmen – but they will be working with it outside Ireland rather than at home.

(NESC, 1976: 20)

Introduction

Economic growth comes from a number of sources: natural factor endowments; human resources; investment; entrepreneurship; and astute political management of this mix. Measuring economic growth is not straightforward since there is no clear agreement about the most appropriate metric to use. Most measures tend to be divided into two rough categories, depending on whether they favour income or consumption-oriented statistics. Whatever the measure, most analysts agree that the Republic of Ireland's performance throughout the post-independence period was poor. Lee (1989: 514) notes that between 1910 and 1970 Ireland recorded the slowest growth of per capita income out of any European country except the UK. For the Republic, every country ranked above Ireland in the early twentieth century pulled much further ahead, and those that were below either overtook or significantly narrowed the gap (ibid.; Haughton, 2000), with the result that 'the Irish growth rate came at the bottom of the European table by a long way' (Lee, 1989: 514).

Although prosperous relative to the Irish Republic until the growth of the 'Celtic Tiger', Northern Ireland's economy was historically also weak, with the direness of its own position only partly alleviated by its location within the United Kingdom. From the inception of the state, unemployment remained stubbornly at least four times above the UK average and never fell below 25 per cent during the 1930s (Kennedy Pipe, 1997). Northern Ireland's main industries of shipbuilding and textiles were in rapid decline after World War II and the region lacked inward investment. American multinational firms began to invest during the 1960s, but the onset of the Troubles slowed such a development. The inadequacies of the economy and the need to modernize were highlighted in the Hall Report (1962) and the Wilson Report (1962) (Wilson, 1989). Instead of modernization, however, there was continued underinvestment and an ongoing sectarian squabble for a marginally superior Unionist share of diminishing spoils.

Thirty years of conflict had a ruinous effect in terms of industrial investment. The UK Government placed faith in large employment subsidies as a means of ameliorating the conflict, but take-up by outside investors was minimal, given the attendant risks. Although the peace process saw a boom in terms of urban regeneration and house prices, the Northern Ireland economy remained hugely dependent upon subsidy, with the level of Treasury allocation per citizen (made mainly according to the Barnett formula) exceeding that of any other part of the UK. Moreover, the economy is nearly bereft of large industry and is overly dependent upon the public sector (more so than any other UK region), leading to the claim that Northern Ireland has 'an economy more collectivised than Stalin's Russia, more corporatist than Mussolini's and more quangoized than Wilson and Heath's governments (Lord Trevor Smith of Clifton, *Hansard*, 20 July 2004, c152; Tonge, 2006a).

Natural Resources

According to Haughton (2000: 26) the Irish Free State could count some important assets:

> It had an extensive system of communications, a developed banking system, a vigorous wholesale and retail network, an efficient and honest administration, universal literacy, a large stock of houses, schools and hospitals, and enormous external assets. By the standards of most of the world's countries the country was well off indeed.

Although in many ways the British colonial legacy to the Republic was relatively benign (Bollen, 1979, 1983; Bollen and Jackman, 1985), still the consequence of partition was that the major industries were left in the northern Irish state. O'Connor (1992) noted that, whereas prior to independence the six northern counties comprised the industrial heartland of the country, after partition as few as 5 per cent of the population in the rest of Ireland was engaged in manufacturing (McLaughlin, 1993: 208). In the absence of much else, it is not hard to figure 'the long-standing significance attached to agriculture by the state, together with a relatively high proportion of the state's labour force employed in agriculture' (Adshead, 1996a: 590; see also Collins, 1994; Greer, 2005). Ireland's comparative advantage was in agriculture, especially pasture over tillage, which was less labour intensive and well-supported by Ireland's climate (Sweeney, 1999: 26). In 1922, half the workforce was involved in agriculture and there was no thought of an industrial policy, despite the continuing decline in agricultural employment (Sweeney, 1999: 29). Given the Republic's limited natural resource endowment, making the shift from primary agricultural production to industrialization and the development of the tertiary sector required for modern economic development was bound to be a challenge – one that could only be addressed by judicious management of other factors of production.

Like its counterpart in the South, Northern Ireland had a strongly agrarian dimension to its economy, with nearly one-third of the population employed in agriculture prior to World War II. Although this represented a lower figure than that found in agriculture in the Irish Republic (around half of the population) it far exceeded the 11 per cent employed in agriculture elsewhere in the UK during this period (Lindsay, 2003). Northern Ireland shared many of the same agricultural land advantages evident to the South, with these accompanied by the industrialization also evident in the province. The percentage employed in industry in Northern Ireland prior to World War II more than doubled the figure in the Irish Free State, at 34 per cent to 13 per cent (Munck, 1993). Although more modern farming techniques were employed in Northern Ireland compared with the South, agricultural productivity from the small farms which dominated the region was modest, whilst wages relative to the UK average were substantially lower, exacerbating problems of demand (Wichert, 1991). Combined with the linen and shipbuilding industries, agriculture accounted for half of Northern Ireland's trade in the interwar years. Agriculture's heightened position after World War II owed much its decline being far less rapid than those of linen and shipbuilding. Belfast's geographical location provided ideal port status, offering a natural arena for shipbuilding, but, as international orders declined, the industry went into steep decline, with a rapidly diminishing workforce, falling from over 20,000 in the 1960s to 4,000 by the 1980s. By 2002, with no orders on its books, shipbuilders Harland & Wolff was effectively a skeletal operation. Subsidies for the linen industry and for Harland & Wolff were obtained from the UK Treasury, but these failed to ameliorate fully the problems of declining demand, lack of competitiveness and Northern Ireland's disadvantaged, peripheral status within the UK. A combination of failing industry and the impact of conflict left Northern Ireland largely bereft of industrial resources. Of the manufacturing portfolio in Northern Ireland, food, drink and tobacco production now accounts for nearly one-third of output, with heavy industry accounting for less than 20 per cent (Bradley, 2007).

Human Resources

Lee (1989: 511) notes that even by the most relaxed criteria the population path followed by Ireland, especially the south, was distinctive. According to FitzGerald (2003: 103), over the last two centuries the Republic has had one of the most unstable demographies in the world, with 'more ups and downs, and twists and turns ... than any other'. The significance of emigration to contemporary demographic shifts is one that should not be underestimated. Emigration is still part of the experience of up to a quarter of each generation (and of every family), but the difference is that the emigrants of today are seen more as 'homing pigeons' (J. Fitzgerald, 2000: 30). Returning emigrants have brought with them the experience of business and culture outside Ireland and across wide areas of Irish society, such as business and academic life, many of those in positions of authority are returned emigrants. FitzGerald (2003: 106) notes that:

> It is a measure of the extraordinary oscillations in Irish economic performance over the past half century that a number of those who have recently returned to work in Ireland after having had to emigrate in the late 1980s had as children been brought back to Ireland by parents who returned here in the 1970s after themselves having had to emigrate in the 1950s or early 1960s!

In more recent times, returning Irish emigrants have been joined by increasing numbers of non-Irish immigrants attracted by good job prospects and a burgeoning economy. The extraordinary elasticity of the Irish labour supply, which has helped contribute to the 'exceptional rate of employment growth', has been noted by Irish economists Clinch *et al.* (2002: 46–7) as perhaps the most significant feature of Ireland's recent economic boom. It was this unusually elastic labour supply that enabled employment to grow so fast and underpin the boom without fuelling inflation. It was not until 1999–2000 that labour shortages finally began to push wage inflation; though this was moderated by the social partnership process, which helped to maintain a degree of wage moderation. In short, the factors that accounted for the highly elastic labour supply lie 'at the heart of the Irish economic miracle' (Clinch *et al.*, 2002: 47). These include: a large initial pool of unemployment; a baby boom in the 1960s and 1970s that facilitated a growth in the working-age population during the boom; an increase in women's participation in the labour force; and last, but not least, significant inwards migration contributing about one half of the growth in the labour force (ibid.).

As has been asserted elsewhere, 'an important factor when examining the employment situation in any country is the proportion of the working-age population that actually seeks work. This is known as the labour force participation rate' (O'Hagan and McIndoe, 2005: 82). In Ireland, the labour participation rate for males is below that in most other states, whilst the participation rate for females is substantially lower (see OECD, 2004). The female participation rate increased considerably in the 1980s and 1990s, due to a large extent by the increasing participation rate of married females (O'Hagan and McIndoe, 2005: 83). Still, between 1994 and 2003, the period of most rapid economic growth, employment in Ireland grew by 3.4 per cent annually, much faster than the 1 per cent annual rise in population occurring over the same period (Haughton, 2005: 121). The rapid rise in employment was due to a large influx of young people into the labour market, a resumption of immigration and a substantial rise in the proportion of adults employed, shifting from 52 per cent of the working-age population in 1994 to 65 per cent in 2003 (ibid.).

If education, training and experience make workers more employable, then there is good evidence to suggest that the Irish workforce is relatively well-educated. Although universal secondary education was not introduced in the Republic until 1968, so that older workers are not necessarily well-educated, there is compelling evidence to show that younger Irish are relatively better-educated than many of their European peers. A standardized OECD test found that 'Irish students scored 527 in reading literacy, 503 in mathematics, and 513 in science, compared to an OECD average of 500' (Haughton, 2005: 122). Though it seems that the Irish education system consistently fails a significant minority (see pp. 205–6), on average it provides a solid base for the majority of the workforce. Moreover, there is a definite correlation between the recent expansion of higher education and the economic growth spurt of the 1990s (ibid.). In short, Ireland now boasts a well-educated cohort of young people with 35 per cent of those aged 25–34 obtaining a third-level qualification in 2002, up from 28 per cent in 1999, and above the EU 15 rate of 26 per cent (ibid.).

The role of immigrant participation in the labour market is particularly significant: as the economy boomed and labour shortages became more apparent, the government responded to requests from employers for additional workers by making it relatively easy to recruit and employ workers from outside the country (NESC, 2006). As a result, since 1996, Ireland has been a net importer of people (OECD, 2008: 101). There are almost 170 nationalities now represented in the state, reflecting the diverse nature of this immigration. On the face of it then, the highly globalized Irish economy is now sustained by a highly globalized workforce (Adshead *et al.*, 2007).

Northern Ireland has had a small net population outflow for several decades, although its pattern has changed. Whereas disadvantaged Catholics were more likely to leave during the first five decades of the state, the onset of conflict saw a greater tendency among middle-class Protestants to leave, often not returning to the region after study at universities in other parts of the UK. Immigrant labour began to arrive at the end of the conflict. Throughout the years of decline, the failings of Northern Ireland's economy were often overshadowed by arguments over its inequities in terms of different skills and employment levels within the labour market.

Discrimination on religious grounds began to be tackled via the Fair Employment Act of 1976, which was extended in 1989 to cover virtually all medium- and large-sized businesses in Northern Ireland. The Fair Employment Acts were accompanied by pressure for religiously proportionate workforces emanating from America via the MacBride Principles, which sought to link United States investment to sanctions against firms apparently reluctant to employ Catholics. Divisive even among nationalists, the MacBride Principles did not radically alter employment patterns, but they did add to the pressure upon the British Government to adopt a more interventionist role in securing fairness in workforce recruitment. Until the 1990s, attempts to ensure equitable recruitment opportunities relied too heavily upon self-regulation by business (which represented the problem, not a solution) and an excessive onus upon individuals to risk being labelled 'troublemakers' by bringing cases to tribunals (Cunningham, 2001). Sectarian harassment remained within some workplaces and there remain problems for particular firms in some working-class areas in achieving equitable community recruitment due to the strength of the communal divide (Shirlow and Murtagh, 2006).

Despite the plethora of fair employment legislative measures, the unemployment rate among Catholics continues to outstrip that endured by Protestants in Northern Ireland, a problem that persisted amid Unionist government, British direct rule and devolved power-sharing. In 2004, six years after the GFA and nearly three decades after the first fair employment legislation, the unemployment figure for Catholics, at 7 per cent, was more than double that found among Protestants (OFDFM, 2002), a differential which had remained unaltered over the previous decade. A higher proportion of Protestants (72 per cent) of working age were in employment compared to Catholics (62 per cent), another stubbornly persistent differential (ibid.). Overall, Northern Ireland's position improved relative to that of the United Kingdom. By the 2000s it was no longer the area of worst unemployment, yet the difference in fortunes within the province seemed impervious to legislative action. In one highly contentious case, that of the Police Service, affirmative action was used in ensuring 50–50 Catholic and Non-Catholic recruitment, but elsewhere the devolved government relied upon the raft of legislative measures in place to ensure equal employment prospects. There remains an ongoing debate between those who see the disparities in unemployment rates as indicative of ongoing sectarian malpractice and those who perceive the differential as a product of one or more of locational or educational problems associated with the Catholic community (Tonge, 2005a).

Beyond the issue of the sectarian divide, economic problems remain, only partly disguised by the rebuilding and reconstruction evident since the conflict subsided. Despite impressive performances on some educational measurements, with the highest levels of state-sector entry to university of any part of the United Kingdom, Northern Ireland has the largest percentage of school leavers devoid of any educational qualifications, its figure of 22.3 per cent nearly double the UK average (DETI, 2007). Living standards for Northern Ireland's citizens remain 20 per cent below those in Britain, a problem caused mainly by lower wages (Nigel Dodds, Minister for the DETI, (www.detini.gov.uk,cgi-bin/more-news?util=1168, 4 February 2008) and high house prices, the latter now the third highest of any UK region. The percentage of working age persons in employment, at 74.5 per cent, is over 5 per cent lower than the UK average, and youth unemployment is high, at 7.7 per cent, in 2008 (www.deti.gov.uk/cgi-bin, 10 February 2008). Manufacturing output is growing in value in real terms (by 20 per cent during 2000–6 alone) but manufacturing remains small, with fewer than 100,000 jobs, less than one-sixth of the total within the service sector, which itself continues to grow at a faster rate (DETI, 2007). There is little incentive to work in private industry, given that public sector wages are almost one-third higher. The public sector provides almost one-third of all Northern Ireland employment and the annual subvention provided by the UK Government amounts to £5–6billion annually, nearly one-quarter of the region's gross domestic product (Oliver and Leonard, 2008: 4–5).

Investment and Enterprise

Since the 1950s, the reorientation of Irish economic policy has been geared to openness, to trade and to foreign direct investment (FDI) – objectives that have been conscientiously and consistently pursued by successive governments. Whereas in the 1960s, FDI helped create a number of 'screw-driver' industries (so-called because of their association with assemblage of products produced elsewhere as opposed to productive processes of their own), by the 1990s FDI in Ireland was of a different calibre and quality altogether and was linked to high-wage jobs in leading multinationals. According to O'Toole (2003: 17), throughout this period 'the frontline troops in the battle for foreign investment were public servants working for the Industrial Development Authority, many of them showing a degree of motivation and enterprise that would have done any swaggering entrepreneur proud'. Both well-networked and well-practised in the external promotion of the state to foreign investors, in the 'second wave' of economic growth associated with FDI state agencies like the Industrial Development Authority (IDA) sought out FDI from sectors they identified with growth potential (IT, pharmaceuticals and healthcare sectors) and marketed Ireland as 'a country with a highly educated and flexible English-speaking workforce, with low taxes on companies' and with 'access to the EU, good financial and professional services and political stability' (Sweeney, 2003: 210).

On a per capita basis, despite its small size, Ireland had benefited disproportionately from FDI, and this was a key contributor to the 1990s 'Celtic Tiger' growth phase (Sweeney, 2003: 211). The fact that such a large part of this FDI is from US multinationals, such as Apple, Intel, IBM, Microsoft and SmithKline Glaxo, has prompted the suggestion that

> it may now be more realistic to think of the Irish economy not as a region of Europe, but as an out-post of the United States attached to the edge of the EU; in recent years four-fifths of foreign direct investment has originated in the United States, and US firms now account for a quarter of manufacturing employment and about a half of manufacturing output and exports.
>
> (Haughton, 2000: 44)

In this respect, Anyadike-Danes *et al.* (2007: 7) demonstrate that whilst Ireland's growth rate was remarkable in the European context, it is roughly comparable to the average growth rate experienced by 23 out of 50 states from the US.

Although the high level of foreign investment is remarkable, it has been suggested that the consistency of Irish governmental approaches to FDI, plus the slow but steady evolution of FDI policy, has had the effect of increasing the confidence of investors in Ireland (Ruane and Uğar, 2005: 167). Foreign investors were lured with generous tax concessions, financial aids and flexible support packages, which over time began to be increasingly disbursed in relation to the 'quality of the project from an Irish perspective', in terms of the number and quality of jobs created by the project (ibid.). This flexibility was slightly undermined in 1982, when the Government was found to be in breach of the Treaty of Rome and had to change its export tax incentive (by harmonizing the corporate tax rate across all manufactured goods) as a result. This, together with other concerns about increasing competition, prompted a major review of industrial policy, the Telesis Report, published in 1982 (Kennedy *et al.*, 1982–3; Nolan, 1983). The decade ended with the commitment of significant EU Structural Funding in Ireland, which provided the support for further development of manufacturing and internationally traded services in the 1990s (Ruane and Uğar, 2005: 170).

During the 1990s, 'as much as 6.5 per cent of Irish GDP consisted of transfers from the European Union – only a third from the much debated Structural Funds and the rest from the distinctly less fashionable Common Agricultural Policy' (Keating, 2006: 436). Nevertheless, it is argued that European investment in the Irish economy has had a considerable impact on economic management, which, together with a 'radical adjustment in the structure of the Irish economy' as a consequence of the Single Market (O'Donnell, 1998: 8), has prompted a reconsideration of economic strategy in the light of further European integration (NESC, 1989). The outcome was 'an unambiguous recognition and acceptance of Ireland's participation in the international economy and the European Union' (O'Donnell, 1998: 14).

Substantial external investment in Northern Ireland has assisted the reconstruction of the region. The EU-funded Northern Ireland Programme for Building Sustainable Prosperity accounts for two-thirds of the Structural Funds programme, which provided over €1.3billion of assistance from 2000 to 2006. The local promotion of inward investment to Northern Ireland has improved as a consequence of the eradication of violence, but the creation of permanent jobs remains difficult. Northern Ireland's Industrial Development Board (IDB) failed to achieve its job creation targets in the majority of years in the decade prior to the GFA (despite spending £500 million from 1988 to 1997), although the situation improved markedly in the latter part of the 1990s (Northern Ireland Audit Office, 1998).

For late developing states such as Ireland (O'Malley, 1989, 1992), the game of 'catch up' with other more economically advanced states, with whom they must compete, makes the task of achieving economic growth all the more difficult. Typically, for late developing states, 'achieving sustained growth has meant first complementing agriculture with industrial capacity and then moving from simple, low value-added manufacturing to more sophisticated, higher return kinds of industrial activities' (Evans, 1997: 63). According to this perspective, it was commonly acknowledged that states could increase the pace of industrialization, so long as they ultimately deferred to the needs of private entrepreneurs (Jacobsen, 1994: 8). This is because 'transformation depends on business' and 'in the contemporary world, citizens of all countries depend on capital to provide them with the means of becoming more productive participants in the global economy' (Evans, 1997: 63). As the gap between earlier industrializers and the so-called late developing states widens, however, the supply of entrepreneurs willing to risk their capital in productive investments becomes crucial.

The crux of the problem faced by late developers is, according to Evans (1995: 147), 'that institutions that allow large risks to be spread across a wide network of capital holders do not exist, and individual capitalists are neither able nor interested in taking them on. Under these circumstances the state must serve as surrogate entrepreneur'. This is the logic that leads White and Wade (1988: 1) to argue that 'the phenomenon of successful "late development" should be understood as a process in which states have played a strategic role in taming domestic and international market forces and harnessing them to a national economic interest'.

In the Republic's case, whilst there is no doubt that 'international market forces' have made a significant contribution to the economic boom, whether or not they have been tamed by the state – or indeed whether the state has been tamed by them – remains contested (see pp. 189–91). Certainly, the Irish state was successful in the creation of a number of strategic state agencies designed to attract FDI and develop indigenous entrepreneurial activity (O'Riain, 2000, 2004), though research into the output and capacity of Irish entrepreneurial activity is very scarce (Anyadike-Danes *et al.*, 2007).

In 1992, the Culliton Report (1992) went some way to addressing the somewhat asymmetrical policy focus on international investment by recommending a reorganization of existing grant awarding agencies into two main agencies: one addressing the needs of indigenous firms (Enterprise Ireland); the other focused on the attraction of foreign owned industry (the IDA). In addition to promoting the growth of industrial clusters and the greater use of equity, as opposed to non-repayable grants, the Report 'placed emphasis on the creation of an overall competitive business environment, with the hope that firms would move away from the grant dependency mentality identified by previous reports' (Andreosso-O'Callaghan and Lenihan, 2006: 279). The subsequent creation of the Government Taskforce on Small Business in 1993 provided an important signal from the Irish Government that it recognized the importance of SMEs as generators of growth and employment in the Irish economy.

Investment in Northern Ireland from overseas firms has been limited, due largely to the impact of the conflict. Businesses were bombed by the IRA during their campaigns and occasionally business leaders were abducted or even killed. The IRA's campaign of assassination against those business leaders it believed would stabilize Northern Ireland by investing in the province impaired the UK Government's ability to 'sell' the merits of investment to the USA. The first American company to invest in Northern Ireland, Du Pont (in 1959) had its (English-born) head of its Derry plant killed by the IRA in 1977. However, American companies did not stop investing in the region, with 46 companies located there by the time the IRA called its first ceasefire. These companies provided 10,000 jobs, but there was less investment from other countries (Tonge, 2002). American firms were attracted by the high levels of subsidy, an approach of the British Government which sometimes failed, the most infamous example being its part-financing of the DeLorean sports car project, which collapsed with large losses in 1982.

By 2002, there were 640 foreign-owned businesses in Northern Ireland, employing 11 per cent of the region's workforce, with wholesale and retail accounting for 30 per cent of foreign owned production, followed by manufacturing at 27 per cent. Most Northern Ireland businesses (98 per cent) are classed as 'small', with fewer than 50 employees (two thirds are family owned), and only 0.3 per cent employing more than 250 employees (a slightly lower figure than elsewhere in the UK) (DETI, 2006). Given the post-conflict rebuilding work and increasing attractiveness of Northern Ireland, it is perhaps unsurprising that construction and property-services firms provide the largest categories of growth within the region's business mix. Great Britain remains the largest market by far for Northern Ireland's 'exports', with 42 per cent heading in this direction, a figure rising to over half for large businesses in the region. The volume of trade with the Republic of Ireland has grown sufficiently for it to become the second largest recipient of goods from small and medium enterprises, higher than sales to the EU, within which France, Spain and Germany are the destinations for almost half of exports.

In an attempt to boost inward investment, the Northern Ireland Executive argued for cuts in corporation tax to create a 'Celtic Tiger' boost to the North's economy, disadvantaged by its land border with a low tax rival. However, the UK Treasury's Varney Review rejected the idea, arguing that 'such a policy would run the risk of encouraging profit-shifting from the rest of the UK to Northern Ireland' (Varney, 2007: 5). The Executive pleaded that Northern Ireland was a special case, estimating in its submission to the Varney Review that 27,000 jobs were lost directly due to the conflict. The Varney Review's rejection of greater fiscal autonomy for Northern Ireland highlighted the problem for the Executive in terms of its lack of manoeuvre in attracting firms to invest in the region. Given that Northern Ireland's economy was growing faster than any other part of the UK under the current tax regime, tax cuts would have been difficult to justify.

Managing Economic Policy

In the early years of the state the growth model pursued by Cumann na nGaedheal government was based on the premise that what was good for agriculture was good for the country (Haughton, 2000: 27). When Fianna Fáil came to office in 1932, they offered an economic policy that differed in two important respects: it was ideologically committed to greater economic self-sufficiency; it was politically committed to reneging on annuities payments to Britain (for land bought by tenants from landlords). Picking an economic war with a state in receipt of 96 per cent of Irish exports (Sweeney, 1999: 32) hit the Irish economy hard. The governmental response was a period of economic protectionism, which although it boosted employment in manufacturing in the medium term, arguably contributed to industrial stagnation in the 1950s, leaving Irish industry uncompetitive and poorly placed to deal with competition that did arrive following a change of policy in the 1960s (Haughton, 2000: 30–5).

That shift in policy is widely associated with the publication, in 1958, of the now renowned government paper entitled *Economic Development* (Government of Ireland, 1958) or 'Whitaker Report' (so called after the Secretary of Finance charged with its composition). In the Executive Summary of the Whitaker Report its author was obliged to admit that:

> After 35 years of native government people are asking whether we can achieve an acceptable degree of economic progress. The common talk amongst parents in the towns, as in rural Ireland, is of their children having to emigrate as soon as their education is completed in order to be sure of a reasonable livelihood … All this seems to be setting up a vicious cycle of increasing emigration, resulting in a smaller domestic market depleted of initiative and skill, and a reduced incentive, whether for Irishmen or foreigners, to undertake and organise the productive enterprises which alone can provide increased employment opportunities and higher living standards.
>
> (Government of Ireland, 1958: 5)

The Whitaker Report advocated a '180 degree reorientation of economic policy, away from the insular and ultimately self-defeating attempts at economic isolation and towards full integration with the international economy through "industrialisation by invitation"' (Adshead, 2008). Arguing for trade liberalization, attracting FDI and state intervention in capital-intensive, export–oriented production, the report advocated a 'highly interventionist' approach and 'marked the beginning of Ireland's move towards export-oriented growth' (Smith, N.,2006: 105). Ireland was one of the first late developing states to adopt this approach (O'Malley, 1989, 1992), which it is argued helped lay the foundations for improved economic performance in the 1990s (Smith, N., 2006: 64–9). Still, it is argued that had the Republic made this decision a decade earlier, it would have joined in the post-war boom that lifted the rest of Europe into the most sustained period of economic growth ever, one which was to last until the early 1970s (Sweeney, 1999: 40).

Ireland's decision to embrace Europe as soon as was politically feasible (given the economic ties with the UK) constitutes a further milestone in government management of the economy. Membership of the EU immediately led to a reduction (and ultimate removal) of trade barriers. Haughton (2000: 37) notes that whilst 'it was recognised that some of Irish industry would wither under the competition', 'it was also expected that Ireland would become a good platform from which companies from outside the EU could serve the European market'. Laffan and O'Mahony (2008) note that until the Republic achieved economic 'catch-up' with its European neighbours in the 1990s, 'Irish politicians and officials adopted a very active approach to European finances and receipts from Brussels', ensuring that they 'consistently achieved the highest per capita transfers from the European budget until enlargement' in 2004. Indeed, it is argued that EU Structural Funding may have increased annual Irish GDP growth by an extra 0.5 to 0.9 per cent during the 1990s (Andreosso-O'Callaghan and Lenihan, 2006: 282).

Further credit is given to the Irish state for realizing the significance of *social* as well as *economic* capital in the drive towards development throughout the late 1980s – a move that was encouraged and supported by the revised EU Structural Funding arrangements from 1988 onwards (Sabel, 1986; Adshead and Quinn, 1998). This, together with the desire to make the best use of Structural Funding – through attempts to coordinate national and EU sponsored development activities so as to avoid duplication of efforts or costs and obtain the maximum EU support available – set the context for a series of national concordats which have since been referred to as Irish 'government by partnership' (Adshead, 2002: 70). Of course, partnership arrangements are not a new phenomenon in continental Europe. What was unusual about their evolution in the Irish context was the relative absence of most acknowledged preconditions for the creation of such neo-corporatist arrangements (Hardiman, 1988). It seemed that in a few short years, the Irish state developed the means for maintaining the necessary macroeconomic discipline and reflexivity to survive as a small open economy in a global market (O'Donnell, 1998; O'Donnell *et al.*, 2007).

Social Partnership

To date, Ireland has experienced seven social pacts, as outlined in Table 10.1. The first, Programme for National Recovery (PNR), involved agreement between employers, trade unions, farming interests and government on wage levels in both the public and private sectors for a three year period (1987–90), with a broader agreement on general developments in some social policy sectors (see O'Donnell, 1998: 11; O'Donnell and Thomas, 1998: 119). The second social pact, Programme for Economic and Social Progress (PESP), running from 1991–3, continued the practice of setting agreed pay increases for public and private sectors, plus a number of agreements on commitments to social equality (following reports made by the Commission on Social Welfare and the Second Commission on the Status of Women) and tax reform. The PESP was also notable for initiating a pilot programme designed to provide an 'area-based response' (ABR) to long-term unemployment. The intention of the ABR programme was to develop 'an integrated approach designed to implement a community response in particular local areas to long-term unemployment and the danger of long-term unemployment' (Government of Ireland, 1991). Twelve ABR

Table 10.1   *Social Pacts and Governments in Office in the Republic of Ireland,*
1987–2008

Programme	Government
Programme for National Recovery (1987–90)	Fianna Fáil minority government Fianna Fáil/Progressive Democrat coalition (formed July 1989)
Programme for Economic and Social Progress (1991–3)	Fianna Fáil/Progressive Democrat coalition Fianna Fáil/Labour coalition (formed January 1993)
Programme for Competitiveness and Work (1994–6)	Fianna Fáil/Labour coalition Fine Gael/Labour/Democratic Left coalition (formed December 1994)
Partnership 2000 (1997–2000)	Fine Gael/Labour/Democratic Left coalition Fianna Fáil/Progressive Democrat coalition (formed June 1997)
Programme for Prosperity and Fairness (2000–2)	Fianna Fáil/Progressive Democrat coalition (re-elected 2002)
Programme for Sustaining Progress (2003–5)	Fianna Fáil/Progressive Democrat coalition
Towards 2016 (2006–)	Fianna Fáil/Progressive Democrat coalition Fianna Fáil/Green Party + independents coalition (formed May 2007)

areas were selected (eight urban and four rural), each with a board of directors comprising six directors from the local community, six from the social partners and six from the state agencies in the area (Adshead, 2002: 79).

The pay provisions of the third social pact, Programme for Competitiveness and Work (1994–6), followed much the same pattern as the two preceding pacts, 'with another local bargaining clause, but with much more attention being given to non-pay issues' (Roche and Cradden, 2003: 80). Whilst both the PNR and PESP contained references to the desirability of worker participation, the Programme for Competitiveness and Work made this ambition more explicit in the terms of refer-ence it provided for a review of the Competitiveness and Employment Protection Unit, which had been established in 1993, within the Department of Enterprise and Employment, to provide advice to employers on alternatives to redundancy (Dáil Debates, 1993: 436/1137). 'What was being sought with increasing insistence was for partnership at national level to be complemented by partnership in the enterprise, plant and office' (Roche and Cradden, 2003: 81).

Negotiated with the Rainbow Coalition (Fine Gael/Labour/Democratic Left), the fourth pact agreement, Partnership 2000 (P2K), was considered by many to be the most ambitious yet and reflected a significant shift of emphasis compared to other programmes. Alongside commitments to pay increases and tax reduction, there was an explicit endorsement that 'developing partnership in the workplace' was key to building a more competitive Ireland (ibid.). Additionally, this pact was notable for its inclusion of representatives from the community and voluntary sector, which, combined with a thematic approach to the identification and prioritization of objectives, tended to broaden the programme's sphere of interest (NESF, 1997). As a result, P2K laid a stronger emphasis on dealing with inequality, long-term unemployment and social exclusion than had been the case in other pacts. It was responsible for the creation of the Equality Authority (which replaced the Employment Equality Agency), a Commission on wage differentials, and one on the family, as well as a review body for Special Education. Additionally, the programme signalled a measure of agreement on action to modernize the public service, enlisting the social partners in support of the Strategic Management Initiative.

The fifth Programme for Prosperity and Fairness (PPF) 2001–2 continued the tradition of pay increases and tax cuts (though it was not responsible for the introduction of national minimum wages, which were introduced by the Government in April 2000). This pact sought to deepen and extend the workplace-partnership process that was begun in the preceding P2K agreement, whilst at the same time acknowledging the more diverse demands created by the inclusion of the 'Community and Voluntary pillar'. As a result, it developed earlier programmes by making provision for the involvement of the 'social partners' in over 20 working groups, under the aegis of five 'frameworks' designed to deal with different dimensions of public and social policy. A Performance Management Advisory Group was set up to oversee the implementation of performance indicators in local government. Additionally, a Public Service Benchmarking Body was established to examine public sector jobs and rates of pay relative to the private sector. The National Framework Committee on Family Friendly Practices was established to oversee the provision of family-friendly policies in the workplace. An initiative providing Targeted Investment in Disadvantaged Areas was later developed into the RAPID programme[1]. Five Pilot Social Inclusion Units were introduced in local authority areas and later increased to nine. Additionally, the programme spawned a range of working groups in areas as diverse as agricultural training, lifelong learning, immigrants, tax credits, public service pensions, social welfare and insurance, services for people with disabilities, housing, health sector implementation, sheltered workshops, community employment, maternity benefit and electronic payment. Arguably, the range and breath of initiatives introduced in the PPF held out the very real possibility that Social Partnership might collapse under the weight of its own enthusiasm.

In consequence, the Programme for Sustaining Progress, from 2003–5, attempted to rationalize the provision of new policy measures with the creation of ten Special Initiatives (namely, Housing and Accommodation; Cost and Availability of Insurance; Migration and Interculturalism; Long-term Unemployed, Vulnerable Workers and those made Redundant; Tackling Educational Disadvantage; Waste Management; Care – children, people with disabilities and older people; Alcohol/Drug Misuse; Including Everyone in the Information Society; and Ending Child Poverty).

The most recent partnership agreement, Towards 2016, attempts to establish a ten-year framework with a number of key objectives for economic and social development. With the specific inclusion of a package of measures to ensure greater compliance with labour standards, according to the General President of the Services, Industrial, Professional and Technical Union (SIPTU) the deal 'represents the maximum that could be achieved at this time through this process' (O'Connor, 2006).

Much of the recent fascination with the Irish 'Partnership State' (O'Donnell, 2008) suggests that the Irish case provides an exemplar of new modes of governance which is 'distinguished by a unique set of institutional innovations for creative, dynamic, and self-reflexive governance for social and economic development' (House and McGrath, 2004; see also Sabel, 2001; Teague, 2006). It has been suggested that 'the willingness of successive Irish governments to relinquish their unique role in policy-making, for the inclusion of agreed "social partners", demonstrates a changing attitude towards government' (Adshead and Quinn, 1998). This alleged shift has been variously characterized: for some it represents a move towards more corporatist styles of policy-making (Hardiman, 1992; Taylor, 1993) involving new governance networks (Hardiman, 2006). For others (O'Donnell and O'Reardon, 1997, 2000), Irish Social Partnership offers something more than traditional quasi-corporatist arrangements, warranting its depiction as a new form of 'post-corporatist concertation', characterized by 'deliberation' and 'problem-solving' between a wider range of interests than the traditional confederations of capital and labour, and where 'the capacity to shape and reshape parties' preferences are seen to be prominent features of the dealings between the social partners, interwoven into a process that also involves "hard-headed" bargaining' (O'Donnell and O'Reardon, 2000: 250).

Whatever the characterization, it is clear that social partnership is becoming embedded in the national system of governance (O'Donnell *et al.*, 2007; Adshead and McInerney, 2008a), though this process of institutionalization is not without a critique. Social Partnership is accused of diminishing democratic accountability and the role of the Dáil (O'Cinneide, 1998; Browne, 2006) and is criticized for providing uneven opportunities for political participation and representation of its constituent partners (Meade and O'Donovan, 2002; Murphy, 2002; McInerney, 2008a, 2008b). Commenting on democratic deficits implicit in social partnership arrangements, Adshead (2008) notes that while Social Partnership surely represents a significant trade-off between democratic accountability and the means to achieve economic growth, 'presumably the consensus regarding the "success" of social partnership reflects the view that this is a price worth paying'.

In Northern Ireland, the ending of direct rule from Westminster has seen a fundamental restructuring of the delivery of economic policy, although responsibility for macroeconomic management remains with the UK government. The Westminster government had operated different rules for Northern Ireland during the conflict than those present elsewhere in the UK, where a tough monetarist strategy and the curbing of aspects of the welfare state were evident. Given the special circumstances pertaining to Northern Ireland, more generous fiscal and social welfare policies were evident, as a means of employment generation and amelioration (Connolly, 1990). Nonetheless, there has been no formal coming together of business, labour and policy-makers during direct rule or since; corporatism in the UK died with the advent of Thatcherism in 1979.

Since the return of devolution, the Department of Enterprise, Trade and Investment (DETI) has been responsible for the development of economic policy. Given Northern Ireland's reliance upon the service sector, the ability of the DETI to promote private sector growth is limited and the amount of primary legislation it initiates is limited (averaging two bills annually, although this may grow). Within the DETI there are four agencies, of which Invest Northern Ireland is the body responsible for promoting inward investment, business growth, training and research. Economic priorities are outlined in the Executive's Programme for Government Budget and Investment Strategy. Invest Northern Ireland assumed the responsibilities of the Local Enterprise and Development Unit (LEDU), which was also based in the DETI. The LEDU was a failure in terms of its aims, of promoting local business growth, and its management, described as a 'profound failure of governance' (Northern Ireland Audit Office, 2006). Invest Northern Ireland has itself achieved only modest results, with only ten foreign firms being attracted to invest in the region through its efforts between 1999 and 2003 (http://bbc.co.uk/1/hi/northern_ireland/ 2911167.stm).

Labour market supply-side issues are addressed by the Department for Employment and Learning (DfEL), which has workforce employability as one of its key agendas and promotes learning and skills training. DfEL's framework is set at Westminster and much of its combating of unemployment has been conducted via the UK-wide New Deal, a package funded initially by a tax on public utilities and aimed at placing the unemployed into training, employment or education. Local economic projects are overseen by the Department for Regional Development, which is responsible for shaping the physical and social environment in Northern Ireland.

The 'Celtic Tiger': Distressed, Developmental or Deluded?

The name 'Celtic Tiger' emerged because Irish growth rates have been sustained at levels close to the phenomenal growth rates achieved by the four 'Asian Tigers' (South Korea, Taiwan, Hong Kong and Singapore), which averaged around 8 per cent per year over three decades before the crash in 1997/8 (Sweeney, 1999: 13). The turnaround was such that in 1997 *The Economist* (17 May 1997: 23) described the Irish Republic as 'one of the most remarkable economic transformations of recent years: from basket-case to "emerald tiger" in ten years'. Not surprisingly, the post hoc rationalization for this remarkable reversal of economic fortunes remains a central concern for many social scientists in Ireland and abroad, as does the lessons that might be learned from an examination of the Irish case (Adshead *et al.*, 2008). Although economic explanations of the 'Irish miracle' are legion (O'Donnell, 1998; Sweeney, 1999; Nolan *et al.*, 2000; Haughton, 2000; Clinch *et al.*, 2002; Ruane and Uğar, 2005; Andreosso-O'Callaghan and Lenihan, 2006), still the conclusions to be drawn from this experience are contested.

Kirby's (2002: 3–7) *Celtic Tiger in Distress* raises three major difficulties associated with mainstream interpretations of the economic boom. He not only questions 'assertions that the Irish economy has been transformed into a high-tech, high-growth economy', but notes that economic success has gone 'hand in hand with glaring social failures', which together suggest that the process of globalization has led to a 'resituating of the state into a subordinate relationship with global market forces'. Using Cerny's (2000) model of the 'competition' state, Kirby (2002: 143) argues that in this new relationship between the state and globalized markets, 'the state's scope of control over the national economy and society diminishes as economies integrate into the international marketplace'.

An alternative view of the state, put forward by O'Riáin's (2004) *The Politics of High-Tech Growth*, contradicts Kirby's (2002) on the grounds that 'it misses the political possibilities that exist within the current economy and polity' (O'Riáin, 2000: 187). In O'Riáin's (2004: 28) interpretation, governments are able to make a real difference in how states may position themselves in the international economic order, 'mediating between the global and the local, connecting them and shaping the nature of their relationship'. In O'Riáin's (2004: 47) opinion, the economic growth of the 1990s was characterized by the intersection of three major dynamics:

> industrial upgrading supported by a national system of innovation, reinforced by a broader set of socioeconomic changes generating local demand for technology goods and a variety of services, underpinned by an increasingly tenuous compromise of solidarity without equality.

Thus, like Kirby (2002), O'Riáin (2004: 47) also questions the evenness of Irish economic development, noting that the Irish 'welfare effort has decreased even as national wealth has increased'. The difference between the two, however, is in the extent to which O'Riáin (2008) believes that the state may (consciously or unconsciously) create spaces for political struggles about the nature and direction of economic development.

Perhaps the harshest critics of the Celtic Tiger phenomenon, however, are those who would contest the very nature of its 'success' at all. O'Hearn (2001) argues that official statistics grossly overstate the extent of the Republic's growth as a result of transfer pricing – the practice used by multinational corporations to depress the price of raw material imports in order to raise their profits artificially, thereby enabling those multinationals located in Ireland to pay relatively low Irish corporation taxes, whilst avoiding higher tax rates that might be due elsewhere. Thus, for example, analysis of the Irish trade figures for 'other ingredients' used by the Coca Cola plant in Drogheda suggest profits as high as £40 million a year, which is remarkably impressive for a factory employing around 200 employees (Sweeney, 1999: 51). For O'Hearn (2001: 84), the significant gap between the state's GNP (measuring the total outputs) and GDP (the same measure but excluding resources that leave the state), combined with 'stunningly low' investment rates, makes the Irish boom much less impressive.

This is a point of view shared to a great extent by Allen (2000, 2007). In *The Celtic Tiger: The Myth of Social Partnership in Ireland*, he argues that throughout the economic boom 'the majority of workers have lost out' as 'social partnership arrangements have ensured that workers received a declining share of the economy' – a situation that has been made possible by trades union complicity in the social partnership project (Allen, 2000: 103–25). In his later work, *The Corporate Takeover of Ireland* (2007: 242), he argues that 'the Irish political elite have embraced neo-liberalism on a grand scale and have offered themselves as a bridgehead for US influence in Europe'. The evidence for this, he argues, is in the increasing subjugation of the public sector to corporate style management, deliberate governmental strategies to weaken the unions and the close alignment of Irish foreign policy 'with the needs of the US empire' (Allen, 2007: 243).

The dominant political and public opinion seemed largely uninterested in the critique, being content to 'make hay while the sun shines'. The Irish were, according to the economist David McWilliams (2005: 1), 'borrowing, spending, shopping, shagging, eating, drinking and taking more drugs than any other nation'. According to him, 'the full-on nation' was 'burning the candle at both ends' (McWilliams, 2005: 13). It was all to end in tears; the Tiger disappeared, banished amid a very austere 2008 budget which reflected global economic crisis.

The possibility of a Celtic Tiger-type dash for growth in the North was always minimal even prior to the onset of global economic problems. Bereft of the power to vary its tax rates from UK levels, the devolved executive remains reliant upon handouts from the Treasury, which tend to be used to allocate welfare priorities rather than stimulate economic growth. Prior to global recession, the region had nonetheless come closer to full employment than at any time in its history, and, from 1998 until 2008 rising house prices and low inflation made Northern Ireland an attractive place to live. However, this did not disguise the excessive reliance upon the state for funding and, amid recession, Northern Ireland's subsidies were increasingly questioned.

Towards an All-Ireland Economy?

The rapid thawing of relations between the two parts of the island since the GFA has raised the prospect of greater all-island economic cooperation. Prior to the Agreement, cross-border trade was limited, falling below the level that might be expected between neighbouring states (Birnie and Hitchens, 2001). Northern Ireland looked to the rest of the UK as its natural market, accounting for nearly 40 per cent of the sale of its goods. North–South trade accounts for only 5 per cent of Northern Ireland's GDP, although this figure is more than double that found in the Irish Republic (Bradley and Birnie, 2001). Since 1990, cross-border trade has improved to account now for nearly one-quarter of Northern Ireland's manufacturing exports, a dramatic rise from the 7 per cent figure at the start of the 1990s (see www.detini. gov.uk). An economic 'cold war' had followed partition, marked by episodic boycotts of the goods of the 'rival' state. Unionist suspicion of political attempts to promote all-island trade sectorally, as in the GFA, is only slowly dissipating. Moreover, whatever the lack of a civil society dynamic for all-island linkages, there is clear support among both communities in Northern Ireland for sectoral cross-border economic cooperation, although this majority in favour disappears among Protestants when extended to the political or security spheres (MacCarthaigh and

Totten, 2001). The success of the Celtic Tiger to the South removed one Unionist argument – that of reduced economic circumstances – against the reintegration of the island, but it made no impact upon national identity or political aspirations.

The NSMC oversees aspects of all-island economic cooperation. Six new cross-border implementation bodies were established under the NSMC's remit: food safety; inland waterways (covering loughs); trade and business development; language; aquaculture and marine matters; and special EU programmes. Other areas of cooperation agreed in the GFA were agriculture, education, environment, transport, health and tourism. However, these areas would not fall under cross-border bodies with executive powers, implementing policies on an all-island basis. Instead, policy implementation would remain within the domain of each jurisdiction under previous arrangements. Thus far, the modest remit of the cross-border bodies (although they employ over 700 staff) has meant that the NSMC's importance has been more symbolic than actual, although it does appoint the boards of half of the all-island bodies. The significance of the NSMC lies in bringing together ministers from the two jurisdictions for annual (thus far) meetings, a visible sign of the defrosting of relationships and an indication that cross-border economic and political activity is diminishing in sensitivity (Coakley *et al.*, 2007; Tannam, 2007). Most of the significant activity takes place within the sectoral meetings in each area of cross-border cooperation. For the NSMC to become more dynamic in presiding over such cooperation, additions to the current set of all-island executive bodies would need to be agreed, a development requiring the approval of the Northern Ireland Assembly and the Dáil Éireann (House of Representatives). Nationalists have not abandoned their hopes, grounded in neo-functionalist ideas, that ever-growing economic cooperation across the island will have the political benefits of diminishing the relevance of the border and advancing the case for unity. Thus far, however, the insertion of formal checks upon growth, which prevent a free-standing dimension to the political promotion of all-island economic cooperation via the NSMC, has inhibited further integration.

Economic cooperation between the two parts of the island is backed by substantial financial support. In 2005, €846m was spent on all-island activity, with national operational programmes accounting for nearly half; the North–South bodies and GFA-agreed areas of cooperation costing 37 per cent and EU programmes providing a further 15 per cent (Centre for Cross Border Studies, 2007). Substantial funding for all-island initiatives has been evident since the International Fund for Ireland was established after the 1985 Anglo-Irish Agreement. Funding for cross-border initiatives, not necessarily economic, increased further with the implementation of the EU's Peace I and II programmes, which contributed over €1.3billion from 1995 to 2006, with further, small assistance available until 2013. The Northern Ireland Executive, via its Structural Funds Plan, and the Irish government, via its National Development Plan, produce a common chapter on all-island development, which guides the SEUPB in its development of all-Ireland economic agendas. Thus far, the common chapter has highlighted the fragmented and piecemeal nature of all-island cooperation, based upon, variously, intergovernmental (British–Irish) arrangement, North–South bodies, EU programmes and other aid programmes, highlighting a need for more integrated, systemic cooperation, a development likely to occur with the improved relations between the respective governments (Magennis, 2007).

Conclusion

Credit for the Republic of Ireland's remarkable economic turnaround was variously ascribed: (i) to a happy coincidence of good luck (making the most of its position mid-way 'between Boston and Berlin' and its experiencing a parallel growth trend with the US economy during the 1990s); (ii) to its good judgement (in developing multi-annual strategic planning in a relatively stable macroeconomic framework that is supported by European Monetary Union (EMU) as well as a consensual approach to the management of the economy, spearheaded by social partnership); (iii) to its fortunate benefiting from significant investment (in terms of the EU Structural Funds and Cohesion Funds); and (iv) to an unusually elastic labour supply (in the form of returning emigrants and new immigrants as well as demographic and structural changes to the labour force). Still, much of this economic boom was spent in construction and driven by the housing sector – both of which were experiencing a significant downturn in the early 2000s. The challenge for economic management in the Irish Republic, therefore, is to maintain economic growth and stability in less serendipitous conditions (Robinson and Adshead, 2008).

Northern Ireland's economy remains overly dependent upon subsidy from the UK Exchequer. Its economic fortunes are closely related to those of the UK in its entirety, within which, despite continuing peripheral status, the region has finally shed its position as its poorest part, courtesy of economic growth and peace monies. At the time that devolved power-sharing was restored in 2007, there was much hype from Northern Ireland's political leaders concerning a supportive economic package from the Treasury. Upon closer inspection, the headline £51.5billion of support measures contained much repackaged material (£35billion would have been allocated under the existing Barnett formula), but nonetheless provided a substantial sum of £18billion for the Executive to promote economic growth and to spend on priority areas. Whilst the package was attractive to the incumbent Executive, Northern Ireland's economic problems remained unaddressed. There remains little industry; there is an over-reliance upon jobs in the public sector and, beyond the 'kick-start' package, it is unclear how the Executive can lever sufficient economic control to generate further growth beyond that generated as part of the 'peace dividend'. Further devolution of responsibilities, including the ability to differentiate taxation rates from the remainder of the UK (a power awarded to the Scottish government, although, as yet, unused), would offer a partial solution.

11

Social Policy and the Welfare State

Want is only one of five giants on the road of reconstruction and in some ways the easiest to attack. The others are Disease, Ignorance, Squalor and Idleness.

William Beveridge (1942: 6)

Introduction

For several decades, social policy varied markedly in the two parts of Ireland, following the introduction of the welfare state in Great Britain and Northern Ireland and the dominance of the anti-state-welfare Catholic Church in the Irish Republic. Until independence the only poverty relief measures that existed in Ireland were the application of a limited number of reforms adopted by the British Government and applied in Ireland (see: Burke, 1999: 19–24) These included, in 1908, the Children's Act and the Old Age Pensions Act, and, in 1911, the National Insurance Act – the first act to provide an insured worker and his family the right to relief. Still, the advent of independence in 1922 did not see an upsurge in social legislation or provisions and it is notable that one of the first acts of the new Irish state was to reduce the rate of old age pension by 10 per cent (Kiely, 1999: 2). Moreover, given that the majority of Irish political institutions and its administrative bureaucracy, as well as such social policy as existed, were all inherited from Britain, it is notable that following independence the evolution of Irish welfare was markedly different to that of the UK (Daly and Yeates, 2003).

When, in 1942, the Beveridge Report was being widely acclaimed as a landmark turning point in the conceptualization of state responsibility for social provision, its impact on Ireland, while reflected in a Green Paper entitled *Social Welfare* in 1949 (Department of Social Welfare, 1949) and the establishment of the Department of Social Welfare by way of the 1952 Social Welfare Act, was otherwise negligible. Ireland did not adopt the Beveridge model of a welfare state that was introduced into Britain in 1948, and for several decades following lagged far behind income maintenance provisions in the UK (Mills, 1999: 8). Whilst it is true to state that the economic resources of the new state were simply not there to support any radical social policy, even if they were, the political desire seems equally lacking. The ideology of the new state was deeply conservative (Burke, 1999: 26).[1]

In Northern Ireland, the Beveridge ideal of 'cradle to grave' care was implemented, albeit with some reluctance. Here, the concerns of the Unionist Government were financial, as universal welfare provision was a costly undertaking. In contrast to the situation in the Irish Republic, however, there was no strong religious opposition to the state's enhanced role in welfare provision. Moreover, the innate conservatism and fiscal rectitude of the Unionist Government was to some extent countered by the realization that a strong welfare state would provide another claim to superiority for Northern Ireland over the confessional state to the South. As elsewhere in the United Kingdom, the NHS was very popular, and its implementation, along with the consolidation of piecemeal unemployment, national insurance and pensions provision into a state welfare package, was a means of ensuring continuing support for the Unionist Party from the Protestant working class. Unionist fears were finally allayed when the UK Government agreed in 1949 to bear most of the cost of unemployment and social welfare provision (Buckland, 1981). The result was the creation of a welfare state in Northern Ireland which provided a strong case against a united Ireland, even though it made scant impact upon constitutional preferences.

Origins and Influences

In the Republic of Ireland and Northern Ireland, the original common origins of the British welfare system soon diverged into two quite distinct welfare regimes. In the UK, Clement Atlee's post-war Government (1945–51) was responsible for the creation of the British welfare state, infused as it was with labour values of solidarity and social reform. According to Harris (1996: 122):

> the rhetorical hallmark of the early years were the replacement of 'charity', 'dependency', 'moralism' and bureaucratic surveillance of private lives by a new ethic of social 'citizenship'. The principle would be universalism as opposed to selectivity, entitlement rather than discretion, and benefits paid on the basis of needs rather than means tests.

In the Republic of Ireland, by contrast, the 1937 constitution, which cemented democratic transition following independence, described a state with a quite different character. In government, the influence of the Catholic Church was evident not only through the impact of Catholic social teaching upon the content of public policy on marriage, divorce, contraception, health services, but also in the degree to which the Church became embedded in the system of social services developing in post-independence Ireland. By far the most important of these was education, which continues to be organized and managed along religious lines (Fuller, 2002: 149–62). The pattern in education was repeated to a more limited extent in a number of other social services, including hospital services, the care of orphaned and homeless children, the 'rescue of fallen women' and a limited range of services for the poor and for unemployed women (Inglis, 1987; Fahey, 1992). In each case, the Church was the only institution capable of sustaining a level of provision comparable to that of the state. The response by the state at some points was hostile or competitive, but, for the most part, partnership of some sort was the preferred option (Fahey, 1992: 252). As a consequence, key areas of the social services became a joint venture between the 'voluntary' Church effort and official funding and administration.

In the stead of more radical or reformist social analysis that might have been provided by the secular left, the Catholic Church in Ireland copper-fastened its position as an influential social force and subsequently maintained and protected its influence by demonizing 'the evils of socialism' (Larkin, 1985). MacMahon (1981: 279) noted that although the clergy were generous and often self-sacrificing in their efforts to help the poor, their response to social misery was determined to a large extent by the prevailing social, political and economic ideas of the time. It was an accepted fundamental belief that there was a natural social order imposed on humankind by the Creator and many clerics were inclined to allocate the responsibility for social problems to 'feckless individuals', wanting in thrift, diligence or common sense (MacMahon, 1981: 266). In this socio-cultural climate, alternative social discourses on poverty soon distinguished the 'deserving' from the 'undeserving' poor (Devereux, 1998) and so helped to reinforce the social stratification that was already being established by a range of means-tested and targeted social provisions. In consequence, although the Irish welfare regime does incorporate some universalized provisions (such as child benefit and old age pensions), on the whole 'Ireland's mix of means-tested, insurance-based and universalist income support and service arrangements' (NESC, 2005: 35) make it difficult to discern any over-arching orthodoxy or attitudes towards social provision. In fact, the most recent major study of the Irish welfare system made a point of acknowledging that even 'describing it as a "system" risks implying the ensemble has more internal logic than is the case', concluding instead that the hybrid nature of the system might be better characterized as 'a mongrel welfare system of mixed parentage' (ibid.).

Initially sceptical of the onset of socialist provision, the post-World War II Unionist regime nonetheless had agreed in the 1945 General Election to implement any welfare reforms supported by voters elsewhere in the UK (Bew *et al.*, 1996). The Unionists were more convincingly persuaded of the merits of the welfare state when favourable financial terms for its implementation were offered by the Westminster Government. As a result, the post-war welfare settlement elsewhere in the UK was replicated in Northern Ireland, along with major programmes of house building. Over 100,000 homes were brought into local authority control, and although not all slums were removed defenders of the Unionist government argued this was impossible given the state of the housing stock inherited by the embryonic welfare state (Wilson, 1989). Social ministries in Northern Ireland mirrored their Whitehall counterparts.

Inevitably, there were some sectarian issues. That Catholic objections to full state provision were over-ridden meant that the Mater Hospital was excluded from assistance, the Unionist Government deciding that hospitals were to be either 100 per cent state funded and controlled or unaided (Buckland, 1981). The Minister for Education was obliged to resign after proposing an increase in funding for voluntary schools (mostly Catholic) from 50 per cent to 65 per cent (Bew *et al.*, 1996). These rows were sideshows, however, and improvements in housing and health were soon evident. Of greater concern than welfare provision, though, was the ailing state of the Northern Ireland economy. A plethora of reports from the late 1950s until the end of the 1990s highlighted the structural vulnerability and economic inefficiency which beset the region (Birnie and Hitchens, 2001). Regional planning proved inadequate, lacking in coherence and vision, whilst local councils were too weak to develop a serious strategic vision (Wichert, 1999). Northern Ireland's 'serious problems as a viable and self-sustaining economic entity' have not disappeared (Munck and Hamilton, 1998: 148). However, generous welfare provision has been mainly funded by the British taxpayer, which has ensured that the region's benefit system has remained largely immune from the pressures which a dysfunctional and dependent economy might otherwise have generated.

Welfare Reform: Critical Junctures and Key Drivers for Change

For the Republic of Ireland, in contrast to most other European states, 'the ending of the second world war was not a moment of great upheaval' (Conroy, 1999: 34). Whilst across Europe, the economic, political and social challenges presented by post-war reconstruction and development provided the impetus for new political alliances and policy approaches (George and Taylor-Gooby, 1996: 2–4), in Ireland the underlying thinking and policies which had developed in the 1930s and 1940s continued on into the 1950s and 1960s (Conroy, 1999: 34). The First Programme for Economic Expansion covering the period 1959–63 (see pp. 184–5) signalled the integration of Ireland into the world economy and the beginning of a new economic context more favourable to the extension of social security (McCashin, 2004: 40). State welfare was expanded through the introduction of insurance and means-tested schemes for groups like the unemployed, deserted wives and unmarried mothers, as well as new benefits including invalidity and death benefit (Kirby, 2007: 6). The introduction of free secondary education in 1967 led to a major increase in the numbers completing the second level: as a consequence educational provision was expanded at the second and third levels. Overall, Ireland's social welfare expenditure increased from 5.5 per cent of GDP in 1960 to 6.8 per cent in 1968 and to 11.4 per cent in 1974 (Kirby, 2007: 7). If spending on education, health and housing is included, overall social expenditure increased from 14.5 per cent of GDP in 1962 to 20.5 per cent a decade later (ibid.).

The pace and scale of change was further accelerated in the 1970s, when 'Ireland's entry into the European Community (EC) in 1973 incurred a series of legal obligations, relating to non-discrimination and equality of pay, which began to challenge attitudes to women, the workplace and the family' (Adshead, 2005: 172). More concretely, the application of Article 119, requiring member states to enforce the principle that men and women should receive equal pay for equal work, meant that Ireland was forced to 'end all sex discrimination in social security schemes that are work related' (ibid.). In partial consequence of this, by the early 1980s, it was clear that a review of social welfare policies was badly needed (Mills, 1999: 13). In 1983, Barry Desmond, the Labour Minister for Social Welfare, established a Commission on Social Welfare (CSW), charged with the task of reviewing the entire social welfare system and related social services. The commission produced a blueprint for consolidation of the existing social welfare system, based on three financial objectives for social security policy: the abolition of poverty, income redistribution and income replacement. In addition, the Commission listed five principles that should both guide the operation of the system and be used in its evaluation. These were: adequacy, redistribution, comprehensiveness, consistency, and simplicity (Adshead and Murphy, forthcoming).

Although the report has been criticized by some for its lack of structural recommendations (Cousins, 1995; McCashin, 2004), it may still be regarded as an important landmark in the story of Irish social policy, introducing the concept of an 'adequacy benchmark' and the promotion of poverty reduction objectives into Irish social welfare. Moreover, its relatively positive tone, which sought to 'expand and significantly improve the present system' (CSW, 1986: 184), went against contemporary international trends for welfare cutbacks and constraint. With over a hundred recommendations, the CSW Report was sufficiently detailed to serve as a 'bible' or frame of reference for senior departmental officials who regularly turned to it as a source of direction. Its adequacy benchmarks framed the debate about income adequacy for the next decade, and the social insurance system developed according to its recommendations. In 1987, the thinking behind the initial social partnership agreement was influenced by the availability of a ready-made analysis that argued for protecting and increasing the incomes of the poorest and expanding social insurance coverage (Adshead and Murphy, forthcoming).

Subsequent social partnership agreements also included commitments designed to tackle poverty and exclusion. In 1990, negotiations for the second social partnership agreement, the Programme for Economic and Social Progress (PESP) 1991–3, included an ABR to long-term unemployment. Established on a pilot basis as 'an integrated approach designed to implement a community response in particular local areas to long-term unemployment and the danger of long-term unemployment' (Government of Ireland, 1991). Twelve ABR areas were selected (eight urban and four rural), and each ABR project had a board comprising six directors from the local community, six from the social partners and six from the state agencies in the area (Adshead, 2002: 78). ABR initiatives were further developed in subsequent agreements and they still remain a key government policy instrument for tackling disadvantage (most recently in the RAPID and DEIS initiatives).

Negotiated with the Rainbow Coalition (Fine Gael/Labour/Democratic Left), the fourth pact agreement, Partnership 2000 (P2K) 1997–2000, was considered by many to be the most ambitious yet, for it reflected a significant shift of emphasis compared to other programmes (O'Donnell *et al.*, 2007). Alongside commitments to pay increases and tax reduction, this pact was notable for its inclusion of representatives from the community and voluntary sector which, when combined with a thematic approach to the identification and prioritization of objectives, tended to broaden the programme's sphere of interest (NESF, 1997). As a result, Partnership 2000 laid a stronger emphasis on dealing with inequality, long-term unemployment and social exclusion than had been the case in other pacts. P2K was responsible for the creation of the Equality Authority (which replaced the Employment Equality Agency), a Commission on wage differentials, and one on the family, as well as a review body for Special Education (O'Donnell *et al.*, 2007). Since then, the extension of social partnership to include the community and voluntary sector has been criticized for not adequately supporting their effective inclusion in policy negotiations (Adshead and McInerney, 2008a). According to Ó'Riáin (2008: 179):

> the extensions of social partnership itself have been damaged by the withdrawal, and subsequent exclusion, of some sections of the community and voluntary sector from partnership processes at the national level and the reassertion of central authority over the local partnerships (for example, in the reconstitution of Area Development Management Ltd around a model of service delivery rather than community empowerment and the sidelining of the Community Workers' Cooperative).

Others have argued that the institutionalization of anti-poverty and social inclusion measures within social partnership has precluded their further growth and development as policy areas in their own right (Connolly, 2007). Whilst in theory, the establishment of a National Anti-Poverty Strategy (NAPS) in 1997 might seem to contradict this view, in practice the impact of the NAPS has been much less significant than was originally intended (Adshead and Millar, 2008; Adshead and McInerney, 2008a).

Formally launched after an extensive consultative process in 1997, the original concept of NAPS was threefold: to achieve greater integration in policy initiatives by identifying cross-cutting themes in government departments; to establish 'poverty proofing' of all government initiatives and key policy areas; and, most significantly from a governance perspective, to develop the participation of people living in poverty whose lived experience might inform policy solutions and bring greater urgency to the debate about poverty (Adshead and Millar, 2008). The absence of such voices in decision-making has in the past been identified as one of the weaknesses in corporatist or neo-corporatist governance mechanisms (Peters, 2004). As such, NAPS was a potentially innovative cross-cutting institutional mechanism that widened the concept of governance by validating consultation with people experiencing poverty and affirming the role of NGOs in policy-making. Although a change of government in 1997 diluted political support for the strategy, the incoming Fianna Fáil/PD Government allowed the institutional mechanisms to remain in place.

In 2005, the publication by the NESC of *The Developmental Welfare State* marked another important milestone in Irish conceptualizations of the rights of citizens and responsibilities of government in terms of social welfare. Originating from a commitment negotiated in the fifth social partnership agreement, Programme for Prosperity and Fairness (2000–2), the 'developmental welfare state' (DWS) framework is underscored by 'the Council's starting conviction ... that Ireland's strong economic performance is a new context within which to seek major improvements in social protection' (NESC, 2005: 197). The conclusion to the report argues that 'good economic performance and improved social protection are neither intrinsically opposed nor compelled to occur together in some automatic way, but that they *can be made to support each other*' (NESC, 2005: 198). In order to achieve this, the Council advises reform of the welfare state along three key dimensions.

The first and most important of these reforms relates to the *provision* of social protection, where an upgrading of both the scope and the quality of the state's 'service effort' is proposed. This will involve increasing the proportion of public versus private social protection provision, so that public sector service providers 'provide high quality services and halt the current erosion in the take up of public services by individuals who have the means to purchase private sector alternatives' (NESC, 2005: 203). The second area for reform relates to *access* to social protection. Advancing the idea of 'tailored universalism', the Council proposes that essentially, 'at the key point of interface between a service professional and the person using the service, there should be neither an incentive nor a reason for the provider to take account of the income circumstances of the client but only of the person's need' (ibid.). Here the challenge for the system is to develop integrated and effectively coordinated social protection policies that may be combined as appropriate or 'tailored' to meet individual need. The final area of reform relates to *income adequacy*, which most crucially is seen as a 'necessary but not sufficient condition' for social inclusion (see Adshead and Murphy, forthcoming, for further details).

Whilst the DWS report is the most conspicuous and most comprehensive attempt to date to re-reorient the current scope and shape of social protection policies in Ireland, opinion varies about the direction that this new orientation may point to. On the one hand, it can be construed as an attempt to develop social solidarity and service effort, characteristic of higher welfare providers such as Nordic and Continental Europeans. On other hand, elements of workfare and 'third way' suggest more UK workfare-inspired reforms associated with more liberal welfare regimes (Murphy and Millar, 2007; Murphy, 2008). More generally, the unambiguous attempt to integrate social protection policies with broader state welfare and employment policies reflects a conscious effort to forge policy (and by their nature political) linkages between state action on employment, health and welfare (Adshead and Murphy, forthcoming). Though in this regard the contradictory tendencies of various social protection policies could be seen as an impediment to large scale reform, the NESC report chooses to make a virtue from what others might see as a vice, arguing that the 'mongrel system' may perhaps prove 'more robust in adapting to globalisation and shifts in values than purebred "pedigree specimens" of welfare states with more accentuated regime characteristics' (NESC, 2005: 35). The key features and contradictory tendencies within the Irish 'hybrid' system are noted in the summary review of the five main realms of state welfare activity considered below.

Noting the origins of the Troubles in the civil rights campaigns against discrimination, economic growth and generous welfare provision were viewed by the British government as potential violence-reducing agents in Northern Ireland. Although such a view leant towards economic reductionism in its partial addressing of conflict causation, there was a clear link between social deprivation and propensity for support for paramilitary groups. In areas controlled by republican and Loyalist paramilitary groups, alternative local states developed, with republicans, in particular, developing political strength by assisting benefit recipients in obtaining maximum benefit entitlements and providing additional 'services' in terms of transport, finance and even policing, all strengthening paramilitary control. Indeed in respect of 'paramilitary policing', it was significant that two-thirds of 'punishments' being exercised were within areas classified as 'very deprived' in terms of income (Monaghan and McLaughlin, 2006: 184).

Northern Ireland's economically weak position within the United Kingdom has placed considerable stress upon the benefit system. Much of the concentration has been upon intercommunity inequality, rather than Northern Ireland's socio-economic position in relation to the rest of the UK. Since the 1990s, there has been a plethora of initiatives aimed at addressing inequality and poverty. The UK government's commitment to the EU Social Chapter has addressed issues of working conditions, health and safety, and gender equality (Bew *et al.*, 1997).

In respect of Northern Ireland's particular problems, in advance of the GFA, the Policy Appraisal and Fair Treatment (PAFT) initiative was designed to ensure that all policies under direct rule would have equitable outcomes across both communities. PAFT was developed under the auspices of the Standing Advisory Commission on Human Rights, which argued for an interventionist approach to fair employment (Dickson and Osborne, 2007). Following PAFT, the Targeting Social Need programme aimed to skew expenditure to address deprivation generally and close the remaining gaps between the two communities, whilst, post-Agreement, 'New' Targeting Social Need has attempted to address unemployment, health, housing and education problems (Shirlow and Murtagh, 2006). These region-wide initiatives have been developed alongside the introduction of an Equality Commission under the GFA, accompanied by neighbourhood initiatives such as the 17 'pockets of deprivation' targeted by the Department for Social Development; and alongside multi-agency economic regeneration groupings such as the West Belfast Task Force and North Belfast Partnership, which have cross-community input, and the implementation of major EU-funded programmes, notably the URBAN and PEACE initiatives.

Despite local, national and European legislation, perceptions of inequality remain. As Mitchell (2003: 69) notes, 'the shift from victimhood to equality is one of the most important changes in contemporary Northern Ireland politics'; but the desire of nationalists to arrive in a 'better place' has not halted demands for transition. The achievement of near parity between Unionists and nationalists has helped transfer focus to other inequalities. Women Assembly members, themselves enjoying only modest representation in a male-dominated Assembly, have highlighted gender inequalities, even though their role on Assembly committees dealing with social issues tends to be stronger (Cowell-Meyers, 2003; Ward, 2007). Social class represents 'one of the most important sources of inequality and division within contemporary Northern Irish society' (Coulter, 1999a: 99–100).

How Does Ireland Compare?

An examination of the five main realms of social protection reveals divergent patterns in the Republic of Ireland and Northern Ireland. In 1992, the Republic of Ireland was spending 23 per cent of its GNP per capita on social protection per capita, a figure that fell to 19 per cent in 2001 (NESC, 2005: 105). Despite a 46 per cent increase in social spending per capita in real terms (due to the phenomenal growth in the economy), when we compare the absolute levels of social spending per capita across the EU, in terms of a common purchasing power standard (PPS),

'Ireland was estimated to be spending 3,875 PPS units per person on social expenditure whereas the average for the EU as a whole was 6,405 units' (NESC, 2005: 106). Put another way, social spending per capita in Ireland in 2001 was 60.5 per cent of the EU15 average (NESC, 2005: 107). Using data for 1998, the OECD (2002: 24–5) observes that Ireland, along with the USA, Japan and Korea, spends significantly less than might be expected, given its level of wealth.

A further distinction to be made in comparative evaluation of social expenditure is the difference between private and public social spending. Some private spending (on mandatory social insurance schemes, for example) provides a significant component to overall expenditure. This is significant, since there are very different distributional consequences attached to private versus public social expenditure. For example, higher private social spending (often by privileged groups of workers in sectoral social insurance schemes) may completely bypass the most vulnerable groups in society who are outside the workforce (elderly, children, unemployed, disabled, etc.). Even when compared with the so-called 'Anglo-Saxon countries', characterized by liberal welfare regimes, Ireland was estimated to have the lowest level of private social spending – a position which is not changed when (generous) tax breaks for pensions are included (NESC, 2005: 112). This, combined with the relatively low expenditure on public social protection, has led the OECD to conclude that Ireland is 'a particularly low spender on social protection by EU and OECD standards' (NESC, 2005: 113). Out of 18 countries studied by the OECD (using 1997 data), only Korea, Japan and New Zealand spend a smaller proportion of their GDP on net social expenditure than Ireland (Adema, 2001). Moreover, despite the inevitable time lag in cross-national data collection and analysis, NESC (2005: 110) notes that, even though this conclusion is drawn in relation to 1997 data, the relatively stable structures of alternative state taxation systems mean that even when newer data appear, the patterns revealed are unlikely to change.

Northern Ireland retains a relatively privileged position in terms of social protection. Although its taxation levels remain attuned to UK levels, the Assembly and Executive being denied this fiscal responsibility, public expenditure on the region by the UK Treasury remains disproportionately high. Such spending accounts for 70 per cent of regional GDP, compared to a UK average of 44 per cent (Centre for Economic and Business Research, 2007; *The Times*, 10 October 2007). State pensions and benefits alone consume 20 per cent of GDP, more than double the comparable percentage in London and South East England (Smith, D., 2006). Northern Ireland's lower GDP compared to elsewhere in the UK can be attributed to several factors: a higher percentage of (economically inactive) under-16-year-olds (23 per cent, compared to 19 per cent in the UK in its entirety); a rate of economic activity among adults that is 5 per cent lower (73 per cent, compared to 78 per cent); and substantially lower (£111 per month in 2007) gross household incomes.

Poverty

Overall, Kirby (2007: 24) notes that between 1987 and 2005 average incomes in the Republic rose by 125 per cent in real terms. On the face of it then, the average Irish person is clearly much better off than they used to be. Crucially, however, it seems that a rising tide has not lifted all boats. In 2001, Ireland had the highest at-risk-of-poverty rate in the EU15 (NESC, 2005: 125). The contrast between trends in absolute poverty, which is steadily declining, and trends in the at-risk-of-poverty rate, which is steadily rising, reflects an important debate about how advanced economies conceive 'poverty'. In the Irish context, 'consistent poverty' used to be defined as being below 50–60 per cent of *average household* income (Department of Social and Family Affairs, 2001), with the experience of basic deprivation being measured by at least one of eight indicators (Whelan *et al.*, 2003: 34–5). Following Irish convergence to agreed common EU indicators, however, consistent poverty is now measured as being below 50–60 per cent of the *median individualized* income. The at-risk-of-poverty rate reflects the fact that, whilst having an income level below 60 per cent of the median income is neither a necessary nor a sufficient condition of being in a state of poverty, it is generally a good indicator of 'poverty risk'. Since 2003, the EU's at-risk-of-poverty rate has been more centrally adopted in measuring poverty in Ireland, which enables us to identify significant clusters of 'relative poverty' as a result.

Children and adults in lone-parent households experienced a 48.3 per cent risk of relative poverty compared to a national average of 19.4 per cent (Murphy, 2007a: 110). Irish people aged 65 years and over had the highest at-risk-of-poverty rate in the EU15 for people of comparable age; and the income of these people was, on average, 69 per cent of those people aged 0–64, a lower proportion than in any other EU member state (NESC, 2005: 129). People with disabilities, who experience a significantly higher risk of poverty, can in particular experience a higher risk of consistent poverty. The CSO (2005: 1) estimated that, in 2004, 21.7 per cent experienced deprivation compared to 6.8 per cent of the total population. Travellers remain one of the most disadvantaged and discriminated against groups in Irish society, faring badly on every indicator of disadvantage including unemployment, illiteracy, poverty, health status, access to decision-making and political representation (Crowley, 2007: 89).

Interestingly, in addition to the young, the old and the vulnerable, whom we might expect to be most at risk, recent labour force data indicates a burgeoning category of employees whose income is not sufficient to lift them out of poverty, which has almost quadrupled over the course of the boom (Kirby, 2007: 27). The conclusion reached by Nolan and Smeeding (2004: 559) that 'only the United States, Russia and Mexico have higher levels of inequality' confirms that 'among the richest OECD nations Ireland has the second highest level of inequality'. Table 11.1 provides the percentage figures for those in poverty, by occupation.

Although a post-conflict boom in Northern Ireland has been visible, there has, as in the Irish Republic, been a section of the population left behind. Indeed, such a trend was evident as the conflict subsided. During the 1980s and 1990s, the percentage of individuals in households with less than 50 per cent of average household income, after housing costs had been accounted for, grew from 9 per cent to 24 per cent (Steele and Shirlow, 1999; Shirlow and Shuttleworth, 1999). In the final 14 years of the conflict, from 1980 until 1994, the top 10 per cent of earners averaged

Table 11.1   *Households in Poverty in the Republic of Ireland (60 per cent or Less of Median Income), 1994–2005 (%)*

Labour force status	1994	1998	2001	2005
Employee	3.2	2.6	8.1	7.0
Farmer	18.6	23.9	23.0	n/a
Other self-employed	16.0	16.4	14.3	n/a
Unemployed	51.4	58.8	44.7	40.6
Ill/disabled	29.5	54.5	66.5	40.6
Retired	8.2	18.4	36.9	20.5
Home duties	20.9	46.8	46.9	27.6

Source: Murphy, M., 2006: 97; EU-SILC, 2006 (in Kirby, 2007: 27).

salaries eight times higher than those of the least wealthy 50 per cent, at the outset, rising to 13 times higher by the time of the paramilitary ceasefires in 1994 (Coulter, 1999a). The GFA's focus on erasing equality, amid a polity of few class politics, was concerned with the eradication of intercommunal inequality, which was relatively minor compared to the gulf in household incomes. This led to criticism of the Agreement as an 'enterprise that has neither the ability nor indeed the intention of creating a just and progressive society on the island' (Coulter, 1999b: 97).

Health

Public expenditure (capital and non-capital) on the health services has increased greatly since 1990 and by almost 200 per cent in real terms since 1997 (Layte *et al.*, 2007: 113). Despite the dramatic increase in public health spending, however, 'there is a generalised concern that the public health services have not only not improved but deteriorated' (NESC, 2005: 118). Moreover, it is clear that health-related outcomes in Ireland leave considerable room for improvement: in 2001, life expectancy was the lowest in the EU15, the infant mortality rate was the highest, and the standardized death rates from diseases of the circulatory system, cancer and diseases of the respiratory system were consistently the highest for both men and women (NESC, 2005: 119). Although, on the whole, the Republic's provision of healthcare is essentially redistributive, with 30 per cent of expenditure going to the bottom quintile of income distribution (Nolan, 1991; O'Shea and Kennelly, 2002: 65), the pattern of provision has led to an extremely stratified system of care. Whilst the Irish state provides a comprehensive good quality healthcare system for public patients, it then subsidizes those with higher incomes who opt out of that system through tax breaks on private care and insurance. In 1990, 34 per cent of the population had private health insurance, increasing to 40 per cent in 1998 and 50 per cent in 2003 (Layte *et al.*, 2007: 120). The fact that so much privately funded care is given in public hospitals has helped 'a structure to evolve whereby the public health services themselves incorporate faster access and arguably better care for half the population, the half with more resources' (*Irish Times*, 29 December 2000). The view that this has helped to promote a 'two-tier' healthcare system that is neither economically sustainable nor socially desirable is a common critique (O'Shea and Kennelly, 2002; Wren, 2003; Wiley, 2005; Millar, 2004).

Although historically enjoying a beneficial position, the Northern Ireland Executive now struggles to maintain health services at levels above those comparable with Britain. The first budget produced after the 2007 restoration of devolution projected an increase in spending of only 12 per cent, compared to 19 per cent in England and Wales, despite battles between the Health Minister (Michael McGimpsey) and the Finance Minister (Peter Robinson) similar to those between ministers and the Chancellor in the UK spending round (Gudgin, 2008). Between 1999 and 2002, spending on health in Northern Ireland fell from 112 per cent to 109 per cent of the UK average, still a favoured position, but one in decline (Midwinter, 2007). Health is the most popular policy area for increases in public expenditure (Department of Health, Social Services and Public Safety, 2002).

The Department of Health, which presides over an excessive 18 delivery organizations, launched its regional strategy, *Health and Well Being; Into the Next Millennium*, shortly after devolution, based upon a detailed plan containing 12 strategic objectives by which health performance could be monitored (McQuade and Fagan, 2002). Most health indicators in Northern Ireland are very close to the UK average, although life expectancy is slightly below that across the UK as a whole, a figure which in turn is marginally below the EU average. Heart failure and cancer remain the two largest causes of death in Northern Ireland, a common picture across the UK. Infant mortality in Northern Ireland remains slightly higher than elsewhere in the UK, although much less markedly than in earlier decades.

Education

When public spending on education is expressed per pupil/student in common PPSs, international comparisons show that Ireland spends relatively large sums for each student in the tertiary level and particularly small sums for each student in the primary and secondary levels (NESC, 2005: 120). Comparatively speaking, the 15 and 21 per cent of GNP per capita being spent at primary and secondary levels respectively in 2001 were the lowest proportionate investments in the EU15; whilst the 32 per cent of GNP per capita spent at the tertiary level (excluding research and development) was the highest (ibid.). This goes some way to explaining the 'notable persistence in educational inequalities by social background' found by Smyth and Hannan (2000: 117): public spending on education is regressive as 'the state spends more on the education of better-off young people, who tend to stay in the system longer, than it does on young people from poorer backgrounds, who tend to leave the system earlier' (Kirby, 2007: 61).

In 2005 a report by the National Council for Curriculum and Assessment (NCCA, 2005) acknowledged that a significant challenge for the current system of provision was 'how to ensure that an education system originally designed to serve the needs of an elite few can be re-shaped to meet the needs of a broader, more diverse group of learners'. It has been argued, however, that despite the reforms, so far 'the schooling system has been slow to respond to change and developments have lagged behind those in wider society' (Smyth *et al.*, 2007: 154).

Considering that UK Treasury expenditure on education in Northern Ireland remains above the UK average (in 2002, the region received 128 per cent of the UK average), Northern Ireland's educational performance is mixed (Midwinter, 2007). For those entering grammar schools, there is the prospect of university education; and the success of those schools has ensured that the private education sector remains tiny, representing only 5 per cent of the sector. Almost 99 per cent of entrants to Northern Ireland's two universities are drawn from the state sector. Given the 'elite' Russell Group status of Queen's University Belfast, this is a striking figure, as the average state sector entrance percentage for the Russell Group in its entirety is 80 per cent. However, the success of grammar schools also made starker the disparities in educational performance. By 2002, over one-third of school leavers achieved three A level passes (Department for Employment and Learning (NI), 2006a:1) Moreover, 13 per cent of all school leavers completed their education with three 'A' grade A levels, but over 5 per cent left school bereft of any qualifications (*Hansard*, 23 February 2004, col. 153W). Grammar schools offer excellent standards and results, but amount to only one-quarter of secondary schools. The devolved Executive embarked upon an education strategy entitled Raising Standards for All, but this ambition tended to be overshadowed by continuing rows over the future of the 11+ transfer test. With Sinn Féin and the SDLP opposed to the test and the DUP and UUP in favour of its retention, the debate at times adopted a sectarian flavour. Sinn Féin's control of the Department of Education from 1998 allowed the party to develop its agenda on the issue and abolish the transfer test, although it appeared that some form of selection at the age of 14 would still be permissible within the revised system.

Another educational concern has been the supposed 'brain drain' of graduate talent from Northern Ireland:40 per cent of students from Northern Ireland who study at university do not remain in the region upon graduation) (Department for Employment and Learning (NI), 2006b: 2). Of the students studying in Great Britain, almost one in five remains there rather than returning to Northern Ireland, whilst the Republic of Ireland accounts for only 3 per cent of graduate employment destinations of Northern Ireland graduates, a figure which may increase with the promotion of teacher qualifications and exchanges under Strand 2 of the GFA (ibid.).

Overall, education in Northern Ireland was described two decades ago as 'largely an adoption of policy in Great Britain', and little has altered in the intervening years to reshape this view (Connolly and Loughlin, 1990: 321). The school curriculum mirrors that elsewhere in the UK, and the much-fabled supposed greater emphasis on science and mathematics in non-Catholic schools is mythical. The growth of citizenship classes, introduced into the national curriculum in the 2000s, may represent an area of difference, as any promotion of British values might be seen as at odds with the spirit of the GFA.

Housing

There are, according to O'Sullivan (2003: 52), three different ways of conceptualizing and measuring housing need: the number of households that apply to local authorities for housing and are deemed in need; the number of households that apply for local authority housing, but are deemed better suited to some other form of social provision; and the numbers of households in the private rental sector in receipt of rent allowance under the Supplementary Welfare Allowance. In 1999, depending on the metric used, the number of households requiring social housing ranged from just under 40,000 to just under 80,000 (ibid.). Measurements of the homeless are similarly contested, with official statistics putting the number of homeless in Ireland at 2,751 in 1991 and 2,667 in 1993 (O'Sullivan, 2003: 43–4). By the late 1990s, however, it was argued that the 'housing crisis' not only affected 'groups for whom affordable accommodation is a perennial problem – the homeless, destitute and economically marginal households', but, 'for the first time in over thirty years, affordable housing was a middle class problem' (Galligan, 1998: 145). The young employed, who in earlier decades would have stepped onto the property ladder as a matter of course, were particularly hard hit by this development (Lane, 2001).

The most usual explanation for this crisis is the ratio of house prices to earnings. In the mid-1990s, average house prices were three to four times average industrial earnings, but by 2003 they were eight to ten times average industrial earnings (Downey, 2005, quoted in Fahey and Duffy, 2007: 131). Whilst the rise in house prices that came with the economic boom was quite disproportionate to the increasing house-building costs (Drudy and Punch, 2001: 248), just as significant were the cutbacks in social housing. Whereas, prior to the 1980s, social housing output usually amounted to some 20–30 per cent of new house construction, this level fell to 6 per cent in 2000 then rose again to 10 per cent in 2002 (Fahey and Duffy, 2007: 136). Taken together, this led to a major reduction in the accessibility of housing for low-income groups, which was only partially compensated by an expansion of rent allowances under the Supplementary Welfare Scheme.

Housing policy in Northern Ireland has followed that elsewhere in the UK in terms of 'right-to-buy', the popular Thatcherite policy introduced at the beginning of the 1980s which allowed those living in council housing ('social housing' in Northern Ireland, due to the removal of local councils from the allocation of provision) to buy their own homes at a discount below market values. Between 1979 and 2007, the Northern Ireland Housing Executive (NIHE) sold over 110,000 homes to their occupants, such sales now totalling almost one-quarter of the owner-occupied sector and 16 per cent of the entire housing market (Department for Social Development, 2007). Critics of such policy note that 32,000 were on a waiting list for social housing in 2007, of which one-third were officially classed as homeless, a figure which has risen in recent years, with the Assembly committee on Social Development instigating an inquiry into the problem (Wilford, 2007). Overall, owner-occupation accounts for three-quarters of Northern Ireland's housing market, as the region, until recently at least, was a repository of good value, affordable housing.

As the cost of private houses in Northern Ireland has soared, substantially outstripping the retail price index for every year since the conflict effectively ended in 1994, the pressure to provide affordable housing has increased. This problem is exacerbated by the lower wages (12 per cent lower) paid in the region compared to elsewhere in the UK. Amid steep price rises, the percentage of homes being sold to first-time buyers fell dramatically, from 60 per cent of the market in 2001 to 36 per cent a mere six years later (Department for Social Development, 2007).

Public housing in Northern Ireland is allocated by the NIHE, a body whose work is overseen by the Department for Social Development (DSD). Although the DSD provides the strategic overview for the work of the NIHE, most (over 90 per cent) of its staff work in the Social Security or Child Support Agencies. These agencies, rather than housing projects, absorb most of the DSD's £4.785million budget (2006–7 figures). The NIHE's own budget amounts to £600million annually, of which two-thirds is absorbed in housing benefits (NIHE, 2007). In addition to the costs to the NIHE of providing social housing, the Executive is obliged to assist the majority (60 per cent) of private sector tenants with housing benefit (University of Ulster, 2007).

Whilst the GFA (p. 17) and the Northern Ireland Executive have recommended initiatives to reintegrate the Unionist and nationalist populations, the NIHE has been reluctant to risk this approach, confining reintegration to a small scale pilot in Enniskillen by 2007, far away from the more acute interfaces, even though measures of deprivation, such as the Noble Index, suggest that segregation and deprivation may be clearly linked. Given that, even ten years after paramilitary ceasefires, half of the population living in sectarian interface areas stated that they would not even walk through areas dominated by the opposite religion, let alone live there, the NIHE faces a difficult task in reintegrating housing (Shirlow and Murtagh, 2006).

Employment

Between 1985 and 2006 the number of persons in employment increased from almost 1.1 million to over 2 million (CSO, 2007a). Within that same period the number of persons unemployed decreased by 128,200 to 91,400 (CSO, 2007b; and see Figure 11.1).

Despite employment growth, decreases in unemployment and inward migration of labour, levels of dependency on social welfare among those of working age remain high. Benefit dependency rose from 12.4 per cent of the working population in 1980 to hold constant at 20 per cent for the period 1985–2005 (Murphy, 2006: 95). Evidently, the increase in employment during the economic boom has been made up from migrant labour, leaving a residual group of the domestic labour force unemployed. The response has been of a number of diverse policy debates that focus on the importance of *participation, activation* and the extension of *conditionality* in social protection payments.

The emphasis on 'participation' refers to the widely held view that a job is the best route out of poverty. This view is espoused by a variety of state and semistate agencies, such as NESF (2000), the Forum on the Future of the Workplace (2005), the revised

Figure 11.1   Labour Force Status in the Republic of Ireland, 1986–2006

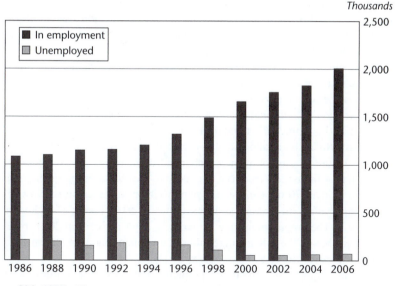

Thousands

Source: CSO (2007b: 25).

NAPS (2002), the National Action Plan for social inclusion (NAPS s/inc) (2003a), the NEAP Annual Reports (1998–2005) and the National Competitiveness Council (2003), which all emphasize the need for greater activation and mobilization of the workforce (O'Connor, 2005). 'Activation' refers to a range of policy measures that are designed to facilitate a welfare claimant in accessing employment. These include, on the one hand, positive reforms to income maintenance to ensure there is a financial incentive to take up work, and on the other hand, the introduction of sanctions in the form of reduced income maintenance for those who 'fail' to take up offers of education, training or employment. This view is also espoused by a variety of non-government organizations such as the NWCI (Murphy, 2003), the INOU (1999b) and EAPN (2006), as well as other state agencies and departments. FÁS reports in 2003, 2004 and 2005 all suggested that the increase in lone parent and disability payments, which outstripped decreased numbers of unemployment payments, could be counteracted by activation measures in order to ameliorate labour market shortages. The same view was put forward by Department of SFA strategy statements, annual reports and internal policy work (O'Connor, 2005), as well as lone parent and disability expenditure reviews (Murphy, 2007a). The emphasis on activation was further supported at the international level by EU employment guidelines, and by OECD analysts Pearson and Jagger (2003) and Grubb (2004) who have argued that low Irish unemployment during the economic boom afforded a political opportunity to introduce more activation in the Irish labour market and that government should introduce work requirements for lone parent and disability benefits (Murphy, 2007a).

In terms of conditionality, the extent to which Irish governments are willing to attach conditions to the receipt of social protection policies is still unclear. In 2006, the Social Welfare Bill renamed unemployment payments as 'job seekers' payments, and in 2007 the Social Welfare Act was amended so as to make social payments for welfare dependant mothers with children over eight subject to new obligations to take up paid employment (Murphy, 2007a). Both of these changes are consistent with a move to more active social policy and they mirror changes in most OECD countries over the past ten years.

Northern Ireland's traditional position as the site of the highest rate of unemployment in the UK (both preconflict and during the conflict) is finally being eroded. By 2007, unemployment had fallen to 3.4 per cent, the lowest rate in the region's history. The nature of employment has changed dramatically, as Northern Ireland has entered a post-industrial era. From the 1960s to the 1990s, employment in manufacturing fell by over 70 per cent, whilst public sector employment rose by 158 per cent and employment in private services grew by 54 per cent (McGovern and Shirlow, 1997). The employment rate for women, at 61 per cent in 2001, remained low, 8 per cent below the UK average, although women made up almost the same percentage of the workforce as men (Black, 2004).

Employment segregation remains a problem, with almost two-thirds of those employees working in private sector firms employed in companies with a religiously skewed workforce, and with Catholics living in overwhelmingly nationalist areas being the least prepared or able to travel far to work (Shirlow and Murtagh, 2006). Successive fair employment legislation acts have done much to reduce overt private sector employment discrimination, as fair employment oversight travelled from being under the wing of a modest quango to becoming an integral part of employment provision (Osborne and Cormack, 1989; Connolly, 1990). Nonetheless, the geography of workforce location remains a barrier to mobility. Affirmative action to address workforce imbalances, in the form of quotas, is illegal, except, ironically, in the case of the police service itself. The legal penalties accruing to non-compliance with fair employment legislation have ensured widespread observation of the law (Bew *et al.*, 1997).

Conclusion

In the Republic of Ireland, it is clear that some elements of contemporary social policy are often far more rooted in ideas from the past than we might think. It is clear, for example, that high levels of inequality are tolerated in a state dominated by a form of Catholic social teaching that focused, in the early years of the state, on more absolutist forms of poverty reduction and charity (McLauglin, 1993; Acheson *et al.*, 2004). Addressing inequality has never been a core objective of Irish social security policy – rather there is political acceptance of 'solidarity without equality' (Ó'Riáin and O'Connell, 2000: 39). This particularly conservative approach to policy goes some way to explaining the slow and cautious pace of social change.

Much of the social agenda in Northern Ireland from the 1970s until the 1990s was concentrated upon the alleviation of discrepancies between the plight of the nationalist and Unionist communities, the latter still perceived until very recently as enjoying marginal advantage. The post-GFA equality agenda has maintained this focus, but it has been accompanied by a broader, cross-community attempt to alleviate the problem of stubborn pockets of deprivation in the region. A fusion of local, national and international financial resources has improved socio-economic fortunes throughout Northern Ireland. Some of the main problems have shifted substantially over recent decades. For example, housing problems have shifted from quality to affordability, whilst employment concerns have been located on the type of employment rather than a high rate of unemployment. Irrespective of the shifting nature of the problem, it is evident that sections of the working class remain overly dependent upon the provisions of the welfare state and that social class, more than ethnic background, is a key determinant of life chances.

12

Ireland in the European Union and Beyond

No single theory can explain the complex politics of policy-making in the European Union. Moreover, no single chapter could summarize adequately the range of contributions made to understanding these complexities.

(Bache, 1998: 16)

Introduction

Ireland joined the European Union (EU) in January 1973, the Republic as a full member state and Northern Ireland as a region of the UK. For Northern Ireland, the fact that the region does not have full member status and that most negotiations with the EU are carried out on its behalf by the UK government, which has always been 'lukewarm' about Europe, has meant that Northern Irish politicians are not as firmly embedded into the EU system as their southern counterparts. For the Republic, integration with the EU has occurred to such an extent that on all major European issues there is a virtual political consensus across all political parties with the exception of Sinn Féin and the Greens, who are more critical of the EU. In Northern Ireland, the scepticism towards the EU elsewhere in the UK has been evident. In the 1975 referendum on whether the UK should remain within the European Community, only 52 per cent of Northern Ireland's voters voted in favour of continuing membership, substantially below the overall UK vote in support of 67 per cent. Many Unionists questioned the value of EU membership, whilst Sinn Féin opposed EU membership until the late 1990s. Only the SDLP among the major northern parties has consistently been strongly supportive of the EU, even briefly advocating a role (during the early 1990s) for the EU Commission in the administration of Northern Ireland. All the other parties have overcome initial opposition to the EU and have become much greater backers, recognizing the financial benefits on offer.

The Irish Republic and pro-Europeanism

From the outset, successive Irish governments have been in favour of further European integration and have been actively involved in all major EU policy initiatives in order to maintain Ireland's position as a core member of the EU. Consequently,

212

considering its size, Ireland has enjoyed disproportionate influence in the EU: as well as supplying a number of prominent Europeanists (James Dooge on institutional reform, Maurice Doyle on regional policy and the EMU, Garret FitzGerald on the Lomé Treaty and regional policy, Ray MacSharry on CAP reform, Peter Sutherland on competition policy, Judge Fidelma Macken in the European Court Court of Justice, John Bruton on institutional reform following enlargement, and Pat Cox as President of the European Parliament). Ireland has also helped to develop a number of EU pilot programmes that were subsequently successfully mainstreamed. These include the LEADER rural development programme and various Community Initiatives run by the European Commission. This, together with good use of size-able aid transfers from EU Structural Funds, and the successful adoption of west European styles of economic management and policy making, has led the Irish to be generally 'pro-European'.

The Irish have traditionally been regarded in Brussels as 'good Europeans', unlike the UK government, which has been viewed as intrinsically hostile to any attempts to expand EU competences. The pro-EU status of the Irish was challenged in the 1990s when the Republic's economic boom led the Government into conflict with the EU over its management of the economy. As the EU entered the final preparations for EMU and required all member states to develop broadly convergent economic policies, the Irish Government was criticized for its refusal to damp down the extremely successful Celtic Tiger economy. The Irish Finance Minister in particular was publicly rebuked for his generous tax concessions to foreign investors, which were regarded by the European Commission as breaking the spirit, if not the law, of the Single Market. Moreover, in May 2001, the Republic's rejection of the Government backed constitutional amendment required to ratify the Nice Treaty heralded a new popular scepticism concerning Irish interests and deeper European integration. The Nice Treaty was the outcome of a complex set of negotiations over the institutional changes necessary to facilitate the proposed enlargement of the EU eastwards. Running to some hundred pages in length, and not even required to be ratified until the end of 2002, the Irish 'no' vote probably represented not so much an outright rejection of the Treaty as a public trouncing of the political parties and government officials who thought that they could rely on the electorate to endorse a series of political changes that had been given a summarily short explanation and only scant public discussion. In the absence of a strong pro-Treaty endorsement, anti-Treaty campaigners were able to promulgate the idea that a vote for Nice would lead a diminution of Irish neutrality and unwanted immigration (O'Brennan, 2003). It took a second referendum to overturn the initial Nice Treaty rejection. In June 2008, history looked set to repeat itself with rejection of the Lisbon Treaty.

Entry into the European Community and Attitudinal Evolution

When Ireland joined the European Community (EC) in January 1973, in addition to significant economic benefits, EC membership offered the Republic a chance to move out from 'Britain's shadow' in international relations. As a consequence, joining the EC did not appear as a threat to national sovereignty, but rather an opportunity for the state to establish itself internationally. Unlike the situation in other countries, the issue of EC membership did not lead to internal splits in the Republic's political parties. Both Fianna Fáil and Fine Gael campaigned in favour of membership and, though the Labour party had been opposed to membership throughout the 1960s, at its annual conference in 1971 even it was recommending some form of EC association (Laffan, 1991a: 197). Moreover, shortly after Ireland's accession to the EC in 1973, the Labour Party had no problem in forming a coalition government with Fine Gael, despite having campaigned on opposing sides of the referendum to join. Instead, 'the Labour party accepted the verdict of the referendum and adjusted to the reality of Ireland's involvement in the European Community' (ibid.). In the Republic, this was no great political concession, since, when the question of membership was put to the Irish people in a referendum the year before, 83 per cent voted in favour from a poll of 71 per cent of the population (Coakley, 1983: 51). This remains the highest 'yes' vote in any EU member state. The fact that Ireland was set to be a net beneficiary of the EC did much to sustain this initial enthusiasm.

The responsiveness of the Irish to European influence is further augmented by the relatively small size of the Irish polity: 'even the people who operate very minor programmes that are EU funded, and who then go over to network communications in Brussels, tend to be influential policy-makers because of the small numbers of people involved'.[1] As a result, the Irish system of policy formation on EC issues is much less institutionalized than in other member states; there are far fewer coordinating committees, and those that exist meet less frequently than their counterparts. 'The small size of the bureaucracy leads to a less formal approach to policy making; civil servants working on the Community know their counter-parts in other government departments and deal with many issues over the telephone (Laffan, 1991a: 193; see also: Adshead, 1996a: 593–601). On the one hand, it may be argued that the small size of Irish bureaucracy, which easily facilitates pragmatic and ad hoc responses to EU policy, leads to 'clear sight over short distances' (Laffan, 1991a: 193). On the other hand, policy-makers argue that the fact that many Irish bureaucrats are by necessity generalists rather than specialists has facilitated a good deal of creativity in Irish policy towards the EU, plus the ready transfer of new ideas between different parts of government (Adshead, 2005).

Northern Ireland's support for the EC was more muted. Of the main parties, only the SDLP offered unequivocal support for a 'yes' vote in the 1975 UK referendum on continued membership. The SDLP envisaged the creation of a Europe of the regions which would diminish the border and create new contexts of sovereignty, removing the tensions in British–Irish relationships. Sinn Féin was an underdeveloped political organization which did not contest elections but strongly opposed EC membership as an abdication of Ireland's sovereignty. For Unionists, the EC represented a potential threat to sovereignty in two respects: firstly, the erosion of Westminster through the transfer of power to EU institutions; and, secondly, the potential transnational implications of being obliged to deal with a 'hostile' EU partner to the South within a context of diminished importance of borders. The mere visit of the Taoiseach, Sean Lemass, to the North had aroused protests in 1965. Eight years later, Northern Ireland's entry into a formal cooperative arrangement with the Irish Republic via the EU was viewed with caution. The UUP was suspicious of the EC, but less overtly than the DUP, which offered strident resistance to the perceived 'Catholic club' of EC members. Paisley's invective included a denunciation of the EC as 'Babylon the Great, the mother of harlots and abominations of the Earth' (Moloney and Pollok, 1986: 405).

Although the membership issue has long been settled, Euroscepticism remains intact, with the UK government steadfast in its reluctance to adopt the euro as its currency. It has utilized five economic 'tests' which need to be passed before entry to the Eurozone will be considered. Given the UK's economic health during the ten years of the Blair Government (far superior to the economies of some of the countries inside the zone), the real utility of these examinations appeared to be to avoid a risky referendum on adoption of the euro. The SDLP's endorsement of the currency is in accordance with the party's long-standing Europeanism, whereas the enthusiasm of Sinn Féin is a more modern feature. Sinn Féin moved rapidly from pre-GFA opposition to the EU per se to a position in which the extension of the eurozone to Northern Ireland was supported as a 'crucial part of the process of the economic unification' (Sinn Féin, 2003: 6). Catholics have been much more in favour of the EU's expansion of competences, favouring, for example, the Maastricht Treaty by a two-to-one majority, whereas a slight majority of Protestants opposed it (Kennedy, 1994). Unionist parties remain opposed to the euro and the issue divides on a sectarian basis even among non-sectarian parties. Catholic Alliance Party members are much more supportive of the extension of the euro to Northern Ireland than are their Protestant counterparts (Tonge, 2005b). Both Unionist parties and Sinn Féin opposed the EU constitution. The DUP (2004: 9) emphasizes its belief in the 'primacy of national sovereignty' and strongly supports the retention of sterling, policies identical to those of the UUP. Despite the growth of EU powers and the establishment of the Northern Ireland Assembly, the UK Government is still seen as the primary location of decision-making, with only 4 per cent viewing the EU as the main repository of decision-making, a figure 3 per cent lower than that recorded for local councils, arguably the weakest in Western Europe (Gilland and Kennedy, 2002).

Administrative Adaptation to EU Membership

In the Republic, Laffan (1991a: 190) argued that the adaptation of the Irish civil and public service to EC membership may have been even more demanding than the original adaptation to the foundation of the state. This is because in 1922 Ireland inherited a well-established administrative apparatus from the British, whereas in 1973 there was a widespread questioning of the capacity of Ireland's public administration to cope with the demands of an industrializing and urbanizing society. Be that as it may, by 1975, when Ireland first held the Presidency of the EC, the administrative machinery was all more or less in place.

From accession to the EU in 1973 to the end of the 1990s, Ireland's system for managing EU business was relatively stable (Laffan and O'Mahony, 2007: 171). The

Departments of Foreign Affairs, Agriculture, Industry, Finance and the Taoiseach's Office were the leading ministries in the management of EC policy (Laffan, 1991a: 191). Each ministry is responsible for those areas of EC policy that fall within their remit, whilst the economic division of the Department of Foreign Affairs keeps a watching brief over the flow of proposals through the EC Council system in all policy areas and directs the flow of information to and from the permanent representation. Throughout the 1970s, all of these departments were expanded as a consequence of EC membership. The Department of Foreign Affairs' economic division, responsible for EC matters, almost trebled in size, and the political division, responsible for European political coordination, was similarly transformed (ibid.).

The expansion of the EU's policy regime to include economic and monetary union, as a consequence of the Maastricht Treaty in 1992, added new domestic actors into the EU management system. With the increased policy-making in areas such as environment and internal security, the Departments of Environment and Justice moved much more to the centre of EU policy-making and became more involved in a range of cross-cutting issues (Laffan and O'Mahony, 2007: 172–3). Added to this, the growing importance of the European Council in EU policy further enhanced the position of the Taoiseach in shaping Irish approaches to the EU.

In Brussels, the cabinet informs decisions in the Council of Ministers and from time to time cabinet subcommittees are created to deal with major areas of interest. This was the case prior to the Intergovernmental Conference leading to the Single European Act (SEA), the Draft Treaty on European Union and the Nice Treaty. The Department of Foreign Affairs continues to exercise its role as overseer of all EC policies, but the Taoiseach's Office plays an important part in setting priorities and in coordinating major negotiations (Laffan, 1991a: 192). Nevertheless, Ireland's permanent representation in Brussels is accorded a high status in the policy process because of the small size of central government. A period working in the unit is perceived as useful from a career point of view. The permanent representative and his or her deputy are always career diplomats from Foreign Affairs, which also supplies the lion's share of remaining officials, usually around 45 per cent (ibid.). The rest come from various domestic departments with relevant expertise.

Generally, the preparation of dossiers and administrative coordination remains the prerogative of the domestic civil service, though the permanent representation in Brussels provides invaluable information regarding the attitudes of other delegations to particular issues and possible negotiating scenarios. The status of the permanent representative also ensures that his or her views are listened to and carry considerable weight in the formation of national policy responses (ibid.). All in all, the governmental machinery to develop and coordinate Irish policy on EU issues has evolved out of that used before. Although for some time the interdepartmental structures for coordination of EU business were characterized by 'institutional fluidity and malleability', it is argued that the rejection of the Nice Treaty in 2001 led to a significant 'ratcheting up of inter-departmental co-ordination and enhanced parliamentary scrutiny' (Laffan and O'Mahony, 2007: 173–8).

In Northern Ireland, the influence of the EU under direct rule came mainly indirectly, as European directives were channelled via Whitehall departments, which were then responsible for ensuring compliance. The Northern Ireland Office lobbied on behalf of the region, but its arguments were filtered via Whitehall, as EU directives affected the entire UK. There is insufficient scrutiny of EU-prompted legislation at Westminster, where Northern Ireland MPs have played little part in scrutiny vehicles (Meehan, 2006). A limited amount of direct representation of the region is made to the European Commission office in Belfast. Birrell (2008) notes how the sheer volume of EU directives has created difficulties and backlogs in adapting these for regional consumption. The post-2007 devolved arrangements have not markedly altered the triangular EU–Whitehall–Northern Ireland relationship, given that relations with the EU are an excepted (i.e. non-devolved) aspect. Nonetheless, it seems reasonable to expect that executive departments in Northern Ireland will assume over time much greater responsibilities for the local adoption and implementation of EU initiatives. Northern Ireland's interests are still articulated within a UK-wide context by the Westminster Government. However, the Joint Ministerial Committee (JMC), which brings together the UK Government with the leaderships of the devolved administrations, helps shape input to EU matters. This is chaired by the Foreign Secretary (McGowan, 2007).

The Executive has an office in Brussels, although it has struggled to make an impact, partly due to lack of resources. Given the absence of a Minister for Europe, the link between the OFDFM Whitehall and the EU is the European Policy Coordination Unit at Stormont, which advises departments on the impact of EU directives and legislation. Within the Assembly, the 'serious lack of knowledge of the EU, its policies and mechanisms ... became all too readily apparent' (McGowan, 2007: 284). There is a strong case for a dedicated standing Assembly committee dealing with European matters. Each local council has a European Liaison Officer, but the Assembly is still playing 'catch-up' in respect of European affairs.

Political Adaptation to EU Membership

Until the mid-1990s, the poor economic situation in the Republic of Ireland was the primary determinant of Irish approaches to the EU. If anything, this approach to governmental negotiations with the EU supported the centralized nature of government. From about 1975, the commitment to regional planning declined not only as a consequence of economic recession, but also because EC membership led to a change of policy emphasis. Instead of focusing on internal regional disparities, the new priority was achieving greater convergence between Ireland as a whole and the more developed parts of the EC (Walsh, 1993: 3). It is argued that Ireland's classification as a single region by the European Union postponed the development of political, representative and administrative structures for regional development (O'Donnell and Walsh, 1995: 225). Despite this, however, government desires to make the best use of Structural Funding, through attempts to coordinate development activities and avoid duplication of efforts or costs, did contribute to a change of governmental style. In 1988, as part of broader EU structural and budgetary reforms (Bache, 1998), the European Commission sought to develop in all structurally funding projects the principles of concentration, programming, partnership, monitoring and evaluation, and additionality (the principle that EU funding should be in addition to, and not instead of, alternative national funding). Following the reforms, it was neces-sary for the Irish Government to prepare a four-year National Development Plan (NDP). This, together with a changing policy style at national level, further advanced the practice of linking EU intervention to regionally based, multi-annual strategic programmes (Adshead and Quinn, 1998: 216).

The primary objective of the first NDP was to achieve improved competitiveness and efficiency in the Irish economy, by tackling problems arising from peripherality, inadequate infrastructure and low population density (O'Donnell and Walsh, 1995). Still, the new principles of programming, partnership, concentration and additionality (as well as the later adoption of subsidiarity in the Maastricht Treaty) drew attention to the need for inclusiveness in decision-making and implementation of development policy. Although it may be true that initially the Irish Government only paid lip-service to these principles (Coyle, 1990: 11), by the time that the second NDP was introduced, covering the period 1994–9, a discernible shift of emphasis was apparent. Instead of concentrating solely on economic targets, such as industrial activity or sectoral growth, there was an increasing acknowledgement of EC oriented goals and objectives. Chief amongst these were the emphases placed by the EU upon strategic programming and planned assistance, together with a desire to build *social* as well as *economic capital*. A range of new metrics was introduced for evaluating public policy: combating social exclusion and marginalization; building infrastructure for innovation and 'social animation' (the term used by community development workers to refer to the enhance-ment and empowerment of human resources) – promoting partnership and commu-nities all became important indicators of the new approach. As a consequence, state development was viewed as a multidimensional process with serious *social* and *polit-ical*, as well as *economic*, implications – a change of emphasis which the government freely acknowledged as 'building upon the experience gained from the implementation of initiatives stemming from EC actions' (Government of Ireland, 1995: 12).

From 1988, the introduction of five-year 'National Development Plans', combin-ing EC Structural Funds assistance with national exchequer funds and outlining the strategic integration of a variety of policy initiatives comprising public, private and voluntary agencies, marked a turning point in the organization of public administra-tion and governance in Ireland. Whilst the institutional mosaic at ground level remained complex, if not even chaotic, the design and direction of their activities began to change (Adshead, 2002). Even without any major institutional overhaul, renewed emphasis on negotiation and partnership in the organization of public policy pointed to a change in governing style. The advent of Irish 'government by partner-ship' has its foundations in changing government approaches to both political and economic management of the state (Adshead and McInerney, 2008a). The introduc-tion of programmatic government required by the reform of EU Structural Funds constitutes the chief *political* element in this change and may be regarded as a direct consequence of Europeanization (Adshead, 2005).

The scale of EU support for Northern Ireland has eliminated initial reservations concerning membership. The region's three MEPs, drawn (one each) from the DUP,

UUP and Sinn Féin, cooperate in representing Northern Ireland. Unionist suspicion of the EU's promotion of cross-border activity has diminished as the EU has declined to involve itself overtly in the creation of new contexts of sovereignty once envisaged by the SDLP. The EU's concern with Northern Ireland has been predominantly based on the alleviation of inequality and the promotion of peace through financial backing. These aspects have been largely uncontroversial. The European Parliament (EP) has been episodically proactive in promoting political remedies to the Northern Ireland problem, which it has been powerless to operationalize. In 1981 the EP established a working party to explore how a resolution of the Northern Ireland problem might be achieved. The Haagerup Report (1984) produced by the EP was an important contribution to the debate over future modes of governance. Long in advance of the GFA, it placed the potential solution within an identity paradigm, contending that only with the legitimation of competing ethnic groups and aspirations could the problem be resolved. Presciently, the Haagerup Report argued for power-sharing and intergovernmental cooperation as the institutional mechanisms that could provide a way forward.

Although the political divisions and violence of the 1980s prevented any operationalization of the Haagerup Report, the EP's interest in Northern Ireland did not disappear. It criticized aspects of the policing of the region, offered symbolic support for the 1985 Anglo-Irish Agreement (endorsing the accord by 150 votes to 28) and, in 1992, launched an investigation into anti-Catholic discrimination. Yet the ineffectiveness of the EP ensured its activism had little impact.

As an economic benefactor, the EU has had significant political impact, in terms of internal relationships within Northern Ireland and in respect of all-Ireland activity. Internally within Northern Ireland, the EU has promoted a 'culture of "civil and social dialogue" in its funding of cross-community groups in Northern Ireland and via its support for groups effecting the transformation from violence, such as former prisoners' organizations' (Bean, 2008: 171). Across the island, the SEUPB is the most significant of the six new cross-border bodies established under the GFA. It operates as the paying and managing agent for the PEACE programmes, contains the most scope to expand all-island activity and enjoys greater autonomy, via a Chief Executive not appointed by the NSMC, than most other cross-border bodies. The SEUPB meets quarterly in sectoral format and promotes cross-border cooperation in implementing the NDP for Ireland and the Northern Ireland Structural Funds Plan.

There remains scepticism over whether the EU, or any other exogenous actors, have had much impact on Northern Ireland's transition from conflict to peace (Dixon, 2006). Indeed perhaps the most important perception of the EU among Northern Ireland citizens is that of a 'cash cow' (McGowan and O'Connor, 2004). Nonetheless, the EU has been an important facilitator of cross-border activity, the-placement of which has made transnationalism seem less threatening to Unionists in what is still viewed as a zero-sum sovereignty game (Meehan, 2006). The impact of the EU has made redundant traditional perceptions of nation-state or garrison-state Ireland, obliging Sinn Féin to move its position from outright opposition to critical engagement (Sinn Féin, 2003).

Economic Impacts of EU Funding

Until the mid-1990s, the poor economic situation in Ireland – both North and South – was the primary determinant of Irish approaches to the EU. Since then, EU assistance to the North has also been bolstered by specific peace process funding, allied to the promotion of cross-border activity.

In the Republic, the motivation for Irish membership of the EU was a direct result of the change in national economic policy taken in 1958 (Laffan, 1999: 92). The failure of attempts to industrialize behind protective barriers became apparent during the economic crises of the 1950s and led in turn to a more outward orientation of policy that focused on export-led growth through the development of manufacturing and the enticement of foreign-owned multinational companies into Ireland (Bradley, 2000). As a small, open and peripheral economy, average incomes were well below the EU average and, as a result, successive Dublin governments argued for solidarity and cohesion between EU members. During the negotiations on the SEA, which facilitated the creation of the European 'Single Market', the Republic joined with other less well off member states to press for a commitment to economic and social cohesion. This was achieved through the addition of a protocol to the SEA and through a renegotiation of the EU budget, giving increased financial and administrative commitments to Structural Funding for disadvantaged regions in the EU. Both the Republic and Northern Ireland were designated as high priority, or Objective One, regions for EU Structural Funds aid for the period 1988–99. Similar pressures were brought to bear in the negotiation of the Maastricht Treaty and resulted in the creation of an EU Cohesion Fund, providing financial assistance for projects in the fields of environment and trans-European networks to member states whose per capita GNP is less than 90 per cent of the overall Union average. In this case, however, Northern Ireland was excluded from a share of the Fund because its provisions related to member states, not regions.

In the Republic, the desire to attract foreign investment obliged the state to accept the challenge of free trade and gain access to European markets. Nevertheless, with the onset of OPEC oil price rises in 1979 and the subsequent world recession, the economy faltered and a period of unstable, mainly negative, growth followed for the years 1982 to 1986 (Bradley *et al.*, 1993: 11). Across Europe, many governments sought to pursue broadly similar strategies, and as they did so they often ended up 'competing against each other for key projects so that the net beneficiaries in this zero-sum game were the large mobile corporations' (Walsh, 1993: 6). As a result policy emphasis changed, reflecting a keener interest in new technologies and product innovation: Irish governments began to place a renewed emphasis on the 'development of the indigenous sector and the development and promotion of small and medium sized enterprises' (Quinn, 1996). At the same time, attempts to create export-led growth led to Ireland's total participation in, and inextricable ties to, the international economy (O'Donnell and Walsh, 1995).

In seeking both to reform the economy and respond to the demands of the international market, Irish governments attempted to introduce greater flexibility in production processes and the organization of labour by introducing a system of national concordat with the major representatives of business and labour. Such a system had been tried before with the 'National Understandings' of 1979 and 1980 (both national wages agreements negotiated directly between the Government, the ICTU and employer organizations), and which arguably marked the beginning of a subtle shift in the nature of Irish decision-making (Lee, 1989: 537–40; Chubb, 1992: 125–30). 'They [the national understandings] began the integration of management and trade unions into the formulation of public policy' (Lee, 1979: 20). This trend was inhibited by the turnover of governments and the recession of the early 1980s, but it was later re-established in a yet more developed form towards the end of the decade.[2] There have since been seven 'social partnership' agreements (see pp. 185–8), continuing 'pretty much unbroken for 20 years', such that 'there seems little doubt that it has been institutionalized in some way' (O'Donnell *et al.*, 2007: 21; see also O'Donnell, 2008).

Certainly, the Irish system of 'government by partnership' is not a direct consequence of EU membership, but was primarily nationally conceived and developed. Still, widespread references to Ireland's 'moving on' from a UK model to a 'European model' for managing the economy point to the increasing salience of European attitudes and approaches. Joining the EU is credited with being 'an essentially liberating' experience, that has 'created a positive, outward-looking attitude that affects business, the educational system, and politics (J. Fitzgerald, 2000: 55; see also Laffan, 1999; Fitzgerald and Girvin, 2000; Laffan and O'Mahony, 2008). It is argued that both the trade union movement and the business community greatly benefited from the stimulus provided by other European models of behaviour (J. Fitzgerald, 2000: 33) and that the successful growth of social partnership owes an intellectual debt to the experiences of countries such as the Netherlands and Germany, rather than to the more traditional channels of influence from the UK (Sexton and O'Connell, 1996). European integration did not introduce partnership government, but it did provide the backdrop and context within which Ireland was able to develop this form of economic management. After the 1988 reform of the Structural Funds and the Treaty on European Union in 1992, EU membership provided Ireland with both a limited range of policy choices and a clear set of policy objectives (R. Fitzgerald, 2000; O'Donnell, 2000). Thus together 'the crisis during the 1980s, the response of the elite to this and the role of the European Union as an agenda-setting agency combined to provide the basis for the political and social consensus that reinforced economic success during the 1990s' (Fitzgerald and Girvin, 2000: 281).

The management of Northern Ireland's economy is undertaken largely beyond the region, by the UK Exchequer, but the problems of the region have ensured it has received special financial treatment by the EU since 1977. Objective 1 status, awarded to those parts of the EU with the most pressing reconstruction needs, was granted during the 1990s, along with PEACE I and PEACE II programmes. As this support diminished, the problem for Northern Ireland was how to continue to develop economically with lesser assistance.

In terms of the impact of EU funding, there has been considerable controversy over the problem of 'additionality', by which the UK Government and the Northern Ireland Executive adjust expenditure on items on the basis that the EU 'shall provideth' (Birrell, 2008). For most of the 1970s and 1980s, the net total benefit of EU membership (money provided, less paid in) was slight, amounting to only £100 million, but this has increased substantially due to the EU PEACE programmes. The PEACE II programme contributed £274million between 2000–04 in Northern Ireland alone, with a further tranche of money under PEACE III promised until 2013, whilst the INTERREG programme of cross-border cooperation provided £52million. Other smaller EU funding was provided via the LEADER programme, worth £10m, designed to promote development initiatives; URBAN, designed to achieve similar ends in towns and cities, and worth £7million; and EQUAL, whose £8million of funding was aimed at eliminating inequalities in access to labour markets. To these sums can be added the amount of money for the application of each of these projects, specifically in the border region, where a further £250m of funding was provided over the same period (Tonge, 2005b). From 1990 to 2005, Birrell (2008) calculates that Northern Ireland received £2.3billion from the EU from its programmes addressing regional equality and a further £500 million of support specifically to bolster the peace process.

The Influence of the EU

Ireland's entry into the EU in 1973 incurred a series of legal obligations, relating to non-discrimination and equality of pay, which began to challenge attitudes to women, the workplace and the family. Article 119 of the Treaty of Rome obliges member states to ensure, and subsequently maintain, the application of the principle that men and women should receive equal pay for equal work. This article's require-ments are amplified by EC Directive 75/117 on equal pay and EC Directive 76/207 on equal treatment, which calls on all member states to end all sex discrimination in social security schemes that are work related. Up until this point Article 40.1 of the Irish constitution, declaring that 'all citizens shall, as human persons, be held equal before the law', had not been entirely successful as a basis for dealing with sex discrimination, since some conservative judges were able to interpret the 'as human persons' as a restriction on its application where other less conservative judges did not (Scannell, 1988: 131). There was now, however, no doubt that the rights subscribed to in the Treaty of Rome could be used to take action on sex discrimin-ation even where Irish constitutional rights proved ineffective.

Typically, it was the need to conform to legal obligations arising as a consequence of EU membership that proved most effective in securing *economic* (and therefore more expensive) rights. The rights of women to work after marriage, to equal pay and to equal opportunities, to maternity leave, and to equal social welfare allowances were only granted by the Oireachtas when, and sometimes long after, it was obliged to grant these rights by EU membership (Galligan, 1998: 68–89). Scannell (1988: 133) argued that 'any advances in women's rights that could cost money were always vigorously resisted by the legislature', and that many of the above mentioned rights 'might have been won by women without the intervention of the EC, had they had the resources and energy to fight for them in the Courts'. In this respect alone, membership of the EU had a direct and definite effect, proving to be a significant challenge to the most discriminatory aspects of Irish conservatism.

In relation to the challenges of conservatism more generally, however, there were also significant interstate dimensions to the Europeanization effect. Throughout the 1970s, foreign travel increased and Irish people began to notice and take an interest in what was happening on the continent. This, combined with influxes of returned emigrants when the economy improved in the 1970s, led to changing social attitudes – a tendency that was even more marked with the influx of returned emigrants associated with the economic boom of the 1990s. This group made up more than 'half of all immigrants in the 1990s, and in 2004 comprised 34 per cent, while another 36 per cent were either EU nationals or US nationals. Only 30 per cent of the total, as of 2004, were from outside the EU' (Garner, 2007: 118).

The publication of the Employment Permits Act in April 2003, which facilitated the access for workers from the ten EU accession countries to the Irish labour market immediately upon EU enlargement (in May 2004), marked the beginning of a more interventionist work permit system in Ireland (Ní Shé *et al.*, 2007: 33). In late 2003, the Government began encouraging employers to give preference to workers from the EU accession countries and, by November 2003, the Department of Enterprise Trade and Employment (DETE) had started to return applications for new work permits for workers from outside the enlarged European Union, whenever workers from the EU accession countries were available to fill the vacancy (ibid.). Between May 2004 and February 2006, 186,000 Personal Public Service Numbers (PPSNs) were allocated to nationals from accession states, out of which more than half went to Polish citizens, (Doyle *et al.*, 2006: 13). Whilst not all of these migrants took up work (a PPSN number is also for access to other state services), cross-matching of PPSN numbers with income tax records indicates that around 70 per cent of those with a PPSN number subsequently took up employment (Doyle *et al.*, 2006: 62).

It is now estimated that one in seven of the Irish population is Polish (OECD, 2008), though anecdotal evidence from 'successful' or 'well-established' UK and Polish immigrants suggests that the Irish model of immigration is better understood as one where separate identities coexist, rather than one where immigrants are easily assimilated into an all-encompassing Irish identity (Ní Shé *et al.*, 2007: 69).

Assessing the impact of the EU on Northern Irish society is an even more difficult task than exploring the institutional changes it has influenced. Meehan (2006) makes a convincing case that the EU has beneficially shaped society in three areas: cross-community cooperation, social legislation and women's representation. The latter-most element is perhaps the most contentious argument, as women remain under-represented in Northern Ireland's political institution; the civic forum has hardly been a showcase for the advancement of women and the Northern Ireland Women's Coalition proved to be a short-lived political party. Notwithstanding problems of the complexity of processes, delays, auditing and lack of accountability, cross-community cooperation has been encouraged by the rules relating to EU funding, which have created consensual and clientelistic relationships between funders and funded which have straddled the sectarian divide. The establishment of District Partnerships as the agents of EU funding has to take place on an inclusive basis and applications for funding are often conditional upon projects being of benefit to the entire community, not merely one side of the ethno-national divide. EU support for prisoner groups, with monies distributed locally by the Community Foundation of Northern Ireland (CFNI), advanced the process of conflict transformation. The CFNI's objectives were required to be in accord with those of the EU's broader PEACE programme, requiring the development of healing, retraining and encouragement of self-help (Shirlow and McEvoy, 2008). Republicans, in particular, forged a more comfortable relationship with the local state in response to the demands of funding agencies. Unionists are more sceptical than nationalists concerning the EU's utility in diminishing violence through its aid programmes, but there is cross-community consensus that such financial assistance has bolstered economic development (Irvin and Byrne, 2002).

Social legislation, including gay equality in terms of the age of consent and the introduction of civil partnerships, might be seen as influenced by the EU and the European Convention of Human Rights, within a conservative polity. Northern Ireland was witness to 'Save Ulster from Sodomy' campaigns during the late 1970s and without European pressure it is possible that liberalizing legislation, beginning with the decriminalization of homosexual acts in 1982, might not have occurred.

Although EU projects and the agreed all-island cooperation of the GFA have been important in linking the two polities and economies on the island, integration remains piecemeal. As Bradley (2007: 79) argues, there 'remains the possibility that, in the absence of explicit, concerted and profitable North–South cooperative initiatives, there will be a tendency for a continuation of the previous process of essentially separate development of the two regions and an inability to complete the island economy, even as conventional North–South trade continues to expand'. Northern Irish industry (a limited entity) tends to look eastwards to its internal UK market, whilst Irish industry has EU and global markets bigger than northern outlets.

Agreement between North and South in terms of the 'common chapter' of all-island economic development based on EU structural funds has led to limited strategic cooperation. Strand 2 of the GFA has created piecemeal sectoral cooperation (Magennis, 2007). Neither will, in present form, greatly alter industrial or economic asymmetries between the two polities. However, gentle, ring-fenced cooperation, with the means of further symmetries resting with the respective legislatures, has moved all-island activity into an unthreatening, less politicized sphere for northern Unionists traditionally hostile to all-island activity as a supposed Trojan horse for political unity.

Beyond Europe: Ireland and the World

Whilst undoubtedly the EU takes up the 'lion share' of Ireland's foreign policy attention, the Republic's long history of emigration and more recent economic development have also led to strong links with the United States, as well as important human and cultural ties with Canada, Australia and New Zealand. A member of the United Nations since 1955, the Republic's foreign policy is committed to the maintenance of international peace and security under the UN Charter, and to respect for international law. For the most part, this commitment is carried out in the context of the EU's Common Foreign and Security Policy, but also in other multilateral contexts, including participation in the WTO, the Council of Europe and the Organization for Security and Co-operation in Europe.

Although the Republic maintains a policy of military neutrality and is not a member of any military alliance, for the last 50 years it has been an active contributor to both UN and UN-mandated peace-keeping operations, where the Republic has gained something of a reputation for its even-handed and effective administration (Skelly, 1997; Ahern, 2006). Nonetheless, there is an on-going political debate over the meaning and status of Irish neutrality (Devine, 2006). During World War II, Ireland's neutrality was 'extremely benevolent towards the allies' and it has been argued that the Republic is better described as non-belligerent rather than strictly neutral (Doherty, 2002: 13). Contemporarily, it is argued that the politically expedient notion of 'active neutrality' – which has allowed for membership of NATO's Partnership for Peace (PfP) consortium (see http://www.nato.int/issues/pfp/) and the EU's 'European Rapid Reaction Force' (Lindborg, 2001) – is in fact an oxymoron (Salmon, 1989: 311). Allegations over the use of Shannon airport as a stop-over for US military rendition flights, which remain unproven because no searches of aircraft are ever made, give further credence to the elasticity of Irish neutrality notions (Coulter, *Irish Times*, 28 July 2008; Horgan, *Irish Times*, 8 August 2008). However, regular opinion polls and explanations of Irish voting behaviour in EU treaty referenda repeatedly evince support for the popular public notion of Irish neutrality (Marsh, 1992; O'Brennan, 2003; Tonra, 2006).

On a more positive note, the Republic's ready recognition as a small (relatively) neutral state, whose colonial experience is as a colony rather than a colonizer, has helped to foster a strong commitment to international development aid. In 2006, the first ever White Paper on Irish aid placed 'the cause of development at the heart of Ireland's foreign policy' (Government of Ireland, 2006: 1). Amongst the new initiatives included in the White Paper was the creation of a Rapid Response Corps for use in humanitarian crises and a Unit for Conflict Resolution in the Department of Foreign Affairs, designed to draw on Ireland's own experience of conflict resolution in support of that in other developing countries. Since 1996, Ireland's Official Development Assistance (ODA) has steadily increased as a proportion of GNP and, at the United Nations summit meeting in September 2005, the then Taoiseach, Bertie Ahern, committed Ireland to reaching the UN target for spending 0.7 per cent of GNP on official development assistance by 2012 (*Irish Times*, 13 November 2006). If this were to be achieved, it would rank the Republic as one of the most generous countries in the world, though whether or not the increase in aid will be maintained in less prosperous times under a new Taoiseach remains to be seen. In July 2008, the Minister for Finance announced a cut of €45million to the ODA budget (*Irish Times*, 9 July 2008), thereby putting the achievement of Irish UN aid commitments into jeopardy.

Conclusion: Assessing the Impact of Europe

In the Republic, the initial tendency for Irish governments to view the European Community as essentially an economic entity (Laffan, 1991b:187) did not prevent them from being enthusiastic supporters of further European integration, both in their own interests and in the interests of the Union as a whole (Laffan, 1999: 91). This is because, for the Republic, both political and economic objectives happily coincided with EC membership. Until Ireland joined the EC, its external economic relations were characterized by a dependent relationship on the UK (J. Fitzgerald, 2000: 33) and the importance of decreasing this dependency by developing economic diversity in a more outwards-oriented economy was just as much a political as an economic objective. Notwithstanding the Republic's openness to EU membership, it may still be noted that in the political and economic spheres Ireland's adaptation to European integration has been carried out largely on its own terms. Ireland's initial rejection of the Nice Treaty and 'No' vote in the 2008 referendum on the EU constitution might be inerpreted as a cooling of a hitherto cordial relationship.

Ireland remains a strongly centralized state with no real regional government and a very weak system of local government. Despite this, however, both the direct and indirect impacts of EU membership have been key drivers for changing the nature of governmental authority at the centre. The advent of 'government by partnership' in Ireland is an interesting example of *shared* centralized government, which perhaps flourishes in Ireland because of the relatively small size of the Irish polity. This 'opening up' of the Irish state is also evidenced in the social and cultural realms of the state. Irish EU membership directly affected the body of Irish law and thereby significantly contributed to changing views about women, work and the family in Ireland (see Chapter 4). Whilst EU law laid down new codes and guidelines relating to sex discrimination, the experiences gained by closer connection with Continental European and modernizing influences laid the basis for a broader cultural shift in attitudes and lifestyles, allowing much of the modernization associated with EU membership and experience to counterpoint the traditional authority of the Church (Adshead, 2005).

The EU has impacted upon Northern Ireland in a similar manner to its effect upon the Irish Republic in terms of a mass of policy directives affecting all aspects of administration. Responsibility for implementation of the directives has finally been transferred from Whitehall and the Northern Ireland Office, the position under direct rule, to a devolved executive. However, the lack of knowledge of EU matters and uncertainty over how to adapt to the overarching EU–UK government framework means that Northern Ireland's institutional relationships with Brussels are still evolving. The EU's influence has extended beyond directives and the generosity of its financial provision has been of considerable importance. Such aid was initially provided because of Northern Ireland's peripheral status and economic problems and was followed during the 1990s and beyond by substantial peace process funding, a feature which will diminish under PEACE III during 2007–13. The EU also provided an institutional context in which British and Irish ministers could bilaterally consolidate a prospering intergovernmental framework. Although the EU has not produced the post-nationalist political perspectives desired by its most fervent cheerleaders, it has contributed to a modest reintegration of the once polarized polities on the island of Ireland.

Conclusion

We have attempted to examine government and politics in Ireland across three dimensions, looking at political institutions, political behaviour and significant elements of public policy. In terms of political institutions, clear similarities exist between the Irish Republic and Northern Ireland. Both have parliamentary structures that have evolved from the Westminster model. Members of representative institutions adopt constituency work as arguably more important than their legislative functions. The Irish Republic and Northern Ireland both utilize the PR-STV voting system and both polities operate under coalition government, within which interparty bargaining shapes policy outputs. Local government powers are low in both states, exceptionally so in Northern Ireland, where local councils are the weakest in Western Europe. The respective civil services operate on similar lines, shaped by the Whitehall model of permanency and neutrality, whilst both have been subject to managerial reforms designed to introduce a more innovative and dynamic culture. Since 1998, political actors in both states have opted for constitutional politics framed directly by the GFA and indirectly by a system of common law and legal jurisprudence common to both polities.

The moves towards decentralization in the Republic and, more significantly, devolution for Northern Ireland have partially addressed the acute cases of centralization which the Irish state and the United Kingdom represented when compared with their Continental counterparts. The centralized nature of the Republic may be a legacy of its colonial past, but it is a tradition that the state has happily maintained. Even when, in November 1998, the Government created two new regional authorities – the Border, Midlands and West (BMW) regional authority, and the Southern and Eastern Authority – this was widely recognized as a 'quick fix' strategy designed to facilitate continued access to EU regional aid by maintaining Objective One status for the less well off BMW region. It did not represent any attempt to reform existing regional structures or to introduce devolved government in any shape or form. Despite this, however, as we have seen, EU membership did introduce new approaches to public administration. In 1988, when the reform of EU regional aid policies required the completion of comprehensive development plans, Irish governments responded with the introduction of five-year 'National Development Plans' outlining the strategic integration of a variety of policy initiatives and public agencies operating at subnational level. Whilst the institutional mosaic at ground level remained complex, if not even chaotic, the design and direction of their activities began to change. Even without any major institutional overhaul, renewed emphasis on negotiation, partnership and subsidiarity in the organization of public policy pointed to a change in governing style. In Northern Ireland, local politicians are adapting to vastly changed circumstances. Whilst devolution is hardly unfamiliar to the region (it has existed for the majority of the state's existence), this form of devolved power-sharing is novel and holding any power was an unfamiliar concept to the younger generation of Northern Ireland politicians. Institutional teething problems were inevitable as the conflict did not wither overnight and the mechanics of government took time to grasp, but the early indications are that the institutional apparatus in the North is now firmly embedded and functioning effectively.

Despite the similarity of their institutions, in terms of political behaviour, relationships between government and governed differ markedly between the two polities. The clearest example of this is the development of 'government by partnership' in the Republic, where much of the recent fascination with the Irish 'Partnership State' (O'Donnell, 2008) suggests that the Irish case provides an exemplar of new modes of governance which is 'distinguished by a unique set of institutional innovations for creative, dynamic, and self-reflexive governance for social and economic development' (House and McGrath, 2004; Sabel, 1996). It has been suggested that 'the willingness of successive Irish governments to relinquish their unique role in policy-making, for the inclusion of agreed "social partners", demonstrates a changing attitude towards government' (Adshead and Quinn, 1998). This alleged shift has been variously characterized: for some it represents a move towards more corporatist styles of policy-making (Hardiman, 1992; Taylor, 1993) involving new governance networks (Hardiman, 2006). For others (O'Donnell and O'Reardon, 1997, 2000), Irish Social Partnership offers something more than traditional quasi-corporatist arrangements, warranting its depiction as a new form of *post-corporatist concentration*, characterized by 'deliberation' and 'problem-solving' between a wider range of interests than the traditional confederations of capital and labour and where 'the capacity to shape and reshape parties' preferences are seen to be prominent features of the dealings between the social partners, interwoven into a process that also involves "hard-headed" bargaining' (O'Donnell and O'Reardon, 2000: 250). In Northern Ireland, as elsewhere in the UK, formal social partnerships have not existed since the 1970s and the devolved Executive is most unlikely to create such arrangements; given the continuing economic dominance of the Treasury in London, local quasi-corporatism would have little impact. This notwithstanding, the devolved administrations in Scotland and Wales have attempted maximum inclusivity in policy formulation and the Northern Ireland Executive may follow those pluralist models.

The two states still share a number of socio-cultural attributes. The Republic of Ireland and Northern Ireland are both states in which the importance of religion has declined. Assisted by the European-wide rise of secularism and more parochial scandals, the Catholic Church's influence upon state policy collapsed rapidly during the 1990s in the Irish Republic, as a liberal and pluralist entity finally emerged from beneath the confessional cloak. Although the correlation between religious affiliation and voting choice in Northern Ireland is the strongest in Western Europe, this does not indicate the strength of religion per se, but is more an indication of religious affiliation (as distinct from practice) as a component of bloc identity. Despite religious opposition, gay equality and civil partnership legislation has been enacted in Northern Ireland, whilst equally strong religious opposition to divorce in the Irish Republic was overcome by the mid-1990s. Nonetheless, both states remain highly religious entities on some measurements. Churchgoing remains a regular feature of life in the North among Catholics and Protestants, whilst, across both countries, the Catholic Church retains its control of many schools and thus influences education from the ages of 5 to 18. Although long in political decline, Orangeism represents an important part of civil-religious life for many Protestants in the North. Abortion remains prohibited across the island.

Whilst civil society in the Irish Republic might be seen as the glue binding a people together, Northern Ireland's civil society remains subject to binary fracture. Within a consociational polity in which an ethnic divide is formally recognized and legitimized (via the GFA) it is perhaps unsurprising that there are effectively two adjacent and largely mutually exclusive societies in Northern Ireland. Educational, sporting, financial (via different credit unions) and cultural divides remain strong below the overarching political-religious fracture. By contrast, the great trick of contemporary politics in the Republic of Ireland is the clear maintenance of public consensus as a consequence of the evolving practice of 'government by partnership' and the parallel development of national Social Partnership arrangements. Even so, whilst the capacity for consensus building that is created by Social Partnership is widely acknowledged, it is also criticized for diminishing debate about the conditions of democracy in the Republic of Ireland. Across both states, for example, women and minorities remain under-represented with no obvious means of redress, and inequality remains unacceptably high.

So what of the prospects for future relations within and between these two states? As far as public policy is concerned, both states have emerged from earlier difficulties to host prosperous economies, even whilst lacking strong industrial bases. Fuelled largely by reduced taxation upon businesses, the Celtic Tiger produced a remarkable turnaround, generating rapid and substantial foreign investment in the Irish Republic. EU membership and attendant financial subsidies have been hugely beneficial for the Republic and this support has been reciprocated by a generally positive outlook towards the EU among its citizens, notwithstanding the recent upset such as the initial rejection of the Nice Treaty and of the EU constitution. The North's economy is much less of a success story in terms of private sector investment, with heavy reliance (almost one-third of jobs) upon the public sector. Northern Ireland's economy is recovering from prolonged conflict, but it remains dependent upon UK subvention and EU PEACE programme money, the third and final round of which will expire in 2013, while the economies North and South are vulnerable to global economic downturn.

It seems inevitable that a combination of the increased global interdependence, the continually evolving influence of the EU, the all-island arrangements of the GFA and cordial Anglo-Irish intergovernmental relations will continue to erase distinctions between the two polities on the island of Ireland. Within a restructured United Kingdom, the Scottish and Welsh administrations are seeking further powers and, controversies over policing and justice notwithstanding, it seems inconceivable that the Northern Ireland Executive will not follow suit. Whether Northern Ireland's Britishness – an always distinctive concept – will be diminished by further remoteness from Westminster is a moot point. Decades of devolution in earlier times did not reduce the sense of 'ultra-Britishness' held by Unionists in the North, but the context is now very different. The state to the South is no longer seen as the clerical, nationalist, irredentist entity once viewed as the antithesis of everything Protestant-British; and the 'zero-sum politics of territorialism' have been replaced by a positive approach to cross-border networks (Coakley and O'Dowd, 2008: p. 308). In the Republic, the political desire for a united Ireland, which infused and inspired successive governments, even if only rhetorically, has been reduced to aspiration rather than imperative.

A thawing of relations between North and South has followed the ending of British–Irish contestation of sovereignty over Northern Ireland, an entity seen by successive Free State/Irish Republic governments as illegitimate from the 1920s until the 1990s. Northern Ireland's place in the United Kingdom is conditional upon the will of its citizens, but this is not novel, such conditionality having been evident since the Sunningdale Agreement of the 1970s. Much more important has been the Irish Government's explicit acceptance of the terms of that conditionality, which have ensured a rapprochement between North and South since the GFA, unprecedented to those generations which lived through political enmity, trade boycotts, sectarian denunciation and considerable violence. A greater coming together of North and South cannot, however, rely solely upon the institutional apparatus of the NSMC and cross-border bodies. For this to occur, more substantial all-island arrangements will need to develop through a coming together of groups in civil society, operating in increasingly 'border-blind' ways.

Notes

1 The Executive

1 Following Garret FitzGerald's decision to appoint a senator as Minister for Foreign Affairs, he was informed by his party chairman that Members of the Dáil (TDs) were insulted that he thought none of them fit for office and that he had as a consequence lost their trust. Thus O'Byrne (1986) argued that much of the goodwill towards FitzGerald from the parliamentary party following his electoral success was lost in the 'botched manner in which he constructed his cabinets'.

2 The National Economic and Social Council, the National Economic and Social Forum and The National Centre for Partnership and Performance, all of which are constituted under the umbrella of the National Economic and Social Development Office and the institutional arrangements to negotiate and monitor national agreements.

3 The minority Haughey administration of 1987–89 was able to maintain office with the support of an independent TD, Tony Gregory, and the Workers' Party, as well as a broad consensus on fiscal and economic policy with the main opposition parties (Farrell, 1993b).

2 The Legislature

1 George Gavan Duffy, J. O'Mara, Seán T. Ó Ceallaigh, E. J. Duggan, Piaras Béaslaoi and Eoin MacNeil.

2 For a critical review of the Public Accounts Committee, 1961–80, see O'Halpin 1985.

3 From 30 June 1981 there was a Fine Gael/Labour coalition, claiming 48.2 per cent of Dail support. From 9 March 1982 there was a Fianna Fáil government, claiming 48.8 per cent of Dail support; this was replaced by a Fine Gael/Labour coalition, with a slim majority of 51.8 per cent of Dail support, on 14 December 1982 (Coakley and Gallagher, 1993: 272).

4 So called after the Dublin suburb in which the policy was announced by the then Fine Gael leader, Alan Dukes.

3 The Bureaucracy

1 The Civil Service Commissioners Act, 1956, and the Civil Service Regulation Act, 1956, granted the Minister of Finance broad regulatory powers, and also some exceptions to the requirement that positions be filled by competition – enabling the appointment of ministerial advisers and personnel secretaries from outside the civil service.

2 This required senior civil servants, as well as members of the Oireachtas and other public servants, to disclose their business interests to the Oireachtas for annual publication.

3 This gave citizens a legal right of access to official and personnel information.

4 This gave Oireachtas committees increased powers of investigation into areas of public concern, including the ability to compel witnesses to respond to questions.

5 Interview with the Chief Executive, Area Development Management (ADM) Ltd, (now *Pobal*) Dublin, 10 November 1997. ADM is the independent body set up by the Irish government to administer and oversee the disbursement of EU Structural Funds.

6 Interview with the Executive Officer, Department of the Taoiseach, Dublin, 3 November 1997.

7 Civil Society, Interest Groups and Pressure Politics

1 Interview with the Irish Business and Employers Confederation, 8 February 2006.
2 Interview with the Irish Business and Employers Confederation, 30 January 2006.
3 Interview with the Irish National Organisation for the Unemployed (INOU) 30 November 2005.
4 Interview with the National Women's Council of Ireland, 19 January 2006.

9 Territorial Administration and Subnational Government

1 In 1898, the Local Government (Ireland) Act transferred the functions of the grand juries (non-elected gentry held responsible for law and order in their own localities) to democratically elected county councils under the same doctrine of *ultra vires* that pertained in Britain.
2 The city acts included the Dublin City Management Act, 1930; the Limerick City Management Act, 1934; and the Waterford City Management Act, 1939.
3 The 1963 Local Government (Planning and Development) Act was intended to give local authorities greater freedom to expand their developmental role without the need of constant referral to central government. In practice, however, it served primarily to strengthen the role of the county managers at the expense of elected council officials.

10 Economic Management

1 Revitalising Areas by Planning, Investment and Development (RAPID) is a government initiative focused on 45 disadvantaged urban areas and provincial towns, designed to increase investment by government; improve delivery of public services; and enhance opportunities for communities to participate in strategic development.

11 Social Policy and the Welfare State

1 This view, typified by Economics Minister Patrick McGilligan's pronouncement that – in order to uphold economic policy – 'people may have to die in this country and may have to die from starvation' (Dáil Debates, vol. 9, p. 562, 30 October 1924), is often referred to by contemporary historians as reflecting the prevailing orthodoxy of the time (Lee, 1989: 127; Ferriter, 2004: 318).

12 Ireland in the European Union and Beyond

1 Interview with the Chief Executive, Area Development Management (ADM) Ltd, Dublin, 10 November 1997. ADM (now *Pobal*) is the independent body set up by the Irish government to administer and oversee the disbursement of EU Structural Funds.
2 Between 1981 and 1982 there were three elected governments in Ireland: from 30 June 1981, a Fine Gael/Labour coalition claiming 48.2 per cent of Dáil support; from 9 March 1982, a Fianna Fáil government claiming 48.8 per cent of Dáil support; and from 14 December 1982, a Fine Gael/Labour coalition with a slim majority of 51.8 per cent of Dáil support (Coakley and Gallagher, 1993: 272).

Bibliography

Acheson, N., Harvey, B., Kearney, J. and Williamson, A. (2004) *Two Paths, One Purpose: Voluntary action in Ireland, North and South*, Dublin: IPA.

Adams, G. (2007) *Presidential Speech to Sinn Féin Special Conference on Policing*, Dublin.

Adema, W. (2001) *Labour Market and Social Policy*, Paris: OECD Occasional Paper No. 52, Directorate for Education, Employment, Labour and Social Affairs.

Adshead, M. (1996a) 'Beyond clientelism: Agricultural networks in Ireland and the EU', *West European Politics*, 19(3), 583–608.

Adshead, M. (1996b) 'Sea change on the isle of Saints and Scholars? The 1995 Irish referendum on the introduction of divorce', *Electoral Studies*, 15(1), 138–42.

Adshead, M. (2002) *Developing European Regions? Comparative governance, policy networks and European Integration*, Aldershot: Ashgate.

Adshead, M. (2005) 'Europeanization and changing patterns of governance in Ireland', *Public Administration*, 83(1), 159–78.

Adshead, M. (2006) 'New modes of governance and the Irish case: finding evidence for explanations of Social Partnership', *Economic and Social Review*, 37(3), 319–42.

Adshead, M. (2008) 'State autonomy, State capacity and the Patterning of Politics in the Irish state' in Adshead, M., Kirby, P. and Millar, M., (eds), *Contesting the State: Lessons from the Irish case*, Manchester: Manchester University Press, 50–72.

Adshead, M., Kirby, P. and Millar, M. (2008) 'Ireland as a model of success' in Adshead, M., Kirby, P. and Millar, M., (eds) *Contesting the State: Lessons from the Irish case*, Manchester: Manchester University Press, 1–24.

Adshead, M., Kirby, P. and Millar, M., eds (2008) *Contesting the State: Lessons from the Irish case*, Manchester: Manchester University Press.

Adshead, M., Lodge, T. and Ní Shé, É. (2007) 'Ireland – Layered Citizenship in a globalised economy', in *Matchpoints in Globalisation Conference*, University of Aarhus, Denmark.

Adshead, M. and McInerney, C. (2008a) 'Institutionalising partnership governance in Ireland', in Considine, M. and Giguerre, S., (eds), *Local Development*, Basingstoke: Palgrave, 233–54.

Adshead, M. and McInerney, C. (2008b) 'Ireland's National Anti-Poverty Strategy as New Governance', *Irish Political Studies*, forthcoming.

Adshead, M. and Millar, M. (2008) *NAPS policy and process – what have we learned?, Research Working Paper 08/02*, Dublin: Combat Poverty Agency.

Adshead, M. and Murphy, M. (forthcoming) chapter in Millar, M. and Adshead, M., eds, *Governance and Public Policy in Ireland*, Dublin: Irish Academic Press.

Adshead, M. and Neylon, G. (2008) 'Irish approaches to ECEC – keeping the politics out of the nursery', in *Paper presented to the Centre for Social and Educational Research (CSER), Early Childhood Care and Education Seminar Series*, Dublin Institute of Technology.

Adshead, M. and Quinn, B. (1998) 'The move from government to governance: Irish development policy's paradigm shift', *Politics and Policy*, 26(2), 209–25.

Aherne, B. (2003) 'The policy implications of social capital', Speech at the launch of the NESF report, 29 November 2003; available at www.taoiseach.gov.ie/index.asp?locID= 365&docID=-I

Ahern, B. (2005) 'Community is the thread that holds together the fabric of our society and our future', *Village Magazine*, 10, 9 September.

Ahern, D. (2006) 'The fiftieth anniversary of Ireland's membership of the United Nations – looking forward', *Irish Studies in International Affairs*, 17, 3–13.

Aldous, R. (2007) *Great Irish speeches*, Dublin: Quercus.

Allen, K. (1997) *Fianna Fáil and Irish Labour, 1926 to the Present*, London: Pluto.

Allen, K. (2000) *The Celtic Tiger. The myth of Social Partnership in Ireland*, Manchester: Manchester University Press.

Allen, K. (2007) *The Corporate Takeover of Ireland*, Dublin: Irish Academic Press.

Almond, G. A. and Verba, S. (1963) *The Civic Culture: Political Attitudes in Five Western Democracies*, Princeton: Princeton University Press.

Andreosso-O'Callaghan, B. and Lenihan, H. (2006) 'Is Ireland a role model for SME development in the new EU member states?', *European Integration*, 28(3), 277–303.

Anyadike-Danes, M., Hart, M. and Lenihan, H. (2007) 'Business formation and survival rates in a rapidly growing economy: the Irish experience', in *Paper presented to the Matchpoints in Globalisation Conference*, University of Aarhus.

Aristotle (1984 [ca. 350 BC]) *The Politics*, tr. Carnes Lord, Chicago: Chicago University Press.

Arkins, A. (1990) 'Legislative and Executive relations in the Republic of Ireland', in Norton, P., ed. *Parliaments in Western Europe*, London: Frank Cass, 90–102.

Arter, D. (1999) *Scandinavian Politics Today*, Manchester: Manchester University Press.

Aughey, A. (1996) 'Local Government', in Aughey, A. and Morrow, D. (eds) *Northern Ireland Politics*, Harlow: Longman, 94–102.

Aughey, A. (2005) *The Politics of Northern Ireland: Beyond the Belfast Agreement*, London: Routledge.

Bache, I. (1998) *The Politics of European Union Regional Policy. Multi-level governance or flexible gatekeeping?*, Sheffield: Sheffield Academic Press.

Bacik, I. (2004) *Kicking and Screaming: Dragging Ireland into the 21st Century*, Dublin: O'Brien.

Bale, T. (2005) *European politics. A comparative introduction*, Basingstoke: Palgrave.

Bannon, M. (1991) 'The contribution of the management system to local and national development' in Barrington, T. J., ed. *City and County Management 1929–1990: a retrospective*, Dublin: IPA, 44–5.

Barrington, T. J. (1980) *The Irish Administrative System*, Dublin: Institute for Public Administration (IPA).

Barrington, T. J. (1987) 'Ireland the interplay of territory and function' in Rhodes, R. A. W. and Wright, V., (eds), *Tensions in the Territorial Politics of Western Europe*, London: Frank Cass.

Bax, M. (1975) 'The political machine and its importance to the Irish Republic', *Political Anthropology*, 1(1), 6–20.

Bax, M. (1976) *Harpstrings and Confessions: An Anthropological Study of Politics in Rural Ireland*, Assen: Van Gorcum.

Bean, K. (2008) '"The economic and social war against violence": British social and economic strategy and the evolution of Provisionalism' in Edwards, A. and Bloomer, S., eds, *Transforming the Peace Process in Northern Ireland*, Dublin: Irish Academic Press, 163–74.

Beveridge, William (1942) *Social Insurance and Allied Services Report*, presented to Parliament by command of His Majesty, November HMSO, Cmnd 6404.

Bew, P., Gibbon, P. and Patterson, H. (1996) *Northern Ireland 1921–1994: Political Forces and Social Classes*, London: Serif.

Bew, P., Gibbon, P. and Patterson, H. (2002) *Northern Ireland 1921–2001: Political Forces and Social Classes*, London: Serif.

Bew, P. and Patterson, H. (1982) *Sean Lemass and the Making of Modern Ireland*, Dublin: Gill and Macmillan.

Bew, P., Patterson, H. and Teague, P. (1997) *Between War and Peace: The Political Future of Northern Ireland*, London: Lawrence and Wishart.

Birnie, E. and Hitchens, D. (2001) 'Chasing the Wind? Half a Century of Economic Strategy Documents in Northern Ireland', *Irish Political Studies*, 16(1), 1–29.

Birrell, D. (2007) 'The Reform Agenda in the Northern Ireland Civil Service: The Influences of Parity, Integration, Devolution and Direct Rule', *Public Policy and Administration*, 22(3), 273–88.

Birrell, D. (2008) *The System of Governance in Northern Ireland*, Manchester: Manchester University Press.

Birrell, D. and Murie, A. (1980) *Policy and Government in Northern Ireland: Lessons of Devolution*, Dublin: Gill and Macmillan.

Black, B. (2004) 'The Changing World of Work' in Lloyd, K., Devine, P., Gray, A. and Heenan, D., eds, *Social Attitudes in Northern Ireland: The Ninth Report*, London: Pluto, 67–80.

Blair, T. (1998) *Leading the Way. A new vision for local government*, London: Institute for Public Policy Research.

Blais, A. (1991) 'The debate over electoral systems', *International Political Science Review*, 12(3), 239–60.

Blondel, J. (1973) *Comparative Legislatures*, London: Prentice Hall.

Bloomer, S. (2008) 'Bridging the Militarist-Politico Divide: The Progressive Unionist Party and the Politics of Conflict Transformation', in Edwards, A. and Bloomer, S., eds, *Transforming the Peace Process in Northern Ireland*, Dublin: Irish Academic Press, 97–113.

Bloomfield, K. (2007) *A Tragedy of Errors. The Government and Misgovernment of Northern Ireland*, Liverpool: Liverpool University Press.

Boal, F., Keane, M. and Livingstone, D. (1996) *Them and Us? A Survey of Catholic and Protestant Churchgoers in Belfast*, Belfast: Central Community Relations Unit.

Bogdanor, V. (1997) 'In checking, we trust', *Times Higher Education Supplement*, 22.

Bogdanor, V. (1999) 'Devolution: Decentralisation or Disintegration?', *Political Quarterly*, 70(2), 185–94.

Boland, J. (1991) 'Dáil can only be reformed if TDs are liberated from multi-seat constituencies', *Representation*, 30, 111.

Bolger, P. (1977) *The Irish Co-operative Movement, its History and Development*, Dublin: IPA.

Bollen, K. A. (1979) 'Political democracy and the timing of development', *American Sociological Review*, 44, 572–87.

Bollen, K. A. (1983) 'World system position, dependency, and democracy: the cross-national evidence', *American Sociological Review*, 45, 468–79.

Bollen, K. A. and Jackman, R. W. (1985) 'Economic and non-economic determinants of political democracy in the 1960s' in Braungardt, R. G., ed. *Research in Political Sociology*, Greenwich, CT: Jai Press.

Borooah, V. (2003) 'Rational actor models, voting and the Northern Ireland Assembly' in Adshead, M. and Millar, M., eds, *Public Administration and Public Policy in Ireland: Theory and Methods*, London: Routledge, 147–64.

Boyce, D. G. (1990) *Nationalism in Ireland*, London: Routledge.

Boyce, D.G. (1996) *The Irish Question and British Politics, 1868–1996*, London: Macmillan.

Boyle, M. (2000) 'Euro-regionalism and struggles over scales of governance: the politics of Ireland's regionalization approach to Structural Fund allocations 2000–2006', *Political Geography*, 19, 737–69.

Boyle, R. (1995) *Towards a new public service*, Dublin: Institute for Public Administration (IPA).

Boyle, R. (1998) '*Governance and accountability in the Irish civil service*', in *Committee for Public Management Research (CPMR) Discussion Paper 6*, Dublin, IPA.

Boyle, R. with T. McNamara, M.Mulreany, A. O'Keefe and T. O'Sullivan (1998/9) 'Review of developments in the public sector in 1997', *Administration*, Vol. 45, No.4, 1998, pp. 3–38.

Boyle, R. (1999) '*The management of cross-cutting issues*', in *Committee for Public Management Research (CPMR) Discussion Paper 8*, Dublin, IPA.

Boyle, R. and Worth-Butler, M. (1999) 'Multi-stream structures in the Public Service', in *Committee for Public Management Research (CPMR) Discussion Paper 9*, Dublin, IPA.

Bradley, J. (2000) 'The Irish economy in comparative perspective' in Nolan, B., O'Connell, P. J. and Whelan, C. T., eds, *Bust to Boom? The Irish experience of growth and inequality*, Dublin: IPA, 4–26.

Bradley, J. (2007) 'Economic development: the textile and information technology sectors' in Coakley, J. and O'Dowd, L., eds, *Crossing the Border: New Relationships between Northern Ireland and the Republic of Ireland*, Dublin: Irish Academic Press, 201–26.

Bradley, J. and Birnie, E. (2001) *Can the Celtic Tiger cross the Border?* Cork: Cork University Press.

Bradley, J., FitzGerald, J. and Kearney, I. (1993) *Stabilization and Growth in the EC Periphery: A Study of the Irish Economy*, Aldershot: Avebury.

Brennock, M. (1997) 'Ministerial titles highlight new priorities for government', *The Irish Times*, 27 June.

Bresnihan, V. (1999) 'The symbolic power or Ireland's President Robinson', *Presidential Studies Quarterly*, 29(2), 250–62.

Briscoe, B. (1982) *The Co-operative Idea*, UCC, Cork: Bank of Ireland Centre for Co-operative Studies.

Briscoe, R. and Ward, M. (2000) *The Co-operatives of Ireland*, UCC, Cork: Centre for Co-operative Studies.

Bromage, A. W. (1954) 'Irish councilmen at work', *Administration*, 2(1), 93–111.

Browne, N. (1986) *Against the Tide*, Dublin: Gill and Macmillan.

Browne, V. (2006) 'Social Partnership is Nonsense', *Irish Times*, 31 May.

Bruce, S. (1986) *God Save Ulster! The Religion and Politics of Paisleyism*, Oxford: Oxford University Press.

Bruce, S. (1994) *At the Edge of the Union*, Oxford: Oxford University Press.

Brunt, B. (1988) *Western Europe Economic and Social Studies, The Republic of Ireland*, London: Paul Chapman.

Buchanan, T. (1969) *Regional studies in Ireland*, Dublin: An Foras Forbatha.

Buckland, P. (1981) *A History of Northern Ireland*, London: Holmes and Meier.

Budge, I. (1985) 'Party factions and government reshuffles: a general hypothesis tested against data from 20 postwar democracies', *European Journal of Political Research*, 13, 327–33.

Bulmer, S. and Burch, M. (1998) 'Organizing for Europe: Whitehall, the British state and European Union', *Public Administration*, 76(3), 601–28.

Burke, H. (1999) 'Foundations stones of Irish social policy 1831–1951' in Kiely, G., O'Donnell, A., Kennedy, P. and Quin, S., eds, *Irish Social Policy in Context*, Dublin: UCD Press, 11–32.

Burton, J. (2003) '10 years on and looking for some sparkle in a dull Dáil', *The Irish Times* 16 August.

Byrne, D., Dully, J., Garvey, D., Kirwan, W., Mulhern, T., O'Hanlon, G., Rogers, S., Ryan, O., Treacy, C., Tuohy, B., and Tutty, M.G. (1995) 'Strategic Management in the Irish Civil Service', Special issue, *Administration*, 3(2), 1–152.

Byrne, E. (2007) *Corruption Report: Ireland*, Dublin: Transparency International.

Byrne, N., McCarthy, O. and O'Connor, R. (2004) 'The development of new rural credit unions in Ireland within a context of service rationalization in rural areas', *Community Development Journal*, 39(4), 401–12.

Byrne, R. and McCutcheon, J. P. (2001) 4th edn, *The Irish legal system*, Dublin: Butterworth.

Campbell, C. and Wilson, K. (1995) *The End of Whitehall? Death of a Paradigm*, Oxford: Blackwell.

Carmichael, P. (2002) 'The Northern Ireland Civil Service: Characteristics and Trends since 1970', *Public Administration*, 80(1), 23–49.

Carmichael, P. (2003) 'Continuities and Change in the Unified British Civil Service: The Northern Ireland Experience', in *Institute of Public Administration of Australia Annual Conference*, Brisbane.

Carmichael, P. and Osborne, R. (2003) 'The Northern Ireland Civil Service under Direct Rule and Devolution', *International Review of Administrative Sciences*, 69, 205–17.

Carnegie Trust (2007) *The Shape of Civil Society to Come, Findings from the Inquiry into the Future of Civil Society in the UK and Ireland*, London: Carnegie UK Trust.

Carty, R. K. (1976) 'Social cleavages and party systems: a reconsideration of the Irish case', *European Journal of Political Research*, 4, 195–203.

Carty, R. K. (1981) *Party and Parish Pump: Electoral politics in Ireland*, Waterloo, Ontario: Wilfred Laurier.

Casey, J. (2000) 3rd edn, *Constitutional Law in Ireland*, London: Sweet and Maxwell.

Cassidy, K. (2005) 'Organic Intellectuals and the Committed Community: Sinn Féin and Irish Republicanism in the North', *Irish Political Studies*, 20(3), 341–56.

Castles, F. G. (1967) *Pressure Groups and Political Culture*, London: Routledge.

CEC (Commission of the European Communities) (1997) *Agenda 2000 – Volume I: for a stronger and wider Union*, Brussels: CEC.

Centre for Cross Border Studies (2007) 'Overview of North/South and Cross-Border Cooperation in the Common Chapter', *Briefing Note 6*.

Centre for Economic and Business Research (2007) *Regional Economic Performance*, London: CEBR.

Cerny, P. G. (2000) 'Restructuring the Political Arena: Globalization and the Paradoxes of the Competition State' in Germain, R. D., ed. *Globalization and its Critics: Perspectives from Political Economy*, Basingstoke: Macmillan, 117–38.

Chubb, B. (1957) 'The Independent Member in Ireland', *Political Studies*, 5, 131–9.

Chubb, B. (1963) 'Going about persecuting civil servants: the role of elected representatives in the Irish legislature', *Political Studies*, 11(3), 272–86.

Chubb, B. (1970) *The Government and Politics of Ireland*, Dublin: IPA.

Chubb, B. (1974) *Cabinet Government in Ireland*, Dublin: IPA.

Chubb, B. (1988) 'Government and the Dáil: Constitutional Myth and Practice' in Farrell, B., ed. *De Valera's Constitution and Ours*, Dublin: Gill & Macmillan.

Chubb, B. (1992) 3rd edn, *The Government and Politics of Ireland*, London: Longman.

Clinch, P., Convery, F. and Walsh, B. (2002) *After the Celtic Tiger, challenges ahead*, Dublin: O'Brien Press.

Coakley, J. (1980) 'The significance of names: the evolution of Irish party labels', *Etudes Irlandais*, 5, 171–81.

Coakley, J. (1983) 'The European dimension in Irish public opinion, 1972–1982' in Coombes, D., ed. *Ireland and the European Communities: ten years of membership*, Dublin: Gill and Macmillan.

Coakley, J. (1984) 'Selecting a prime minister: the Irish experience', *Parliamentary Affairs*, 37(4), 403–17.

Coakley, J. (1993a) 2nd edn, 'Society and political culture' in Coakley, J. and Gallagher, M., eds, *Politics in the Republic of Ireland*, Dublin: PSAI Press.

Coakley, J. (1993b) 2nd edn, 'The foundations of Statehood' in Coakley, J. and Gallagher, M., eds, *Politics in the Republic of Ireland*, Dublin: PSAI Press, 1–24.

Coakley, J. (1999) 2nd edn, 'The foundations of Statehood' in Coakley, J. and Gallagher, M., eds, *Politics in the Republic of Ireland*, London: Routledge, 1–31.

Coakley, J. (2003) 3rd edn, 'Society and Political culture' in Coakley, J. and Gallagher, M., eds, *Politics in the Republic of Ireland*, London: Routledge, 32–70.

Coakley, J. (2005a) 4th edn, 'Society and Political culture' in Coakley, J. and Gallagher, M., eds, *Politics in the Republic of Ireland*, London: Routledge, 36–71.

Coakley, J. (2005b) 4th edn, 'The foundations of Statehood' in Coakley, J. and Gallagher, M., eds, *Politics in the Republic of Ireland*, Abingdon: Routledge, 3–35.

Coakley, J. and Gallagher, M., eds (1993) 2nd edn, *Politics in the Republic of Ireland*, Dublin: PSAI Press.

Coakley, J. and Gallagher, M., eds (2005) 4th edn, *Politics in the Republic of Ireland*, Abingdon: Routledge.

Coakley, J. and O'Dowd, L. (2008) 'The Irish border in the twenty-first century', in J. Coakley, J. and L. O'Dowd, eds (2008) *Crossing the Border: New Relationships between Northern Ireland and the Republic of Ireland*, Dublin: Irish Academic Press.

Coakley, J. and O'Dowd, L., eds (2008) *Crossing the Border: New Relationships between Northern Ireland and the Republic of Ireland*, Dublin: Irish Academic Press.

Coakley, J., O'Caoindealbhain, B. and Wilson, R. (2007) 'Institutional cooperation: the North-South implementation bodies' in Coakley, J. and O'Dowd, L., eds, *Crossing the Border: New Relationships between Northern Ireland and the Republic of Ireland*, Dublin: Irish Academic Press, 32–60.

Cochrane, F. (2001) 'Unsung Heroes? The Role of Peace and Conflict Resolution Organisations in the Northern Ireland Conflict' in McGarry, J., ed. *Northern Ireland and the Divided World*, Oxford: Oxford University Press, 137–56.

Cochrane, F. (2006) 'Two cheers for the NGOs: building peace from below in Northern Ireland' in Cox, M., Guelke, A. and Stephen, F., eds, *A Farewell to Arms? Beyond the Good Friday Agreement*, Manchester: Manchester University Press, 253–67.

Collins, N. (1994) 'Agricultural policy networks of the Republic of Ireland and Northern Ireland', *Political Studies*, 43/4:664–82.

Collins, N. and O'Shea, M. (2003) 'Clientelism: facilitating rights and favours' in Adshead, M. and Millar, M., eds, *Public Administration and Public Policy in Ireland. Theory and methods*, London: Routledge, 88–107.

Collins, S. (1993) *Spring and the Labour Story*, Dublin: O'Brien.

Collins, S. (2005) *Breaking the Mould. How the PDs changed Irish politics*, Dublin: Gill and Macmillan.

Collins, S. (2006) 'Ruling restores authority of Oireachtas', *Irish Times*, 10 March.

Collins, S. (2008) 'Rich legacy recalled in tributes as Hillery is laid to rest', *Irish Times*, 16 April.

Collins, S. and Hennessy, M. (2007) 'Ahern gives Greens two top ministries in Cabinet', *Irish Times*, 15 June.

Colomer, J., ed. (1996) *Political institutions in Europe*, London: Routledge.

Commins, P. (1986) 'Rural Irish society' in Clancy, P., Drudy, S., Lynch, K. and O'Dowd, L., eds, *Ireland: a sociological profile*, Dublin: IPA, 47–69.

Commission on the Status of Women (1972) *Report of the Commission on the Status of Women*, Dublin: DSO.

Commission on the Status of Women (1993) *Report of the Second Commission on the Status of Women*, Dublin: DSO.

Connaughton, B. (2005) 'The impact of coalition government on politico-administrative relations in Ireland 1981–2002' in Peters, G. B., Verheijen, T. and Vass, L., eds, *Coalitions of the unwilling? Politicians and civil servants in coalition governments*, Bratislava: NISPAcee.

Connaughton, B. (2006) 'Reform of politico-administrative relations in the Irish system: clarifying or complicating the doctrine of ministerial responsibility?', *Irish Political Studies*, 21(3), 257–76.

Connolly, E. (2005) 4th edn, 'The government and the governmental system' in Coakley, J. and Gallagher, M., eds, *Politics in the Republic of Ireland*, London: Routledge, 328–83.

Connolly, E. (2007) *The Institutionalisation of Anti-Poverty and Social Exclusion policy in Irish Social Partnership*, Dublin: Combat Poverty Agency (CPA) Research Working Paper 07/01.

Connolly, L. (1999) 'Feminist Politics and the Peace Process', *Capital and Class*, 69, 145–59.

Connolly, L. (2003) *The Irish Women's Movement, from revolution to devolution*, Dublin: Lilliput Press.

Connolly, M. (1990) *Politics and Policy Making in Northern Ireland*, London: Philip Allan.

Connolly, M. and Loughlin, S. (1990) *Public Policy in Northern Ireland: Adoption or Adaptation*, Belfast: Policy Research Institute.

Conroy, P. (1999) 'From the fifties to the nineties: social policy comes out of the shadows' in Kiely, G., O'Donnell, A., Kennedy, P. and Quin, S., eds, *Irish Social policy in context*, Dublin: UCD Press, 33–50.

Cooney, T. (2006) 'Determining when a judge is deemed unfit for office', *Irish Times*, 18 March.

Coughlan, A. (1984) 'Ireland's welfare state in time of crisis', *Administration*, 32(1), 37–54.

Coulter, C. (1999a) *Contemporary Northern Irish Society*, London: Pluto.

Coulter, C. (1999b) 'The Absence of Class Politics in Northern Ireland', *Capital and Class*, 69(1), 77–100.

Cousins, M. (1995) *The Irish Social Welfare System: Law and social policy*, Dublin: Round Hall.

Cousins, M. (1997) 'Ireland's place in the worlds of welfare capitalism', *Journal of European Social Policy*, 7(3), 223–35.

Cousins, M. (2005) *Explaining the Irish welfare state*, Lewiston, NY: Edwin Mellen Press.

Cowell-Meyers, K. (2003) 'Women in Northern Ireland Politics: Gender and the Politics of Peace-Building in the New Legislative Assembly', *Irish Political Studies*, 18(1), 72–96.

Coyle, C. (1990) 'Irish local bureaucracies in national and European Communities', in *ECPR workshop on local and regional bureaucracies in European states*, University of Limerick, Ireland.

Coyle, C. (1994) 'Irish local administration in the national and European policy process', *Research in Urban Policy*, 5, 21–41.

Cradden, T. (1999) 2nd edn, 'Social partnership in Ireland' in Collins, N., ed. *Political Issues in Ireland Today*, Manchester: Manchester University Press, 46–63.

Cradden, T. and Erridge, A. (1990) 'Employers and trade unions in the development of public policy in Northern Ireland' in Connolly, M. and Loughlin, S., eds, *Public Policy in Northern Ireland*, Belfast: Policy Research Institute, 99–123.

CRG Constitutional Review Group (1996) *Report*, Dublin: Stationery Office.

Criminal Justice Review Group (2000) *Review of the Criminal Justice System in Northern Ireland*, Belfast: HMSO.

Cromien, S. (2000) 'Serving in new Spheres' in O'Donnell, R., ed. *Europe the Irish experience*, Dublin: Institute of European Affairs, 148–60.

Cronin, M. and Kirby, P., eds (2008) *Transforming Ireland: challenges, resources, opportunities*, Manchester: Manchester University Press.

Crotty, R. (1986) *Ireland in Crisis: a study in capitalist colonial undevelopment*, Dingle: Brandon.

Crowley, U. (2007) 'Boundaries of citizenship: The continued exclusion of Travellers' in Hayward, K. and MacCarthaigh, M., eds, *Recycling the State: The Politics of Adaptation in Ireland*, Dublin: Irish Academic Press.

CSO (2005) *EU Survey on Income and Living Conditions*, Dublin: CSO.

CSO (2007a) *Ethnic or Cultural Background (including the Irish Traveller Community)*, vol. 5, Dublin: CSO.

CSO (2007b) *Measuring Ireland's Progress 2006*, Dublin: CSO.

CSW (Commission on Social Welfare) (1986) *Report of the Commission on Social Welfare*, Dublin: DSO.

Culliton Report (1992) *A Time for Change: Industrial Policy for the 1990s*, Dublin: Stationery Office.

Cunningham, M. (1997) 'The Political Language of John Hume', *Irish Political Studies*, 12(1), 13–22.

Cunningham, M. (2001) *British Government Policy in Northern Ireland*, Manchester: Manchester University Press.

Curtin, C. and Varley, T. (2002) 'Communitarian populism and the politics of rearguard resistance in rural Ireland', *Community Development Journal*, 37(1), 20–32.

CWC (Community Workers Co-operative) (2003) 'Sustaining Progress – also sustains poverty and inequality', *News and Views*, Galway: CWC.

CWC (Community Workers Co-operative) (2005) 'Government censures dissent: funding to the Community Workers' Co-operative axed', *Press release*, 25 January.

Dáil Éirean, vol. 270, 12 February 1974.

Dalton, R., J. (2000) 'The decline of party identification' in Dalton, R. J. and Wattenberg, M. P., eds, *Parties without Partisans: political change in advanced industrial democracies*, Oxford: Oxford University Press.

Daly, M. and Yeates, N. (2003) 'Common origins, different paths', *Policy and Politics*, 31(1), 86–97.

Daly, S. (2007) 'Mapping civil society in the Republic of Ireland', *Community Development Journal*, 1–20.

Damgaard, E., Gerlich, P. and Richardson, J. J. (1989) 'Policy change, ideological change and the persistence of problems' in Damgaard, E., Gerlich, P. and Richardson, J. J., eds, *The Politics of Economic Crisis*, Aldershot: Avebury, 184–95.

Damgaard, E., Gerlich, P. and Richardson, J. J., eds (1989) *The Politics of Economic Crisis*, Aldershot: Avebury.

Deakin, N. (2001) *In Search of Civil Society*, Basingstoke: Palgrave.

Democratic Unionist Party (2004) *European Election Manifesto 2004*, Belfast: DUP.

Department for Employment and Learning (NI) (2006a) *Compendium of Northern Ireland Education Statistics 1992–3 to 2004–5*, Belfast: DfEL.

Department for Employment and Learning (NI) (2006b) *Destinations of Leavers from Higher Education 2004/5*, Belfast: DfEL.

Department for Social Development (2007) *Affordability Review*, Belfast: DfSD.

Department of Enterprise Trade and Investment (DETI) (2006) *Small and Medium Enterprises: December 2006*, Belfast: DETI.

Department of Enterprise Trade and Investment (2007) *Quarterly Economic Review: Winter 2007*, Belfast: DETI.

Department of Enterprise Trade and Investment (DETI) (2008) *Labour Market Summary*, Belfast: DETI.

Department of Finance and Personnel (2004) *Fit for Purpose: The Reform Agenda in the Northern Ireland Civil Service*, Belfast: HMSO.

Department of Health and Social Security (1998) *Building Real Partnership: Compact between Government and the Voluntary and Community Sector in Northern Ireland*, Belfast: DHSS.

Department of Health, Social Services and Public Safety (2002) *Health and Social Care in Northern Ireland: a Statistical Profile*, Belfast: DHSSPS.

Department of Social Community and Family Affairs (DSCFA) (2000) *The White Paper on a Framework for Supporting Voluntary Activity*, Dublin: DSCFA.

Department of Social Welfare (1949) *Social Welfare*, Dublin: DSO

Department of the Taoiseach (1996) *Delivering Better Government*, Second report to the Government of the co-ordinating group of secretaries – A programme of change for the Irish civil service, May 1996, pdf available at: http://www.bettergov.ie/index.asp? docID=83.

Desmond, B. (1975) *The Houses of the Oireachtas – a Plea for Reform*, Leinster House Dublin: Parliamentary Labour Party.

Devereux, E. (1993) 'The lonely furrow: Muintir na Tire and Irish Community 1931–1991', *Community Development Journal*, 28(1), 45–54.

Devereux, E. (1998) *Devils and Angels: television, ideology and the coverage of poverty*, London: John Libbey Media.

Devine, K. M. (2006) 'The myth of "the myth of Irish neutrality": deconstructing concepts of Irish neutrality using international relations theories', *Irish studies in international affairs*, 17, 115–39.

Devlin, L. S. J. (1969) *Report of the Public Services Organization Review Group, 1966–1969*, Dublin: Stationery Office.

Dickson, B. (2007) 'Revisiting rights', *Fortnight*, 452(2).

Dickson, B. and Osborne, B. (2007) 'Equality and human rights since the Agreement' in Carmichael, P., Knox , C. and Osborne, R., eds, *Devolution and Constitutional Change in Northern Ireland*, Manchester: Manchester University Press, 152–66.

Dixon, P. (2006) 'Rethinking the international and Northern Ireland: a critique' in Cox, M., Guelke, A. and Stephen, F., eds, *A Farewell to Arms: Beyond the Good Friday Agreement*, Manchester: Manchester University Press, 409–26.

Doherty, R. (2002) *Ireland, Neutrality and European Security Integration*, Aldershot: Ashgate.

Donelan, E. J. (1992) 'The role of the parliamentary draftsman in the preparation of legislation in Ireland', *Dublin University Law Journal*, 14(1), 1–18.

Donoghue, F. (1998) 'Defining the non-profit sector in Ireland' in Salamon, L. and Anheier, H. K., eds, *Working papers of the John Hopkins Comparative nonprofit sector project, No. 28*, Baltimore: John Hopkins Institute for Policy Studies.

Donoghue, F., Anheier, H. K. and Salamon, L. M. (1999) *Uncovering the Nonprofit Sector in Ireland: Its Economic Value and Significance*, Baltimore: John Hopkins Institute for Policy Studies.

Donoghue, F., Prizeman, G., O'Regan, A. and Noel, V. (2006) *The Hidden Landscape – first forays into mapping non-profit organisations in Ireland*, Dublin: Centre for non-profit management, TCD.

Donohoe, M. (2007) 'Labour criticises extra junior ministers', *Irish Times*, 16 June.

Doolan, B. (1994) 3rd edn, *Constitutional and Legal Rights in Ireland*, Dublin: Gill and Macmillan.

Dooney, S. and O'Toole, J. (1992) *Irish Government Today*, Dublin: Gill and Macmillan.

Dowding, K. (1995) *The Civil Service*, London: Routledge.

Doyle, J. (1996–7) 'Freedom of Information: lessons from the international experience', *Administration*, 44(4), 64–82.

Doyle, N., Hughes, G and Wadenjso, E. (2006) *Freedom of Movement for Workers from Central and Eastern Europe: Experiences in Ireland and Sweden*, Stockholm: Swedish Institute for European Policy Studies.

Drudy, P. J. and Punch, M. (2001) 'Housing and inequality in Ireland' in Cantillon, S., Corrigan, C., Kirby, P. and O'Flynn, J., eds, *Rich and poor: perspectives on tackling inequality in Ireland*, Dublin: Oak Tree Press, 235–61.

DSFA (Department of Social and Family Affairs) (2001) *NAPS Background Note*, Dublin: DSFA.

Dunphy, R. (1998) 'A group of individuals trying to do their best: the dilemmas of Democratic Left', *Irish Political Studies*, 13(1), 50–75.

Dunphy, R. and Hopkins, S. (1992) 'The organisational and political evolution of the Workers' Party of Ireland', *Journal of Communist Studies*, 8(3), 91–118.

Duverger, M. (1954) *Political Parties: their organization and activity in the modern state*, London: Methuen.

Duverger, M. (1980) 'A new political system model-semi-presidential government', *European Journal of Political Research*, 8, 165–87.

EAPN (European Anti-Poverty Network) (2006) *Setting Minimum Social Standards across Europe, summary of research and papers, summer 2006*, Dublin: accessed at www.eapn.ie.

Eckstein, H. (1963) 'Group theory and the comparative study of pressure groups' in Eckstein, H. and Apter, D. E., eds, *Comparative Politics*, London: The Free Press.

Eckstein, H. (1966) *A Theory of Stable Democracy*, Princeton: Princeton University Press.

Eckstein, H. (1967) 'The determinants of pressure group politics' in Eckstein, H. and Apter, D., eds, *Comparative Politics*, London: Macmillan.

Edwards, A. (2007) 'Democratic Socialism and Sectarianism: The Northern Ireland Labour Party and Progressive Unionist Party compared', *Politics*, 27(1), 24–31.

Edwards, M. (2004) *Civil Society*, Cambridge: Polity Press.

Electoral Commission (2004) *The Northern Ireland Assembly elections 2003*, Belfast: Electoral Commission.

Elgie, R. and Fitzgerald, P. (2005) 4th edn, 'The President and Taoiseach' in Coakley, J. and Gallagher, M., eds, *Politics in the Republic of Ireland*, Abingdon: Routledge, 305–27.

Elliott, S. and Flackes, W. (1999) *Northern Ireland: a Political Directory*, Belfast: Blackstaff.

Ellis, D. (1994) 'Freedom of Information: a welfare rights perspective', in *National Social Services Board (NSSB) annual conference*, Dublin Castle, 9 December.

English, R. (2003) *Armed Struggle. A History of the IRA*, London: Palgrave Macmillan.

Epstein, L. D. (1967) *Political Parties in Western Democracies*, New York: Frederick A. Praeger.

Esping-Andersen, G. (1990) *The Three Worlds of Welfare Capitalism*, Cambridge: Polity.

Eurostat (2004) *Portrait of the Regions*, Brussels: European Commission.

Evans, G. and Duffy, M. (1997) 'Beyond the sectarian divide: the social bases and political consequences of Nationalist and Unionist party competition in Northern Ireland', *British Journal of Political Science*, 27(1), 47–81.

Evans, J. and Tonge, J. (2003) 'The future of the radical centre in Northern Ireland after the Good Friday Agreement', *Political Studies*, 51(1), 26–50.

Evans, J., Tonge, J. and Murray, G. (2000) 'Constitutional Nationalism and Socialism in Northern Ireland: the Greening of the SDLP', *British Elections and Parties Review*, 10, 111–32.

Evans, P. (1995) 'The state as problem and solution: predation, embedded autonomy, and structural change' in Haggard, S. and Kaufmann, R., eds, *The Politics of Economic Adjustment*, Princeton, NJ: Princeton University Press.

Evans, P. (1997) 'State structures, government-business relations, and economic transformation' in Maxfield, S. and Schneider, B., eds, *Business and the State in Developing Countries*, Ithaca, NY: Cornell University Press, 63–87.

Examiner (1999) 'Taoiseach must come clean on Sheedy case', Online, 4 May, accessed at *http://archives.tcm.ie/irishexaminer/1999/05/04/opinion.htm*.

Fahey, T. (1992) 'Catholicism and industrial society in Ireland' in Goldthorpe, J. H. and Whelan, C. T., eds, *The Development of Industrial Society in Ireland*, Oxford: Oxford University Press, 241–63.

Fahey, T. and Duffy, D. (2007) 'The housing boom' in Fahey, T., Russell, H. and Whelan, C. T., eds, *Best of times? The social impact of the celtic tiger*, Dublin: IPA, 123–38.

Fahey, T., Hayes, B. C. and Sinnott, R. (2006) *Conflict and Consensus. A study of values and attitudes in the Republic of Ireland and Northern Ireland*, Leiden: Brill.

Fanning, B. (2002) *Racism and Social Change in the Republic of Ireland*, Manchester: Manchester University Press.

Fanning, R. (1978) *The Irish Department of Finance*, Dublin: Gill and Macmillan.

Fanning, R. (1986) 'The great enchantment: uses and abuses of modern Irish history' in Dooge, J. A., ed. *Ireland in the contemporary world*, Dublin: Gill and Macmillan, 146–60.

Fanning, R. (1988) 'Mr de Valera drafts a constitution' in Farell, B., ed. *De Valera's Constitution and Ours*, Dublin: Gill and Macmillan, 33–45.

Fanon, F. (1963) *The Wretched of the Earth*, trans Farrington, F, New York: Grove Press.

Farrell, B. (1969a) 'A note on the Dáil constitution', *Irish Jurist*, 4(1), 127–38.

Farrell, B. (1969b) 'Labour and the Irish political party system: a suggested approach to analysis', *Economic and Social Review*, 1(4), 477–502.

Farrell, B. (1970) 'Labour and the Irish party system: a suggested approach to analysis', *Economic and Social Review*, 1, 477–502.

Farrell, B. (1971a) *Chairman or Chief? The role of Taoiseach in Irish Government*, Dublin: Gill and Macmillan.

Farrell, B. (1971b) *The founding of Dáil Éireann*, Dublin: Gill and Macmillan.

Farrell, B., ed. (1973) *The Irish Parliamentary Tradition*, Dublin: Gill and Macmillan.

Farrell, B. (1973) 'The first Dáil and after' in Farrell, B., ed. *The Irish parliamentary tradition*, Dublin: Gill and Macmillan, 208–20.

Farrell, B. (1983a) 'Ireland: From friends and neighbours to clients and partisans: some dimensions of parliamentary representation under PR STV' in Bogdanor, V., ed. *Coalition government in Western Europe*, London: Heinemann.

Farrell, B. (1983b) *Séan Lemass*, Dublin: Gill and Macmillan.

Farrell, B. (1985) 'Ireland: from friends and neighbours to clients and partisans: some dimensions of parliamentary representation under PR-STV' in Bogdanor, V., ed. *Representatives of the People? Parliamentarians and constituents in western democracies*, Aldershot: Gower, 237–64.

Farrell, B., ed. (1988) *De Valera's Constitution and Ours*, Dublin: Gill and Macmillan.

Farrell, B. (1988) 'Ireland. The Irish Cabinet system: more British than the British themselves' in Blondel, J. and Müller-Rommel, F., eds, *Cabinets in Western Europe*, London: Macmillan, 33–46.

Farrell, B. (1993a) 'Cagey and Secretive: Responsibility, executive confidentiality and the public interest' in Hill, R. J. and Marsh, M., eds, *Modern Irish Democracy*, Dublin: Irish Academic Press.

Farrell, B. (1993b) 'The formation of partnership government' in Gallagher, M. and Laver, M., eds, *How Ireland Voted 1992*, Dublin/Limerick: Folens/PSAI, 146–61.

Farrell, B. (1994) 'The political role of Cabinet ministers in Ireland' in Laver, M. and Shepsle, K. A., eds, *Cabinet Ministers and Parliamentary government*, Cambridge: Cambridge University Press, 73–87.

Farrell, B. (1996) 2nd edn, 'The Government' in Coakley, J. and Gallagher, M., eds, *Politics in the Republic of Ireland*, Limerick: PSAI Press, 167–89.

Farrell, D., McKerras, M. and McAllister, I. (1996) 'Designing Electoral Institutions: STV Systems and their consequences', *Political Studies*, 44(1), 24–43.

Farrell, M. (1980) *Northern Ireland: The Orange State*, London: Pluto.

Fearon, K. and Rebouche, R. (2006) 'What happened to the women? Promises, reality and the Northern Ireland Women's Coalition' in Cox, M., Guelke, A. and Stephen, F., eds, *A Farewell to Arms? Beyond the Good Friday Agreement*, Manchester: Manchester University Press, 280–301.

Felle, T. and Adshead, M. (2009) 'Democracy and the Right to Know', in *Proceedings from the PPA Conference marking the 10th anniversary of Freedom of Information in Ireland*, Department of Politics and Public Administration Working Papers, University of Limerick, Paper No. 18.

Ferriter, D. (2004) *The Transformation of Ireland 1900–2000*, London: Profile Books.

Financial Times (1997) 'Sell-off strategies in the spotlight', 9 September.

Financial Times (1997) 'Continent of shareholders?', 15 October.

Fine Gael (2000) *A Democratic Revolution*, Leinster House Dublin: Fine Gael Parliamentary Party.

Finer, S. E. (1958) *Anonymous Empire*, London: Pall Mall.

Finlay, F. (1998) *Snakes and Ladders*, Dublin: New Island.

FitzGerald, G. (1959) 'PR – the great debate', *Studies*, 48(1), 1–20.

FitzGerald, G. (1991) 'The Irish electoral system: defects and possible reforms', *Representation*, 30(111), 49–53.

FitzGerald, G. (2003) *Reflections on the Irish State*, Dublin: Irish Academic Press.

FitzGerald, G. (2004) 'The role of the Taoiseach: chairman or chief?' in Garvin, T., Manning, M. and Sinnott, R., eds, *Dissecting Irish Politics, essays in honour of Brian Farrell*, Dublin: UCD Press, 66–81.

Fitzgerald, J. (2000) 'The story of Ireland' failure – and belated success', in Nolan, B., O'Connell, P. J. and Whelan, C. T., eds, *Bust to Boom? The Irish experience of growth and inequality*, Dublin: IPA, 27–57.

Fitzgerald, R. (2000) 'Ireland and European integration, 1985–1998' in Steininger, R. and Gehler, M., eds, *Die Neutralen und die europaischen Integration 1945–1998*, Wien: Bohlau.

Fitzgerald, R. and Girvin, B. (2000) 'Political culture, growth and the conditions for success in the Irish economy' in Nolan, B., O'Connell, P. J. and Whelan, C. T., eds, *Bust to Boom? The Irish experience of growth and inequality,* Dublin: IPA, 268–309.

Fitzsimons, J. (1984) *Democracy be Damned!,* Kells Meath: Kells Publishing Co.

Fuller, L. (2002) *Irish Catholicism since 1950: The undoing of a culture,* Dublin: Gill and Macmillan.

Gafikin, F. and Morrisey, M. (1990) *Northern Ireland: the Thatcher Years,* London: Zed.

Gallagher, M. (1977) 'The presidency of the Republic of Ireland: implications of the "Donegan affair" ', *Parliamentary Affairs,* 30(4), 373–84.

Gallagher, M. (1978) 'Party solidarity, exclusivity and inter-party relationships in Ireland 1922–1977', *Economic and Social Review,* 10(1), 1–22.

Gallagher, M. (1981) 'Societal change and party adaptation in the Republic of Ireland 1960–1981', *European Journal of Political Research,* 9(3), 269–95.

Gallagher, M. (1985) *Political Parties in the Republic of Ireland,* Manchester: Manchester University Press.

Gallagher, M. (1987) 'Does Ireland need a new electoral system?', *Irish Political Studies,* 2, 27–48.

Gallagher, M. (1988) 'The President, the people and the constitution' in Farrell, B., ed. *De Valera's Constitution and Ours,* Dublin: Gill and Macmillan, 375–92.

Gallagher, M. (1993) 'The Constitution' in Coakley, J. and Gallagher, M., eds, *Politics in the Republic of Ireland,* Dublin: Folens/PSAI Press, 49–66.

Gallagher, M. (1996) 'Electoral systems' in Constitution Review Group, ed. *Report of the Constitution Review Group*, Dublin: DSO, 499–520.

Gallagher, M. (2003) 'Stability and turmoil: analysis of the results' in Gallagher, M., Marsh, M. and Mitchell, P., eds, *How Ireland voted 2002,* Basingstoke: Palgrave, 88–118.

Gallagher, M. (2005a) 4th edn, 'The Constitution and the Judiciary' in Coakley, J. and Gallagher, M., eds, *Politics in the Republic of Ireland,* London: Routledge, 73–101.

Gallagher, M. (2005b) 'Parliament' in Coakley, J. and Gallagher, M., eds, *Politics in the Republic of Ireland,* Abingdon: Routledge, 211–41.

Gallagher, M. and Komito, L. (1993) 2nd edn, 'Dáil Deputies and their constituency work' in Coakley, J. and Gallagher, M., eds, *Politics in the Republic of Ireland,* Dublin: PSAI Press.

Gallagher, M. and Komito, L. (1999) 'The constituency role of TDs' in Coakley, J. and Gallagher, M., eds, *Politics in the Republic of Ireland,* London: Routledge.

Gallagher, M. and Komito, L. (2005) 4th edn, 'The constituency role of Dáil deputies' in Coakley, J. and Gallagher, M., eds, *Politics in the Republic of Ireland,* London: Routledge, 242–72.

Gallagher, M., Laver, M. and Mair, P. (1992) *Representative Government in Modern Europe,* London: McGraw-Hill.

Gallagher, M., Laver, M. and Mair, P. (1995) 2nd edn, *Representative Government in Modern Europe,* London: McGraw-Hill.

Galligan, Y. (1998) *Women and Politics in Contemporary Ireland, from the margins to the mainstream,* London: Pinter.

Ganiel, G. (2007) 'Preaching to the Choir? An Analysis of DUP discourses about the Northern Ireland Peace Process', *Irish Political Studies,* 22(3), 303–20.

Garner, S. (2007) 'Ireland and Immigration: Explaining the absence of the far right', *Patterns of Prejudice,* 41(2), 109–30.

Garvin, T. (1974) 'Political cleavages, party politics and urbanisation in Ireland: the case of the periphery-dominated centre', *European Journal of Political Research,* 2(4), 307–27.

Garvin, T. (1976) 'Comment on Dr Carty's rejoinder', *European Journal of Political Research,* 4(2), 204.

Garvin, T. (1977) 'Nationalist elites, Irish voters and Irish political development: a comparative perspective', *Economic and Social Review,* 8, 161–86.

Garvin, T. (1978) 'The destiny of the soldiers: tradition and modernity in the politics of de Valera's Ireland', *Political Studies,* 26(3), 328–47.

Garvin, T. (1981) *The Evolution of Irish nationalist politics*, Dublin: Gill and Macmillan.

Garvin, T. (1987) 'The Politics of Language and Literature in pre-independent Ireland', *Irish Political Studies*, 2, 49–63.

Garvin, T. (1991) 'Democracy in Ireland: collective somnambulance and public policy', *Administration*, 39, 42–54.

Garvin, T. (1996) *1922 the Birth of Irish Democracy*, Dublin: Gill and Macmillan.

Gay, O. and Mitchell, J. (2007) 'Stormont, Westminster and Whitehall' in Carmichael, P., Knox, C. and Osborne, R., eds, *Devolution and Constitutional Change in Northern Ireland*, Manchester: Manchester University Press, 243–60.

George, V. and Taylor-Gooby, P. (eds) (1996) *European Welfare Policy: Squaring the Welfare Circle*, London: Palgrave Macmillan.

Geoghegan, V. (1994) 'Socialism, national identities and post-nationalist citizenship', *Irish Political Studies*, 9(1), 61–80.

Giddings, P. ed. (2005) *Parliamentary Accountability: A Study of Parliament and Executive Agencies*, Basingstoke: Macmillan.

Gilland, K. and Kennedy, F. (2002) 'Data Yearbook 2002', *Irish Political Studies*, 17.

Gilland-Lutz, K. (2003) 'Irish party competition in the new millennium: change or plus ca change?', *Irish Political Studies*, 18(2), 40–59.

Girvin, B. (1986) 'Social change and moral politics: the Irish constitutional referendum 1983', *Political Studies*, 34, 61–81.

Girvin, B. (1987) 'The divorce referendum in the Republic: June 1986', *Irish Political Studies*, 2, 93–8.

Girvin, B. (1997) 'Political culture, political independence and economic success in Ireland', *Irish Political Studies*, 12, 48–77.

Girvin, B. (1999) 'Political competition, 1992–1997' in Marsh, M. and Mitchell, P., eds, *How Ireland Voted 1997*, Oxford: Westview/PSAI Press.

Girvin, B. (2002) *From Union to Union: Nationalism, Democracy and Religion in Ireland-Act of Union to EU*, Dublin: Gill and Macmillan.

Gladdish, K. (1997) 'The Government of the Netherlands' in Curtis, M., ed. *Western European Government and Politics*, New York: Longman, 341–92.

Goth, P., McKillop, D. and Ferguson, C. (2006) *Building Better Credit Unions*, Bristol: Policy Press/Joseph Rowntree Foundation.

Government of Ireland (1958) *Economic Development*, Dublin: Stationery Office.

Government of Ireland (1972) Proceedings from the Joint Committee on European Affairs, Orders of Reference, available at http://www.oireachtas.ie/Viewpoint.asp?

Government of Ireland (1985) *Serving the country better*. White paper on the public service, Dublin: Stationery Office.

Government of Ireland (1991) *Local government reform and reorganisation*. Dublin: DSO.

Government of Ireland (1994) *Government of Renewal – 1994 programme for government*, Dublin: Stationery Office.

Government of Ireland (1995) *Operational Programme: local urban and rural development 1994–1999*, Dublin: Stationery Office.

Government of Ireland (Dept of the Taoiseach) (1996) *Delivering Better Government*, Second Report to the Government of the Co-ordinating Group of Secretaries – A Programme of Change for the Irish Civil Service, available at – http://www.bettergov.ie/index/asp?docID=83.

Government of Ireland (1996a) *Better Local Government. A programme for change*, Dublin: DSO.

Government of Ireland (1996b) *Devolution Committee Interim Report*, Dublin: Stationery Office.

Government of Ireland (2006) *Towards 2016:Ten-Year Framework Social Partnership Agreement 2006-2015*, Dublin: Taoiseach Department/Stationery Office.

Government of Ireland (2008) *Stronger Local Democracy: Options for change, Green paper* Dublin: Department for the Environment.

Grant, W. (2000) *Pressure Groups and British Politics*, Basingstoke: Macmillan/Palgrave.

Greer, A. (1994) 'Policy Networks and State-Farmer relations in Northern Ireland, 1921–72', *Political Studies*, XLII, 396–412.

Greer, A. (1996) *Rural Politics in Northern Ireland: Policy Networks and Agricultural Development since Partition,* Aldershot: Avebury.

Greer, A. (2005) *Agricultural Policy in Europe: National Politics and Political Integration,* Manchester: Manchester University Press.

Grubb, W.N. (2004) *Career Guidance and Public Policy: Bridging the Gap,* Paris: OECD.

Gudgin, G. (2008) 'Budget reckoning', *Fortnight,* 457, 2.

Haagerup, N. (1984) 'Report Drawn Up on Behalf of the Political Affairs Committee on the Situation in Northern Ireland', *European Parliament Working Documents,* 1–1526/83.

Hadfield, B. (2001) 'Seeing it Through? The Multifaceted implementation of the Belfast Agreement' in Wilford, R., ed. *Aspects of the Belfast Agreement,* Oxford: Oxford University Press.

Hainsworth, P. (1990) 'The European Community as a Policy Arena in Northern Ireland' in Connolly, M. and Loughlin, S., eds, *Public Policy in Northern Ireland: Adoption or Adaptation?,* Belfast: Policy Research Institute, 77–97.

Hall Report (1962) *Report of the Joint Working Party on the Economy in Northern Ireland,* London: HMSO, Cmnd 1835.

Hall, P. (1992) 'The movement from Keynesianism to Monetarism' in Steinmo, S. Thelen, K. and Longstreth, F., eds, *Structuring Politics: historical institutionalism in comparative analysis,* Cambridge: Cambridge University Press.

Hanson, D. (2007) 'RPA:The Minister replies', *Fortnight,* 45, 10.

Hardiman, N. (1988) *Pay, Politics and Economic Performance in Ireland 1970–1987,* Oxford: Clarendon Press.

Hardiman, N. (1992) 'The state and economic interests: Ireland in comparative perspective' in Goldthorpe, J. H. and Whelan, C. T., eds, *The Development of Industrial Society in Ireland,* Oxford: Oxford University Press, 329–58.

Hardiman, N. (2006) 'Politics and Social Partnership: Flexible Network Governance', *ESRI,* 37(3), 343–75.

Hardiman, N. and Lalor, S. (1984) 'Corporatism in Ireland: an exchange of views', *Administration,* 32(1), 76–88.

Harney, M. (2006) in the *Irish Times,* 6 June 2006. www.decentralisation.gov.ie.

Harris, J. (1996) 'Political ideas on the welfare state' in Marquand, D. and Seldon, A., eds, *The Ideas that Shaped post-war Britain,* London: Fontana.

Harvey, B. (2003) *Report on the implementation of the White Paper Supporting Voluntary Activity,* Presented to the CV12, Dublin.

Harvey, B. (2008) 'Funding and the Strings Attached', in Paper Presented to an All Ireland Conference for the Community Sector, Dublin.

Haughton, J. (2000) 'The historical background' in O'Hagan, J. W., ed. *The Economy of Ireland, policy and performance of a European region,* Dublin: Gill and Macmillan, 2–49.

Haughton, J. (2005) 'Growth in output and living standards' in O'Hagan, J. and Newman, C., eds, *The Economy of Ireland, national and sectoral policy issues,* Dublin: Gill and Macmillan, 107–35.

Hayward, K. (2004) 'The Politics of Nuance: Irish Official Discourse on Northern Ireland', *Irish Political Studies,* 19(1), 18–38.

Hazleton, W. (1994) 'A Breed Apart. Northern Ireland's MPs at Westminster', *Journal of Legislative Studies,* 1(4), 30–53.

Hederman O'Brien, M. (1989) 'Whatever happened to rates? A study of Irish tax policy on domestic dwellings', *Administration,* 37(4), 334–51.

Heenan, D. (2004) 'Culture in Northern Ireland' in Lloyd, K., Devine, P., Gray, A. and Heenan, D., eds, *Social Attitudes in Northern Ireland: The Ninth Report,* London: Pluto, 81–91.

Heidar, K. and Koole, R. (2000) 'Parliamentary party groups compared' in Heidar, K. and Koole, R., eds, *Parliamentary Party Groups in European Democracies: political parties behind closed doors,* London: Routledge, 248–70.

Henderson, J. and Teague, P. (2006) *'The Belfast Agreement and Cross Border Economic Cooperation in the Tourist Industry'*, in *Mapping Frontiers, Plotting Pathways Working Paper 4*, Institute of British-Irish Studies, University College Dublin and Institute of Governance, Centre for International Borders Research, Queen's University Belfast.

Henig, S. and Pinder, J. (1969) *European Political Parties,* London: George Allen and Unwin.

Hennessey, T. (2000) *The Northern Ireland Peace Process: Ending the Troubles?,* Dublin: Gill and Macmillan.

Hennessy, T. (2005) *Northern Ireland: The Origins of the Troubles,* Dublin: Gill and Macmillan.

Heywood, A. (2002) 2nd edn, *Politics,* London: Palgrave.

Heywood, P. and Wright, V. (1997) 'Executives, bureaucracies and decision-making' in Rhodes, M., Heywood, P. and Wright, V., eds, *Developments in West European politics,* London: Macmillan, 75–94.

Hillyard, P. (1997) 'Security strategies in Northern Ireland: Consolidation or reform?' in Gilligan, C. and Tonge, J., eds, *Peace or War? Understanding the Peace Process in Northern Ireland,* Aldershot: Avebury, 119–32.

Hogan, G. (2001) 'Directive principles, socio-economic rights and the Constitution', *Irish Jurist,* XXXVI, 174–98.

Hogan, G. and Morgan, D. G. (1998) 3rd edn, *Administrative Law in Ireland,* Dublin: Round Hall Sweet and Maxwell.

Hogan, G. and Whyte, G. (2003) 4th edn, *J.M. Kelly: the Irish Constitution,* Dublin: Butterworths.

Holland, K. M., ed. (1991) *Judicial Activism in Comparative Perspective,* Basingstoke: Macmillan.

Holmes, M. (1994) 'The establishment of Democratic Left', *Irish Political Studies,* 9, 148–56.

Horgan, J. J. (1926) 'Local government developments at home and abroad', *Studies,* 15.

Horowitz, D. (2001) 'The Northern Ireland Agreement: Clear, Consociational and Risky' in McGarry, J., ed. *Northern Ireland and the Divided World,* Oxford: Oxford University Press.

House of Commons (1999) 'Local Elections: Proposals for Reform', *Research Paper* 99(46).

House of Commons (2002) *The Justice (Northern Ireland) Bill, Research Paper 02/07,* London: House of Commons.

House, J. D. and McGrath, K. (2004) 'Innovative Governance and Development in the New Ireland: Social Partnership and the Integrated Approach', *Governance: An International Journal of Policy, Administration, and Institutions,* 17(1), 29–57.

Hughes, I., Clancy, P., Harris, C. and Beetham, D. (2007) *Power to the People? Assessing Democracy in Ireland,* Dublin: TASC.

Humphreys, P. C. (1998) *'Improving public service delivery'*, in *Committee for Public Management Research (CPMR) Discussion Paper 7,* Dublin, IPA.

Humphreys, P. C. and O'Donnell, O. (2006) 'Public service decentralisation. Governance opportunities and challenges', CPMR Discussion Paper No. 33, Dublin, IPA.

Hussey, G. (1993) *Ireland Today: Anatomy of a changing state,* Dublin: Townhouse/Viking.

Hutchinson, J. and Smith, A.D. (1992) *Nationalism: Critical Concepts in Political Science,* London; Routledge.

ICCL – (Irish Council for Civil Liberties) (2006a) *Equality for all Families,* Dublin: ICCL.

ICCL – (Irish Council for Civil Liberties) (2006b) *Protecting Civil Liberties, Promoting Human Rights. 30 years of the Irish council for civil liberties,* Dublin: ICCL.

Immergut, E. M. (1998) 'The theoretical core of new institutionalism', *Politics and Society,* 26(1), 5–34.

Independent Commission on Policing (1999) *A New Beginning: Policing in Northern Ireland (The Patten Report),* Belfast: HMSO.

Information Commissioner (2005) *Annual Report of the Information Commissioner,* Dublin: DSO.

Inglehart, R. (1977) *The Silent Revolution: changing values and political styles amongst Western publics,* Princeton: Princeton University Press.

Inglis, T. (1987) *Moral Monopoly: the Catholic Church in modern Irish society,* Dublin: Gill and Macmillan.

INOU (1999) 'Supplementary Welfare Allowance', pre-budget submission to government, April 1998, available at www. INOU.ie/publications.

IPA (1997) *Annual Directory,* Dublin: IPA.

Irish Times (1997) 'How a government sailed into a storm over clerical abuse', 23 August.

Irvin, C. and Byrne, S. (2002) 'Economic aid and its role in the Peace Process' in Neuheiser, J. and Wolff, S., eds, *Peace at Last? The Impact of the Good Friday Agreement on Northern Ireland,* London: Berghann, 132–52.

Jackson, A. (1999) *Ireland 1798–1998,* Oxford: Blackwell.

Jacob, H. (1996) 'Conclusion' in Jacob, H., Blankenburg, E., Kritzer, H. M., Prôvine, D.M, and Sanders, J., eds, *Courts, Law and Politics in Comparative Perspective,* Cambridge: Cambridge University Press, 195–240.

Jacobsen, J. K. (1994) *Chasing Progress in the Irish Republic,* Cambridge: Cambridge University Press.

Jarman, N. (1997) *Material Conflicts: Parades and Visual Displays in Northern Ireland,* Oxford: Berg.

Jarman, N. (2008) 'Ordering Transition: The Role of Loyalists and Republicans in Community-based Policing Activity' in Edwards, A. and Bloomer, S., eds, *Transforming the Peace Process in Northern Ireland,* Dublin: Irish Academic Press.

Jeffery, K. and Arthur, P. (1996) *Northern Ireland since 1968,* Oxford: Blackwell.

Katz, R. S. (1980) *A Theory of Politics and Electoral Systems,* London: Johns Hopkins University Press.

Katz, R. S. and Mair, P. (1995) 'Changing models of party organisation and party democracy: the emergence of the cartel party', *Party Politics,* 1, 1, 5–28.

Kaufmann, E. (2007) *The Orange Order: A Contemporary Northern Irish History,* Oxford: Oxford University Press.

Kavanagh, D., David, R., Smith, M. and Geddes, A. (2006) *British Politics,* Oxford: Oxford University Press.

Kavanagh, R. (2001) *Spring, Summer and Fall. The rise and fall of the Labour Party,* Dublin: Blackwater Press.

Keane, R. (2004) 'Judges as Lawmakers: the Irish experience', *Judicial Studies Institute Journal,* 4(2), 1–18.

Keating, M. (2006) 'Irish explanations', *European Political Science Reviews,* 5, 434–39.

Kelly, D (1993) 'Public Administration in a mature democracy', *Administration,* 41(1), 72–9.

Kelly, D. (2000/1) 'Public Administration in a mature democracy', *Administration,* 48(4), 65–77.

Kennedy, D. (1988) *The Widening Gulf: Northern Attitudes to the Independent Irish State 1919–49,* Belfast: Blackstaff.

Kennedy, D. (1994) 'The Northern Ireland Question and the European Union' in Barton, B. and Roche, P., eds, *The Northern Ireland Question: Perspectives and Policies,* Aldershot: Ashgate.

Kennedy, F. and Sinnott, R. (2006) 'Irish social and political cleavages' in Garry, J., Hardiman, N. and Payne, D., eds, *Irish Social and Political Attitudes,* Liverpool: Liverpool University Press, 60–78.

Kennedy, K., Giblin, T. and McHugh, D. (1988) *The Economic Development of Ireland in the Twentieth Century,* London: Routledge.

Kennedy, K., Ruane, F. and White, P. (1982–3) 'Symposium on industrial policy in Ireland', *Journal of the Statistical and Social Inquiry Society of Ireland,* vol. XXIV, part V, 33–51.

Kennedy, L. (1989) *The Modern Industrialisation of Ireland, 1940–1988,* Dublin: Economic and Social History Society of Ireland.

Kennedy-Pipe, C. (1997) *The Origins of the Present Troubles in Northern Ireland,* Harlow: Longman.

Kenny, S. (2001) 'Tensions and dilemmas in community development: new discourses, new Trojans?' *Keynote paper presented to the International Community Development Conference,* Rotorua, New Zealand.

Kiely, G. (1999) 'Introduction: from colonial paternalism to national partnership: an overview of Irish social policy' in Kiely, G., O'Donnell, A., Kennedy, P. and Quin, S., eds, *Irish Social Policy in Context,* Dublin: UCD Press, 1–10.

King, A. (1994) 'Chief Executives in Western Europe' in Budge, I. and McKay, D., eds, *Developing Democracy,* London: Sage.

Kirby, P. (1988) *Has Ireland a Future?,* Cork: Mercier Press.

Kirby, P. (2002) *The Celtic Tiger in Distress. Growth with Inequality in Ireland,* Basingstoke: Palgrave.

Kirby, P. (2005) 'The Death of Innocence: Whither Now? Trauma in Church and State', *Studies,* 84(335), 257–64.

Kirby, P. (2007) *UNRISD Poverty Reduction and Policy Regimes,* Country paper on Ireland, UN. O'Riain, S. (2008) 'Competing state projects in the contemporary Irish political economy' in, Adshead, M. Kirby, P. and Millar, M., eds, *Contesting the State: Lessons from the Irish Case,* Manchester: Manchester University Press, 165–85.

Kirchheimer, O. (1966) 'The transformation of the Western European party systems' in LaPalombara, J. and Weiner, M., eds, *Political Parties and Political Development,* Princeton: Princeton University Press.

Kissane, B. (2002) *Explaining Irish Democracy,* Dublin: UCD Press.

Kitschelt, H. (1994) *The Transformation of European Social Democracy,* Cambridge: Cambridge University Press.

KMPG (1991) *Report on the Financing of Local Government,* Dublin: DSO.

Knox, C. (2001) 'A civil service and a civil society' in Wilson, R., ed. *Agreeing to Disagree? A Guide to the Northern Ireland Assembly,* Belfast: HMSO.

Knox, C. and Carmichael, P. (2006) 'Improving Public Services: Public Administration Reform in Northern Ireland', *Journal of Social Policy,* 35(1), 97–120.

Knox, C. and Carmichael, P. (2007a) 'His critics respond', *Fortnight,* 450, 11.

Knox, C. and Carmichael, P. (2007b) 'Rethinking the RPA', *Fortnight,* 452, 9.

Knox, C. and Carmichael, P. (2007c) 'The Review of Public Administration' in Carmichael, P., Knox , C. and Osborne, R., eds, *Devolution and Constitutional Change in Northern Ireland,* Manchester: Manchester University Press, 202–18.

Komito, L. (1984) 'Irish clientelism: a reappraisal', *Economic and Social Review,* 15(3), 173–96.

Komito, L. (1989) 'Voters, politicians and clientelism: a Dublin survey', *Administration,* 37(2), 171–96.

Komito, L. (1992a) 'Brokerage or friendship? Politics and networks in Ireland', *Economic and Social Review,* 23(2), 129–45.

Komito, L. (1992b) 'Dáil deputies and their constituency work' in Coakley, J. and Gallagher, M., eds, *Politics in the Republic of Ireland,* Galway: PSAI Press.

Labour Party (2003) *Putting Our House in Order: Dáil Reform, Parliamentary Oversight and Government Accountability,* Leinster House Dublin: Parliamentary Labour Party.

Laffan, B. (1991a) 'Government and administration' in Keatinge, P., ed. *Ireland and EU Membership Evaluated,* London: Pinter, 190–6.

Laffan, B. (1991b) 'Sovereignty and national identity' in Keatinge, P., ed. *Ireland and EC Membership Evaluated,* London: Pinter, 187–9.

Laffan, B. (1991c) 'The political process' in Keatinge, P., ed. *Ireland and EC Membership Evaluated,* London: Pinter, 197–205.

Laffan, B. (1999) 2nd edn, 'The European Union and Ireland' in Collins, N., ed. *Political Issues in Ireland Today,* Manchester: Manchester University Press, 89–105.

Laffan, B. (2000) 'Rapid adaptation and light co-ordination' in O'Donnell, R., ed. *Europe. The Irish experience,* Dublin: Institute for European Affairs, 125–47.

Laffan, B. (2001) 'Organising for a Changing Europe: Irish Central Government and the European Union', *Studies in Public Policy,* TCD, Dublin: The Policy Institute.

Laffan, B. and O'Mahony, J. (2007) 'Managing Europe from an Irish perspective: critical junctures and the increasing formalization of the core executive in Ireland', *Public Administration,* 85(1), 167–88.

Laffan, B. and O'Mahony, J. (2008) *Ireland and Europe,* Basingstoke: Palgrave.

Laffan, B. and Payne, D. (2002) 'The EU in the domestic: Interreg III and the Good Friday Institutions', *Irish Political Studies,* 17(1), 74–96.

Laffan, B. and Tonra, B. (2005) 4th edn, 'Europe and the international dimension' in Coakley, J. and Gallagher, M., eds, *Politics in the Republic of Ireland,* London: Routledge, 430–61.

Lalor, S. (1982) 'Corporatism in Ireland', *Administration,* 30(4).

Lane, J.-E. and Ersson, S. (1998) 4th edn, *Politics and Society in Western Europe,* London: Sage.

Lane, P. R. (2001) *On the Provision of Incentives to Save,* Dublin: Irish Association of Investment Managers.

Larkin, L. (1985) 'Socialism and Catholicism in Ireland', *Studies,* 74(293), 66–92.

Lasswell, L. D. (1951) *Democratic Character*, Glencoe: The Free Press.

Latham, E. (1952) *The Group Basis of Politics*, Ithaca, NY: Cornell University Press.

Laughlin, E. (2002) 'Ireland: From Catholic corporatism to social partnership', in A. Cochrane, J. Clarke and S. Gewitz (eds) *Comparing Welfare States: Britain in international context,* Milton Keynes: Open University Press, 223–60.

Laver, M. (1986a) 'Ireland: politics with some social bases: an interpretation based on aggregate data', *Economic and Social Review,* 17, 107–31.

Laver, M. (1986b) 'Ireland: politics with some social bases: an interpretation based on survey data', *Economic and Social Review,* 17, 193–213.

Laver, M. (2000) 'Coalitions in Northern Ireland', in Democratic Dialogue Conference, Belfast.

Laver, M. (2002) 'The role and future of the upper house in Ireland', *Journal of Legislative Studies,* 8(3), 49–66.

Laver, M. (2005) 4th edn, 'Voting behaviour' in Coakley, J. and Gallagher, M., eds, *Politics in the Republic of Ireland,* London: Routledge, 183–210.

Layte, R. and Nolan, B. (2004) 'Equity in the utilization of health care in Ireland', *Economic and Social Review,* 35(2), 111–34.

Layte, R., Nolan, A. and Nolan, B. (2007) 'Health and health care' in Fahey, T., Russell, H. and Whelan, C. T., eds, *Best of times? The social impact of the celtic tiger,* Dublin: IPA, 105–22.

Leach, R. (1994) 'Restructuring local government', *Local Government Studies,* 20(3), 345–60.

Leach, S. (1993) *Local Government Review: a crisis of credibility,* London: European Policy Review Forum.

Leach, S. (1994a) 'The local government review: a critical appraisal', *Public Money and Management,* 14(1), 11–16.

Leach, S. (1994b) 'The local government review: from policy drift to policy fiasco', *Regional Studies,* 28(4), 537–43.

Lee, A. (2003) 'Community development in Ireland', *Community Development Journal,* 38(1), 48–58.

Lee, J. J. (1979) *Ireland 1945–70,* Dublin: Gill and Macmillan.

Lee, J. J. (1989) *Ireland 1912–1985: Politics and Society,* Cambridge: Cambridge University Press.

Lemass, S. F. (1961) 'The organisation behind the economic programme', *Administration,* 9(1), 3–10.

Levine, J. (1985) *Sisters, the personal story of an Irish feminist,* Dublin: Attic Press.

Lijphart, A. (1977) *Democracy in Plural Societies: a comparative exploration,* New Haven: Yale.

Lijphart, A. (1996) 'Unequal participation: democracy's unresolved dilemma', *American Political Science Review,* 91(1), 1–14.

Lijphart, A. (1999) *Patterns of Democracy: government forms and performance in thirty-six countries,* London: Routledge.

Lindborg, C. (2001) 'The EU Rapid Reaction Force: Europe takes on a new security challenge', Occasional papers on international security policy. Basic Papers No.37, available at: http://www.basicint.org/pubs/Papers/BP37.htm.

Lindsay, C. (2003) 'A century of labour market change: 1900 to 2000', *Labour Market Trends,* 111(3), 133–44.

Lindborg, C. (2001) 'The EU Rapid Reaction Force: Europe takes on a new security challenge', Occasional Papers on International Security Policy, Basic papers No. 37.

Linz, J. J. and Stepan, A. (1996) *Problems of Democratic Transition and Consolidation. Southern Europe, South America, and post-communist Europe,* London: John Hopkins University Press.

Lipset, S. M. (1959) 'Some Social Requisites of Democracy: Economic Development and Political Legitimacy', *American Political Science Review,* 53, 69–105.

Lipset, S. M. and Rokkan, S. (1967) 'Cleavage structures, party systems and voter alignments: an introduction' in *Party Systems and Voter Alignments,* Glencoe: Free Press.

Little, A. (2004) *Democracy and Northern Ireland: Beyond the Liberal Paradigm?,* Basingstoke: Palgrave Macmillan.

Lochner, K., Kawachi, I. and Kennedy, B. (1999) 'Social Capital: a guide to its measurement', *Health and Place,* 5(4), 259–70.

Longley, L. D. and Davidson, R. H. (1998) 'Parliamentary Committees: changing perspectives on changing institutions' in Longley, L. D. and Davidson, R. H., eds, *The New Roles of Parliamentary Committees,* London: Frank Cass, 1–20.

Loughlin, P. (2006) ' "it's a United Ireland or nothing": John Hume and the Idea of Irish Unity, 1964–72', *Irish Political Studies,* 21(2), 157–80.

Lynn, B. (1998) *Holding the Ground: the Nationalist Party in Northern Ireland,* Aldershot:: Ashgate.

Lynn, B. (2002) 'Tactic or Principle? The Evolution of Republican Thinking on Abstentionism in Ireland, 1970–1998', *Irish Political Studies,* 17(2), 59–73.

Lyons, P. and Sinnott, R. (2003) 'Voter turnout in 2002 and beyond' in Gallagher, M., Marsh, M. and Mitchell, P., eds, *How Ireland Voted 2002,* Basingstoke: Palgrave, 143–58.

MacCarthaigh, M. (2005) *Accountability in Irish Parliamentary Politics,* Dublin: IPA.

MacCarthaigh, M. and Totten, K. (2001) 'Irish Political Data 2000', *Irish Political Studies,* 16, 287–352.

MacGinty, R. (2001) 'Anticipating Multi-Level voting in Northern Ireland?', in PSA Elections, Public Opinion and Parties annual conference, University of Sussex.

MacMahon, J. A. (1981) 'Catholic clergy and the social question in Ireland, 1891–1916', *Studies,* 70(280), 263–88.

Magennis, E. (2007) 'Public policy cooperation: the "common chapter" – shadow or substance?' in Coakley, J. and O'Dowd, L., eds, *Crossing the Border: New Relationships between Northern Ireland and the Republic of Ireland,* Dublin: Irish Academic Press, 245–62.

Maguire, M. (1976) 'Pressure groups in Ireland', *Administration,* 25.

Maillot, A. (2004) *New Sinn Féin,* London: Routledge.

Mair, P. (1977) 'Labour and the Irish party system revisited: party competition in the 1920s', *Economic and Social Review,* 9(1), 59–70.

Mair, P. (1986) 'Locating Irish political parties on a left-right dimension: an empirical enquiry', *Political Studies,* 39, 456–65.

Mair, P. (1992) 'Explaining the absence of class politics in Ireland' in Goldthorpe, J. H. and Whelan, C. T., eds, *The Development of Industrial Society in Ireland,* Oxford: Oxford University Press, 383–410.

Mair, P. (1993) 'Fianna Fáil, Labour and the Irish party system' in Gallagher , M. and Laver, M., eds, *How Ireland Voted 1989*, Galway: Centre for the Study of Irish Elections and PSAI Press, 162–73.

Mair, P. (2003) 3rd edn, 'Party competition and the changing party system' in Coakley, J. and Gallagher, M., eds, *Politics in the Republic of Ireland*, London: Routledge, 127–51.

Mair, P. and Weeks, L. (2005) 'The party system' in Coakley, J. and Gallagher, M., eds, *Politics in the Republic of Ireland* (4th edn), London: Routledge, 135–59.

Maloney, O. (1992) 'A response to Micheal McDowell's views on the value of Catholic socio-economic theory', *Studies*, 81(322), 163–70.

Manning, M. (1972) *Irish Political Parties, an introduction*, Dublin: Gill and Macmillan.

March, J. G. and Olsen, J. P. (1997) 2nd edn, 'Institutional perspectives on political institutions' in Hill, M., ed. *Theories of the Policy Process: a reader*, London: Harvester Wheatsheaf.

Marsh, D. (1992) *Irish Public Opinion on Neutrality and the European Union*, Dublin: TCD Occassional Papers.

Marsh, D. and Rhodes, R. A. W. (1992) *Policy Networks in British Government*, Oxford: Clarendon Press.

Marsh, M. (1993) 'Selecting party leaders in the Republic of Ireland', *European Journal of Political Research*, 24(3), 295–316.

Marsh, M. and Mitchell, P. (1999) 'Office, votes, and then policy: hard choices for political parties in the Republic of Ireland, 1981–1992' in Muller, M. C. and Strom, K., eds, *Party, Office or Votes? How political parties in Western Europe make hard decisions*, Cambridge: Cambridge University Press.

Marsh, M. and Weeks, L. (2005) 4th edn, 'The party system' in Coakley, J. and Gallagher, M., eds, *Politics in the Republic of Ireland*, London: Routledge, 135–59.

Martin, F. (2005) 'The changing face of family law in Ireland', *Judicial Studies Institute Journal*, 5(1), 16–41.

Martin, M. (1991) 'Fianna Fáil has a problem – it's time to deal with it', *Sunday Tribune*, 4 August.

McAllister, I. (2004) 'The armalite and the ballot box: Sinn Féin's electoral strategy in Northern Ireland', *Electoral Studies*, 23(1), 123–42.

McAuley, J. (2004) *The Politics of Identity: A Loyalist Community in Belfast*, Aldershot: Avebury.

McAuley, J. (2005) 'Whither New Loyalism? Changing Loyalist Politics after the Belfast Agreement', *Irish Political Studies*, 20(3), 323–40.

McAuley, J. (2008) 'Constructing Contemporary Loyalism' in Edwards, A. and Bloomer, S., eds, *Transforming the Peace Process in Northern Ireland*, Dublin: Irish Academic Press, 15–27.

McAuley, J. and Tonge, J. (2007) 'For God and for the Crown: Contemporary Political and Social Attitudes among Orange Order Members in Northern Ireland', *Political Psychology*, 28(1), 33–52.

McBride, L. W., ed. (1999) *Images, Icons and the Irish Nationalist Imagination*, Dublin: Four Courts Press.

McCafferty, N. (1984) *The Best of Nell: selected writings*, Dublin: Attic Press.

McCashin, A. (2004) *Social Security in Ireland*, Dublin: Gill and Macmillan.

McCracken, J. L. (1958) *Representative Government in Ireland: a study of Dáil Éireann 1919–1948*, Oxford: Oxford University Press.

McDermott, P. A. (2000) 'The separation of powers and the doctrine of non-justiciability', *Irish Jurist*, XXXV, 280–304.

McDonald, F. (2006) 'Dempsey proposals to reduce number of TDs from 166 to 120 or less in Dáil debates', quoted in 'Clientelist system must be replaced by effective alternative', *The Irish Times*, 21 April.

McDonald, H. and Cusack, J. (2005) *The UDA: Inside the Heart of Loyalist Terror*, London: Penguin.

McDowell, M. (1991) 'The questionable value of Catholic socio-economic theory', *Studies,* 80(319), 253–8.

McEvoy, J. (2008) *The Politics of Northern Ireland,* Edinburgh: Edinburgh University Press.

McEvoy, K. (2006) 'Restorative justice, politics and local communities', *Fortnight,* 442, 8–9.

McGarry, J. (2001) 'Northern Ireland, Civic Nationalism, and the Good Friday Agreement' in McGarry, J., ed. *Northern Ireland and the Divided World,* Oxford: Oxford University Press, 109–36.

McGarry, J. and O'Leary, B. (1995) *Explaining Northern Ireland,* London: Blackwell.

McGarry, J. and O'Leary, B. (1999) *Policing Northern Ireland: Proposals for a new start,* Belfast: Blackstaff.

McGarry, J. and O'Leary, B. (2004) *The Northern Ireland Conflict: Consociational Engagements,* Oxford: Oxford University Press.

McGovern, M. and Shirlow, P. (1997) 'Counter-insurgency, De-industrialisation and the Political Economy of Ulster Loyalism' in Shirlow, P. and McGovern, M., eds, *Who are 'the People'? Unionism, Protestantism and Loyalism in Northern Ireland,* London: Pluto.

McGowan, L. (2007) 'The European Dimension' in Carmichael, P., Knox, C. and Osborne, R., eds, *Devolution and Constitutional Change in Northern Ireland,* Manchester: Manchester University Press, 278–91.

McGowan, L. and O'Connor, J. (2004) 'Exploring Eurovisions: Awareness and Knowledge of the European Union in Northern Ireland', *Irish Political Studies,* 19(2), 21–42.

McInerney, C. (2007) 'Social Partnership in Ireland – Diluting or Deepening Democracy?', in Paper presented to the Matchpoints in Globalisation Conference, Aarhus, Denmark.

McIntyre, A. (1995) 'Modern Irish republicanism: the product of British state strategies', *Irish Political Studies,* 10, 97–121.

McIntyre, A. (2001) 'Modern Irish Republicanism and the Belfast Agreement: Chickens Coming Home to Roost, or Turkeys Celebrating Christmas?' in Wilford, R., ed. *Aspects of the Belfast Agreement,* Oxford: Oxford University Press, 202–22.

McLaughlin, E. (1993) 'Ireland: Catholic Corporatism' in Cochrane, A. and Clarke, J., eds, *Comparing Welfare States: Britain in International Context,* London: Sage, 205–37.

McManus, M. (1993) 'The Republic of Ireland' in Chandler, J. A., ed. *Local Government in Liberal Democracies,* London: Routledge, 28–52.

McNamara, T. (1990) 'A conversation with Donal Creedon, Secretary, Department of Agriculture and Food (1988–1989)', *Administration,* 38(1), 70–86.

McQuade, O. and Fagan, J., eds (2002) *The Governance of Northern Ireland,* Moira: Lagan.

McWilliams, D. (2005) *The Pope's Children,* London: Pan Books.

Meade, R. (2005) 'We hate it here, please let us stay! Irish social partnership and the community/voluntary sector's conflicted experiences of recognition', *Critical Social Policy,* 25(3), 349–73.

Meade, R. and O'Donovan, O. (2002) 'Editorial introduction: Corporatism and the ongoing debate about the relationship between the state and community development', *Community Development Journal,* 37(1), 1–9.

Meehan, E. (2006) 'Europe and the Europeanisation of the Irish question' in Cox, A., Guelke, A. and Stephen, F., eds, *A Farewell to Arms? Beyond the Good Friday Agreement,* Manchester: Manchester University Press, 338–56.

Midwinter, A. (2007) 'The financial framework' in Carmichael, P., Knox, C. and Osborne, R., eds, *Devolution and Constitutional Change in Northern Ireland,* Manchester: Manchester University Press, 186–200.

Millar, M. (2004) 'Health care: consumer purchase or social right?', in Collins, N. and Cradden, T., eds, *Political issues in Ireland today* (3rd edn), Manchester: Manchester University Press, 62–80.

Mills, F. (1999) 'Income maintenance' in Kiely, G., O'Donnell, A., Kennedy, P. and Quin, S., eds, *Contemporary Irish social policy,* Dublin: UCD Press, 5–26.

Mitchell, C. (2003) 'From Victims to Equals? Catholic Responses to Political Change in Northern Ireland', *Irish Political Studies,* 18(1), 51–71.

Mitchell, C. (2006) *Religion, Identity and Politics in Northern Ireland,* Aldershot: Ashgate.

Mitchell, P. (1999) 'Coalition discipline, enforcement mechanisms, and intraparty politics' in Bowler, S., Farrell, D. M. and Katz, R. S., eds, *Party Discipline and Parliamentary Government,* Columbus: Ohio State University Press, 269–87.

Mitchell, P. (2000) 'Ireland: from single party to coalition rule' in Wolfgang, C., Muller, C. and Størm, K., eds, *Coalition Governments in Western Europe,* Oxford: Oxford University Press, 127–57.

Mitchell, P. (2001) 'Divided government in Ireland' in Elgie, R., ed. *Divided Government in Comparative Perspective,* Oxford: Oxford University Press, 182–208.

Mitchell, P. (2003a) 'Ireland: "O what a tangled web…" – delegation, accountability, and executive power' in Størm, K., Wolfgang, C., Bergman, M. and Bergman, T., eds, *Delegation and Accountability in Parliamentary Democracies,* Oxford: Oxford University Press.

Mitchell, P. (2003b) 'Government formation in 2002: "You can have any kind of government as long as it's Fianna Fáil" ' in Gallagher, M., Marsh, M. and Mitchell, P., eds, *How Ireland voted 2002,* Basingstoke: Palgrave Macmillan, 214–29.

Mitchell, P. (2003c) 'Ireland, from single party to coalition rule' in Muller, W. and Størm, K., eds, *Coalition Governments in Western Europe,* Oxford: Oxford University Press, 126–57.

Mitchell, P. (2007) 'Party competition and voting behaviour since the Agreement' in Carmichael, P., Knox, C. and Osborne, B., eds, *Devolution and Constitutional Change in Northern Ireland,* Manchester: Manchester University Press, 110–24.

Mitchell, P. and Gillespie, G. (1999) 'The Electoral Systems' in Mitchell, P. and Wilford, R., eds, *Politics in Northern Ireland,* Oxford: Westview, 66–90.

Mitchell, P., O'Leary, B. and Evans, G. (2009) 'Extremist Outbidding in Ethnic Party Systems Is Not Inevitable: Tribune Parties in Northern Ireland', *Political Studies,* forthcoming

Moloney, E. (2003) *A Secret History of the IRA,* London: Penguin.

Moloney, E. and Pollok, A. (1986) *Paisley,* Dublin: Poolbeg.

Monaghan, R. and McLaughlin, S. (2006) 'Informal Justice in the City', *Space and Polity,* 10(2), 171–86.

Montesquieu, C. L. (1949 [1748]) *The Spirit of the Laws,* New York: Hafner.

Morgan, D. G. (1985) *Constitutional Law of Ireland,* Dublin: Round Hall Press.

Morgan, D. G. (1999) 'Mary Robinson's Presidency: Relations with the Government.', *Irish Jurist,* 34, 256–75.

Morison, J. (2006) 'Constitutionalism, civil society and democratic renewal in Northern Ireland' in Cox, M., Guelke, A. and Stephen, F., eds, *A Farewell to Arms? Beyond the Good Friday Agreement,* Manchester: Manchester University Press, 253–67.

Morrisey, M. (1986) 'The Politics of Economic Management 1958–1970', *Irish Political Studies,* 1, 79–95.

Moss, W. (1933) *Political Parties in the Irish Free State,* New York: Columbia University Press.

Moss, W. (1968) *Political Parties in the Irish Free State,* New York: AMS Press.

Mudde, C. (1996) 'Defining the extreme right party family', *West European Politics,* 19(2), 225–48.

Müller, W. C. and Størm, K. (1999) *Policy, Office, or Votes? How political parties in Western Europe make hard decisions,* Cambridge: Cambridge University Press.

Munck, R. (1993) *The Irish Economy: results and prospects,* London: Pluto.

Munck, R. and Hamilton, D. (1998) 'Politics, the economy and peace in Northern Ireland' in Miller, D., ed. *Rethinking Northern Ireland,* Harlow: Longman.

Murphy, C. (1989) *The Women's Suffrage Movement and Irish Society in the Early Twentieth Century,* London: Harvester Wheatsheaf.

Murphy, G. (1998) 'Towards a Corporate State? Seán Lemass and the Realignment of Interest Groups in the Policy Process 1948–1964', *Administration,* 1, 86–102.

Murphy, G. (2003) 'Pluralism and the politics of morality' in Adshead, M. and Millar, M., eds, *Public Administration and Public Policy in Ireland, theory and method,* London: Routledge, 20–36.

Murphy, G. (2006) 'Assessing the relationship between neo-liberalism and political corruption: the Fianna Fáil-Progressive Democrat coalition, 1997–2006', *Irish Political Studies,* 21(3), 297–318.

Murphy, M. (2002) 'Social Partnership – is it the only game in town?', *Community Development Journal,* 37(1), 80–90.

Murphy, M. (2006) 'Towards a Workfare State: implications for local development ' in Jacobsen, D., Kirby, P. and O Broin, D., eds, *Emerging from the Shadow of the Celtic Tiger,* Dublin: New Island Press & TASC.

Murphy, M. (2007a) *Reframing the Irish Activation Debate: accommodating care and safeguarding social rights and choices,* Studies in Public Policy 23: The Policy Institute, Dublin: TCD.

Murphy, M. (2007b) 'Working Aged' in Cousins, M. eds., *Welfare Policy and Poverty,* Dublin: Combat Poverty Agency.

Murphy, M. (2008) 'Towards a more equitable society: the role of civil society' in Cronin, M. and Kirby, P., eds, *Transforming Ireland: challenges, resources, opportunities,* Manchester: Manchester University Press.

Murphy, M. and Millar, M. (2007) 'The Developmental Welfare State: A glass half full?', *Administration,* 55(3), 75–100.

Murphy, T. V. and Roche, W. K., eds (1997) *Irish Industrial Relations in Practice,* Dublin: Oak Tree Press.

Murray, C.H. (1990) *The Civil Service Observed,* Dublin: Institute for Public Administration.

Murray, F. and Teahon, P. (1998) 'Irish Political and Policy-making System and the Current Programme of Change', in Papers delivered to the OECD meeting of Senior Officials from Centres of Government, Institute of Public Administration 45(4) (Winter 1997–98), 39–58.

Murray, G. (1998) *John Hume and the SDLP: Impact and Survival in Northern Ireland,* Dublin: Irish Academic Press.

Murray, G. and Tonge, J. (2005) *Sinn Féin and the SDLP: From Alienation to Participation,* London: Hurst.

NAPS (2002) *National Action Plan for Social Inclusion,* Dublin: Office for Social Inclusion.

National Competitiveness Council (2003) *Annual report.* Accessed at http://www.forfas.ie/ncc/about_competitiveness.html NCCA (National Council for Curriculum and Assessment) (2005) *Proposals for the Future development of Senior Cycle Education in Ireland,* April 2005, Dublin: NCCA.

NCCA (National Council for Curriculum and Assessment) (2005) *Proposals for the Future Development of Senior Cycle Education in Ireland,* April, Dublin: NCCA.

NCCRI (2001) *The Review of Immigration and Residence Policy,* Dublin: NCCRI.

NEAP (National Employment Action Plans) (1998–2005) *National Employment Action Plans for the Years 1998–2005.* Reports accessed from the Department of Enterprise, Trade and Employment at http://www.entemp.ie/labour/services/neapstrategy.htm.

Neary, J. P. and 'O'Gráda, C. (1986) 'Protection, economic war and structural change: the 1930s in Ireland', CEPR Discussion Papers 58.

Neary, J.P. and O Gráda, C. (1991) 'Protection, economic war and structural change: the 1930s in Ireland', *Irish Historical Studies,* l. 27,.250–66.

NESC (1976) *Prelude to Planning,* NESC Report No.26, Dublin: NESC.

NESC (1989) *Ireland in the European Community: performance, prospects and strategy,* NESC Report No. 88, Dublin: NESC.

NESC (National Economic and Social Council) (2005) *The Developmental Welfare state,* Dublin: Stationery Office.

NESC (The National Economic and Social Committee) (2006) *Managing Migration in Ireland: A Social and Economic Analysis,* NESC Report No. 116, Dublin: NESC.

NESF (National Economic Social Forum) (1997) *A Framework for Partnership – Enriching Strategic Consensus through Participation,* Dublin: NESF.

NESF (National Economic and Social Forum) (2000) *The National Anti-Poverty Strategy, Report Number 8,* Dublin: NESF.

NIEC (National Industrial Economic Council) (1965) *Report on Economic Planning,* no. 8, Dublin: NIEC.

Ni Eigeartaigh, A. (2007) 'Mise Eire: recycling nationalist mythologies' in Hayward, K. and MacCarthaigh, M., eds, *Recycling the State. The politics of adaptation in Ireland,* Dublin: Irish Academic Press, 18–42.

Ní Shé, É., Lodge, T. and Adshead, M. (2007) *A Study of the Needs of Ethnic Minorities in County Clare,* Ennis/Limerick: Research Report for Health Services Executive.

Nolan, B. (1991) *The Utilisation and Financing of Health Services in Ireland,* Dublin: ESRI.

Nolan, B. and Smeeding, T.M. (2004) 'Ireland's income distribution in comparative perspective', *Review of Income and Wealth,* 51/4: 537–60.

Nolan, B., O'Connell, P. and Whelan, C. T., eds (2000) *Bust to Boom: the Irish Experience of Growth and Inequality,* Dublin: Institute for Public Administration.

Nolan, S. (1983) 'The Telesis Report – a review essay', *Economic and Social Review,* 281–9.

Northern Ireland Audit Office (1998) *Industrial Development Board for Northern Ireland: Inward Investment,* Belfast: HMSO, HC1096.

Northern Ireland Audit Office (2006) *Governance Issues in the Department of Enterprise, Trade and Investment's Former Local Enterprise Development Unit,* Belfast: HMSO, HC 817.

Northern Ireland Civil Service (1999) *Code of Ethics,* Belfast: NICS.

Northern Ireland Civil Service (2000) *Equal Opportunities in the Northern Ireland Civil Service: Seventh Report,* Belfast: NICS.

Northern Ireland Housing Executive (2007) *36th Annual Report, 2006–7,* Belfast: NIHE.

Norton, P., ed. (1990a) *Legislatures,* Oxford: Oxford University Press.

Norton, P., ed. (1990b) *Parliaments in Western Europe,* London: Frank Cass.

NWCI (National Women's Council of Ireland) and Murphy, M. (2003) *A Woman's Model for Social Welfare Reform,* Dublin: NWCI.

NWCI (National Women's Council of Ireland) (2005) *An Accessible Affordable Childcare Equality Anti-poverty Model,* Dublin: NWCI.

O'Brennan, J. (2003) 'Ireland's return to 'normal' voting patterns on EU issues: the 2002 Nice Treaty Referendum', *European Political Science,* 2(2), 5–13.

O'Byrnes, S. (1986) *Hiding behind a face: Fine Gael under FitzGerald,* Dublin: Gill and Macmillan.

O'Callaghan, M. and O'Donnell, C. (2006) 'The Northern Ireland Government, the "Paisleyite Movement" and Ulster Unionism in 1966', *Irish Political Studies,* 21(2), 203–22.

O'Cearbhaill, D. and Varley, T. (1996) 'An Irish community development movement's experience of crisis conditions: Munitir na Tire's struggle for survival', *Community Development Journal,* 27(1), 1–16.

O'Cinneide, S. (1998) 'Democracy and the Constitution', *Administration,* 46(4), 41–58.

O'Connell, P. J. and Rottman, D. (1992) 'The Irish Welfare State in Comparative Perspective' in Goldthorpe, J. H. and Whelan, C. T., eds, *The Development of Industrial Society in Ireland,* Oxford: Clarendon Press, 205–40.

O'Connor, J.S. (2005) 'Policy coordination, social indicators and the social policy agenda in the European Union', *Journal of European social policy,* 15/4: 345–61.

O'Connor, P. (2008) 'The Irish Patriarchal state: continuity and change' in Adshead, M., Kirby, P. and Millar, M., eds, *Contesting the State: Lessons from the Irish case,* Manchester: Manchester University Press, 143–64.

O'Connor, E. (1992) *A Labour History of Ireland, 1824–1960,* Dublin: Gill and MacMillan.

O'Connor, E. (2002) 'Ireland in Historical Perspective: The Legacies of Colonialism – Edging Towards Policy Concertation' in Berger, S. and Compston, H., eds, *Policy Concertation and Social Partnership in Western Europe*, Oxford: Berghahn Books.

O'Connor, F. (1993) *In Search of a State: Catholics in Northern Ireland*, Belfast: Blackstaff.

O'Connor, J. (2005) 'Policy coordination, social indicators and the social policy agenda in the European Union', *Journal of European Social Policy,* 15 (4), 345–61.

O'Connor, J. (2006) 'Marathon talks process has finally ended, so now it's over to you', Special supplement on the proposals for a new national agreement, *Liberty*, 5(2).

O'Connor, P. (2008) 'The Irish patriarchal state: continuity and change' in Adshead, M., Kirby, P. and Millar, M., eds, *Contesting the State: lessons from the Irish case,* Manchester: Manchester University Press, 143–64.

O'Donnell, P. (1963) *There Will be Another Day*, Dublin: Dolmen Press.

O'Donnell, R. (1998) *Irelands Economic Transformation: Industrial Policy, European Integration and Social Partnership*, Centre for West European Studies: University of Pittsburgh, Working Paper, no. 2, available at: www.nesc.ie.

O'Donnell, R. (1999) 'Social Partnership: Principles, Institutions and Interpretations' in O'Connell, P., ed. *Astonishing success; Economic Growth and the Labour Market in Ireland,* Geneva, International Labour Organisation: Employment and Training Papers no. 44.

O'Donnell, R. (2000) 'The new Ireland in the new Europe' in O'Donnell, R., ed. *Europe, the Irish experience,* Dublin: Institute of European Affairs, 161–214.

O'Donnell, R. (2001) *Social Partnership: Prospects for Future Development,* Dublin: Forfás Policy Paper.

O'Donnell, R. (2008) 'The Partnership state: building the ship at sea' in Adshead, M., Kirby, P. and Millar, M., eds, *Contesting the State: Lessons from the Irish Case*, Manchester: Manchester University Press, 73–99.

O'Donnell, R., Adshead, M. and Thomas, D. (2007) *The Emergence and Insitutionalisation of Social Pacts: Ireland,* 'New Modes of Governance', EU Framework 7 Integrated Project Priority 7 Citizens and Governance in Knowledge Based Society, Project No. CITI-CT-2004–506392.

O'Donnell, R. and O'Reardon, C. (1997) 'Ireland's Experiment in Social Partnership 1987–96' in Fajertag, G. and Pochet, P., eds, *Social Pacts in Europe,* Brussels: European Trade Union Institute.

O'Donnell, R. and O'Reardon, C. (2000) 'Social Partnership and Ireland's Economic Transformation' in Fajertag, G. and Pochet, P., eds, *Social Pacts in Europe – New Dynamics,* Brussels: European Trade Union Institute.

O' Donnell, R. and Thomas, D. (1998) 'Social Partnership and Policy Making' in Healy, S. and Reynolds, B., eds, *Social Policy in Ireland; Principles, Practices, Problems,* Dublin: Oak Tree Press., pp. 109–32.

O' Donnell, R. and Thomas, D. (2002) 'Ireland in the 1990s: Policy Concertation Triumphant' in Berger, S. and Compston, H., eds, *Policy Concertation and Social Partnership in Western Europe,* Oxford: Berghahn Books.

O'Donnell, R. and Walsh, J. (1995) 'Ireland: region and state in the European Union' in Rhodes, M., ed. *The Regions and the New Europe,* Manchester: Manchester University Press, 200–28.

O'Dwyer, L. (2006) *Chief Executive of the Irish League of Credit Unions, Presentation to the Oireachtas Joint Committee on Finance and the Public Service*, 13 September, accessed at http://debates.oireachtas.ie/DDebate.aspx?F=FIJ20060913.xml&Page=1&Ex=172.

OECD (2002) *Annual Report 2002*, Paris: OECD.

OECD (2004) *Employment Outlook*, Paris: OECD.

OECD (2008) *OECD Economic surveys: Ireland 2008*, Issue 5, Paris: OECD.

OFDFM (2006) *Labour Force Survey 2002*, Belfast: Office of First and Deputy First Minister.

Office for National Statistics (2007) *Key Statistics for Northern Ireland: Regional Trends 38*, London: ONS.

O'Hagan, J. and McIndoe, T. (2005) 'Population, employment and unemployment' in O'Hagan, J. and Newman, C., eds, *The Economy of Ireland, National and Sectoral Policy Issues,* Dublin: Gill and Macmillan, 76–106.

O'Halpin, E. (1985) 'The Dáil committee of Public Accounts, 1961–1980', *Administration,* 32(4), 483–511.

O'Halpin, E. (1986) 'Oireachtas committees: experience and prospects', *Seirbhís Phoiblí,* 7(2), 3–9.

O'Halpin, E. (1991) 'The Civil Service and the Political System', *Administration,* 38(3), 283–302.

O'Halpin, E. (1997) 'Partnership programme managers in the Reynolds/Spring coalition, 1993–4: an assessment', *Irish Political Studies,* 12(1), 78–91.

O'Halpin, E. (1998) 'A changing relationship? Parliament and Government in Ireland' in Norton, P., ed. *Parliaments and Governments in Western Europe,* London: Frank Cass, 123–41.

O'Hearn, D. (2001) *The Atlantic Economy: Britain, the US and Ireland,* Manchester: Manchester University Press.

O'Kane, E. (2007) *Britain, Ireland and Northern Ireland since 1980: The Totality of Relationships,* London: Routledge.

O'Leary, B. (1990) 'Setting the record straight: a comment on Cahill's Country Report on Ireland', *Governance,* 3, 98–104.

O'Leary, B. (1991) 'An Taoiseach: the Irish prime minister', *West European Politics,* 14(2), 133–62.

O'Leary, B. (2001) 'Comparative Political Science and the British-Irish Agreement' in McGarry, J., ed. *Northern Ireland and the Divided World,* Oxford: Oxford University Press, 53–88.

O'Leary, B. and Peterson, J. (1990) 'Further Europeanisation and realignment: the Irish general election, June 1989', *West European Politics,* 3(1), 124–36.

O'Leary, C. (1979) *Irish Elections 1918–1977: parties, voters and proportional representation,* Dublin: Gill and Macmillan.

O'Leary, J. (1999) 'Regional income estimates for Ireland 1995', *Regional Studies,* 33, 805–15.

O'Leary, O. and Burke, H. (1998) *Mary Robinson: the authorised biography,* London: Hodder and Stoughton.

O'Loan, D. (2007) Department of Finance and Personnel Committee Report, October, accessed at www.bbc.co.uk/1/hi/northern_ireland/7.

Oliver, Q. and Leonard, A. (2008) 'Taking responsibility for prosperity', *Fortnight,* 459, 4–5.

Olson, D. M. and Norton, P., eds (1996) *The New Parliaments of Central and Eastern Europe,* London: Routledge.

Olson, M. (1971) *The Logic of Collective Action. Public goods and the theory of groups,* London: Harvard University Press.

O'Malley, E. (1989) *Industry and Economic Development: the challenge for the latecomer,* Dublin: Gill and Macmillan.

O'Malley, E. (1992) 'Problems of industrialisation in Ireland' in Goldthorpe, J. H. and Whelan, C. T., eds, *The Development of Industrial Society in Ireland,* Oxford: Oxford University Press, 31–52.

O'Malley, E. (2006) 'Ministerial selection in Ireland: limited choice in a political village', *Irish Political Studies,* 21(3), 319–36.

O'Muilleoir, M. (1999) *Belfast's Dome of Delight: City Hall Politics 1981–2000,* Belfast: Beyond the Pale.

O'Muimhneachain, M. (1959) 'The functions of the Department of the Taoiseach', *Administration,* 7(4), 277–93.

O'Neill, B. (2000) 'The Referendum process in Ireland', *Irish Jurist,* XXXV, 280–304.

O'Regan, M. (2004) 'Socialist Bertie not yet for turning', *Irish Times,* 1 December.

Ó'Riáin, S. (2000) 'The flexible developmental state: globalization, information technology and the "Celtic Tiger" ', *Politics and Society,* 28(2), 157–93.

Ó'Riáin, S. (2004) *The Politics of High-Tech Growth: developmental network states in the global economy,* Cambridge: Cambridge University Press.

Ó'Riáin, S. (2006) 'Social partnership as a mode of governance: introduction to the special issue', *Economic and Social Review,* 37(3), 311–18.

O'Riáin, S. (2008) 'Competing state projects in the contemporary iIrish political economy' in, Adshead, M. Kirby, P. and Millar, M., eds, *Contesting the State: Lessons from the Irish Case,* Manchester: Manchester University Press, 165–85.

Ó'Riáin, S. and O'Connell, P. (2000) 'The Role of the State in Growth and Welfare' in Nolan, B., O'Connell, P. and Whelan, C., eds, *Bust to Boom? The Irish Experience of Growth and Inequality,* Dublin: ESRI/IPA.

Osborne, R. and Cormack, R. (1989) 'Fair employment: towards reform in Northern Ireland', *Policy and Politics,* 17(4), 287–94.

O'Shea, E. and Kennelly, B. (2002) 'The welfare state in Ireland – challenges and opportunities' in Taylor, G., ed. *Issues in Irish public policy,* Dublin: Irish Academic Press, 52–79.

O'Sullivan, E. (2003) 'Marxism, the state and homelessness in Ireland' in Adshead, M. and Millar, M., eds, *Public Administration and Public Policy in Ireland: Theory and Methods,* London: Routledge, 37–53.

O'Toole, F. (1995) *Meanwhile Back at the Ranch. The politics of Irish Beef,* London: Vintage.

O'Toole, F. (2003) *After the Ball,* Dublin: TASC, Dublin: New Island Books.

Panebianco, A. (1988) *Political Parties: organization and power,* Cambridge: Cambridge University Press.

Patterson, H. (1996) 'Northern Ireland 1921–68' in Aughey, A. and Morrow, D., eds, *Northern Ireland Politics,* Harlow: Longman, 1–10.

Patterson, H. (2002) *Ireland since 1939,* Oxford: Oxford University Press.

Patterson, H. and Kaufmann, E. (2007a) *Unionism and Orangeism in Northern Ireland since 1945: The Decline of the Loyal Family,* Manchester: Manchester University Press.

Patterson, H. and Kaufmann, E. (2007b) 'From deference to defiance: popular unionism and the decline of elite accommodation in Northern Ireland' in Carmichael, P., Knox, C. and Osborne, B., eds, *Devolution and Constitutional Change in Northern Ireland,* Manchester: Manchester University Press, 83–95.

Pearson, R. and Jagger, N. (2003) *Human Resources in Science and Technology Policy,* Paris: OECD.

Peillon, M. (1995) 'Interest Groups and the State' in Clancy, P., Drudy, S., Lynch, K. and O'Dowd, L., eds, *Irish Society; Sociological Perspectives,* Dublin: Institute of Public Administration.

Peters, B. G. (1987) 'Politicians and bureaucrats in the politics of policy making' in Lane, J. E., ed. *Bureaucracy and Public Choice,* London: Sage, 256–82.

Peters, B. G. (2004) 'Governance and Public Bureaucracy: New Forms of Democracy or New Forms of Control', *Asia Pacific Journal of Public Administration,* 26(1), 3–16.

Powell, F. and Geoghegan, V. (2004) *The Politics of Community Development,* Dublin: A&A Farmer.

Prager, J. (1986) *Building Democracy in Ireland. Political order and cultural integration in a newly independent nation,* Cambridge: Cambridge University Press.

Puirséil, N. (2007) *The Irish Labour party 1922–73,* Dublin: UCD Press.

Putnam, R. (1993) *Making Democracy work: civic traditions in modern Italy*, Princeton, NJ: Princeton University Press.

Putnam, R. (2000) *Bowling Alone*, New York: Simon & Schuster.

Pyne, P. (1969) 'The third Sinn Féin party: 1923–1926', *Economic and Social Review,* 1/1, 29–50.

Quinn, R. (1996) 'Address to the Regional Affairs Committee of the European Parliament by the Minister of Finance for Ireland', delivered in Brussels, 7 May.

Rallings, C., Thrasher, M. and Downe, J. (1996) *Enhancing Local Government Turnout,* London: Joseph Rowntree.

Regan, M. C. and Wilson, F. L. (1986) 'Interest group politics in France and Ireland: comparative perspectives on neo-corporation', *West European Politics,* 9(3), 393–411.

Review of Public Administration (2006) *Better Government for Northern Ireland: Final Decisions of the Review of Public Administration,* Belfast: HMSO.

Rhodes, R. A. W. (1997) *Understanding Governance. Policy networks, governance, reflexivity and accountability,* Buckingham: Open University Press.

RIA (Royal Irish Academy) (2006) *Third Sector Research Programme,* Dublin: RIA.

Richardson, J. J. (1994) 'Doing less by doing more: British government 1979–93', *West European Politics,* 17(3), 178–97.

Richardson, J. J. (2000) 'Government, interest groups and policy change', *Political Studies,* 48, 1006–25.

Robinson, M. T. W. (1974) 'The role of the Irish Parliament', *Administration,* 21(3), 3–25.

Robinson, N. and Adshead, M. (2008) 'Towards a political economy of "post-celtic tiger" Ireland', in Paper presented to the Irish Social Science Platform (ISSP) conference, 'After the Celtic Tiger', Dublin: City University.

Roche, B. and Cradden, T. (2003) 'Neo-corporatism and social partnership' in Adshead, M. and Millar, M., eds, *Public Administration and Public Policy in Ireland: theory and methods,* London: Routledge, 69–87.

Roche, W. K. (1992) 'The liberal theory of industrialisation and the development of industrial relations in Ireland' in Goldthorpe, J. H. and Whelan, C. T., eds, *The Development of Industrial Society in Ireland,* Oxford: Oxford University Press, 291–328.

Roche, W. K. (1994) 'Pay determination, the state and the politics of industrial relations' in Murphy, T. V. and Roche, W. K., eds, *Irish Industrial Relations in Practice,* Dublin: Oak Tree Press.

Roche, W. K. and Ashmore, J. (2000) 'Irish Unions in the 1990s: Testing the Limits of Social Partnership' in Griffin, G., ed. *Changing Patterns of Trade Unionism,* Sydney: Mansell.

Rose, R. (1991) 'Prime Ministers in parliamentary democracies', *West European Politics,* 14(2), 9–24.

RTÉ News (1999) 'Justice Minister addresses the Dáil on Sheedy Affair', 20 April, accessed at www.rte.ie/news/1999/0420/dail.html.

RTÉ News (1999) 'Taoiseach denies improper actions in Sheedy affair', 5 May, accessed at www.rte.ie/news/1999/0505/sheedy.html/.

Ruane, F. and Uğar, A. (2005) 'Trade and foreign direction investment in manufacturing and services' in O'Hagan, J. and Newman, C., eds, *The Economy of Ireland, National and Sectoral Policy Issues,* Dublin: Gill and Macmillan, 162–87.

Saalfeld, T. and Müller, W. C. (1997) 'Roles in legislative studies: a theoretical introduction' in Saalfeld, T. and Müller, W. C., eds, *Members of Parliament in Western Europe. Roles and Behaviour,* London: Frank Cass.

Sabel, C. (1996) *Ireland: local partnerships and social innovation,* Paris: OECD.

Sabel, C. (2001) 'A quiet revolution of democratic governance: towards democratic experimentalism', in Michalski, W., ed., *Governance in the 21st Century,* Paris: OECD, 121–48.

Sack, P. (1976) *The Donegal Mafia: an Irish political machine,* New Haven, CT: Yale University Press.

Salmon, T. (1989) *Unneutral Ireland: a unique and ambivalent security policy,* Oxford: Oxford University Press.

Sartori, G. (1976) *Parties and Party Systems,* Cambridge: Cambridge University Press.

Sartori, G. (1986) 'The influence of electoral systems: faulty laws or faulty method?' in Grofman, B. and Lijphart, A., eds, *Electoral Laws and their Political Consequences,* New York: Agathon Press, 43–68.

Sabel, C. (2001) 'A quiet revolution of democratic governance: towards democratic experimentalism' in, W. Michalski (ed) *Governance in the 21st century: power in the global knowledge economy and society,* Paris: OECD, pp. 121–48.

Scannell, Y. (1988) 'The Constitution and the role of women' in Farrell, B., ed. *De Valera's Constitution and Ours,* Dublin: Gill and Macmillan, 123–36.

Scharpf, F. W. (1988) 'The joint decision trap: lessons from German federalism and European integration', *Public Administration*, 66, 229–78.

Seanad Éireann Committee on Procedure and Privileges: Sub-Committee on Seanad Reform (2004) *Report on Seanad Reform*, Dublin: Stationery Office, Government of Ireland.

Sexton, J. J. and O'Connell, P. J. (1996) *Labour Market Studies: Ireland*, Luxembourg: European Commission.

Sharp, P. (1989) 'External challenges and domestic legitimacy: Ireland's foreign policy, 1983–1987', *Irish Political Studies*, 4.

Shatter, A. J. (1997) *Shatter's Family Law in the Republic of Ireland*, Dublin: Wolfhound Press.

Sheridan, K. (2002) 'Dáil needs to swap rhetoric for reform', *Irish Times*, 18 October.

Shirlow, P., ed. (1995) *Development Ireland: contemporary issues*, London: Pluto.

Shirlow, P. and McEvoy, K. (2008) *Beyond the Wire: Former Prisoners and Conflict Transformation in Northern Ireland*, London: Pluto.

Shirlow, P. and Murtagh, B. (2006) *Belfast: Segregation, Violence and the City*, London: Pluto.

Shirlow, P. and Shuttleworth, I. (1999) ' "Who is going to toss the burgers"? Social Class and the Reconstruction of the Northern Irish Economy', *Capital and Class*, 69, 27–46.

Sinn Féin (2003) *Sinn Féin and the European Union*, Dublin: Sinn Féin.

Sinnott, R. (1984) 'Interpretations of the Irish party system', *European Journal of Political Research*, 12, 289–307.

Sinnott, R. (1986) 'Party differences and spatial representation: the Irish case', *British Journal of Political Science*, 16, 217–41.

Sinnott, R. (1995) *Irish Voters Decide. Voting behaviour in elections and referendums since 1918*, Manchester: Manchester University Press.

Sinnott, R. (1999) 3rd edn, 'The electoral system' in Coakley, J. and Gallagher, M., eds, *Politics in the Republic of Ireland*, London: Routledge, 99–126.

Sinnott, R. (2001) *Attitudes and Behaviour of the Irish Electorate in the Referendum on the Treaty of Nice*, Flash Eurobarometer Survey for the European Commission. Institute for the Study of Social Change, University College Dublin.

Sinnott, R. (2002) 'Cleavages, parties and referendums: relationships between representative and direct democracy in the Republic of Ireland', *European Journal of Political Research*, 41, 811–26.

Sinnott, R. (2005) 4th edn, 'The rules of the electoral game' in Coakley, J. and Gallagher, M., eds, *Politics in the Republic of Ireland*, London: Routledge.

Skelly, J.M. (1997) *Irish Diplomacy at the United Nations 1945–1965*, Dublin: Gill and Macmillan.

Smith, D. (2006) *Living with Leviathan. Public Spending, Taxes and Economic Performance*, London: Institute of Economic Affairs.

Smith, N. (2006) *Showcasing Globalisation*, Manchester: Manchester University Press.

Smith, N. and Hay, C. (2007) 'Mapping political discourses of globalisation and European integration empirically in the UK and Ireland', *European Journal of Political Research*, 47(3), 359–82.

Smyth, E. and Hannan, D. F. (2000) 'Education and Inequality' in Nolan, B., O'Connell, P. J. and Whelan, C. T., eds, *Bust to Boom? The Irish Experience of Growth and Inequality*, Dublin: IPA.

Smyth, E., McCoy, S., Darmody, M. and Dunne, A. (2007) 'Changing times, changing schools? Quality of life for students' in Fahey, T., Russell, H. and Whelan, C. T., eds, *Best of Times? The social impact of the Celtic tiger*, Dublin: IPA, 139–54.

Smyth, J. (1999) 'Policing Ireland', *Capital and Class*, 69, 101–23.

Southern, N. (2005) 'Ian Paisley and Evangelical Democratic Unionists: An Analysis of the Role of Evangelical Protestantism within the Democratic Unionist Party', *Irish Political Studies*, 20(2), 127–46.

Spencer, G. (2008) *The State of Loyalism in Northern Ireland*, Basingstoke: Palgrave Macmillan.

Stapleton, J. (1991) 'Civil Service Reform, 1969–87', *Administration,* 38(4), 303–35.

Staunton, E. (2001) *The Nationalists of Northern Ireland 1918–1973,* London: Columba.

Steele, T. and Shirlow, P. (1999) 'Review of Deprivation in Northern Ireland' in Hastings, T., ed. *Deprivation in Europe,* Brussels: Political Economy Unit.

Stepan, A. with Skach, C. (2001) 'Constitutional frameworks and democratic consolidation: parliamentarianism versus presidentialism' in Stepan, A., ed. *Arguing Comparative Politics,* Oxford: Oxford University Press, 257–75.

Stone Sweet, A. and Weiler, J. H. H., eds (1998) *The European Court and National Courts – Doctrine and Jurisprudence: legal change in its social context,* Oxford: Hart.

Storey, E. (2002) *Traditional Roots,* Dublin: Columba.

Størm, K. (1998) 'Parliamentary committees in European democracies' in Longley, L. D. and Davidson, R. H., eds, *The New Roles of Parliamentary Committees,* London: Frank Cass, 21–59.

Suiter, J. (2008) 'The Irish Dáil Election 2007', *Irish Political Studies,* 23(1), 99–110.

Sweeney, P. (1999) 2nd edn, *The Celtic Tiger. Ireland's continuing economic miracle,* Dublin: Oak Tree Press.

Sweeney, P. (2003) 'Globalisation: Ireland in a global context' in Adshead, M. and Millar, M., eds, *Public Administration and Public Policy in Ireland: theory and methods,* London: Routledge, 201–18.

Taagepera, R. and Shugart, M. S. (1989) *Seats and Votes: the effects and determinants of electoral systems,* New Haven, CT: Yale University Press.

Taillon, R. and McCann, M. (2002) *An Assessment of the Impact of the Loss of Services Provided by WSN and other Women's Organisations in NI,* Report for OFMDFM, Belfast: Women's Support Network.

Tannam, E. (1999) *Cross-border Cooperation in the Republic of Ireland and Northern Ireland,* Basingstoke: Palgrave Macmillan.

Tannam, E. (2004) '*Cross-border Cooperation between Northern Ireland and the Republic of Ireland: Neo-functionalism revisited*', in *Mapping Frontiers, Plotting Pathways,* Working Paper 4, Institute of British-Irish Studies, University College Dublin and Institute of Governance, Centre for International Borders Research, Queen's University Belfast.

Tannam, E. (2007) 'Public Policy: the EU and the Good Friday Agreement' in Coakley, J. and O'Dowd, L., eds, *Crossing the Border: New Relationships between Northern Ireland and the Republic of Ireland,* Dublin: Irish Academic Press, 104–24.

Taylor, G. (1993) 'In search of the elusive entrepreneur', *Irish Political Studies,* 8, 89–105.

Teague, P. (2006) 'Social partnership and local development in Ireland: the limits to deliberation', *British journal of industrial relations,* 44/3: 421–43.

Tocqueville A. de (1947 [1856]) *The Old Regime and the French Revolution,* Oxford: Blackwell.

Todd, J. (1987) 'Two traditions in Unionist political culture', *Irish Political Studies,* 2, 1–26.

Tonge, J. (2000) *The New Civil Service,* Tisbury: Baseline.

Tonge, J. (2002) *Northern Ireland: Conflict and Change,* London: Pearson.

Tonge, J. (2005a) *The New Northern Irish Politics?,* Basingstoke: Palgrave.

Tonge, J. (2005b) *The EU and the Irish Border: Shaping Aid and Attitudes?,* Belfast, Queen's University: Centre for International Borders Research Working Paper WP05–1.

Tonge, J. (2006a) *Northern Ireland,* Cambridge: Polity.

Tonge, J. (2006b) 'Sinn Féin and "New Republicanism" in Belfast', *Space and Polity,* 10 (2), 135–47.

Tonge, J. (2008) 'Commentary' (on Cunningham's The Political Language of John Hume)' in McGrath, C. and O'Malley, E., eds, *Irish Political Studies Reader,* London: Routledge, 142–49.

Tonge, J. and Evans, J. (2001) 'Faultlines in Unionism; Division and Dissent within the Ulster Unionist Council', *Irish Political Studies,* 16, 111–31.

Tonge, J. and Evans, J. (2002) 'Party Members and the Good Friday Agreement in Northern Ireland', *Irish Political Studies,* 17(2), 59–73.

Tonge, J. and McAuley, J. (2008) 'The Orange Order in contemporary Northern Ireland' in Busteed, M., Neal, F. and Tonge, J., eds, *Irish Protestant Identities,* Manchester: Manchester University Press, 289–302.

Tonra, B. (2006) *Global citizen and European Republic. Irish foreign policy in transition,* Manchester: Manchester University Press.

Tormey, R. (2006) *Social and Political Education in Senior Cycle. A background paper,* Dublin: National Council for Curriculum and Assessment (NCCA).

Transparency International (2006) *Global Corruption Report,* Cambridge: Cambridge University Press.

Tucker, V. (1983) 'A history of workers' cooperatives in Ireland and the UK', in Linehan, M and Tucker, V, eds, *Workers' Cooperatives: Potential and Problems*, Cork: Bank of Ireland Centre for Co-operative Studies and University Studies, 1983, 26–43.

Trench, A. (2004) 'The More Things Change, The More They Stay the Same: Intergovernmental Relations Four Years On' in Trench, A., ed. *Has Devolution Made a Difference?,* London: Imprint, 165–92.

University of Ulster (2007) *Northern Ireland Quarterly House Price Index for Q4 2007,* Belfast: UU.

Varney, D. (2007) *Review of Tax Policy in Northern Ireland: The Varney Review,* London: HMSO.

Walker, G. (2004) *A History of the Ulster Unionist Party: Protest, Pragmatism and Pessimism,* Manchester: Manchester University Press.

Walsh, D. (1986) *The Party. Inside Fianna Fáil,* Dublin: Gill and Macmillan.

Walsh, J. (1992) 'The Republic of Ireland' in Townroe, P. and Martin, R., eds, *Regional Development in the 1990s: the British Isles in transition,* London: Jessica Kingsley.

Walsh, J. (1993) *Models for Local and Regional Development in Ireland,* Maynooth, Co. Kildare: St Patrick's College, Centre for local and regional development.

Waltman, J. L. and Holland, K. M., eds (1988) *The Political Role of the Courts in Modern Democracies,* Basingstoke: Macmillan.

Ward, A. J. (1974) 'Parliamentary procedures and the machinery of government in Ireland', *Irish University Review,* 4(2), 222–43.

Ward, A. J. (1996) 'The constitution review group and the "executive state" in Ireland', *Administration,* 44(4), 42–63.

Ward, M. (1983) *Unmanageable Revolutionaries,* Dublin: Brandon Press.

Ward, M. (2007) 'The changing role of women in the context of devolution' in Carmichael, P., Knox , C. and Osborne, B., eds, *Devolution and Constitutional Change in Northern Ireland,* Manchester Manchester University Press, 138–51.

Ward, R. (2006) *Women, Unionism and Loyalism in Northern Ireland: From 'Tea-Makers to Political Actors,* Dublin: Irish Academic Press.

Ware, A. (1996) *Political Parties and Party Systems*, Oxford: Oxford University Press.

Whelan, C. T., Layte, R., Maitre, B., Gannon, B., Nolan, B., Watson, D. and Williams, J. (2003) *Monitoring Poverty Trends in Ireland,* Dublin: ESRI.

Whelan, Y. (2001) 'Symbolizing the state: the iconography of O'Connell Street and environs after independence', *Irish Geography,* 34(2), 135–56.

White, G. and Wade, R. (1988) 'Developmental states and markets in East Asia: an introduction' in White, G., ed. *Developmental States in East Asia,* London: Macmillan.

White, T. d. V. (1948) *Kevin O'Higgins,* London: Methuen.

Whyte, J. (1983) 'How much discrimination was there under the unionist regime 1921–68?' in Gallagher , T. and O'Connell, J., eds, *Contemporary Irish Studies,* Manchester: Manchester University Press.

Whyte, J. (1990) *Interpreting Northern Ireland,* Oxford: Clarendon.

Whyte, J. H. (1974) 'Ireland: politics without social bases' in Rose, R., ed. *Electoral Behaviour: a comparative handbook,* New York: The Free Press, 619–51.

Whyte, J. H. (1980) 2nd edn, *Church and State in Modern Ireland, 1923–1979,* Dublin: Gill and Macmillan.

Wichert, S. (1991) *Northern Ireland since 1945,* Harlow: Longman.

Wiley, M. M. (2005) 'The Irish health system: developments in strategy, structure, funding and delivery since 1980', *Health Economics,* S169–S186.

Wilford, R. (2001) 'The Assembly and Executive' in Wilford, R., ed. *Aspects of the Belfast Agreement,* Oxford: Oxford University Press, 107–28.

Wilford, R., ed. (2001) *Aspects of the Belfast Agreement,* Oxford: Blackwell.

Wilford, R. (2007) 'Inside Stormont: the Assembly and the Executive' in Carmichael, P., Knox , C. and Osborne, R., eds, *Devolution and Constitutional Change in Northern Ireland,* Manchester: Manchester University Press, 167–85.

Wilford, R. and Elliott, R. (1999) 'Small Earthquake in Chile: The First Northern Ireland Affairs Select Committee', *Irish Political Studies,* 14(1), 23–42.

Wilford, R. and Wilson, R. (2001) 'Northern Ireland: endgame' in Trench, A., ed. *The State of the Nations 2001,* Thorverton: Imprint Academic, 77–106.

Wilford, R. and Wilson, R. (2003) *A Route to Stability? The review of the Belfast Agreement,* Belfast: Democratic Dialogue.

Wilford, R. and Wilson, R. (2006) 'From the Belfast Agreement to Stable Power-Sharing', in *PSA Territorial Politics conference,* Queen's University Belfast.

Williams, T. (1993) 'Local government role-reversal in the new contract culture' in Bennett, R. J., ed. *Local Government in the New Europe,* London: Belhaven Press, 95–108.

Wilson Report (1965) *Economic Development in Northern Ireland,* Belfast: HMSO, Cmnd. 479.

Wilson, T. (1989) *Ulster: Conflict and Consent,* Oxford: Blackwell.

Wolff, S. (2002) 'The Peace Process since 1998' in Neuheiser, J. and Wolff, S., eds, *Peace at Last? The Implementation of the Good Friday Agreement on Northern Ireland,* Oxford: Berghahn, 202–32.

Wood, I. (2006) *Crimes of Loyalty: A History of the UDA,* Edinburgh: Edinburgh University Press.

Wren, M.-A. (2003) *Unhealthy State Anatomy of a Sick Society,* Dublin: New Island Books.

Wright, V. (1994) 'Reshaping the state: the implications for public administration' in Müller, W. and Wright, V., eds, *The State in Western Europe: Retreat or Redefinition?,* London: Frank Cass, 102–34, accessed at www.rte.ie/news/1999/0505/sheedy.html.

Zimmerman, J. F. (1997) 'The changing roles of the Irish Department Secretary', *Public Administration Review,* 57(6), 534–41.

Index

Note: where terms are defined the page number is **emboldened**.